On The Road
Drew's Station,
City and Fairbank

By John D. Rose

Table of Contents

Acknowledgments

There are many I would like to thank for their assistance as I assembled this book. Linda Reib at the Arizona State Archives, and Katherine Reeve of the Arizona Historical Society have always been ready to offer their records knowledge. I would also like to acknowledge Cochise County Recorder Christine Rhodes for her friendly and enthusiastic approach to researchers. To my surprise, research at the Pima County recorder's office is unduly difficult. After calling and confirming beforehand that they did have research materials from the era that this book relates to, I traveled to Tucson, and when I arrived there, was told that they had no such records, though later they found what they claimed they did not have. The Pima County Recorder's office could learn much from the Cochise County Archives, as run by Kevin Pyles and the Cochise County Recorder's office, as run by Christine Rhodes. Pima County Treasurer Beth Ford could not have been more helpful, guiding me into her "dungeon" vault as she refers to it to look through original records.

Kevin Pyles, who runs the Cochise County Archives, is a true records expert, and his understanding of the records to which he tends so well is of great value to anyone who cares about Cochise County history. He has been instrumental in locating a number of key records that grace this book. Over decades of research, I have dealt with archives across Arizona and the U.S. As a Cochise County taxpayer, it pleases me greatly that our local archive holds its own against the best anywhere, and in some cases, far surpasses many other larger operations, likely with larger budgets.

In his off time, Kevin has been an immense help in doing the layout of this book, formatting it for publication, and arranging the position of photos, as well as designing the cover. I have enjoyed this process of working on the final steps of the book with him a great deal. I wish that Kevin's late brother Erich Pyles, could see the fine work that he is doing on these many fronts.

Those who were not involved with the book, but to whom I'd like to acknowledge are John and Shirley Ray, parents of my wife Stephanie. Thanks to Michael Pestes for always doing more for others than he will allow them to do for him. The Drew family has been very generous in sharing their family archive with me, and I wish to thank them for this honor.

Special thanks to my wonderful wife Stephanie Rose, who devoted countless hours proofing this book. –John D. Rose

ON THE ROAD TO TOMBSTONE: DREW'S STATION, CONTENTION CITY, AND FAIRBANK

This book is dedicated to my beloved daughter, Aubrey Summer Rose. May she find in her future the wonders of the past.

By John D. Rose

Introduction

During the writing of my first book, "Charleston and Millville A.T., Hell on the San Pedro," I noticed something missing in newspaper as well as personal accounts-the story of Contention City. Information about this key location in the Tombstone Mining District was conspicuous by its absence. Whereas Charleston had far more newspaper ads and news in the Tombstone and Tucson press, Contention rarely entered that portion of the historical record. Like Charleston, Contention City never had its own banking, or its own newspaper. Records from both are helpful when trying to bring to life an all but forgotten location. Contention was a similar size in population to Charleston, a similar distance from Tombstone, and both communities began with reduction mills for rich Tombstone ores. Even as a collector, I've found that Charleston photos and documents are highly prized and scarce, but Contention City is scarcer yet.

Sometimes what is not found can be almost as important as what is found. In the 1880's, Charleston and Tombstone would challenge each other to baseball games, and even in the 1930's letters between former Charleston residents to those still living in Tombstone enhanced the record of those times. Such interplay between those in Tombstone and Contention was not as prolific. With this in mind, I found it a unique challenge to seek out and bring to life the story of elusive Contention, but the telling of its story would be incomplete without the context of two key locations nearby-Drew's Station, and later, Fairbank.

These three key locations would serve as successors to each other. The rich silver strikes at Tombstone demanded that a roadway be created by which over five thousand people could move to Tombstone at a rapid pace, along with their worldly possessions. This primitive roadway would not only supply the massive shipments of food, clothing, furniture, and other supplies, but more importantly, the machinery and material that would turn Tombstone's rich ore into mines and mills that offered jobs to support such a population. Tucson was and still is the key city nearest the southeast where Tombstone and these related sites would be built. With the founding of railroad town site Benson, A.T. in June of 1880, the trip from Benson to Tombstone would still have to be broken into two legs by a stage stop for travelers to rest, as well as a change for weary horses pulling all those wagons filled with people and their possessions, and harder yet, heavy mining equipment.

The first of these locations to appear would be Drew's Station, and it was of critical importance. Later, just over a mile to the south, Contention City would appear, not for the purpose of competing with Drew's Station as the key stage stop on the journey to Tombstone, but rather as a milling site for three of Tombstone's mines, two of which were the very richest of all: the Grand Central and the Contention. The mills of Contention City would be of little use to these travelers, but the related businesses that were created in their wake - the restaurants and hotels - offered a more comprehensive place to stop, and so Drew's Station would fade in importance on the sojourn to Tombstone in favor of this newer, larger location. A railroad would soon grace Contention City with further options for travelers. Ironically, the construction of this railroad required the purchase of an easement from the Drew family of Drew's Station, which they granted.

While Contention appeared of a more substantial and lasting importance, a small railroad camp just to the south, which would later become known as Fairbank, would thrive into the 20th Century, with a longevity far beyond that of its two predecessors, Drew's Station and Contention City. In the 19th Century Fairbank would remain the closest point on a railroad to Tombstone, and at the dawn of the 20th Century, it would become the point at which a new railroad would spur off and finally link Tombstone to the rest of the world. For passengers heading south to Tombstone, this effectively ended the entire era of commercial stage coach travel, of which Drew's Station, Contention, and Fairbank, had been such a memorable part.

The connection of these locations to Tombstone and its history cannot be overstated, and for far too long has been understated, if addressed at all. The story of travel to and from any community will always remain part of its history, especially in the case of a history such as that of Tombstone, which in today's popular culture, is as personality driven as it is driven by actually what occurred so many years ago.

That names like Ike Clanton, Frank and Tom McLaury, Wyatt, Morgan, and Virgil Earp, along with Doc Holliday, and so many others traveled to and from these places should at least pose a curiosity about these sites. But their real story is one of far more intrigue and depth than just a handful of names who are remembered more for the unfortunate situations in which they found themselves, but rather the achievements of so many who were alongside them at the same time and place, and are hardly remembered at all.

Although the story of these locations is to a degree known, this book's purpose is to bring them to life as much as possible, showing that their stories are key to the Tombstone story, so that they may take their place of well-deserved prominence in that larger saga.

NICE LANDSCAPE, BAD NEIGHBORHOOD

From the inception of these towns sprawling along the San Pedro, it was clear that the area offered fine grass lands for ranching, and industrial sites for milling rich Tombstone ore. Newly arriving settlers were not the first to notice such attributes, or that this was a tough neighborhood to settle in, regardless of the opportunities that it afforded. Traveling with Father Kino, Captain Juan Mateo Manje recorded details of this area where the Spanish had hoped to unlock potential mineral wealth and utilize its agriculture resources. On November 9th, 1697, Manje and party "traveled to the north through a valley and down the river [The San Pedro River]. At a league distance we arrived at the settlement of Quiburi, located on the banks of the river with a large valley, plains covered with pasture, and lands where corn, beans and cotton are harvested. The Indians are dressed in cotton. All the lands are under irrigation. Captain Coro, chief Indian of the Pima nation, together with his people, received us splendidly. We lodged in an adobe and beamed house; and they gave us presents as is their custom. We counted 100 houses and 500 persons of both sexes. The chief celebrated our arrival by giving a dance in a place arranged in circular form. Hanging from a high pole in the center were 13 scalps, bows, arrows and other spoils taken from the many Apache enemies who they had slain." [1]

Nearly two hundred years later, the discovery of silver would lead thousands to populate these lands that Manje had hoped to develop. The Spanish certainly would have found such wealth for themselves, but Apache raids gave them little time to locate the land's treasures, and they would remain intact awaiting the arrival of the Tombstone boom that was to come. That boom occasioned the need for a new network of roadways, stage stops, and milling towns on the very lands that Captain Manje had admired in 1697. Instead of local Indian tribes and the Spanish Conquistadors fighting for the valley's rich resources, the American settlers would now take up the task. As the Los Angeles Herald reported on July 1st, 1880, "Several mines in the neighborhood of Tombstone are claimed by a number of parties, and there have been shot-gun demonstrations among the claimants. Titles to some of the locations are getting very much mixed…"

One settler, William H. Drew, could see in the late 1870's what Manje could only imagine in the late 1600's - a wealth of silver providing new opportunity in this "large valley, plains covered with pasture…" Years after the failure of these mining and milling exploits, the area was still rich for pasture and stock raising, along with agriculture, just as Manje had envisioned so long before.

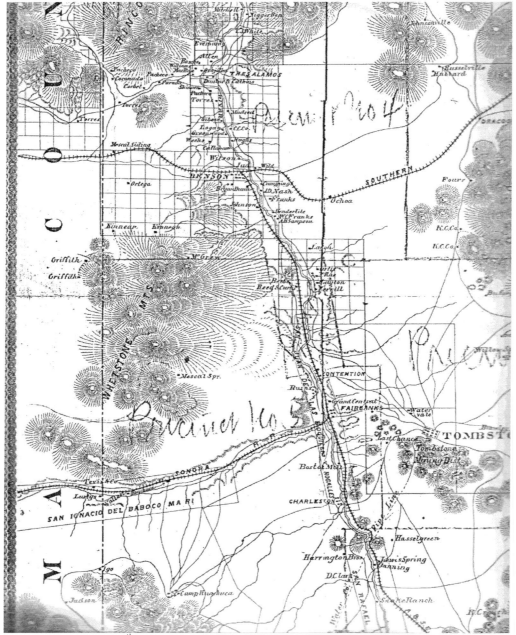

Cropped image of a late 19th Century map showing Tombstone, Fairbank, and Contention among others. Copy from the collections of John D. Rose.

CHAPTER 1

THE SMALL ADOBE BUILDING WITH A BIG STORY

"Then they had a fist fight. Virge thumped the pudding out of him, knockin' him down as fast as he could get up." -Allie Earp

William H. Drew left Montana with his wife, family, and a small herd of cattle, with intentions of heading to California. As his daughter Cora wrote, "Our first stop of any duration was Signal, Arizona, where we remained all that summer and winter." This proved a fortuitous place to stop, as Signal was in a great state of excitement over the fresh silver strikes at Tombstone. Ed Schieffelin had gone to Signal to find his brother Al, and in the process met Dick Gird, forming the very partnership at the core of Tombstone's beginnings. Ed recounted, "I told my brother and Mr. Gird, if any one wanted to know where we were going, to say they did not know, because neither one of them did know where they were going at the time we went. What is known as the Tombstone District was kept entirely secret. The reason for that was because I wanted an opportunity to make full prospects before others could get in. We wanted to get the best mine. After that we calculated to let our friends get a portion of the country." [2] Subsequently, many who left for Tombstone kept in touch with friends at Signal.

William H. Drew, courtesy of the Drew Family Archive.

Talk of such contact would have been all over the streets of Signal when William Drew and family arrived there, and may well have influenced his decision to open a much needed stage stop in the growing Tombstone District of the Arizona Territory (A.T.).

There already existed a stage stop at the confluence of Tres Alamos wash and the San Pedro River, operated by Billy Ohnesorgen, to the north of where Benson, A.T., would later be established, and it would remain viable as a stage stop until the founding of that town in June of 1880. By that point in time, not even Ohnesorgen's well-run operation could compete with all that an actual town had to offer. This would establish the pattern that would one day make Drew's Station obsolete as well. It is a myth that Drew's Station became obsolete because of the

1

building of the railroad. Rather, it was the building of Contention City just over one mile to the south that made this memorable stage stop of little use. Likewise, the historic Tres Alamos site, also known as "The San Pedro Station," had long offered a respite to tired travelers and hurried freighters attempting to cross Arizona. It had been built for use in the overland mail route (now commonly known as the Butterfield Stage route), but it too would be lost in favor of a newly created town. Ohnesorgen would later throw his lot into the competitive stage coach business of the Tombstone District, nearly losing his ranch at Tres Alamos in the process.

But before Benson and Contention City could enter the spotlight, these stage stops played a key role in moving along the fledgling commerce that would build the Tombstone District at a remarkable rate. The population of Tombstone would go from nothing in 1877 to over 5300 in 1882, an almost unimaginable rise, making it larger than Phoenix, A.T. The Tres Alamos site, Spanish for "three cottonwoods," was key to the trip to Tombstone, but it was not enough. Ideally, teams of horses or mules that hauled stages and their passengers should travel no more than ten to twelve miles at a time to keep the animals from injury. The trip from Tres Alamos to Tombstone was nearly double that acceptable mileage.

So William Drew's choice of where to locate was not a random one. With no Benson to the north, and no Contention City and Fairbank to the south, Drew's remote site proved a viable and necessary link between Tres Alamos and Tombstone.

Further to the south of Drew's Station, the climb toward Tombstone rises significantly in elevation. The crossing of Willow wash, south of where Contention would later be built, would necessitate that passengers get out of the coach and push. Drew picked a location in view of the San Pedro, as the topography was a gentle rise from Tres Alamos at 3,402 feet to his station at 3,773 feet, a climb of 371 feet. Then at Drew's Station, the stage would receive a fresh change of horses for the final and most arduous leg of the journey rising over 700 feet to Tombstone, which was 4534 feet in elevation. The location he had chosen was a wise one, but it was not without its issues, especially given its remoteness.

DREW AND A SHOVEL READY PROJECT

In the summer of 1878 The Pima County Board of Supervisors ordered a road survey to be completed into the wilderness that was about to become the thriving Tombstone District. Knowing that the Tombstone silver strikes would soon draw a dramatic population boom, a proper road was essential to progress. A party of three men, William Drew, Robert Mason and H. Lawrence set about the task as a team. Drew and Mason were neighbors, and the roadway that they marked out would traverse their properties.

Mason's Ranche San Pedro Aug 13th 1878

To the honorable board of Supervisors.

Tucson Arizona.

Gentlemen.

In compliance with your notice to us under date of July 22/78. we beg leaf to offer the following report.

We have viewed, layed out and flagged, rout for a wagon road leading from Tucson, to the Upper San Pedro Settlements as follows.

Commencing at a point about four (4) miles East of the Cienaga, on the Tres Alamos road, and running a little East of South to the San Pedro. Sixteen miles above Ohnesorgen's. Shortening the distance fifteen (15) to Sixteen (16) miles.

We have estimated the expense of building this road carefully as possible, and find that it will require about Six hundred to Six hundred and fifty Dollars ($650.00) to complete the work in a first class manner. Trusting that your honorable body may take some action that will cause the building of this Road at an early date.

We Remain yours with Respect.

Estimate for the stage road construction through Drew's Ranch. Copy from the collections of John D. Rose.

Their written report to the Board was dated August 13th, 1878. "Gentlemen. In compliance with your notice to us under [the] date of July22/78, we beg…to offer the following report.

"We have viewed, layed out and flagged, route for a wagon road leading from Tucson, to the Upper San Pedro Settlement as follows.

"Commencing at a point about four (4) miles east of the Ciennaga on the Tres Alamos road, and running a little East of South to the San Pedro, Sixteen miles above [south of, or upstream on the river] Ohnesorger's. Shortening the distance fifteen (15) to Sixteen (16) miles.

"We have estimated the expense of the building of this road carefully as possible, and find that it will require about Six hundred to Six hundred and fifty Dollars…to complete the work in a first class manner. Trusting that your honorable body may take Some actions that will cause the building of this Road at an early date." The trio billed the county for days worked, but without noting a price per day, for fees due.

"Masons Ranch San Pedro Aug 13/78 Pima Co AT To

R. [Robert] Mason, W.H. [William H.] Drew & H. F. Lawrence Dr. for Services rendered in viewing and laying out a wagon Road as per report herewith. Eight (8) days each." [3]

Bill for laying out the stage road across Drew's and Mason's ranch. Copy from the collection of John D. Rose.

Although William Drew and Robert Mason were working partners on the wagon road survey, Drew and others would see a darker side to Mason not previously revealed. "Robert Mason was tried before Justice C.M. Hooker, of Tres Alamos on the 1st instant, for assault and battery on the person of George Eddy. He was tried by a jury of twelve, found guilty and

4

sentenced to sixty days in jail." [4] Mason was by no means through with the local legal system. "Territory of Arizona vs Robert Mason. Appeal from Justice's court, judgement[sic] reversed and case remanded for further proceeding." [5] Charges against Mason were later dismissed by the District Court, First Judicial District Pima County on September 8th, 1879. [6]

And Drew would see firsthand Mason's violent temper over the issue of water use from the limited flow of the San Pedro River, nearby to the homes of both men.

William Drew was utilizing river water to raise corn and other food to feed his family.

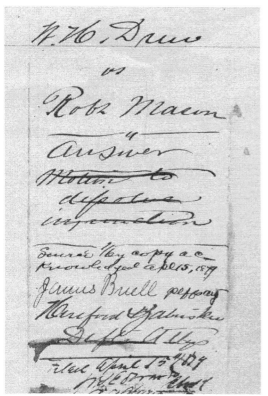

Unfortunately for him, Mason's legal issues the previous November appeared to have had little effect on his behavior. "Water Troubles. Mason and Drew, farmers on the San Pedro, have had troubles about the use of water, and the former was put under bonds to keep the peace in connection with their original difficulty. About a week ago to-day, as we are informed, the trouble broke out anew, in which Mason fired at and nearly hit Drew..." Apparently Harrison was unarmed, but he proved that was not be trifled with, even when outgunned, as he quickly "... got in a lick on his opponent with a shovel, doing some damage. There was some further hostile demonstrations on the part of Mason, which resulted in his [Mason's] arrest and trial at Tombstone, with the privilege of giving a bond for $700 to keep the peace or be imprisoned. Not being able to give the bail, he was brought to Tucson, where he now is, in charge of a Deputy Sheriff." [7]

One of the many documents from the Drew vs. Mason case. Courtesy AHS.

This ongoing conflict would again make news… "Drew vs. Mason; on trial before a jury of three, J.C. McDermott, David Hershaw, and George R. King…The case of Drew vs. Morgan [Mason] was concluded Saturday night. Verdict for plaintiff, $20 damages. Adjourned until Tuesday." [8] Twenty dollars was not much of a penalty when considering that had Mason's aim been better, he would have been up on the possible charge of murder for shooting William Drew.

The related court proceedings offer great insights to Drew's Station and its environs, and also proof that further confirms the correct location of this now very famous station. Court records quote Wm. H. Drew as stating that on April 10th, 1878 he "settled upon and improved as a homestead a certain tract of public land of the United States in the San Pedro valley in said Pima County Territory of Arizona, about one mile South of what is known as the old Califorina [sic] crossing of the San Pedro river, and about three miles North of the old San Pedro ruins..." The location of the old California crossing is an ongoing debate and others arguing for a number of different areas.

That Drew referred to it as the old California crossing is likely from local hearsay that he was told as a new arrival, so such a reference is far less reliable than the second one, since the distance from Drew's homestead to the old California crossing is an indeterminate marker by which the location of Drew's Station and ranch cannot be reliably confirmed. But the "old San Pedro ruins" are a very different matter. They existed long prior to Drew's arrival, dating to 1775, and still exist today. This presidio in ruins was correctly known as "Santa Cruz de Terranate," also referred to as Quiburi Mission, the San Pedro ruins, old ruins, etc. Drew would have known of these ruins and may well have visited them, as they were not only a local landmark but a source of historical curiosity, having been a Spanish settlement whose inhabitants were continually harassed and finally driven out by the Apaches.

The ruins were such a well-known marker on the valley floor that they were even referenced in the original claim document establishing the Tombstone District, signed by Ed and Al Schieffelin and Dick Gird. They are noted on a number of maps from the period. The site of Drew's station measures 2.8 miles northward from Terrenate, as the crow flies. Given the bends in the horseback route between these two points, Drew's estimate of "about three miles" is remarkably close and accurate.

Drew further added that his homestead began "at a point 20 rods East of [the] irrigating ditch known as the upper San Pedro ditch, and east from the North line of the defendants [Mason's] ranch, and running North 880 yards, then West 880 yards, then South 880 yards, then East 880 yards along the North line of Masons ranch to the place of the beginning, containing 160 acres."

Although Drew and Mason had worked together on the road survey through their area, they would later end up in court, as tensions over irrigation water rose between the two neighbors. Prior to Drew's arrival, an irrigation ditch, referred to as the Upper San Pedro Ditch Company, had been dug which ran south to north, giving water access to a number of ranches, including Mason's. One of Drew's neighbors who also had access to the ditch as its waters flowed to and past his property was D. [Daniel] N. Cable. It was he who approximated the point of the ditch's beginning as "about one half mile north of the Contention Mill or Contention City...", ultimately reaching Mason's (and later Drew's) ranch.

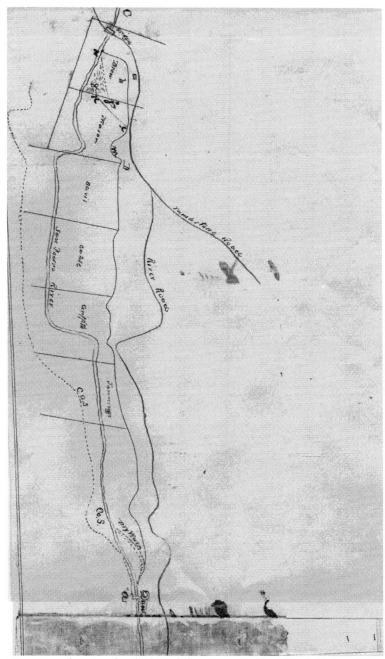

Map drawn by Wm. Drew showing the ditch and dam. As noted by D.N. Cable's mill site claim, the dam began one half mile north of Contention City, proving that Drew's Station was the northern most point as noted on the map. Courtesy AHS.

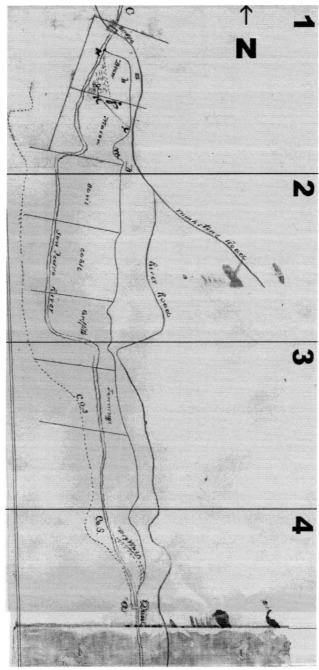

Above, the Drew map is divided into four pieces, and the following pages each shows those areas so that the reader may better understand the maps contents, given its small scale. We have added N for north to the map, as well as the numbers 1-4.

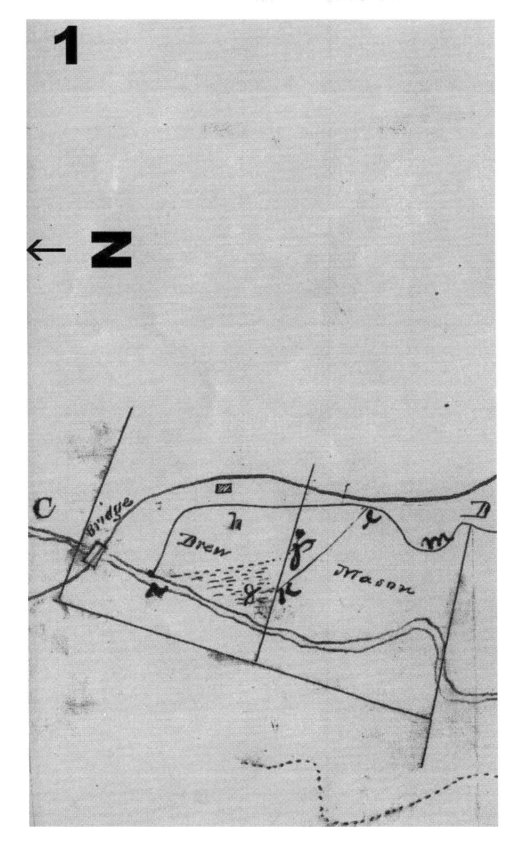

9

2

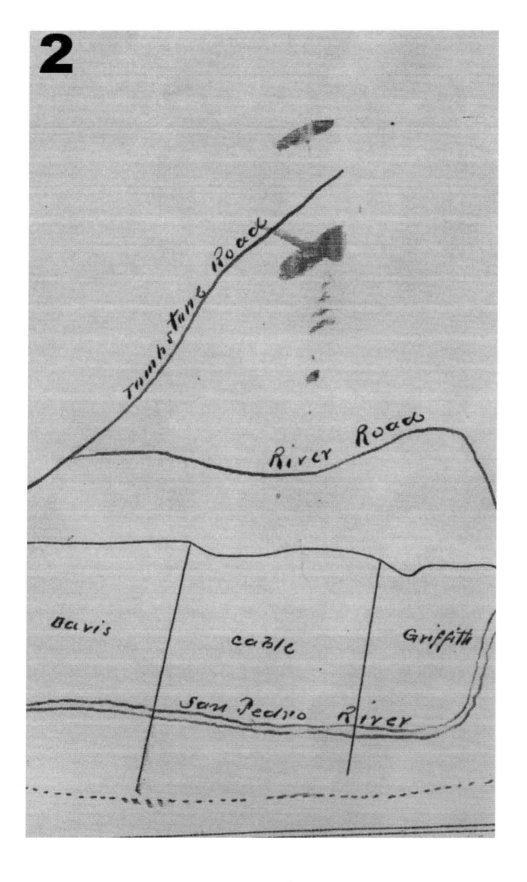

3

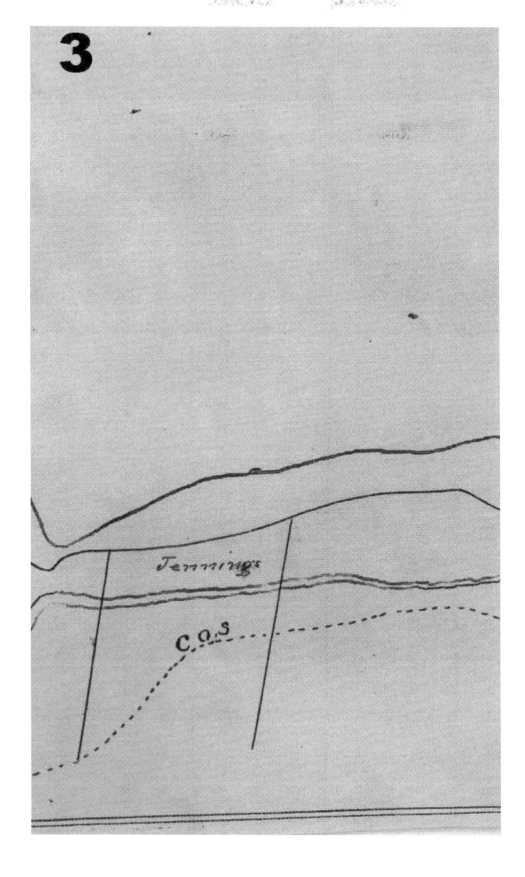

Jennings

c o s

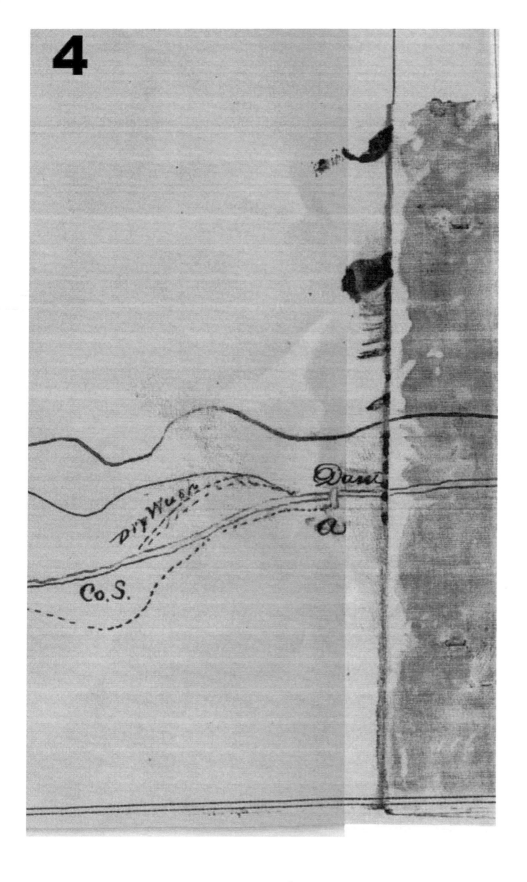

4

Dry Wash

Co. S.

Dam

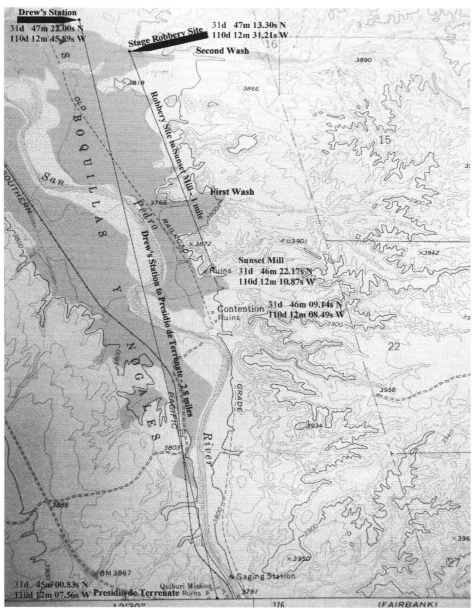

This USGS map shows Quiburi Mission at the location of Santa Cruz de Terrenate, aka, the San Pedro Ruins. As Wm. Drew noted, he located his home "about three miles North of the old San Pedro ruins..." Traveling the contours of the San Pedro River, this 2.8 distance is almost exactly three miles just as Drew estimated. We have added "Presidio de Terrenate" to the map for easy reference. The correct location of Drew's Station is settled. At the north side of Contention, the distance from the Sunset Mill to the robbery site is exactly one mile, just as Bob Paul described. Map research annotations by John D. Rose, computer graphics by D.H.

13

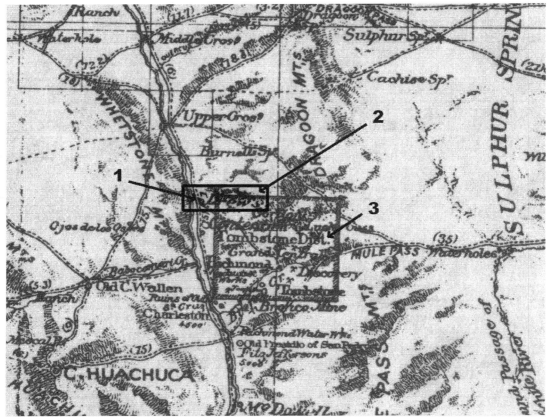

Cropped from the Eckhoff and Riecker map of the Arizona Territory, first published in 1880. The large square shown is the outline of the Tombstone Mining District. Note that the bottom left corner of the District's outline is at the "Ruins of old St. Cruz," aka, Santa Cruz de Terranate, a site wrongly noted as Quiburi Mission by Dr. Charles Di Peso in the 1950's. At the top left of the District's boundary, the word "Drew's", which we have darkened to make it make it more distinct to the reader, is visible with the northern line of the district running through it.

Arrow 1 notes the small circle that marks Drew's Station. Note that it is not directly on the bank of the San Pedro River. Given the scale of this map, Drew's was a fair distance from the river bank, disproving the claim that it was located directly on the river. Arrow 2 points to the word "Drew's" and arrow 3 points to the title "Tombstone Dist." Copy of map in the collections of John D. Rose. Computer graphics by Kevin Pyles.

Google Earth image of the area of Contention City. The first wash to the north was one half mile, and the second wash to the north of Contention is 1.25 miles, which is very close to Bob Paul's estimate of the wash where Philpot was shot as being "one mile the other side of Contention," meaning north of Contention. Measuring from the north side of Contention (instead of its southern side) it is exactly one mile, just as Paul described. Drew's Station was another 1600 feet northwest of the wash, but an outbuilding on Drew's ranch was closer to 200 yards from the wash, as also noted in the Bob Paul account, as published in the Tombstone Epitaph.

Nearly a full mile north of the correct location of Drew's Station is the TTR/Sosa site (see index on Drew's Station), which simply is disqualified by the primary sources. Wm. Drew did not say he lived about four miles from the old ruins, he said about three, therefore his testimony further disqualifies that site, and makes clear that the site as marked is the correct location of Drew's Station.

Research annotations by John D. Rose, computer graphics by D.H.

Drew needed access to the water in the irrigation ditch for his crops on the western section of his land, so at an early time after his arrival, he made an arrangement with Mason. The landscape of the area was such the Drew requested to run a ditch across Mason's property that is noted on his drawing running from the letters "l" to "k." Drew offered free labor to maintain the entire ditch. He spent a month during the summer of 1878 working on the ditch from point "a," where it began at the dam that had been built to pool the San Pedro, down to point "d," which was where Robert Mason received the flow. To further secure his right to this key water source, on November 27th, 1878, Drew purchased an undivided one quarter interest from "said C C Cafflin [?]" in the ditch and dam that fed it. According to Drew, his work on the trench was valued at $50.00, and in return for his labor, Mason would allow him to run a feeder ditch across his ranch to Drew's. So in 1878 Drew began to use the ditch noted on his map as running from "l" to "k."

But by March of 1879, Mason was no longer happy with the arrangement. As the court records continued, "That on or about the first day of March A D 1879 the defendant [Robert Mason] plowed up said ditch and filled it up from 'K' to 'L'…" Another witness told that in cutting off Drew's irrigation supply, Mason had also repeatedly put a "tub" in the ditch to block water flow. When Drew attempted to restore the water flow by clearing the ditch of the fill Mason had dumped in it, the real trouble began—Mason confronted him with a gun. (Wm. Drew referred to guns. One of his sons, George Harrison Drew, was seventy five yards away. "…I saw for certain it was a Gun, it was a patent Winchester Gun…")

Now that he had cut off water to Drew's crops with at least one gun barrel pointed at him, Mason taunted Drew, telling him that his seven acres were "sown in wheat but it has nearly all died out for want of water, and another portion is plowed up for wheat but cannot be sown for want of water, and another portion is set apart for …[Drew's]…garden but cannot be planted for want of water; that on said three acres around 'L' is over half [an] acre of alfalfa which has died out for the want of water…"

Rather than fighting it out with firearms, Drew sought a court injunction. He had to move quickly as his crops were dying before his very eyes. To better explain his case, Drew made a drawing of the area, showing the dam, ditch, and the spatial relationships between himself and the other neighbors using the same water. (Though not to scale, it provides valuable insights.)

Drew then argued his case, both on legal grounds, and also as a man laboring on his family's behalf. "…Plaintiff [William H. Drew] has a family consisting of a wife and four children depending upon him for support, and plaintiff has no other land or property or means of support outside of said ranch, and plaintiff with his family is now living upon said ranch…last year[referring back to 1878] , upon said ranch….[he] dug a well, and built a dwelling house, stables, [a] corn crib, hay corrall [sic] and stock corrall, and cleared about seven acres of ground."

(Drew would later clear an additional three acres for crops, a move which may have sparked the trouble with Robert Mason.)

Mason argued that he had only agreed at the time to allow Drew to use his waste water. If this were true, it is hard to imagine that Drew would have agreed to maintain the entire ditch, knowing that waste water alone could not raise enough crops to support his family. Drew had dug a well on his ranch, and though it supplied all the household water the family needed, it could not irrigate seven acres of land. The issue was whether or not Drew had a legal right to extend the ditch across Mason's property and access the Upper San Pedro Ditch Company water. Once Mason had granted water access across his property to Drew, he had established a precedent. So Mason's arguments were not found credible by the court.

On March 3rd, 1879, Judge French ruled in Drew's favor. "It is therefore ordered by me, the Judge of said District Court of the First Judicial District that until further order…Robert Mason…do absolutely desist and refrain from using or taking out of the upper San Pedro irritating ditch…more than one half [of] the water that flows to defendants [Mason's] ranch in said ditch…"

Mason was unimpressed by the Judge's ruling, and told Drew that "…by the Gods no white man should turn that water on." Worse yet, Mason was by no means through demonstrating his contempt for the court, and soon made matters worse for himself. "On April 12th, 1879, Special Deputy E.S. Penwell traveled to Mason's ranch and personally served him the injunction. Mason told Penwell "That the Judge who issued the Injunction…had no authority in the premises, and that no living white man should divert the water flowing in the ditches in said Injunction described, until the Supreme Judge of the United States so ordered it…"

Judge French soon ordered Mason to his court to explain himself. Oddly, the injunction would later be dissolved, then reinstated. In the end Drew would win his case, and the court upheld his undivided one fourth claim to the water and dam on June 5th, 1879. He would see his reimbursable expenses reduced by the court to the point where he did suffer a financial loss. But he had secured a legal right to a critical water supply for his ranch and his family, just five months before his family could no longer depend on him. He would die in November [1879] of typhoid. For more on this site see WyattEarpExplorers.com, "New Drew's?" [9]

News from Drew's Station of a lighter nature would be reported a short time later, as a sergeant in the army would lose prisoners while resting at the stage stop. "They tell a joke on an army sergeant. He stopped at Drew's [Station] a few nights since, being in charge of two deserters under irons, and having one man as a guard. Mr. Sergeant takes his siesta, leaving the guard to watch the prisoner; but the guard is also tired of the service, so he knocks off the irons of his fellow soldiers and all three make off, taking with them the officer's horse. The sergeant, reduced from cavalry to infantry, made a sad march of thirty miles back to camp." [10]

17

William Drew had a daughter named Cora who, later in her life, wrote of her early years at the station. "From Signal [AT] we moved to a spot on the San Pedro River about eighty miles north of Tucson [Drew's Station is 61 miles southeast of Tucson on the roads of the day] which was our closest trading post." Cora's older brother who helped build the family home/stage station was George Harrison Drew. Harrison, as she called him, was living in Contention City working as a teamster in 1882. Of their home/stage station she later recalled, "Father and my oldest brother Harrison-with the help of two Mexicans, built a three-room adobe house. It had dirt floors and doors made of logs with thick canvass covering the window openings. That year we had a nice garden and a good crop of corn.

Cora Drew had lived at Drew's Station as a child. Courtesy of the Drew Family Archive.

"We were able to secure the stage stop...The four horses were changed at our place and Mama would give the passengers breakfast for a dollar apiece. We also had the Tombstone stages to change. Tombstone ran two stages daily, one second class four-horse stage and one first class six-horse stage."

Cora also recalled her family's financial status of a year later. "I am not sure but I think at this time we were very poor people. For Christmas of 1880 the only thing that Santa left me was a plain dark blue bottle. To me it was the most beautiful thing a child could have and I kept it for many months. Using is as a doll, and it being my only plaything I was heartbroken when I accidently broke it on a rock one day." [11]

The Drew children along with others living in the area had a school to attend, without having to travel to Tombstone. "School At Drew's Station. Miss Lizzie Felter, daughter of Judge

Felter, passed a very creditable examination before Judge Lucas and takes charge this week of the public school at Drew's Station, on the San Pedro." [12]

Cora Drew described the school houses she attended in the Arizona Territory as primitive. "My first schooling was in a three-wall brush shed with a neighbor-woman as the teacher. School was only held when the weather was pleasant and warm. Next I attended a school made of bear grass. This is a fine blade palm which will turn wind and water away. It grows in patches all over Arizona. You separate it as one would celery and tie it to poles, roots up [to avoid the re-rooting that some desert plants are believed capable of]. Both Indians and Mexicans make their homes from this."

She also recalled early experiences learning to ride horses on the ranch that was home to Drew's Station. Although the ranch was located on a declining mesa that drained to the San Pedro River and fronted it, the station and road were wisely built further to the east. This allowed the stage road and those who depended on it the convenience of avoiding washout issues that would later plague the New Mexico and Arizona (N.M. & A.) Railroad. Despite the number of engineers on its payroll, the railroad had not chosen as wise a route as the one lain out by Drew, Mason, and Lawrence. Cora Drew noted that the river was the one area the Drew children were not allowed to traverse on horseback. "The only place we children were not allowed to ride was across the San Pedro River as Topsy [one of their horses] would always get in midstream and roll us off." The familiar shooting heard from desperados across the river may have also figured into this rule imposed by her parents. [13]

CONTENTION CITY ON THE HORIZON

The building of the Contention Mill in the summer of 1879 would not only give Contention City its beginning, but would also give Drew's Station the beginning of its end. "A smelter was built and material was brought in by mule teams. Before the smelter was completed my father passed away in November of 1880 [William H. Drew died in December of 1879]. I was then eight years old. Soon afterwards, my brother Ed was able to secure the contract to deliver wood for the smelter. He hired Mexicans to cut the wood from the Chiricahua Mountains." [14] Early on in their enterprise, their personal tragedy was reported by a Tucson paper: "William H. Drew, of Drew[s] Station on the San Pedro, is dead." [15] This would leave his family to face the many challenges already existing in the area at the time.

About this time, another family was traveling through the Drew ranch and on to Tombstone. Traffic was nearly all one way - heading for the silver strikes. "The wagons spread out one behind the other and tried to keep in the same tracks. We only met one wagon comin' toward us, and then in the afternoon the stage from Benson [Benson did not yet exist; Allie's mention of it is based on her recollection of this event at a later time] caught up with us," as Allie Earp recalled of her journey to Tombstone, accompanied by Wyatt and Mattie Earp, her husband Virgil, and James Earp and his family. The Earps were five miles south of the last stage stop

Virgil Earp, years before his fist fight at Drew's Station during his move to Tombstone. Copy from collections of John Rose.

before reaching Tombstone. On the road approaching Drew's Station, they were drawn into their first conflict in the Tombstone District. "Virge and me were in the front wagon. Lookin' back I saw Wyatt and Jim's wagons both almost in the ditch and on the road passin' them the stage. The driver was crackin' his whip, shoutin' and makin' a big hullabaloo. Right away Virge pulled off to the side. 'Look out! You'll fetch us in the ditch!' I hollered to Virge when the wagon tipped. 'We've got to get over,' said Virge. 'The U.S. Mail has got the right to the road over everybody. Nothing can stop it.'"

Virgil's prompt yielding of the right of way apparently wasn't enough for the stage driver.

"When we were as far as we could get, Virge stopped the horses to let the stage get by. The driver, with plenty of room, kept crackin' his whip, shoutin' and actin' real smart. When he got opposite us, out of meanness and showin' off, he passed so close he ran into our team and raked one of the horses so bad it began to bleed. Then with a laugh, the driver whipped up his own horses and the stage rattled off in a cloud of dust."

Virgil Earp was not to be trifled with, nor would he allow such an act to stand without a response. As Allie added, "Virg didn't say anything. He took one look at the bleeding horse and laid on his whip. They jumped forward and in a jiffy we were racin' down the road after the stage. Wyatt and Jim behind us must have thought somethin' was wrong and whipped their horses into a run after us.

"In about five miles we caught up with the mail stage where it had stopped at a stage-station to change horses. The passengers had all got out to stretch and the driver was standin' with them outside. Virge tied up the reins, got down and walked up to the driver. I got down and followed him just in time to see him knock the driver down. The driver got up and Virge knocked him down again. Then they had a fist fight. Virge thumped the pudding out of him, knockin' him down as fast as he could get up. Finally the driver just laid there. All the people had gathered around. Wyatt and Jim had come up and stood there sayin' nothin'. After a time the driver got on his hands and knees, spit out some blood and teeth, and looked up.

"Don't you get up until you say you're sorry you hurt my horse,' Virge told him. 'You know we were out of your way.'

"I've had enough, the driver grumbled. 'Maybe it was my fault!'" From there the Earps returned to their wagons and the stage road, closing in on their final destination of Tombstone. After leaving Drew's the stage road would soon climb in elevation and a few more miles down the road their new home would come into view. "We all got back in our wagons and started out. We were on top of a hill. I might have known, with a fight on our hands already, what was down there in the Valley. We could see it-it was Tombstone." [16]

TENSIONS BEGIN TO RISE

Since September of 1880, thievery and related issues that plagued Charleston and other areas did not exclude Contention; in fact, they were noticeably on the rise. Further, they appeared to be changing into a criminality of a more organized nature, with many in the stock trades being coerced into paying protection money, and/or joining in the movement and sale of contraband stock. Failure to do so could cause serious repercussions. It was becoming hard for the honest ranchers in the area to contend with such forces. A Contention City butcher and cattle dealer would not be intimidated by these times, but it appears that he gave up on the stock trade in and around Contention City, as a year later he would move to Tombstone, work at a livery stable, and give up running his own beef business. But before leaving Contention he would write a letter complaining of cattle theft and the dangers it posed to his and other businesses in the area. While writing this letter, he learned of a much greater crime.

T.W. [Thomas Webb] Ayles wrote, "I am not a growler or chronic grumbler, but I own stock, am a butcher and supply my immediate neighborhood beef, and to do so must keep cattle on hand, and do try to, and could do so always if I had not to divide with unknown and irresponsible partners, viz: 'Cow Boys,' or some other cattle thieves. Since my advent into the Territory, and more particularly on the San Pedro River, I have lost fifty head of cattle by cattle thieves. I am not the only sufferer from these marauders and cattle robbers on the San Pedro, within the last six months. Aside from 50 head of good beef cattle that I have been robbed of, Judge Blair has lost his entire herd. P. McMinnimen has lost all of his fine fat steers (oxen). Dunbar, at Tres Alamos, has lost a number of head. Burton, of Huachuca, lost almost his entire herd, and others—and in fact all engaged in the stock business—have lost heavily from cattle thieves. And not always do these thieves confine themselves to cattle; horses and mules are gobbled up by these robbers, as well as cattle. Is there no way to stop this wholesale stealing of stock in this vicinity or in the county?

"There seems to be an organized band, and their connections seem to extend to and over the Mexican border and to the borders of New Mexico and across both. Their late raids into Sonora may make that border too hot for them to cross, but their confederates who purchase from them and hide the 'ear marks' may be reached by some organization or the vigilance of the authorities. I am ready to join any organization that will lead to detection and conviction and prompt punishment of these cattle thieves or their confederates who purchase of them. Honest dealers in stock must either have protection or join the band of robbers and their accessories…If there were no cash market for stolen beef cattle, there would be no cattle thieves."

Ayles had put forth an argument for an aggressive but lawful approach to dealing with cattle rustlers. It happened in a coincidence of timing that Eddie Drew, from Drew's Station, actually walked in on Ayles as he was writing this letter, informing him of the murder of a stage coach driver just over a mile from his Contention City home, news which had a profound effect on him. "If this is not convincing proof that the law and order element in Cachise, [Cochise County; many at the time thought that "Cachise" was the correct way to spell and pronounce the Apache chief's name] and throughout the Territory, should deal with thieves and robbers in a summary manner, I am not the person I thought I was when I commenced this article, especially for the benefit of cattle and horse thieves. Yours, T.[Thos.] W. Ayles, Cattle Dealer." [17]

Ayles echoed what many had been saying for quite some time, and his letter is fascinating as it reveals a sea change in his thinking. For him, the shooting of an innocent and well liked stage driver, as well as a passenger, meant that his belief in the lawful approach to such matters was no longer feasible in the face of such outlawry.

ONE MAN BACKS AWAY FROM THE STAGE COACH COMPETITION

Ayles was not alone in his appraisal of the situation in the area. Wyatt Earp, in discussions with Forrestine Hooker, would relate an atmosphere that echoed Ayles' concerns. "…at that time there were many bands of horse-thieves, cattle rustlers and hold-up men infesting Tombstone, Willcox [sic], Gayleyville and their favorite headquarters, Charleston, on the San Pedro River. These combined forces aggregated between two and three hundred men and though all of them might not be implicated in an identical crime at a specified time or place, there was close co-operation among them. Information and warnings were passed along, and officers of [the] law were handicapped by not knowing who was friendly to the outlaws. Another difficulty was to obtain conviction of these criminals after an arrest had been made. There were countless men, apparently reputable citizens, ready to prove an alibi and swear that the accused had been a hundred miles from the scene of [the] crime at the time it had been committed. Then, too, many

22

ranchers who were reputable, honest men, though anxious to see the lawless element controlled, would not come out openly against them for fear of retaliation, which might mean loss of [their] stock on the range, or even a bullet in the back through a window at anytime. It was an easy matter for any man or body of men to hide in the rugged mountains, where cattle, wild game, grass for horses could be found." [18]

Wyatt Earp himself would narrowly avoid risking his own finances in the Tombstone District's brisk stage company competition, of which J.D. Kinnear was a key player. "I intended to start a stage line when I first started out from Dodge City, but when I got there [Tombstone] I found there was two stage lines and so I finally sold my outfit to one of the companies, to a man named Kinnear. But I intended to start this stage when I went there," as Wyatt Earp later recalled. [19]

KINNEAR CHOOSES PASSENGER SAFETY OVER REVENUE

Kinnear himself understood that there were dangers of operating a stage line in the area, and wisely refused to carry bullion shipments in his passenger coaches that could endanger both the lives of his drivers and customers. But heated competition would cause Kinnear to re-think what had been a wise decision. "The mine owners, notably the Gird and Schieffelin interests, were among the first to benefit from the improved freight express. From the inception of Kinnear's line, the principal mining and milling companies tried to negotiate an arrangement for the transport of bullion…by stage to Tucson. Kinnear had steadfastly refused to carry this dangerous cargo, so the miners, themselves, were obliged to haul the heavy bars of precious metal. The slow wagons bristled with their own guards, protecting shipments valued up to twenty-five and thirty thousand dollars. By the first of November, the new competition had driven the Tucson and Tombstone Mail and Express [Kinnear's company] to seek all the business and prestige it could get. Kinnear concluded an agreement with the Tombstone Mill and Mining Company to carry the valuable ingots on his stagecoaches." [20] Kinnear would later be compelled to reverse this decision, running passengers separate from his coaches carrying bullion. But it was a compromise that would come too late to avoid a tragedy.

Tucson and Tombstone Stage Line,

Doing a General
STAGE AND EXPRESS BUSINESS.

J. D. KINNEAR, Proprietor.

PRINCIPAL OFFICE, - - TUCSON, A. T.

Tombstone

~~Tucson~~ A. T., Jan 30th 1880

Dear Father

I just got out of bed the first time for five days I have been down with "Pneumonia" Had a pretty tough time the first two days the doctors did not expect me to live. But I had good physicians and I comenced doctoring in time So that the doctors checked the deasease from the Start but oh I am awful Sore yet. Blistered from head to foot almost with mustard plastrs but I am out of danger unless I expose myself and catch a fresh cold and I aint going to do that for I am going to Stay in the house for two or three days longer. I cant write any more now I must lay down I am getting nervious. Dnt worry I am out of danger — Love to all

Your Affte Son
Jacob Eaton

Original Kinnear letterhead from the collections of John D. Rose.

CHAPTER 2

FATEFUL RIDE ON A MOONLIT NIGHT

"We're just thirteen miles out from Tombstone," was the reply. "That's an unlucky number." –
Peter Roerig

     March of 1881 would bring a tragedy to the Contention area which would have far reaching repercussions for Contention, Drew's Station, and Tombstone's soon to emerge Earp-related controversies. It was an event that the children of Drew's Station would long remember as well. The Kinnear and Company Stage, the line between Benson and Tombstone, was no longer using Drew's Station as a stage stop. This pioneering stage station predictably proved no competition for all that Contention City had to offer: restaurants, stores, a stage station of their own, and the option of staying over in a hotel if a weary traveler wished to break the trip into smaller legs. The care of a doctor was also available. But the stages would still pass within close proximity to Drew's along their course.

     Bud Philpot had been in Arizona for a year, spending most of that time as a driver working for Kinnear. He loved to tell passengers of his "old stage days" when California was more of a frontier. As with many others in his profession, Bud had more than one brush with the "Knights of the Road," aka the stage robber. On one memorable occasion he outsmarted his would-be robbers in grand style. He had shown "his rare presence of mind in moments of excitement. Like every other old stage-driver who ever drove in the mountain counties of California, 'Budd' met his share of 'stoppages.' On one occasion he was halted and confronted with the cold muzzle of a six-shooter and a peremptory command to 'throw out the box.' He threw it out and immediately applied the lash to his horses. Imagination is necessary to depict the chagrin of the road-agents when they found, instead of the treasure-box, a green wooden band-box belonging to a female passenger, which had happened to be near at hand in the boot. For this clever ruse 'Budd' for a long time wore a handsome gold watch, presented to him by Wells, Fargo & Co." [21]

     It was also said of Philpot that "He was proud and fond of his team and the big new coach" and known for treating his horses "as if they were human, and the horses always seemed to know when 'Budd' was at the other end of the lines." [22] That big new coach was named the "Grand Central," in honor of Tombstone's greatest mine, and Contention City's largest mill. Like some who had been on the frontier moving from one boom town to the next, he was viewed as "outwardly rough, but inwardly brave, [a] truehearted man." The children of Drew's Station seemed to take a shine to Philpot as well, Cora Drew noting that "Bud Philpot was the driver of the first class stage, and we children always got up and waved goodby [sic] when he left late at night."[23]

When Bud moved to Tombstone, his young family opted to remain in Calistoga, CA. In early 1881, while driving with his friend and co-worker, "a bullet sent whizzing between him and Jack Allman" when the stage was stopped between Tombstone and Contention. From that incident forward, Bud had "a present[i]ment of coming evil ever since that night." So much so that on Monday, March 14[th], 1881, Bud had asked Allman to mail a letter home to his family. This outwardly tough stage driver had written a "long and loving letter to dear ones at home," according to Allman. [24]

The following day, while Bud's letter home was slowly en route back to California, he was again driving the down coach from Tombstone through Contention to Benson. It was the evening of March 15th, 1881, and it was unusually well illuminated by the moonlight. Jack would have

Bob Paul noted that Bat Masterson was a passenger on the stage when Philpot was shot. Copy photo from the collections of John D. Rose.

been with him, but due to the withdrawal of an opposition stage line, he was given the night off. Without Allman, Philpot left Tombstone with Bob Paul next to him atop the stage. Paul was already a well-established lawman from his California days, as well as a current guard for Wells Fargo. Along with Paul's formidable reputation he also carried his double-barreled Winchester and his pistol.

Paul would have regularly been well-armed on such a trip, but on this journey security was of unusual importance to him. It was later reported that he "was acting messenger at the time and had in his charge a load of bullion beside about $13,000 which the Wells Fargo had declined to accept on account of the danger which attended the transmission of money at that particular time. Mr. Paul had assumed the personal responsibility of carrying that large sum." [25]

According to Bob Paul the stage had left Tombstone with four passengers, one of them being Bat Masterson. Also inside the coach were Thomas Walker and his wife. Walker was a distant relation of Dick Gird's who had helped to load the wagon that the Schieffelin brothers and Gird drove from Signal to seek out the silver discoveries that would create the Tombstone District. He had followed this fledgling expedition uninvited and later delivered to Tucson the first eight bars of bullion ever created in the district, from Gird's Mill at Millville. [26]

The stage, having left Tombstone with four passengers inside, now took the short trip to Watervale, a small settlement on the east side of the stage road just north of Tombstone. Here they added two more passengers, Canadians both: Riley who went inside the coach, and Peter Roerig, who found a spot on top of the coach near Philpot and Paul. Roerig was a Tombstone miner who had worked at the Vizina, Naumkeag, and Tranquility mines. French Canadian by birth, he had a mining partner in Montana he was on his way to meet and look after some mining interests they had in the area. [27]

After leaving Watervale, they headed toward Contention. The majority of this trip is a drop in elevation, with occasional climbs in and out of arroyos. That is why this trip was known as the "down coach." As the stage drove along the main road, it would soon take a left that was used primarily by the ore wagons delivering ore to the Contention Mill at Contention City. They drove to the back of the mill, and while they waited receipt of the bullion, they had a commanding view of the town. [28] Any lanterns glowing from the inside of cabins or businesses as the night fell on Contention City would be easily viewed from this vantage. Here they gained six more bars of bullion, turned the team around toward the main stage road, and headed north. Shortly they exited the road, slowly dropping directly into Contention City itself on its north side. At Contention they changed horses, as was now the custom, rather than traveling just over another mile to Drew's as had been done in earlier days. With the exception of a few ranches, Philpot's next landmark to be passed was Drew's Station. But before he got there, he would have to cross two washes north of Contention City.

He traversed the first wash north of Contention without incident. Conversation inside the coach could be heard by Philpot, Bob Paul and Peter Roerig, who was sitting on the dickey seat. "To occupy this place meant sitting on the top of the coach facing backward while one's legs dangled or braced against a footboard." At some point during this leg of the journey, Roerig asked Philpot, "How far have we come?"…"We're just thirteen miles out from Tombstone," was the reply.

"That's an unlucky number," commented Roerig. "Well, we'll soon make it fourteen," Philpot laughed. [29] While Philpot continued northward toward the next wash, a coach from the low budget Smith line was heading south from Benson toward Contention, then on to its Charleston destination. It was south of Drew's Station at the same time that Philpot was traveling northward from Contention. When the Smith stage arrived in the area of Drew's Station, "a man approached the stage and after peering in discharged a pistol five times in the air. After driving a little further one of the passengers called the attention of the others to five men lying concealed in the brush near the road."

Philpot was still south of this wash in which the Smith stage had witnessed the concealed group, but Smith passengers would soon see Philpot approaching them and passing by as he headed to what they already knew had the appearance of an ambush. He may have still been far enough away to have not heard the five shots. "Shortly after this they passed the stage [Philpot's] bound for Benson, and in the course of a few minutes shots were heard in the direction which it

27

had taken." The two stages passed after the Smith Stage had exited the wash, and before Philpot had reached the same location. It is tragic that knowledge of the concealed men was not passed on to Philpot and Bob Paul as the stages came within a few feet of each other, and at a distance far enough before the wash that they could have escaped what was about to come.

As Philpot drove on, "The team settled down to a swinging trot…The only sounds were the shuffling hoofs of the horses in the sandy road and the indistinct murmur of voices inside the coach…" Bob Paul later recalled this second wash north of Contention City, noting, "A short distance from the ranch [Drew's] was a 'wash' about ten feet deep which lay in the road of the stage." As Philpot drove into the second wash, he slowed again as was necessary when crossing its sandy bottom. Such spots were well known to robbers, as a stage's momentum is lost going into the sand, and is further reduced as it climbs back out. As Philpot entered the wash, less than fifty feet in width, he was very much alive, experiencing a seemingly routine trip and about to reach the opposite side. But that feeling of safety was short lived, as seconds later he and Paul soon noticed "…four men, two on each side of the road, standing on the elevation they were approaching. The men were armed and the driver and messenger knew that it was to be a fight to the death."

Philpot began to drive up out of the wash, and the attackers made their move. As the stage was "going up a small incline about two hundred yards this side of Drew's Station and about a mile the other side of Contention City a man stepped into the road from the east side and called out 'Hold!'…Bob Paul cooly reached for his gun, exclaiming, 'By God, I hold for nobody.'… Mr. Paul has been a terror to the road agents, and it is thought his recognition on the stage prompted the robbers to attempt his life…At the same moment a number of men-believed to have been eight [actually four]-made their appearance, and a shot was fired from the same side of the road, instantly followed by another. One of these shots struck 'Budd' Philpot, the driver, who fell heavily forward between the wheelers, carrying the reins with him...a large number of shots were fired by the assailants at the coach, one bullet passing through the cushion under Detective Paul…Paul emptied both barrels of his gun, and also his revolver while the stage was rattling along as fast as the horses could haul it…"

Paul didn't hesitate to fire on the assembled criminals. "While in the bed of the 'wash' Mr. Paul had recognized one of the men as the notorious Bill Leonard, as he stood upon the bank, his form outlined against the [moonlit] sky. He took a single shot at him before the furious race set in. His own clothing [Paul's] had been twice grazed by bullets."

Paul also made a risky attempt to keep Philpot from falling off the stage, but to no avail. He "endeavored to catch 'Budd' as he was falling over the foot-board, and barely saved himself from falling over also…The horses immediately sprang into a dead run. Meanwhile, Bob Paul, Wells, Fargo & Co's messenger, one of the bravest and coolest men who ever sat on a box-seat, was ready with his gun and answered back shot for shot before the frightened horses had whirled the coach out of range. It was fully a mile before the team could be brought to a stand, when it was discovered that one of the shots had mortally wounded a passenger on the coach named Peter Roerig." As Paul later told, "The coach was soon out of the reach of the robber's bullets and death seemed as imminent from the terrible speed as it had a few minutes before amidst the deadly bullets…"

"There were no means of checking [slowing] the horses except by the application of the brake…" It was only after getting the runaway team under control that Paul learned of the second tragedy of that attack. "Turning his head for the first time he saw [Peter] Rohrig [sic] lying on top of the coach mortally wounded. Finally, when the horses, fatigued by the awful burst of speed had relapsed into a trot, one of the passengers alighted and gathered up the dragging reins."

The passenger handed Paul the reins, and he drove rapidly to Benson, dropping off a group of shocked travelers, and in the few moments that followed their arrival in Benson, Peter Roerig, whose only mistake was being willing the take the seat on top so that his traveling companion could sit inside, died at Benson. Paul "immediately started back for the scene of the murder. At Benson a telegram was sent to Marshall Williams at the Tombstone Wells Fargo office, stating the Roeri[n]g could not possibly live." This telegram would serve as the basis for the Tombstone Epitaph article covering the event on the following day. "There were eight passengers on the coach, and they all united in praise of Mr. Paul's bravery and presence of mind." [30] As the stage raced by Drew's Station, the sound of gunfire brought Eddie Drew quickly to the exact spot where Philpot had just been murdered. "…the shooting sounded as if a bunch of firecrackers were going off," Cora Drew recalled. [31]

"At Drew's Station the firing and rapid whirling by [sic] of the coach sent the men [Eddie Drew was but a teenager at the time] of the station to the scene of the tragedy, when they found poor 'Budd' dead lying in the road, and by the bright moonlight saw the murderers fleeing rapidly from the place." [32] Interestingly, the Epitaph notes that the telegraph from Benson telling of the event didn't reach Marshall Williams in Tombstone until 11 o'clock that evening, and Cora Drew refers to the stage in the area of Drew's at 9pm, and the stage had passed through Contention at 8pm.

Cora recollected, "Ed saddled a horse and went to Contention to tell of the holdup and murder, and shortly men came from Tombstone and took Bud away in a spring-wagon…The bright Arizona moonlight made it possible for Mama and us children to see…the holdup men ride around the hill and off into the distance." [33]

Young Drew would become the first to bring news of this tragedy to Contention City. T.W. Ayles recounted more of his meeting with him: "Right here I am stopped by the entrance of a messenger who reports that the down coach from Tombstone to-night, and which passed here at 8p.m., had been shot into, and 'Budd,' the driver, is now lying on the road-side, dead, with his whip alongside of him. And just now Eddie Drew, a young son of the Station keeper at Drew's station, informs me that he saw the dead man and recognized him as 'Budd,' the driver of the coach. If this proves true, 'Budd' ha[s] been shot, and falling from his seat must have carried the lines with him, and the probabilities are the six horse team has runaway and we can only conjecture what may happen to the passengers, coach, and horses....This occurred at what is known as the 'wash,' just below Drew's Station..."

Ed Landers Drew, years after being the first to discover Bud Philpot's remains. Courtesy of the Drew Family Archive.

Ayles' prediction of dire results for the surviving passengers was logical, but remedied by the bold actions of Bob Paul that evening, whom Ayles referred to as "Bob Paul, Wells, Fargo's old reliable..." [34] By the time Paul returned to the site of Philpot's murder, his body had already been removed.

Once Drew had spread the news at Contention, A.C. Cowan, the Wells Fargo agent there, began his flight to Tombstone on the Contention to Tombstone stage road. Although telegraph wire was strung through and past Contention in July of 1880, there was not yet a station there to send and receive messages. As Cowan rode through the moonlit darkness approaching Tombstone in the distance, Marshall Williams of the Tombstone Wells Fargo office had just received Bob Paul's first report via telegraph from Benson.

Before Cowan had left for Tombstone, he dispatched "nearly thirty well-armed volunteers after the scoundrels." With armed and eager men riding across the expanse from Tombstone to Contention to Drew's Station to Benson, it was indeed fortunate that no posse shot at another by accident. [35]

30

The reaction in Tombstone was one of outrage, as consummate diarist George Parsons recorded. "Wednesday, March 16th, 1881: A most terrible affair of last evening. First intimation I had of it was when Doc. Goodfellow burst into [my] room and asked for [my] rifle. Abbott finally let him have his upon Doc's assurance he didn't want to kill any one. I stopped our chess, got [my] revolver and followed him up, not wishing him to get hurt if I could help it. Men and horses were flying about in different directions, and I soon ascertained the cause. A large posse started in pursuit-$26,000 specie [coined money] reported on [the] stage. Bob Paul went as shot gun messenger and emptied both barrels of his gun at the robbers, probably wounding one. 'I hold for no one,' he said and let drive. Some 20 shots fired-close call for Paul. Capt Colby wished me to form one of another posse, to head the robbers off at San Simon if we could get necessary information upon arrival of [the] stage, and we worked the thing up. Got rifles and horses, and I got [Mayor John] Clum and Abbott to go with us. Probably six in all. Information didn't come as we expected, so delayed, and several of us shadowed several desperate characters in town, one known as an ex-stage robber. Couldn't fix anything. Bud Philpot, the driver, was shot almost through the heart and the passenger, a miner, [Peter Roerig] through the back. Doc showed me the bullet that killed him-an ugly .45 calibre." Parsons and others would soon find that the trail, for his group anyway, had gone cold. "Some more tracking tonight. Our birds have flown." [36] The Earp posse had struck the trail early and was still in pursuit after Parsons and his group had given up the chase. While that pursuit was carried on, additional news surfaced related to the tragedy.

Mr. Derre, the Smith line passenger who told of the preview that he and his fellow passengers had just before the murders took place, later made an additional discovery. "While in Benson several days ago, Derre recognized [Luther] King, the stage robber in the custody of Sheriff Behan, as the one who had peered into the stage. The five shots fired by him were evidently a signal, but for what purpose it is as yet not known; probably to let the robbers understand that it was the wrong stage." What constituted "the right stage" to shoot at is still a source of debate, some asserting that it was really an attempt on the life of Bob Paul, who had contested an election result which would make him Pima County Sheriff, others asserting that it was just a robbery gone very, very badly. It was also argued at the time that "Those acquainted with the cow-boys…stoutly [argue] that had they known that Paul was upon the stage, no attempt would have been made upon it."

If true, this would prove that the cowboys had a more advanced sense of self-preservation than many had believed prior, or since. Having arrived safely at his destination, Bob Paul "transferred the Wells & Fargo treasure box and the United States mail intact to J.D. Kinnear, the agent [and owner of the line] at Benson…accompanied by four men, to the scene of the attack.…it is becoming believed that, Detective Paul becoming aware of the secret intentions of the cow-boys to attack the stage at a favorable moment, brought Mr. Roswell here in haste, and even in ill health, to help thwart their plans. The occurrence last night conclusively proves that Wells, Fa[r]go's officers have been well advised, and were well prepared to defend their treasure box…The Anglo-California Bank lately shipped [a] very heavy treasure to their Tombstone correspondent, which the company alleges as the reason for the extra precautions…"[37]

The attackers had taken their own precautions as well. "They had arranged two 'blinds,' made of brush, one on each side of the road, and commenced firing almost simultaneously after the order to halt. The chances of their capture are favorable, as some of the 'nerviest' men in the Territory are on their track. Sheriff Behan is with the party, which includes Detective Paul, Marshal Williams, the Earp brothers, 'Doc' Holliday, and two others whose names were not learned. " Bob Paul would later claim that one of these two men was Bat Masterson, the Hooker Manuscript confirming the same. [38]

CHASING MURDERERS

The headlines told the story. "A Good Man Gone to Meet His Maker. Brave Bob Paul on Deck as Usual. He Answers the Robbers Shot for Shot. Contention City, Tombstone and Benson Aroused. Three Bands of Armed Men After the Robbers. Probability that They Will be Soon Captured." [39] That last line would prove easier to write than to carry out.

Intriguing reports surfaced in the wake of the tragedy. "It is well known that a Vigilance Committee was lately formed at Tombstone backed by all the money necessary to take these parties in hand and teach them a lesson." [40] But this did not translate into a well provisioned posse in pursuit, members of which included the Earps.

For Bob Paul, his battle with the killers started at the wash just south of Drew's Station when he fired on them and later continued in pursuit, the trail leading to Tres Alamos and to the nearby ranch of Len Redfield. "Detective R.H. Paul telegraphed from Tres Alamos Tuesday to Mr. Van Fleet, Wells Fargo & Co.'s agent here [Tucson], that he tracked the stage robbers to that place [Tres Alamos] last night, and would take the trail this morning. His return would depend upon circumstances. Mr. Paul is following them like a sleuth hound, and when [he] overtakes the fugitives there will be a short reckoning unless the robbers discreetly surrender." [41]

"Sheriff Behan returned yesterday from the chase, having in his custody Lew [Luther] King, who is charged with being an accomplice in the matter, although he was not an actual participant in the shooting. He was captured at Redfield's ranch, on the San Pedro, and it is believed that he was on his way to join the fleeing murderers with ammunition and intelligence of the pursuit. Billy Leonard's horse was also captured, he having broken down and beed [been] abandoned. There is little doubt that Detective Paul and his associates will be successful, and from Sheriff Behan's statements it was not thought necessary to send out additional aid." [42] Behan's decision to not send out additional aid would later be revisited, but now events took a surprising turn, even for those who were not enemies of Behan.

"Escape of an Arizona Murderer. Between 7 and 8 o'clock last evening Luther King, the man arrested at Redfield's ranch charged with being implicated in the recent murder and attempted stage robbery, escaped from the Sheriff's office by quietly stepping out of the back door, while Harry Jones, Esq., was drawing up a bill of sale for a horse the prisoner was disposing of to John Dunbar. Besides Jones, there were present Under Sheriff Woods and John Dunbar, and he had been absent but a few seconds before he was missed, and all stepped into the back yard, but King was nowhere to be seen. His confederate on the outside probably had for him a horse in re[a]diness and he decamped into the darkness, in what direction no one knows... While there might at the time have been more watchfulness on the part of those in charge of him, still through day and night since his arrest, a guard has been kept over him, and in a single unguarded moment he got away, but not without the aid of accomplices on the outside." [43] Parsons had no question as to the responsible party for King's escape, noting that "King, the stage robber, escaped tonight early from H. Woods who had been previously notified of an attempt at release [escape] to be made. Some of our officials should be hanged. They're a bad lot." [44]

The Nugget was attempting to defend the indefensible. There was no outward assault on the jail with guns blazing to gain freedom for King; he was simply allowed to walk out without conflict. The attempt by the Nugget to deflect responsibility away from Under Sheriff Harry Woods and John Dunbar, who was also at the jail and could have shown some civic diligence as well, was just as inexplicable. (Harry Woods would also serve as the editor of the Nugget.)

Now with King on the loose reports of his escape showed him heading in opposite directions. "Several parties started out after him towards Charleston." But a contrary report surfaced that he was seen making for Helm's ranch in the Dragoons. "Every effort will be made to secure his capture." "The Epitaph says: It is a fair supposition that, despite the efforts being made to recapture King, he will make good his escape." [45]

"Gave Leg Bail. Lew King, the cow-boy, who was captured by the Sheriff's posse, suspected of being an accomplice in the recent murders and attempted stage robbery, escaped from the custody of under sheriff Harry Woods, at Tombstone on Monday evening. From the particulars given in the newspapers of that place, the escape was the result of inexcusable and culpable negligence on the part of the officer in charge, as he had been notified of the intended escape of King. It is supposed that the prisoner was aided by a confederate, as the statement was overheard that a fresh horse would await him at Helm's ranch in the Dragoons." [46]

No. $25.00.
LICENSE TAX RECEIPT FOR CACHISE COUNTY.
—○FEE. $1.50.○—
This Certifies that I. Isaacs & Co. Loer this
day paid the sum of Twenty-Five Dollars, which entitles them to
do business as Keepers of Banking Game for the Quarter month
ending August 15, 1881
J. O. Dunbar
COUNTY TREASURER.
J. H. Behan
SHERIFF.
Dated July 25, 1881
H. Woods
DEPUTY.

On July 25th, 1881, Tombstone firefighter and professional gambler Ike Isaacs purchased the above license for his local gambling enterprise. The receipt is for "Keepers of Banking Game," meaning gambling. Note that although the license was preprinted on a quarterly basis, the word Quarter has been crossed out and the word month written above it, making such licensing even more expensive.

The license is signed by three players who were involved with escaped prisoner Luther King. J. H. [John Harris] Behan signs as Sheriff, who brought King to the Tombstone Jail after his capture at Redfield's Ranch. Tombstone Nugget Editor Harry Woods signs as Deputy, and J.O. [John] Dunbar signs as County Treasurer. Both Harry Woods and John Dunbar were present when King was allowed to leisurely walk out of the jail making good his escape. The license was preserved by Ike Isaacs himself, in his personal scrapbook, now in the collections of John D. Rose.

TROUBLE ON THE TRAIL

On March 22nd, Parson noted that "Another party started out today for robbers-just three or four men but amongst them two of the best trailers and plainsmen in the U.S. so said F. Leslie and [Billy] Breakenridge." The chase for the killers of Philpot and Roerig would prove an exhausting one, and Helm's Ranch would again be part of the drama. "Yesterday forenoon Sheriff Behan and all of his party, with the exception of Bob Paul, returned to Tombstone and received the welcome which is due to brave men who have done their whole duty. An Epitaph reporter last evening called up Virgil Earp and from him elicited the following account of the trip:

"Sheriff Bob Paul, of Pima county, Deputy United States Marshal Virgil Earp and his brother Morgan Earp were joined at Helm's ranch on the 24th ult. by Sheriff Behan, 'Buckskin Frank' Leslie, the well-known Government scout and plainsman, and the party took up the trail of Crane and Head, the latter having several days the start of them, and having, moreover, the additional advantage of about eight fresh horses, which they had stolen from Helm's ranch, including Bob Archer's racer. The trail was followed

Fly's Gallery, Tombstone, A. T.

As Parsons wrote, "Yesterday Earps were taken to Contention to be tried for the killing of [Billy] Clanton. Quite a posse went out. Many of Earp's friends accompanied armed to the teeth." Parsons photo Courtesy of Roy Young.

into the Sulphur Spring[s] valley, through which the robbers passed, crossing the Chiricahua mountains near Fort Bowie, in the direction of San Simon. Knowing that the murderers would head for the latter section, and desiring to gain as much time as possible, the pursuers left the trail in [the] Sulphur Spring[s] valley and took a 'short cut' for Galeyville…

"Here they learned that two of the gang had a ranch at a place known as Cloverdale Springs, in southwestern New Mexico. Judging that they would naturally make for this, the posse at once set out for the locality. The first point they reached was San Simon ranch, in the valley known by that name, owned by Barlow & Pierce." Arriving at the San Simon ranch, they were told of a ranch fifty miles to the southeast, and they found this ranch deserted, without food. Conditions only worsened. "Nothing daunted, they pushed ahead about fifty miles further…hoping to find a ranch. At the end of two long, hungry days they were practically lost. They had had no water since leaving the deserted ranch, a space of 24 hours, and a 'council of war' resulted in a hunt for water. After searching unsuccessfully for half a day, Virgil Earp's horse which he had ridden since leaving Tucson, seventeen days before, gave out, and Morgan

35

Earp dismounted, packed all the played out horse's traps on his own animal, and the two brothers, refusing to abandon the noble animal which had done so well, took to the original mode of locomotion, and drove the tired horses before them.

"That night, almost exhausted-having been sixty hours without food and thirty-six without water-the party reached a spring. Here another council was held, and it was determined that Behan, Leslie and Bre[a]kenridge [should] start back to Barlow & Pierce's ranch, 100 miles distant, for food and water, leaving the others to follow as best they could. When the first-mentioned gentlemen reached the ranch, they immediately dispatched a man on a fresh horse on the back trail with provisions and water for Paul and the Earp boys. The messenger met them about 9 o'clock at night. They had been four days and a half in that almost trackless desert, and the only morsel of food which had passed their lips was a solitary quail which one of the party had shot.

"The remainder of the eventful trip is easily told. Arriving at Galeyville, it was found impossible to obtain horses for a fresh start, and the privations which the party had undergone rendered them unfit for immediately resuming the trail. So they returned home, having reason to feel well satisfied with the manner in which they acquitted themselves." [47]

As Breakenridge later wrote of the same event, "Sheriff Behan started with Frank Leslie and myself to hunt them." Of the troubles that the pursuers had, he added that "As none of us had ever been in that part of the country before, we had to inquire the way to Cloverdale, and were directed wrongly as we ought to have expected. [The] next morning, taking a lunch with us, we started on the trail we were directed to take, and that night reached a deserted ranch house known as the double 'dobe. This was forty miles from the Cienaga. The following day we started out early and, passing through a gap in a mountain, found ourselves on a wide open plain with no trees or water in sight. We made a dry camp that night and [the] next morning found the stakes of the…Railroad line that was being surveyed toward Benson.

"We followed them and about noon came in sight of the double 'dobe, where we had stayed the first night out. We went there for water for ourselves and horses. We had seen no one since we left Joe Hill's; we had no provisions, having eaten the last of our lunch the night before, so we let our horses graze and rest until evening. Although both posses camped together at night, we did not travel together, as our party was better mounted and we were more used to the saddle. We reached the water some time before the others. Our horses were tired and we did not know the way, or where there was a ranch at which we could get aid, and after a consultation I decided that my horse was able to carry me back to the San Simon Cienaga that night as he would be in the morning. Behan and Leslie thought the same, but the marshal's posse decided to wait until morning. We saddled up and struck out after dark, and reached Joe Hill's ranch about daylight. We got Hill's people up and hired a man to take some provisions back to the marshal's party. He met them on the way and they were glad to see him. We lay at Hill's ranch one day, then returned to Tombstone.

36

"This was my first trip with Frank Leslie. He was the life of the party; he had a good voice and sang well, told good stories, never complained of being tired, was always ready to go. He was a much better companion out in the country than he was in town." [48]

While Wyatt, Morgan, Virgil Earp, and Doc Holliday as well as the Behan posse remained in pursuit of the killers, the murder victims were medically examined at Benson. "Dr. G.E. Goodfellow and Coroner Mathews went down to Benson on Tuesday night and returned yesterday." The Coroner held an inquest on both of the murdered men, and reports as follows: "'Budd' received the fatal shot in the left arm above the elbow." This evidence proves that the fatal shot for Philpot came from the attackers on the west side of the wash. As the report continued, "The bullet passed through the arm, shattering the bone, entered the left side between the third and fourth ribs, passed through and cut the descending aorta, penetrated the spinal column and lodged under the skin of the back." The evidence on the examination of Roerig showed the attackers to be capable of additional wickedness. Roerig, "who was sitting in the 'dickey' seat, behind the box-seat, was shot in the back after the stage passed the robbers." Roerig, upon hearing the first shot, may have turned to face forward to investigate the commotion in the front seat. Having lost their chance at robbing the stage, if that was their true intent, the robbers then shot at him as the stage passed by them, this shooting offering no advantage in gaining the treasure box of the stage.

Following the examination of Philpot's remains, his body was taken back to Tombstone, where his fateful journey had begun, to be prepared for burial in California. Ironically, it would travel through the very same wash that he was murdered in. "The body of the murdered driver was brought to Tombstone yesterday, and cared for in such [a] manner as his best friends could wish. A splendid hermetically sealed coffin encloses his remains, and the vacant store on Fremont street, formerly occupied by R. Cohen was selected as the most suitable place for the body to await the journey to California. During the day, until the coach carries the remains to Benson, friends will be permitted to take a last look at all that is left of one of the best hearted men and truest friends that this world very often has the good fortune to know." [49]

THE AFTERMATH OF A TRAGEDY

"Poor 'Bud' at Rest. Calistoga, Cal., March 22.-The remains of Eli [Bud] Philpot, who was shot last week near Tombstone, A.T., arrived here yesterday, and were buried to-day, the funeral being largely attended." [50] By the time Bud's final letter arrived home, news of his death would have already made it there via the telegraphic news reports to both individuals and newspapers of the day.

While the stage attack was still fresh in their memories, the Drew children soon made a discovery. "A week or so later we three children went to a small cluster of trees west of the wash where the holdup had been and we found a black horse tied to a tree, and all but dead from thirst and hunger. We had to take his feed to him for days before he could be brought to the stable. We told the sheriff but the horse was never claimed." [51] Understandably so. Who would want to claim a horse that might implicate the owner in the shooting deaths of Bud Philpot as well as Peter Roerig? From there Cora argued that the horse somehow proved that Doc Holliday, or "Hollydan-an Earp henchman," as she referred to him, must have been involved, as were the Earps, without any further proof than the accusation. She also claimed that the Earps were fed breakfast by her mother the morning after the shooting of Philpot, though contemporary accounts show them far from Drew's station and very much in pursuit of the remaining robbers. Whether or not Cora Drew or others in her family witnessed the fist fight between Virgil Earp and the overly aggressive stage driver on December 1, 1879, she always remembered the Earps with disdain.

After the tragedy more was brought to light about Philpot's nature. "Budd Philpot, the stage driver who was killed on the San Pedro, below Contention City, night before last, was strictly a frontier man. He was born in an immigrant wagon on the Platte river on a cold, blistery day in April, 1850. It may be said of him, like Victor Hugo, that 'he was born on the march.' He was raised in California, and spent his life on the frontier. He was an honorable man, and made many friends, who will not soon forget him. It would be a gracious act on the part of Tombstone to raise a purse for his wife and four children, who live in Calistoga California." [52]

Philpot's employer would soon come under criticism for printing up posters which he thought would be of benefit to Bud's widow. "In order to satisfy the curiosity of the [Evening] Gossip (which the name of the paper indicates) and the Nugget, so they may rest at ease and once more have a good night's sleep (if their consciences will admit of it), I, J.D. Kinnear, of the Arizona Mail and Stage Co., issued the circulars for the benefit of the widow of 'Budd' Philpot, the driver who was killed by the stage robbers. Now it seems to me that it would have a more honorable impression upon the public for the Gossip and Nugget to contribute to the widow of 'Budd' Philpot than to condemn me for what I have done in good faith. This is the last notice that I shall take of this affair. Yours, J.D. Kinnear." [53] Notice of a large benefit for Philpot's family was announced on March 22nd, 1882. "The Benefit for 'Budd's Widow.' The benefit proposed for the family of 'Budd' has taken definite shape, and is announced to come off on Friday evening next. The affair is in the hands of R.J. Clarke, than whom there could be no better manager...A fine orchestra will also be in attendance. The Turn-Verein have donated the use of their hall. Tickets will be $1, with an additional charge of 50 cents for reserved seats. They will be for sale at the office of Wells, Fargo & Co., in whose hands all money will be placed." [54]

The benefit did take place as planned, and was considered a success, offering the Philpot family a heartfelt donation to their harsh new reality. Some in Tombstone purchased tickets without planning to attend. "As there should have been, the attendance at the benefit to the widow and orphans of Budd Philpot last night was all that could be desired, Turn-Verein Hall being crowded...By the entertainment there was realized probably not less than $375, as quite a number of reserved seats were sold to persons who were not able to attend, while tickets and cash taken in at the door represented $332." [55]

Kinnear's simple attempt at raising local aid for Budd's family had created a fire storm of controversy. Given that the circular as printed by Kinnear listed the Wells Fargo office as the place to drop off donations, it was assumed that Wells Fargo was trying to get the public to pay for the burial expenses of one of their employees, thus shirking their responsibility to take care of one of their own who had died in their service. There were multiple falsehoods in this reaction, not the least of which was that Philpot was not a Wells Fargo employee when he died, as he was working for J.D. Kinnear and not Wells Fargo. The Epitaph was quick to address the growing controversy.

Local frustrations over the murder, and a lack of perpetrators to be seen publicly punished, added to the fury wrongly directed at Wells Fargo. "A Mistake. Yesterday a number of circulars were distributed through the city asking that contributions be left at Wells, Fargo & Co.'s office for the aid of the widow and children of 'Budd' Philpot, the stage-driver who was murdered on the Benson road on Tuesday night. The object of the contributions was also stated to be the defraying of expenses of sending the remains home to California. The circulars created quite a storm of indignation among persons who perhaps were not over anxious to contribute, which storm found vent in the columns of the evening paper [The Evening Gossip Newspaper] in a violent and abusive attack on Wells, Fargo & Co. The indignation and attack were in very bad taste for the following reasons: First-The circular was not issued by Wells, Fargo & Co. Second-

"It called only on the 'friends of Budd' for contributions. Third-'Budd' was not an employe[e] of Wells, Fargo & Co. Fourth-J. D. Kinnear received a dispatch in the forenoon from J.J. Valentine, Superintendent of Wells, Fargo & Co.'s Express at San Francisco, requesting him to purchase a suitable coffin and forward the remains of the murdered man to his home at the expense of the company-which telegram the 'kickers' [those raising the false controversy] could have seen had they taken the pains to call at the local office of the company. Fifth-Not one of the growlers can point to an instance where the express company failed to do its whole duty in such cases." [56] Even though Philpot was not a Wells Fargo employee, they still had decided to pay for his burial, before slander to the contrary had surfaced in Tombstone. Also, Wells Fargo records reveal that they made a payment to Tombstone merchant P.W. Smith for $19.25 related to the "Death of Bud Philpot." Also listed was T.W. Ayles who paid $10.00 related to a robbery. [57]

The capture of King by Bob Paul and the Earps at Redfield's ranch was the high point of the pursuit, and King's rather curious "escape" while in the custody of Sheriff John Behan and his staff would expose serious fault lines in the relationship between the Earps, Behan, and others. This would set in motion other events that amplified tensions leading eventually to the gunfight near the O.K. Corral. Wyatt Earp would later state that he saw the capture of these men as his ticket to becoming sheriff, and that he asked Ike Clanton to help him set them up for capture. Then when Clanton grew fearful that word might leak of his deal with Earp to betray dangerous friends, he went about threatening the Earps and Doc Holliday on October 25th and 26th in Tombstone. The tragic events that occurred between Contention City and Drew's Station on that fateful night would deeply inform the history that was about to transpire on October 26, 1881.

The second wash north of Contention City, the exact location where Bud Philpot was shot. Note the cut in the bank of the wash made by countless wagon crossings over 130 years ago. Collections of John D. Rose.

John Rose stands at the last remaining wall of Drew's Station. Collections of John D. Rose.

CHAPTER 3

END OF THE DREW'S STATION ERA

"Molly ran away with me and it was no easy feat riding a racing horse bareback down steep hills…" -Cora Drew

On December 22nd, 1881, just over nine months after the shooting tragedy of Bud Philpot near her Drew's Station home, Georgianna [spelled Georiann on her grave marker] Drew, Harrison's widow, sold an easement across her ranch to the New Mexico and Arizona Railroad, signing the deed as "Ann Drew." Her ranch extended down to the river, and this became part of the route that was necessary to build from Benson to Contention. She received $70 for the land. The sale of a portion of land on which Drew's Station was built to a railroad marked a transition from one era to the next. This pioneering stage stop had first been made obsolete by the building of Contention City, resulting in stages driving past Drew's without stopping. With the arrival of the railroad, commercial stage travel between Tres Alamos and Contention had become obsolete as well. Coaches now only ran passengers round trip from Contention to Tombstone. Private travelers would still use the old road for many years to come, but its days as a key artery bringing people and commerce to and from the still prospering Tombstone were over.

As for the "Grand Central," the coach that Philpot last piloted on that fateful evening, it was on display in Phoenix eleven years later. "There is standing in the street in front of Ward's livery stable at the corner of Center and Madison streets an object of interest and curiosity. It is an old stage coach concerning which a well-known and well authenticated story is told…The old stage was re-christened after the Grand Central which name yet appears on the side in letters dim with age and weather…" It was noted at the time that this stage represented more than just an old coach for which there was now little use, but rather a symbol of a different Arizona that even in 1892, no longer existed. "The civilizing influence of railroads and commerce and the strong hand of law has created in a decade a new community and an entirely new people." It might have been an Arizona and accompanying populace that Bud Philpot may not have recognized, or enjoyed being a part of had he lived to see it. "This old coach figured in several hold-ups before and after, but without the accompaniment of blood shedding. It is scarred with the bullets of desperadoes and the box, though massive shows the effect of time and sun and rain, but the wheels, the heavy, leather springs, in fact all parts of it except the box, are apparently in as good [a] condition as when it was new. Its original cost was $1,500. Last spring the present owner refused an offer of $300." [58] The value of this wonderful link to the past, if for sale today, would easily sell in the six figure range, and perhaps more.

In the 20th century an elderly Cora Drew Reynolds took time to write a brief reminisce of that memorable little adobe stage station on the Arizona desert, in view of the San Pedro River. She recounted many events and some of the colorful characters she encountered, names that in her old age had now become known historical figures, bearing a history that was already slipping

41

away in favor of legend and myth. "I knew Curly Bill well; he was tall, blonde and heavy set and wore his hair like a girl in long curls and ringlets. The Earps, Harry Head [who was involved in the Kinnear stage attack as was Jim Crane], Doc Ha[sic]lliday, Jim Crane, Frank and Ed Lowery, and Billie and Ike Clanton were frequent visitors to our ranch. They gave my mother their word and they kept it that she need never worry about our cattle being rustled." She also told that not long after the shooting of Philpot near their home, "Ike Clanton came to our house and wanted to give me a diamond ring that had belonged to his mother; Mama would not let me have it. Ike said 'Let Cora have it as it is only a matter of time until the Earps and Hollydan [Doc Holliday] get me'…Desperados frequently came to our place…" Cora recalled the times before the shooting of Philpot, when he would visit their stage stop on his route, before horses were changed at Contention City. [59]

As for the Drew family, they would later move near Charleston, where the Drew Brothers were known to run night herds from that locale as did the Clanton boys. [60] Cora Drew wrote of the family's inevitable adjustment to the changes that surrounded what had been their home and their livelihood. In just a few short years, the long trip from Tucson to Tombstone by stage coach was history. They saw the creation of Benson and with it the arrival of the railroad. Then Contention City rose from the desert floor and stage coaches now drove by Drew's Station in favor of the new city to its south. Then came the railroad to Contention, and the days of stage travel and those memorable little stage stops further retreated with the advance of progress. It was time to move on.

"When the railroad came through to Contention…we sold our home and we moved near Charlestown [Charleston] on D.T. Smith's old place (he had been killed in the Bisbee Massacre)…In going to Charlestown we stayed all night at a friend's house near Contention, and the next morning Mama put me on Molly, a large blue-roan mare, and sent me back to our old ranch as we had discovered that Molly's colt had been left behind. Molly ran away with me and it was no easy feat riding a racing horse bareback down steep hills; I remember of thinking of trying to jump off, but we made the ranch and the return trip. This was my first really wild ride. Next day we went on to the Smith ranch, Mama driving one team and me the other with my brothers following along with the cattle and horses. I rushed out to greet the boys when they arrived and ran into a bull coming around an adobe wall. He picked me up and carried me off into a field but did not hurt me. While we were on the Smith place, which was only a few months, David, Charley and I had to ride the range and try and take care of the horses and cattle." [61]

Ed Drew, who as a teenager found Bud Philpot dead in the wash, would later dedicate his life to law enforcement, and he would lose his life in this high-minded pursuit.

Bob Paul, who so boldly faced off against Luther King, Jim Crane, Bill Leonard and Harry Head in the wash near Drew's Station would soon win his contested election battle and also devote himself to law enforcement. "Sheriff-elect, Bob Paul, of Pima county, has taken possession of the office, and justice has been done." [62]

In the wake of the Philpot shooting, J.D. Kinnear sought damage control to calm the fearful traveling public upon which his business depended. "Kinnear & Co. have added a large and powerful bullion wagon to their outfit, and now the bullion, express, treasure, messenger, trunks, baggage, etc., goes to Benson separately from the regular stage. This will be a relief to timid travelers, as there is now no danger of the road agents 'jumping' the regular coach." [63]

Not only was Kinnear communicating to his customers, he was also sending a message to the would-be robbers infesting the area, that his stages would no longer make for profitable targets. But robberies in the area would continue regardless, even if it meant stealing the personal items of the passengers themselves. As the Drew family left behind their station, one era had closed, and another had begun. But theirs was a location which will always remain key to this landscape and its story.

A DREW FAMILY MEMBER HEADS EAST

And what became of little Cora Drew, the girl who was heartbroken when her sole Christmas present from 1880 of a purple bottle was broken into pieces? "I went to my first riding contest when I was sixteen and shortly held the championship of Arizona and New Mexico." She added that "My show horse was a magnificent bay with a black mane and tail by the name of Quirty...Early in 1892 Buffalo Bill urged me to join his Wild West Show which he was taking to Chicago for the World's Columbian Exposition. Mama wouldn't let me go but to compensate for my disappointment she allowed me to go to the Fair with friends." [64]

At the fair, Arizona had its own building with a registry for those from home to sign while seeing the sights in Chicago. Names in that registry would be listed in local newspapers. "ARIZONA AT THE FAIR. Additional List of Visitors at the Territorial Building." Among many others from all over the Arizona Territory, was a group from Wilcox, Arizona. "-Cora Drew, R.B. Parks, Geo. Hooker, J. Jones, Joe Hooker." [65] Given the Drew family knew the Hooker family well, the two listed may have been the friends that Cora referred to when she traveled to the fair. The sites of that event must have been quite remarkable for the little girl who had once called Drew's Station home.

Cora had seen the authentic west with all of its many contradictions, its beauty and its harsh realities. Now she was in contact with a key player in the romantic commercialization of the west, and the advance of its growing mythology. "I saw Buffalo Bill many times that next year in Chicago. It was while in Chicago that I met and married R.J. Reynolds." The rest of Cora's life had little to do with her western roots. After marrying, "except for vacation periods, the Old West became but a memory as new and different horizons opened up for me in the East." [66] She was still enjoying horseback rides at the age of 70.

Although Cora left the west behind, future generations of Americans would continue to delight in stories such as hers, and as long as anyone cares about the Tombstone/Earp saga, they'll care about Drew's Station, and the family who once lived there.

Top left, Cora Drew Reynolds, her mother Georgiann top right; Ed Drew bottom photo. All Drew family photos on this page, and the pages that follow generously shared by the Drew Family.

1895, David Stuart Drew long after leaving Drew's Station.

Charles William Drew, who later died in 1921.

In 1894 Ed Landers Drew at the Sierra Bonita Ranch.

1895, David Stuart Drew working at the Monk Ranch.

Edward Landers Drew in front of Ray Stable c 1910

"This is me Riding a Bronko," writes Ed Drew, on this Sierra Bonita sketch.

Sheriff's Office, Pinal County

FLORENCE, ARIZONA

Territory of Arizona, ()
                     ()
County of Pinal,   () ss.
                     ()
Office of the Sheriff.()

       I hereby appoint E. L. Drew a Deputy Sheriff in
and for the County of Pinal, Territory of Arizona.

                        Jas. E. McGee, Sheriff

****

Territory of Arizona, ()
                     () ss.
County of Pinal.   ()

       I, E. L. Drew, do solemnly swear that I will
support the Constition of the United States and the Laws
of the Territory of Arizona, that I will true faith and
allegiance bear the name and defend them against all enemies whatsoever and that I will faithfully and impartially discharge the duties of the office of Deputy Sheriff in
and for the County of Pinal, Territory of Arizona, according to the best of my ability, so help me God.

                        Signed.
                          E. L. Drew.

Subscribed and sworn to before me this 11th day of February
A. D. 1911.
    (*)
    (SEAL.)   C.G. Mardorf, Notary Public
    (*)
                    My Com Expires Oct. 24th, 1911.

Nearly twenty years after he discovered Bud Philpot's remains near his home of Drew's Station, Ed Drew becomes a lawmen, which will later cost him his life.

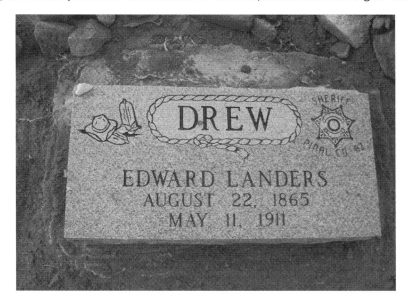

Above, the transit permit for the remains of Ed Drew, killed while serving as a lawman.

The grave marker and final resting place of Ed Drew, Pearce Arizona.

Above, the latter home of George Harrison Drew, who helped construct Drew's Station.

David Stuart Drew, seated in front, 1895.

CHAPTER 4

TRES ALAMOS, ON THE WAY TO DREW'S STATION

"Plenty of money in those days. You could see it hanging on the bushes." –Billy Ohnesorgen

Contention City was founded coincidental to the stamp mills built there, and its ideal location would shortly establish it as a transportation hub. In 1880 it gained the distinction as the closest milling point in the district to the railroad route Southern Pacific (S.P.R R.) was building through Arizona. In early 1882 it would be the first city in the Tombstone District to receive its own railroad connection and accompanying depot.

It would all begin with one mill, the Contention, whose construction began in the summer of 1879 to refine the very rich ore from the Contention Mine at Tombstone. These Tombstone satellite towns created a lively transportation circuit that vitalized the entire area. Teamsters traveled back and forth on a daily basis, management traveled from mine to mill for meetings and consultations, and business of all kinds took place in the process, including trade between the territory and Mexico. Although Contention City merchants would soon offer a great deal of goods for purchase, some residents would still be drawn to the comparative metropolis that Tombstone would become, just to see what the "big city" had to offer.

While Contention City was yet a fledgling development, a stage station operator at Tres Alamos saw an opportunity. News of Tombstone's rich mines could only mean growth and possibly more towns in the area - a concentrated populace was sure to spring up from the desert floor to his south. Located at the confluence of Tres Alamos wash and the San Pedro River, Billy Ohnesorgen's station, a building left over from the days of the Overland Mail route (today commonly known as the Butterfield Stage), had for years thrived, supplying travelers heading from Tucson to Mesilla, New Mexico. But the discovery of rich ore at Tombstone, and the inevitable creation of milling towns like Contention and Charleston, opened a new opportunity for additional business.

On September 15, 1879, Ohnesorgen would join forces with stage operator H.C. Walker to form Ohnesorgen & Walker, going into direct competition with J.D. Kinnear. [67] Ohnesorgen traveled a long way from the land of his birth to end up in the "back woods" of the Arizona Territory. "I was born in the Hartz [Harz] Mountains, Provence of Hanover, Germany, in 1849. My father was employed by the government as mine superintendent, when the revolution broke out, in 1848, and that upset everything. So we set sail for America. I think it was in 1853…It was a sailing vessel and it took 40 days before it landed in New Orleans. The boat sank on the return trip. From New Orleans we went around the Gulf of Texas coast, then by ox team to San Antonio. There I spent my early childhood."

But as he became of age, young Ohnesorgen found San Antonio dull, and wanted to venture further west, and an opportunity to do so presented itself. "I was 16 and had been clerking for my uncle, who was on his way to Messilla, New Mexico, to close out his business. I came more for adventure than anything else-it was a new country and little was known about it." He would arrive in Arizona in February of 1868, working for the Lesinskys in Tucson, but in three years his brother bought an isolated stage stop, and asked Billy to run it for him. This move to Tres Alamos, also known as the "San Pedro Station," would affect much of his life from then on. "The station, like most of them, was made of adobe walls 18 inches thick, arranged in the form of a hollow square with port holes in each corner and no windows. How did we get light? Well, we had the doors and if we wanted lots of light we went outside. The wall of the corral was eight feet [in height], for we were on flat country."

Life in the Tres Alamos area could be a hard one, as he recalled, "The first people to settle at Tres Alamos, was a colony of 25 Americans, but they were all killed in time. I remember, in 1871, four were killed in one day, one, a big Missourian named Long. Then the Mexicans settled there, but the water gave out. In 1876, or '77 William Gibson came and he stayed, he and a man named Roberts. They stayed by the cattle and made good." Of Gibson, Ohnesorgen recalled the lengths he'd go to just to have a partner in late night card games. "Gibson loved to play cards. He would come to my place and pay a man $2.50 to sit up with him all night and play."

Even though the settlements along the San Pedro such as Tres Alamos, Drew's Station, Contention, and later Fairbank often became tough neighborhoods, they proved highly lucrative. "We kept supplies, forage, etc. Plenty of money in those days. You could see it hanging on the bushes. I paid $3.00 a pound for butter at Las Cruces; bacon, $1.50 a pound; lard, 50[cents]; flour, $10 a hundred-got it from Sonora in ox carts-good too. Needles, we sold them one at a time." [68]

OHNESORGEN MEETS TOM JEFFORDS BUT AVOIDS APACHES

Ohnesorgen did attempt aesthetic improvements to the location, but to no avail. "I planted willows and things on either side of the river but the beaver cut down all but one cottonwood which grew to be some three feet in diameter." But operating this key stage stop, especially once Tombstone began, brought him into contact with some long remembered personalities. "I knew most of the noted characters...I knew Captain Jeffords. He was an Indian agent at one time-no good, filthy fellow,-filthy is his way of living-lived right among those damn things (Apache Indians). Once in a while he would go down and haul one home with him,- was a blood brother or something of Cochise. He was very bright. His clerk did all the work when he was agent. He could not even keep the Indians on the reservation. Jef was a tall, lanky fellow of about six feet and his face was full of hair." Ohnesorgen's opinion of Jeffords may have been informed by his dislike of Apaches, and he took precautions to avoid them. "If I wanted to go to Tucson, went on horseback at night or traveled with an ox train." The historical record recalls

Jeffords in a far better light than did Ohnesorgen then; Jeffords' place in history is secured by his unique and very close relationship with Apache chief Cochise.

Soldiers would sometimes be assigned at the stage station for protection in case of Apache attacks. "The government kept a picket of eight or ten soldiers at the station to protect us and the ranchers around us as well as the emigrants. Indians never attacked the station while I was there, but they did before I went there and killed two soldiers."

OHNESORGEN RECALLS J.B. ALLEN OF TOMBSTONE FAME

Ohnesorgen would also make the acquaintance of a well-remembered merchant of the Tombstone District, though his time there was brief. "Pie Allen (J.B. Allen) was a funny genius. He came out with the California Column, made pies on the way and sold them at one dollar a piece. They called them 'Washington Pies' and were made of dried apples. He started a little store in Tucson…He got to be Adjutant General under Governor McCormick. That is where he got the title of 'Colonel.'"

SHE'S HOW OLD?

"At that time of the gold excitement at Planches de Plata, in Mexico, he [Allen] bought a couple of barrels of whisky and went down. When that excitement was subsided, Tombstone was on the boom and he went there…There he married a Mexican girl twelve years old….Had to get a doctor's certificate, etc. But she quit him and he went to Tucson." Allen left Tombstone with the main street bearing his name, settling north of Tucson. "There he got a house and a few cows near the point of the mountains north of town. Made butter. I went there to see him and to collect a bill. He said, 'You would not take all a man has, would you?' and he pulled out $27.00. I said, 'no, keep it. If I had all the money standing out, I would be rich.' He certainly was an enterprising fellow if changing from one thing to another and keeping him on the go is enterprise. He was a fellow who never drank. Old age got away with him." [69] [70]

It was fortunate for Allen that press notes regarding him didn't include the assertion that he "married a Mexican girl twelve years old…" Instead, he presented himself as a successful pioneering merchant, without the hint of personal scandal. "Gen. J. B. Allen returned to Tombstone today where he is doing a large business, and no man in Arizona is more deserving of prosperity than he." [71]

ONE MEMORABLE EVENING IN TOMBSTONE MAY BE ENOUGH

Given Tombstone's notoriety, Ohnesorgen of course paid the boomtown a visit, walking right down the dusty thoroughfare known as Allen Street, named in honor of his acquaintance. Of his visits there, he recalled that "Tombstone was a hard town and a busy one. You could hardly cross the street about the time the miners came off shift because there were so many people. I went to the Bird Cage once-yes, just once, that was enough. Even then they dress better than they do now-didn't show so much....Three elevators [dumbwaiters] went up and down to the boxes carrying drinks and the women delivered them-got a rake for selling them. I only saw one scrap. A gambling boss by the name of Rickenbaugh [sic] knocked a fellow down with his pistol. The damn thing went off and the bullet stuck in a post, just over my head." [72] Lou Rickabaugh was a well-known Tombstone gambler and partner of Wyatt Earp at a gambling concession in the Oriental Saloon.

Note that Ohnesorgen points out that the women working the Bird Cage in the 1880's dressed " better than they do now," and that they "didn't show so much," implying that women dressed more conservatively at the very height of the Bird Cage's success. This evidence contradicts the oft repeated claim today that the Bird Cage was a brothel; it was one raucous night club though, as the bullet discharged by Lou Rickabaugh's gun illustrates.

The back of this check, pictured above, bears the signatures of Doctor G. [George] Goodfellow, D. [David] Calisher, and finally L.[Lou] Rickabaugh. It was a bullet from Rickabaugh's gun that came close to wounding Billy Ohnesorgen at the Bird Cage one raucous evening. The multiple signatures likely indicate that the check was used in a card game between the three signors, with professional gambler Lou Rickabaugh, gambling partner of Wyatt Earp, winning as the final signor. Original check from the collections of John D. Rose.

54

RIDING DICK GIRD'S BARREL SHAPED MULE TO TRES ALAMOS

Although Ohnesorgen found Tombstone an acquired taste, he was a witness to the movement of the enterprising pioneers who formed it. The sojourn that thousands would soon be making to the Tombstone District would begin with a trio nervous about Indian attacks and claim jumpers, a trio destined for a success few would ever know.

As a partner of Dick Gird and the Schieffelin brothers (Ed and Al), John Vosburg was on an excursion not only with his partners, but the Corbin brothers, who would later contribute to the success of the Tombstone District by building the second of two mills at Millville. Of this key time, Vosburg recalled that after a luncheon the Corbins "started in the ambulance [coach] and would drive on to Tucson…yours truly stayed to make an agreement with the owners, Ed, Al and Gird, which I did…then the time said 3.30 or 4 o'clock. Dick Gird let me take 'Molly' his favorite mule and I started for Tucson seventy miles away.

"This Molly was a pet and had been loafing for some months on fairly good pasture and showed it. It was like riding a barrel, spread eagle-wise. I made the crossing of the San Pedro river, where the Town of Benson now is, about 7:30 p.m. Billy Ohnesorgen (and his swamper) were the total population of [the] 'San Pedro Crossing' at that time." Given the width of Molly, Vosburg still recalled later, "when I got down to the river I was so cramped, I said 'Billy come and help me off this mule'…further riding was out of the question. The stage line crossed the San Pedro at Tres Alamos…and was due at that place between twelve and one that night." Vosburg added, "Billy's only transportation was a two horse wagon…" [73] It took the aid of Ohnesorgen and his "swamper" to free Vosburg from Molly's back, or depending on the perspective, the other way around.

TOMBSTONE'S DISCOVERER MAKES THE TRIP FIRST

Tombstone District discoverer Ed Schieffelin recalled Tres Alamos. He was heading on the expedition that would make himself and those traveling with him, brother Al and Dick Gird, rich. They were being tailed by those at Signal who could not understand why Gird would suddenly leave after being offered the General Superintendency of the mine. Even before Tombstone, Gird was a mining man of formidable reputation, whereas Ed Schieffelin was an unknown. That was about to change. "They followed the same road we were taking, and left Tucson one day ahead of us. Beyond Tucson about 40 miles the road forks, one road leading to Tres Alamos, and another to where Benson now is. The former [Tres Alamos] was the mail route and most of the travel went that way, this party turned into the other road, the one I was to take, and went down to where there was an old stage station, where we passed them. We saw their wagons and mules in the corral, but there was only one of the party, named White, in the house, who was sick, and though he heard us as we went by, did not come to the door. Parsons, who was one of the party, had gone off towards the Whetstone Mountains to prospect, and he told me afterwards, if he had learned that Gird was with me, he would have followed us. We went on up the river some distance and camped that night; the next day we arrived within three miles of the Broncho Mine." [74]

Tombstone discoverer Ed Schieffelin, copy photo from the collections of John D. Rose.

Gird echoed Billy Ohnesorgen's report on Indian troubles in the area. After leaving Tucson, the trio arrived at "Pantano, or at least the place that since has been named Pantano…At this point was an old stage station, showing with bullet-marks and with other signs the sieges it had stood against the Indians. From here on we knew that we were in hostile Indian Country." Gird noted the precautions that he took as they headed toward Tres Alamos. "…I insisted on putting out fires, and, in addition, I got up before daylight every morning and scouted the high points around the camp until daylight…From Pantano on, our route was by the old stage-road. I recall how Al and myself suffered from the crossing of this windswept ridge. Before noon of the same day the San Pedro river was crossed at Onasogins, [Billy Ohnesorgen's] which was an old stage-station." The day before reaching Ohnesorgen's the trio made a grim discovery. "Having, the day before, passed rather recently-made graves of two persons that had been killed by the Indians, I deemed it even more prudent to take even more precaution against surprises…"

In the area of Tres Alamos they left the stage road to avoid inquiries, and pushed up the eastern side of the San Pedro, passing the area where their discoveries would soon cause William Drew to open Drew's Station. From there they continued to traverse a wilderness that would soon be home to Contention City, setting up camp where Fairbank would later be located. Gird continues, "The morning after breaking camp at Fairbanks [contemporary accounts use both Fairbank and Fairbanks] with visions of the freshly made graves in my mind, I kept my rifle loaded for quick action, instead of removing the cartridges, which was our custom. On starting I placed my gun in the wagon with the butt on the foot-board. A heavy jolt while crossing a steep wash bounced the gun off the foot-board, and the hammer striking the double trees discharged the ball, which passed under my right arm, through my coat, vest and shirt, but fortunately for me, merely grazing the skin. Ed was greatly frightened, but Al, who was riding ahead, took it as a matter of course with his usual sang-froid." [75]

Al Schieffelin upper left, and Richard Gird upper right. These two, along with Ed Schieffelin, reached great discoveries and success following their trek to Tombstone. This adventure included an errant gun shot that could have ended in tragedy. From the collections of John D. Rose.

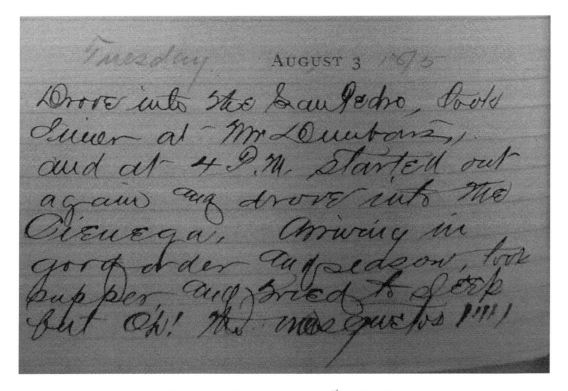

From John Clum's personal diary, dated Tuesday, August 3rd, 1875: "Drove into the San Pedro, took dinner at [Thomas] Dunbar's, and at 4 P.M. started out again and drove into the Cienega. Arriving in good order and season, took supper and tried to sleep but Oh! The Mosquitos!!!" Courtesy of the U of A Special Collections.

A BRIDGE OVER SHALLOW, MUDDY WATERS

In November of 1878 the Pima County Board of Supervisors was petitioned by Thomas Dunbar to build a bridge at Tres Alamos. Dunbar operated a stage stop competing with Billy Ohnesorgen, and understood as did others the need for a reliable bridge during unpredictable flash flooding caused by summer rains. Dunbar wrote the Board that "After having examined the Bridge I think the following material needed [is] 4 stringers 24 feet long…it will take about 300 feet of 3 inch plank to cover it…cost about $550…Thomas Dunbar." [76] (Note that Dunbar states that "after having examined the Bridge" which may mean that one already existed but was in disrepair, or it was a projection of what would be needed, or poor wording on his part, as much of the letter is written in broken sentences.) The "stringers" mentioned were the long beams of

58

wood which would cross the span of the river, and then planks would be nailed into those beams creating a bridge that wagons could easily cross. That Dunbar notes that the stringers needed to be 24 feet long indicates that the width of the river at Tres Alamos, at that time, was narrow, as the stringers would have to rest on the solid ground of both banks of the San Pedro.

The need for a proper crossing at Tres Alamos would be met not by Pima County with tax dollars, but by the private funding and initiative of Billy Ohnesorgen. In August of 1879 Ohnesorgen advertised that he had "completed a good and substantial bridge across the San Pedro River, at San Pedro Station, A.T., at his own expense, and will, therefore, collect toll from those using it until he is reimbursed. High water hereafter will be no obstruction to freight and travel." [77] The ad was written to address prescient issues, and may have been a response to the construction of a new stage road from Tucson to Contention. A bridge wasn't as necessary at Tres Alamos is it would be for traffic between Charleston on the west side of the San Pedro, and Millville on the opposite bank. Charleston was known for having repetitive quicksand issues in the river, whereas Tres Alamos didn't seem to be plagued with the same problem and to the same degree. The only time when this bridge would matter was if a summer monsoonal or other rainstorm raised waters on the San Pedro, but such occurrences were rare. Also, substantial freight shipments had traveled from Mesilla, New Mexico to Tucson, A.T. for years, with drivers crossing the bottom of the river, often without incident.

But Ohnesorgan's bridge would be of valuable use for the shipments of industrial mining and milling equipment heading for Contention, Millville, and Tombstone. "In the winter of 1878-79, I built the toll bridge. There was no cut in the river then. You could have stooped down and drank out of it at any point. The bridge only had a 25-foot span. I bought four stringers from the sawmill in the Huachucas [the saw mill that William Gird founded with help from Richard Gird, later sold to Jimmy Carr] and they cost me $55.00 each. I built the bridge myself, of course, and that did not cost me anything. The thing [the bridge] did not pay until 1880, when they were bringing in machinery for Contention, Charleston…That year was high water and one month I took in $400.00."

Ohnesorgen's ad noted that he had constructed the bridge "at his own expense, and will, therefore, collect toll from those using it until he is reimbursed." The point needed to be made publicly as he later recalled…"My, how people hated to pay [the] toll. They declared it was a public highway. I told them the highway went through the river and they could use it if they wished, but the bridge was on my land and if they used it they would have to pay toll." But given that he had paid $220.00 for the four stringers which were the key to the bridge, it appears that in 1880 he had more than made his investment back, and yet was still charging for the use of the bridge. This is contrary to his earlier statement that he only planned to collect the toll "from those using it until he is reimbursed." [78]

An early customer of this toll bridge enterprise would be the Contention mill. So substantial were the early shipments to the Contention Mill that the freighting firm hired to haul the equipment from the end of railroad to the site had lacked the capacity to move all of it at once. "Buckalew's [freight line] passed through town [Tucson] this morning with another load of machinery for the Contention mill, the weight of which aggregated 114,000 pounds. They expect to arrive at the mill site on the San Pedro in about four days. There is still about sixty five thousand pounds at the end of the railroad." [79]

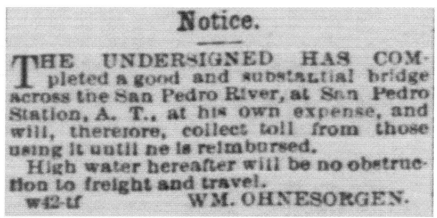

Notice.

THE UNDERSIGNED HAS COMpleted a good and substantial bridge across the San Pedro River, at San Pedro Station, A. T., at his own expense, and will, therefore, collect toll from those using it until he is reimbursed.
High water hereafter will be no obstruction to freight and travel.
w42-tf WM. OHNESORGEN.

Notice of Billy Ohnesorgen's bridge, from the Daily Arizona Citizen, August 6, 1879. Original in the collections of John D. Rose.

A delay in stage coach travel through Drew's Station would occur when this bridge was damaged in the summer monsoons of 1880. "Delayed. The non-arrival of the stages on time from Benson was caused by heavy roads [rains] and the delay was caused by the carrying away of the bridge across the San Pedro River, this latter occurring some days since." [80]

Writing a letter to her hometown newspaper, Clara Spalding Brown offered a vivid description of the storms that had caused the damage to Ohnesorgen's bridge. "Last year the rainy season was inaugurated by smart shows last in June, and July and August were very wet months…Sometimes they would appear to center over Tombstone, the thunder would roll as if some mighty giant were patronizing a mammoth bowling alley close at hand, and the lightning would flash almost continually, and every one would be pleased with the prospects of a terrific shower; yet soon the threatening clouds would disperse in all directions, and, at different points along the horizon, we could discern where the fury of the elements was spent." [81]

CHAPTER 5

FIRST IT TAKES A MILL, THEN IT TAKES A VILLAGE

"…when money came easy and went easy, all kinds of men and women flocked there, and it was soon a lively camp." –Billy Breakenridge

The Contention Mill, photo taken by Carleton Watkins, spring of 1880. Copy photo from the collections of John D. Rose.

The Contention Mill had its first official beginnings on July 24th, 1879. "Notice is hereby given the undersigned have this day located and do claim five acres of land for milling purposes to be held in connection with the Contention Mine…This Mill Site is situated on [The] San Pedro River and about one mile North of [the] old ruins." [82] (The "old ruins" refer to the Spanish Presidio near Contention known as Santa Cruz de Terranate.) The claim was signed by Josiah H. White, who had offered Ed and Al Schieffelin and Dick Gird a scant $10,000 for the Contention Mine, a mine which produced millions. Also witnessing the signing of this document was Charleston town site and Head Center mine surveyor A.J. Mitchell, along with F. Mason and R. Mason. It was filed at the request of Lord & Williams, a Tucson firm of substantial significance,

61

the same store in which John Vosburg had given a $300.00 line of credit to the Schieffelins and Gird the previous year…a $300.00 investment that would make him wealthy as well.

But even before all the equipment for Contention's first mill had arrived on site, Contention City had already begun to take primitive shape, in the summer of 1879. "The star of enterprise has located another town-site on the banks of the San Pedro, and its name is Contention City. It is at the mill site selected by the owners of the Contention mine. The grading of this, under the superintendence of Mr. Foss, is nearly completed. The machinery for the mill will arrive during the present week and very soon everything will be in readiness to commence crushing the Contention ore." In truth this was overly optimistic, as shipments to the construction site would still be en route two months later, but such misinformation did serve at least one purpose: it drew would-be construction, milling and fortune seekers of all kinds to this remote spot along the San Pedro, and they were very much in place when the mill began to dole out paychecks, which merchants were more than happy to help workers spend, locally.

There was plenty to be optimistic about, given early reports of a "cash crop" of ore at the Contention Mine at Tombstone awaiting its mill along the river. "It is estimated that $ 4,000,000 is now in sight in the mine, with sufficient [amounts] on the dump to employ the mill for three months. The contract for hauling the ore from the mine to the mill is let, and all other arrangements made by the owners to start up, when the world will be astonished at the amount of ore produced by the Contention." [83]

Billy Breakenridge, a former deputy Sheriff turned author, later recalled the exciting atmosphere in which Tombstone and Contention were born. "The interesting period in Tombstone was during the fall of 1879, and the early eighties. In those few years Tombstone was born a mining town, lived a mining town and died a mining town. Like all mining towns in their beginning, when money came easy and went easy, all kinds of men and women flocked there, and it was soon a lively camp. The Contention Mill and Mining Company built a quartz mill on the San Pedro River about eight miles from Tombstone, and a town sprang up there called Contention." [84]

A hunting party from Tucson headed into the Tombstone mining district and brought back their impressions of the dynamism of the place. "Last evening returned a party of wanderers consisting of Count Mabry, Duke Gardner, Gen. Gough, Chaplain Cummings and Col. Carpenter commanding. The party left here [Tucson] about a month ago and have been to Patagonia, Huachuca, Sonora, Charleston, Tombstone

Deputy Sheriff Billy Breakenridge. From the collections of John D. Rose.

62

and Contention City. The mines in every section are looking nicely. Three saw mills are in full blast on the Huachucas. Patagonia is filling up rapidly with busy people. Tombstone booms as usual and Contention City is growing with a rush. Lumber is arriving there in large quantities and everything is moving on in good shape. They killed a bear, two antelope and a deer, besides a quantity of small game. They had a good time and came back strong and hearty." [85]

"A new village called Contention City is assuming considerable importance about the site of the Contention mill-Western Mining Company." [86]

CONTENTION CITY NOW HAS A REAL ESTATE MARKET

Just the construction of the mill and those that it employed drew a small populace to its doors. "The town called Contention City has been laid out, surveyed and mapped, and the enterprising proprietors, D.T. Smith and John McDermott, are selling lots to all who desire to invest in the new city, and although it is not one week since the survey of the town was made, a number of lots have sold and preparations to build are going on as fast as material can be had. Already there are in operation one store, one hotel and restaurant, one saloon, one meat market, one Chinese laundry, and some dozen or more shanties which are buildings in embryo. From the very nature of things Contention City must grow and flourish to be the rival even of Tombstone. In addition to the mill which is now being erected, sites for two other mills have been selected here, and the prospects are that a third, for custom use will be located here; then every man can have his 'grist ground' and turned into bullion, and every one will have money who has ore and the multitude of miners will be independent of the few." [87]

Such was the optimism, often well beyond reasonable expectations, that occasioned the beginnings of many such towns, and Contention was no exception. But the idea that Contention could ever come close to the wealth and population of Tombstone as its "rival," was simply impossible. Even at its peak, Contention City's populace numbered less than 10% of Tombstone's 5380. The concentration of wealth in the Tombstone mining district would always remain at Tombstone, and a portion of it would fan out across the valley to wood cutting camps and the milling sites along the San Pedro.

As the shipments rolled in by wagon, the construction of the mill soon began in earnest. "John McDermott is at present at the Contention hoisting works, putting the machinery in order. Lumber is coming rapidly from the saw mills at Chiricahua [mountains], and the Contention mill will now be pushed forward without delay. It is thought the company will erect another 20 stamp mill. Tully & Ochoa's train landed the balance of the machinery a few days since and the timbers are arriving. Millsite for the Head Center mill has been selected and [the] mill contracted for. Men will soon be at work on the ditch, running the water to the Contention mill. Bowers has turned out one of the best kilns of brick (70,000) ever made in the Territory, which settles the question as to material for brick in this vicinity." [88] While McDermott assembled the mill, he took notice of its surroundings, knowing that a town would spring up around it, an opportunity that he had identified, and was sure not to miss.

The town site itself was described in more accurate terms. "Contention City is on the San Pedro river, nine miles northwest of Tombstone. It is laid out on a flat with just decline enough to give good drainage, has a ditch running along its front, is surrounded by ranches, convenient to wood and saw-mills, is on the road from Tucson to Tombstone, (will have the coaches plying between the two points…), the road to Charleston passes here, and take it all in all, has equal advantages with Tombstone and Charleston for a good, healthy, permanent business location." [89]

By December of 1879, McDermott had become agent for J.D. Kinnear's expanding stage line. It was a smart move on the part of Kinnear, and McDermott had already and would continue to enhance his place as an early player in Contention City and its progress. [90]

Contention City developer and real estate magnate John McDermott as well as E. Martin Smith borrow from the Tombstone bank, on July 20th, 1880, promising to repay the bank two hundred dollars in sixty days. As is noted on the document, E. Martin Smith finally repays the loan nearly a year later, on July 29, 1881. Original Pima County bank document bearing the signatures of John McDermott and E. Martin Smith from the collections of John D. Rose.

Although both Charleston and Contention City were located on the river and engaged in the same industry, each begat its own unique atmosphere. Charleston would benefit and suffer from its proximity to the Mexican border: its merchants would reap great rewards from cross border trade, but it would also be plagued by outlaws, mostly American, who committed crimes in the U.S. and quickly fled to Mexico as a safe haven. Contention to the north of Charleston still had its share of lawlessness, but not on the scale that Charleston would endure. Yes, it was further from the border, but it also became known as a community less tolerant of the excesses that would make Charleston legendary. Contention's trade with Mexico would not come into play in a major way until the later arrival of the railroad.

NOW WE'RE IN BUSINESS!

The first mill at Contention was nearing completion, and it was welcome news. "The Western Mining Company's new mill for working the ores of the Contention mine (by which name it is better known) is situated at Contention City, about ten miles down the San Pedro from Charleston and the same distance from the mine. The mill-site is one of the best on the river, and everything about the mill is the best that can be made. The twenty stamps are in place and a very powerful engine ready to set them in motion. Hundreds of cords of wood are piled about the mill, the ore road is completed and hauling will begin this week. The stamps will probably commence their thunder one week from next Monday, March 8th." [91]

Much earnest planning and labor began to pay off. By March of 1880, the Contention Mill and Contention City would see a milestone. "CONTENTION MILL. A $820,000 Shipment of Bullion-The First Run from the Mill. Contention City, A.T., March 22nd., 1880. Editor Nugget: -At precisely 8 a.m. to day, Walker & Co's. six-horse coach came bounding down the grade and turned up at the Contention Mill, where there were stacked up nine silver bricks, a part of the production of the mill since it steamed up a few days ago. Mr. E. Huhn, of the firm Huhn & Luckbardt, mining engineers of San Francisco, and who is here as an expert in the starting up of the Contention mill, informed me, that the bricks, nine in number, assayed from 900 to 969 fine, silver, and 11 to 13, gold. That the probable value of the whole was $20,000." [92]

Such was the rush to get their bullion to market that the Contention mill shipped out silver bars without the benefit of its own scales-they had to approximate the weight of their shipment, and hope that it didn't cost them any revenue. "The bullion scales for the mill had not arrived, and the correct weight could not be had, but the bricks would weigh from 105 to 112 pounds each." [93]

But the fact that this bullion, which by the standards of the rich ores in the Contention mine proved to be of a high grade, showed that the best from the Contention mine and mill was yet to come. "When it is understood that only a poor class of ore was crushed in the starting up of the mill for trial, the results are enormous. Aside from these 'adobes' of silver shipped to-day, there are several more on hand, and the next shipment will probably be larger and of more intrinsic value, as a greater depth is attained in the mine. The arrival in Tucson of these 'adobes' of silver just at the time when the advent of the S.P Railroad to that point is being celebrated there will have a great effect in the near future of Arizona. A more convincing proof of the mineral wealth of Arizona could not be exhibited. The result from the Contention mine is simply a confirmation of what the Corbin & Gird Mills, as they are called, have already demonstrated, and shows further that [the] Tombstone district is champion. If Walker & Co. propose to carry to Tucson, or to rail connection, all the bullion that the above-mentioned three mills turn out…They will have to duplicate their present turn-out of six-horse coaches, and Ham Light will have to add more mules to supply the greed of the quartz gormandizer, the Contention Mill.

"As the machinery, and all other parts connected with the reduction of the ore is being regulated and tested, and the various employees become practiced in their several duties to form a perfect whole, then the full capacity of this mill will be put to the test and the results will be astonishing. It is an old but true maxim that 'you can't make a kid glove out of sows' ear.' So it is equally true that you cannot make experts out of John Doe or Richard Roe by simply dumping them on the pay-roll. The various departments here are being filled up by men who understand their business, and economy is not consulted when it applies to skilled labor. The permanent mill superintendent and assayer, Mr. R. Burnham, understands his bussiness [sic], and is getting things in shape. The night boss, as he is called, Mr. Al Barber, has had long experience as superintendent of quartz mills in Nevada and elsewhere, and what he don't know about the running of mills neither you or I will learn. Gradually all the positions connected with the mill are being filled up by the right men in the right place, and in all its workings men and things are getting into their respective grooves. Soon there will be nothing new about it except the increase of dividends, and even the increase of bank accounts of stockholders will grow…" [94]

"The Contention mill had on the 19th something over 600 pounds of refined silver. They are crushing about sixty tons per day. A new mill will be commenced in a few days. There will be over fifty men and a number of teams employed in grading [foundational grading]. Business is lively. The restaurants, especially Hopkin's Delmonico, is always crowded." [95]

MONEY ALWAYS MOVES

The Contention mill provided jobs inside its walls as well as far beyond them. The Drew family of Drew's Station fame was struggling financially. The death of William Drew left his wife and children to fend for themselves. Referring to the Contention Mill, Cora Drew later noted that "A smelter was built and material was brought in by mule trams. Before the smelter was completed my father passed away…Soon afterwards, my brother Ed was able to secure the contract to deliver wood for the smelter. He hired Mexicans to cut the wood from the Chiricahua Mountains." Harrison's wife would now handle the rough element that plagued the area herself. "…one day we heard the familiar sound of gunplay across the river and shortly thereafter four of five wild-eyed men arrived and demanded a horse of Mama saying, 'Any horse will do as we shall soon get a good one.' Of course Mama had to let them have a horse and they gave her a hundred dollars." [96]

As for the stage buildings at Tres Alamos, they suffered a more decisive fate than the slow deterioration of Drew's Station. "The old station buildings were washed away by a flood which came down eight feet high." [97]

J.D. KINNEAR BUILDS A NEW STATION AND ROAD CLOSER TO CONTENTION

Although Ohnesorgen's bridge proved a valuable undertaking, he may have constructed it to even out competition between him and Kinnear. Ohnesorgen had formed a new stage company with H. C. Walker on September 15th, 1879. His route ran from Tucson to Tres

Alamos and south to the milling towns and Tombstone. Adding insult to injury was the fact that Walker had just left the employ of Kinnear. At this time, track for the Southern Pacific Railroad was approaching Tucson from the west. In a bold move, Kinnear constructed a road from Tucson heading in a southeasterly direction to Contention City and Tombstone, negating the need to travel east to Tres Alamos. It was completed by mid-summer of 1879, reducing mileage and travel time, and as a side benefit, virtually cutting out the need for Ohnesorgen's stage stop and bridge.

Kinnear would learn of an attempt to take public control of the road that he himself had funded. A petition to the Pima County Board of Supervisors with fifteen signatures, including Tucson and Tombstone Bank owner Lionel M. Jacobs, asked that Kinnear's private road become public. "We the undersigned Citizens and taxpayers of Pima County respectfully petition your honorable body that the road lately built by Mr. J D Kinnear from the Cienega to the San Pedro river and Tombstone District be declared a public County road and that a bridge be constructed across the San Pedro river where the road intersects it. Tucson July 7 1879" [98]

Kinnear had further increased his grip on this time saving roadway by purchasing a ranch with good spring water near the northern end of the Whetstone Mountains, as a stage stop. His stages would still have to cross the San Pedro River without the benefit of bridging, as Pima County was reticent to return any tax dollars it received from the Tombstone District. The creation of a new county, with the relative metropolis of Tombstone as its seat, was already being openly discussed, and Pima county felt it was better to receive than to give in such matters.

"Having occasion to visit Tombstone recently, I took Kinnear's line, leaving here [Tucson] at 7 a.m., and reaching the station at 2:30, and after partaking of an excellent dinner, started with six fine horses for Contention over the new road. The Odometer was placed on the wheel of the coach, at Contention, was examined, and indicated the distance to be ten miles. This certainly is a fine road, and passes near the magnificent scenery of the Whetstone mountains. The road is certainly the shortest, and must become a popular route to Tombstone." [99]

The railroad arrived in Tucson in March of 1880. Kinnear installed his station and accompanying roadway, all at his own expense, knowing that soon (in fact, by June of that year), the S. P. would be making runs to the newly-established city of Benson. This would bypass the need for a stage run from Tucson, making his fledgling stage stop obsolete. This shows just how determined was the fight over the money to be made while time still allowed. By June of 1880, Kinnear's ranch, his new roadway, and Billy Ohnesorgen's bridge and historic stage stop at Tres Alamos had little commercial value, now benefitting only locals moving about on old roads that once were of great importance, or those intending to travel east from Benson. Now the key stage route would be south from the railroad terminus at Benson to Contention, and on to Tombstone.

INVITATION.

In behalf of the Citizens of Tucson, the Mayor and Common Council respectfully invite yourself and family to participate in the ceremonies of celebating the event of the Completion of the

Southern Pacific Railroad

to this City, and to receive the officers of the Company, and their friends, at the Depot, upon their arrival at 12 o'clock, noon,

Saturday, March 20th, 1880.

Also, to meet them at a Ball and Banquet at Levin's Park Hall the same evening at 8 o'clock.

Very Respectfully,

R. N. Leatherwood, Mayor,
C. R. Drake,
C. T. Etchell,
M. G. Samaniego,
Alex. Levin.

Tucson, March 18th, 1880.   Councilmen.

John Clum's personal invitation to the celebration of the railroad's arrival in Tucson. Stage lines always retreated as railroads advanced into the same areas, and this celebration would remind Kinnear and his competitors that their routes would soon be shortened, eliminating their portion of the trip from Tucson to what was about to become Benson, Arizona. Tres Alamos would cease to function as a viable stage stop once Benson was founded by the Southern Pacific Railroad. From the personal scrapbook of John Clum, courtesy of the U of A Special collections.

THAT TEAM OF HORSES HAS A MIND OF ITS OWN

By the start of 1880, competition between these two companies was so heated that at one point the Kinnear Company was suspected of loosening hub nuts on Ohnesorgen and Walker stages. It is indeed ironic that they would also share a humorous incident that showed that the Ohnesorgen & Walker Company was willing to help stranded passengers, even those who purchased tickets from their competition. As the Kinnear stage headed from Contention toward Tombstone, a mishap occurred that caused the passengers to stop and look for a missing axle part. But the unattended horses saw no point in the delay, and soon continued on their journey, without the benefit of the driver, the passengers, or the missing wheel that had fallen off. "While rolling along the fine road about six miles out from town Sunday, one of the axle burrs of Kinnear's coach from Tombstone came off and let the wheel down. Driver and passengers got out and joined in the search for the burr, and so did the driver of Ohnesorgen & Walker's stage which was just behind its rival. Kinnear's team being left alone concluded to come to town on their own account, and started thither at a lively rate." New found freedom was not enough to satisfy this group of runaway horses, as they also insisted on remaining in the lead. "After running three miles on three wheels, they attempted to pass a freight team, and in so doing upset the coach and made a bad mess of it. The Kinnear passengers and driver came in by the O. & W. Coach, and the wrecked vehicle went to the repair shop." [100] At least no one could accuse the team of not being devoted to reaching their destination, and in a timely manner at that.

By December of 1879, Billy Ohnesorgen was experiencing severe financial losses due to fare wars and was forced to refinance his ranch on the San Pedro at Tres Alamos wash for $3,000. With his home now on the line, he and partner H.C. Walker approached Dick Gird, as seemed to be a bit of a local custom. Ohnesorgen was still seeking an infusion of badly needed capital into their cash-strapped enterprise. Although Gird had shown great confidence in them by recently awarding a shipping contract to them which had been Kinnear's, he also kept his options for a better deal open, and protected the interests of his mill first and foremost.

In a letter to his bank in Tucson (the Safford Hudson & Co.) dated January 30, 1880, Gird wrote of the matter… "Mess. Chuesorgen [sic] & Walker wish us to advance them $1000 under a bank plan, their agreeing to carry our bullion until same is paid. This we cannot do as by the conditions of our previous contract either party can terminate it at ten days notice, and we do not wish to place ourselves in a position that will prevent our taking advantage of the better facilities and terms that would certainly offer should Wells Fargo & Co. put on."

Even at that, Gird was still willing to help them, provided they put up security against the loan. After all, he was running a mill, not a bank. "We will however advance them the amount, provided they can give security for its payment that will protect us, in the event of either party annulling the contract. With such security, approved by you, please advance them the amount, charging same to us." [101] For Billy Ohnesorgen, giving his home as security may have been as far

69

as he was willing to go, and a further request for collateral by Gird may have pushed him to a decision. Though his partnership with Walker was to be a full year, he sold out to Walker on March 9, 1880.

As Dick Gird considered this request, it is unlikely that he knew Ohnesorgen and Walker were also seeking cash from other sources, making them less than a desirable credit risk. On July 2nd, 1880, they were granted a six month, one thousand dollar loan from John Wild at the princely interest rate of two percent per month. [102] [103]

A QUICK WAY TO BECOME A DIVORCED STAGE COACH OPERATOR

Kinnear's new line and stage stop were an immediate success, but he was also in the middle of a brutal fare war with Walker and Company. An over-filled stage may have helped him remain competitive, but it nearly cost him one of his coaches, and the safety of his own wife. "Accident on the Kinnear Line. The coach on the Kinnear line, coming from Tucson on Wednesday, capsized just after leaving Kinnear station, and Mr. Ray and Mrs. Kinnear were quite severely injured. Dr. Mathews went down to attend the injured. There were on board, Will. Watson…S. Marks & son, A. Fortlouis, M. Rahn, T.E. Farish, Mr. Ray, G.M. Perrine, E.J. Scully and lady, J.S. Maginnees, Mrs. J.P. Colp, W. Felton, and Mrs. Kinnear. Most of the passengers were more or less bruised and cut, but none were hurt seriously, only the two mentioned above, who are now at Kinnear's ranch."

The Nugget was quick to offer constructive criticism that Kinnear would have been wise to adhere to. He may have heard the same from his wife. "The cause of the accident may have been carelessness, but when they come to load nine passengers on top of a coach to go up and down the steep hills and around short turns in the road, it is fortunate we do not hear of more accidents." [104] With six passengers in the bottom of the coach, and a total of nine crammed on top, it is of little surprise that the crash occurred, and a wonder that it had not caused more injuries than it did.

Wells Fargo understood the relational value of Contention City to its interests in Tombstone, which at the time was one of the most promising mining camps in all the west. "We learn that H.C. Walker & Co have signed a contract with Wells, Fargo & Co., and will hereafter carry their freight and bullion to all the points where their stages run. Walker & Co s. agents will act for W., F. & Co. at Millville and Contention City." [105]

Mrs.Kinnear would recover well enough from her injuries to take up a pursuit that few woman of the day ever did. "Lady Prospectors. Parties from the Whetstones inform us that Mrs. J.D. Kinnear and [a] lady companion are among the most indefatigable of the prospectors now in that neighborhood, and can be seen almost any day, pick in hand, clambering over the hills in search of a bonanza." [106]

THE CONTENTION MILL STRIKES ITS FIRST BLOW FOR LOCAL PROSPERITY

Much excitement was generated at the first run of the Contention mine, a welcome sound which would remain for a few years to come. Contention City had become a milling town, and a key part of the wealth of the Tombstone District. "Yesterday was a lively day in Contention City, it was the day the Contention mill started for business, and much curiosity and interest was felt to see this mill in operation. Trials, of course, were had previously as to how it worked, and everything working satisfactorily, on yesterday, the 8th of March, 1880, everything being ready, the Corliss engine was started, and under the charge of engineer McCormick, who has put it up from its foundation, and will continue as chief engineer, the whole machinery was started, the stamps (20) pounded away on the ore, and all went off satisfactorily fully. From the first moment that the stamps were put in motion, there has been no stop. The pound, pound, pound goes on, and will go on until the Contention mine fails to supply the grist to the mill, which from first appearance will last to the end of time. The result from this mill, will have a mighty influence on the future of Arizona, and particularly Southern Arizona.

"Capitalists are watching these results, and will be more confident when the Contention comes to the front with her silver bricks. Enough about the mill. Messrs. Maltie & Lynn, the contractors have accomplished what they agreed to do, and more, and they may well be classed as first-class in their business. What Mr. Lynn, one of the firm of Maltie & Lynn, don't know about a quartz mill with his able chief of staff, W.H. Carrol, to execute his plans, is not worth knowing. We hope that the same contractors may have the building of most if not all of the additional mills completed here.

"The site for the Sunset, it is understood, has been determined on. Our visitors to see the mill start up were many, the Tombstone delegation were, to use a mild phrase, a jolly set; they took in the entire situation and seemed to appreciate it. Among the visitors were [Roderick] F. Hafford, Cosmopolitan saloon. Hafford is tall, stout, and jolly, and made many friends here, the 'boys' will remember him when they go to Tombstone. Mr. James Vogan, of Tombstone, another congenial gentleman was here, Vogan is so well known that all meet him with pleasure. W.B. Hooper & Co. were represented by Mr. Auld, and a jolly good fellow is he. Maj. Struhm, of Tucson, represented himself, and did it well: A.W. Say and B. Frank Hall, W.B. Scott and a host of others. Amongst our guests, and last but not least, was the editor of the Nugget, Mr. [Artemus Emmett] Fay."

Lady visitors to the mill opening were also warmly welcomed. "The deputation [representation] on the part of our lady fellow Citizens at large, was a feature in which we all appreciated. Their names I do not know, but it struck me forcibly that civilization was a fact; right here was the evidence. This deputation probably received marked attention than other…The gentleman outside Superintendent, Mr. F[oss] extended to them the hospitality of the camp, they were shown through the mill, the assaying office, etc., to the ore dump, where from the height of their position, they presented a rare picture to us far beneath, dressed in a tasty way with their white skirts visible, all eyes of the genus male was attracted toward them. It is to be regretted that Mayor McDermott was away until late in the day. All of our visitors without distinction of sex, color, or former condition, called upon Mayor McDermott, and in his absence, Mr. W.F. [William Franklin] Bradley did the honor most faithfully, particularly to the femenines, [sic] who called in a body. Bradley is a jolly fellow, but seemed nervous when the ladies called, but it soon wore off, and every body seemed happy."

WE'LL GET USED TO THE NOISE, JUST KEEP THE BULLION COMING

"The people are getting accustomed to the sound of the stamps already, and the process of reducing ore to silver goes on in the even tenor of its way, a fixed fact, and will no further be a wonder, but its results will soon be felt through every artery of trade throughout Arizona. We wish the Contention Mill and mine success. The company has purchased 500 acres of land, including the mill-site, right here on the San Pedro, and have also purchased two ranches containing 320 acres. This last purchase gives the Contention company the control of the water in the upper San Pedro. D.T. Smith, who had a leg broken some time ago, we regret to learn, will probably lose that limb, Dr. Handy, of Tucson, was sent for, but could not come; Surgeon [J.B.W.] Gard[i]ner, U.S.A. stationed at camp Huachuca, has been sent for, and it is to be hoped that his skill may save both limb and life." [107] (The original deed for the Contention Mill states "five acres.")

The Contention Mill site began with the above document, making claim to the land on which the Mill was built. From the Pima County Millsites, Courtesy of the Arizona State Archives.

Contention was relishing its new growth, and, feeling its collective oats, let the Tombstone press know that it didn't appreciate being ignored. "CONTENTION CITY. The Mill Pounding Away.---Mill-Sites for the Grand Central and Sunset Mines Selected.---A Cold Snap.---Promising Crops.---Happy Ranchers. Contention City, March 14, 1880. Editor Nugget:- What has Contention done to you that we do not receive our Nugget? Your last issue has not been received by your subscribers; in fact we have not received a number of the Nugget for a month. If two stages daily cannot bring us the paper, you had better employ a pack animal, which are slow but sure.

"Since the starting up of the Contention mill it has gone on pounding the rich ore from the Contention mine incessantly, and is now working in all its machinery smoothly and perfectly.

The working force, under manager and assayer Burnham and Mr. Foss, have been sy[s]tematically put into day and night shifts, and with chief-engineer McCormick in charge of the steam department, all goes well. You can look for evidence (in the shape of silver bricks) very soon of the wealth in the Contention ore.

"We will lose Mr. McDermott for a time; he goes to the Grand Central to put in the machinery for the hois[t]ing works at that mine, which it is understood will be on the ground in a very short time after the railroad reaches Tucson.

"The Grand Central has selected the location here for their mill, which will give Contention City three mills-the Contention, Grand Central and Sunset.

"We have had another cold snap; last night it rained, which finally turned to snow, and a regular old fashioned snow storm set in and lasted until daylight. Mountains about us are covered with a white mantle and the air is cold and bracing. After old Sol resumes away and it becomes warmer, our hills and valleys will be covered with grasses green and our flocks and herds will laugh and grow fat. Our ranchmen are delighted at their fine prospects for good crops, and take it all in all, nearly all are happy.

"D.T. Smith, who unfortunately had his leg broken and which at a time seemed serious for him, is now improving and will get well; thanks to the skill of Dr. Handy, of Tucson, and Surgeon Gardner [sic], U.S.A., stationed at [Camp] Huachuca, who were called in as a forlorn hope…"[108] (J.B.W. Gardiner testified at the Spicer hearing, relating to the gunfight near the O.K. Corral, and was also a very close associate of E.B. Gage of the Grand Central)

THE JUDGE AT CONTENTION IS BORED, A GOOD SIGN

"We are having a rest from contentions and litigations-our justice of the peace has gone prospecting and our irrepressible[s] are quiet. We have no bad whisky (some is a little better than others but none bad), most everybody is at work, and all is peace along the San Pedro."

While Contention City celebrated the opening of its first mill, John McDermott, who played a key role in its construction, readied himself for a project of greater substance: the building of the Grand Central Mill. "The hoisting works for the Grand Central mine will arrive here about the 20th inst. [this month] John McDermott, of Contention, has been engaged to put the works in running order. [109]

The Grand Central filed a claim for their mill site in April of 1880. "The undersigned claims by virtue of An Act of congress. Approved May 10th 1872." The 1872 Mining law allowed lands belonging to the United States, both surveyed or not, to be free and open to exploration and purchase. This filing would have been completely legal had the land on which Gage built the Grand Central Mill been the public property of the United States. Given that it was private property inside the Boquillas Land Grant, this filing was not legally based. As the claim made by Gage continued: "Five acres of Ground for a Mill Site situated in Tombstone District-on the San Pedro River. Near and north of the Contention Mill…and shall be known as the 'Grand Central' Mill Site dated on the ground this 26th day of April 1880 E.B. Gage." [110]

McDermott hadn't missed the opportunity of building Contention's first and second mills, and he also wouldn't miss being the target of an odd attack from the Nugget's correspondent in Charleston. "…one draw-back if found below here, McDermott of Contention City uses so much of the water [San Pedro River] that a scarcity is feared, especially during the 'dry' season which is most of the time at the last-mentioned place." [111] Given that the San Pedro River flowed first between Millville and Charleston, continuing northward to Contention, Charleston and Millville had nothing to fear from McDermott's amount of water use. In fact, the opposite was true. Dick Gird had constructed a dam south of Millville to divert water for the use of his and the Corbins' mills, which didn't please those to the north of him, including Contention City residents and its Mayor, John McDermott.

THE TOMBSTONE PRESS IGNORES CONTENTION

Those issues aside, Contention had much to celebrate, as it was gaining a sense of its own significance, which some in Contention felt was lost on the Tombstone Nugget, yet again.

"Your subscribers in Contention City received their Nuggets of the 18th inst. yesterday, the first received for nearly one month. We have an idea right here on the San Pedro that we are entitled to some atten[t]ion; we are the grand centre where mill facilities for our extensive and rich mineral district will have to come eventually, and our city, called Contention, will grow to be recognized as a Bullionville. Here the silver bricks will start on their groove which penetrates commerce and all business arteries throughout the world; controls nations, empires and continents. On yesterday the first bullion was retorted from the Contention mill. It has not been as yet run into bricks and I cannot give the result, but the mass of bullion took many men to handle it. When I am informed of the result officially I will inform you. The Contention Mill and Mining Company have every confidence in all their operatives, and 'he who runs may read,' and has access to all parts of their mill.

"The near approach of the railroad to this section of country has brought to us in advance men who are anxious to take and make contracts for the delivery of all sorts of 'truck,' which includes bacon, butter, etc., including fresh vegetables. I conclude from being an old resident on the San Pedro at this point, that when the railroad crosses the San Pedro our raising of vegetables for market will have to be abandoned for the reason we have too late frosts for early vegetables, and the seasons are short. Southern California can furnish vegetables cheaper and better by rail than our people can furnish at present rates of labor. I suggest to our ranchmen and local farmers to plant vineyards, fruit trees, and to a large extent alfalfa or other grasses, for hay, where irrigation can be economically had. There is no question that our farmers on the San Pedro cannot compete with Southern California for the next year in producing barley, corn, or vegetables, but FRESH vegetables will pay this year. [This is an interesting and insightful comment about how the railroad would affect industry and competition in growing areas. It shows the changes in the quality of life that the railroad would effect, many of them good, as well as posing challenges to others who would have to learn to adapt their businesses, as did the stage lines.]

"In my communication of the 14th I alluded to the case of D.T. Smith who had his leg broken in which Dr. Handy and Surgeon Gard[i]ner, U.S.A., were spoken of as being called in as a 'forlorn hope,' and by their skill, etc. I have been informed that the paragraph reflected upon the attending physician, Dr. McKee. I had no motive in reflecting on that gentleman or to praise particularly Dr. Handy or Surgeon Gard[i]ner. Dr. McKee I do not know personally; Gard[i]ner I am not personally acquainted with; Handy I know slightly, but did not see him while here until he was boarding the coach on his return to Tucson. Mr. D.T. Smith I have not seen since the accident. I hope he will get well. I hope this will prove satisfactory to Dr. McKee's friends and to him personally. I understand he still has charge of the case, and has the full confidence of Mr. Smith. Now, Mr. Nugget, we propose to give you the news as we get it. We are no regular correspondent, and don't work for pay, but having idled our time away right here for a number of months, we propose to give your Nugget and others our opinion and the current news occasionally. We take these as they are floated to us and from facts, and will continue to do so. Varied interests, from the near approach of the railroad are springing up. Time, tide and money will settle these, but this whole country seems to be underlined with mineral and all the capital we can get here either by rail or otherwise, will only develop in this decade..." (Supreme optimism aside, within a decade, Contention's best days were far behind it.)

C.W. Hopkins was serving patrons at his restaurant, an early eatery at Contention. "C.W. Hopkins has opened the Delmonico Restaurant at Contention City, a very complete establishment, and an eating house which deserves the patronage of the public. Mr. H. is a thorough hotel man, prompt and reliable in business, and will serve the public with the best the market affords. He is also agent for the H.C. Walker & Co's. stage line." [112] Now that the Contention's production was in full swing, reports would come on a regular basis as to bullion shipments that would become a welcome routine. "The Contention mill ran twenty-one days last month, and during that time turned out $71,000 in bullion." [113]

IRRATIONAL EXHUBERANCE SETS IN, AGAIN

Optimism in Contention had reached an irrational pitch. It was understandable that the outlook was a promising one, with a major mill in operation, and two more planned, and talk of a railroad. "The mill-site for the Grand Central Mining Company has been surveyed, lying just south and adjoining that of the Contention, on the San Pedro. The site for the Sunset mill is a little to the south of the Grand Central's [south of the Contention Mill, and Contention City as well]. From the way the sites along the San Pedro are being taken up it cannot be long until they occupy the entire distance from Contention to Charleston. From twelve to twenty mills will

76

probably be put up during the next year." [114] Three mills at Contention (the Sunset and the Head Center in the planning stages at this point), the Boston Mill north of Millville, and the two mills at Millville would constitute the six key mills in operation during the Tombstone District's milling peak along the San Pedro, a far cry from what was originally projected.

Of the Sunset the Nugget reported, "Mr. J.W. Pender, an experienced engineer, has now the plans for their 20-stamp mill completed. It is a splendid work of art and will reflect great credit upon the designer." [115] Contention earned another badge of validation as John McDermott was assigned another key role. "John McDermott, Generalissimo of Contention City, was sworn in as postmaster of that place, at Tucson, on Saturday last. John will make an excellent Nasby [nickname for U.S. postmasters]." [116]

By the summer of 1880 the Contention mill had established an impressive record of production in just over three months of operations. "This mill has been running since the ninth day of March last, and during that time has produced nearly or quite one half million dollars in bullion. The daily average is $4,000 to $5,000. It is now a twenty stamp mill, but ten more stamps will soon be added." [117]

BENSON IS BORN AND THE RAILROAD IS CLOSER TO CONTENTION

Benson's Wells Fargo office. Copy photo from the collections of John D. Rose.

77

The sizzling heat of June 1880 was no deterrent to the establishment of Benson as the S. P. Railroad terminus. The railroad was now within reach of Contention. Travelers now preferred to take the train from Tucson to Benson, bypassing the dusty trails, and lengthy and sometimes hazardous stagecoach journeys. While stages were still necessary to reach Tombstone, character differences between that town and Contention would begin to appear. For most travelers, Contention became simply a through point on the way to their destination.

"The long-talked-of Benson City was duly inaugurated on Monday last, and of course we went down to see the sights, but not to invest in town lots! The excursion train from Tucson brought 250 passengers, and for a time there was a bustle in Benson which looked like business. Logan's lunch house was stampeded, and [the] most excellent meals were obtained there. Bob Steward, (Fatty) in his 'A.A.' house, has most excellent quarters, and cheers up the inner man with the best the market affords. These establishments are in tents, probably waiting to see what is to become of Benson. After dinner Judge Underhill, the financial agent for the Company, and Mr. Shannon, auctioneer, commenced the sale of lots. There were sixty-four lots in all sold, from $20 to $177.50, the average price being from $70 to $90."

But the land rush at Benson left much to be desired, as there wasn't one. "There was little enthusiasm over the matter, and the sale closed for want of purchasers. The forwarding firms of Barnett & Block, E. Germain & Co., Davis and Webb, moved up from Pantano on Monday last, and will now erect quarters at Benson for forwarding purposes. One gentleman from Los Angeles was looking for a place to locate a blacksmith shop. Most of the lots were purchased on speculation. The railroad company are pushing ahead with the grading and track-laying, and the company building the road from Benson to Tombstone have already graded four or five miles this side of the river, so that Benson will soon cease to be the terminus, and the company building this way will lay a broad gauge, so that goods will be shipped direct. In Benson the S.P.R.R. Co. are sinking a well down 310 feet, without the least sign of water, which has a damaging [e]ffect to the town, and the Company will not guarantee to supply the town with water. By means of pipes leading to the river water is now brought to the town." [118] Tombstone's hopes were short lived, as S.P. would continue to build toward the New Mexico border.

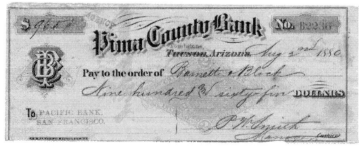

A Tombstone check for Benson Merchants Barnett and Block. Original check from the collections of John D. Rose.

CHAPTER 6

CIVILIZATION IN A GOD-FORSAKEN LAND

"…near Contention, the wheels dropped into a mud hole, and the stage laid over on its side." - Epitaph

The establishment of a mill and town site would necessitate law enforcement and a justice system. Charleston certainly had one. Citizens there were familiar with the chronic "law for profit" principles of "Justice" Jim Burnett, and his dubious second-in-command, Jerry Barton. [119] In a letter from Charleston dated July 4th, 1880, the writer spoke of Jerry Barton's attempts "to fire some sky-rockets yesterday evening, all of which showed a propensity to seek the ground as soon as possible." But the writer also told of a trip that was made by a group of Charleston residents to Contention. "Several parties went down to Contention City yesterday to attend a trial there and came back with a unanimous expression that the said burg has one of the best Justices that a frontier country can boast of. Messrs. Peel and Hunsaker were in attendance for the defense. The Judge took until Monday to give his decision, consequently all are in a state of glorious uncertainty at present." [120] Uncertainty was all but glorious in Charleston, experiencing Burnett in action, as his only predictable thread was what served *himself* the best, not the scales of justice.

While Judge Edwin Augustus Rigg impressed his Charleston visitors, he was also adding to his already extensive Contention City resume. "Col. E.A. Riggs of Contention City, in addition to the offices of Justice of the Peace and assistant Postmaster, has been appointed a Notary Public. The Colonel may also take charge of the school soon to be established there." [121]

TIME FOR SCHOOL AT CONTENTION

The summer of 1880 would also see the beginnings of a school at Contention. This was an important sign that actual civilization was taking hold. The early days of such communities were plagued by violence as the populations were largely male dominated. But once respectable women showed up with their children, a taming effect would often occur, making the dynamic less volatile. This by no means meant that every act of violence and conflict would suddenly and permanently disappear, especially in Charleston. "Prof. M.H. Sherman, Superintendent of Public Instruction for Arizona, arrived last evening from Tucson. To-day he is visiting Charleston and Contention City, and will establish a school at the latter place. Mr. Sherman will spend several days in this [the Tombstone] district and take a run over to Harshaw. He is devoted to schools, and Arizona could not have a better superintendent." [122]

THE TELEGRAPH ARRIVES AT CONTENTION, AND BYPASSES CONTENTION

During that summer, telegraph wire was run from Benson to Tombstone which provided a convenience for the milling area that had not existed. It brought some excitement to

Tombstone, but left Contention disappointed. "The Western Union Telegraph Company's construction force completed putting up the wire from Benson to Tombstone last Tuesday, thus placing us for the first time in direct communication with the rest of the world. This is an event of no ordinary importance to our city. Heretofore mining operators have had to often subject themselves to the annoyance and inconvenience of going to Tucson when it became necessary for them to have speedy communication with parties on the outside…The line is about 35 miles in length, following up the San Pedro from Benson to Charleston and thence partially doubling back on itself to Tombstone. An office was established at Charleston yesterday. Contention will not for the present be connected with the wire; though the line passes through, but the business of the mills there will probably soon justify an office." [123] It was another disappointment for Contention which had, on more than one occasion, felt its importance was not recognized, but a year later it would receive satisfaction in this regard. The Grand Central and Contention mills would be the first in the Tombstone District to receive an invention of far greater advance - the telephone.

WHO'LL STOP THE RAIN?

The substantial summer rains of 1880 would enhance area ranches and their grazing opportunities. But it also wreaked havoc elsewhere. "The telegraph has a tough time in its efforts to brace up against these July storms. It is now down between Charleston and Benson…High water in the San Pedro last Saturday washed out the dam, and both the Tombstone Company's mills are shut down in consequence. Three shifts of workmen are now repairing the dam, which will be itself again in a few days. The five new stamps in the Corbin mill are ready for use. The mill men are improving this opportunity for putting the machinery, belting, etc., of both mills in complete repair…and when they start up again on Monday next those 30 stamps will tell a silver tale." [124]

The waters that had blown through Gird's dam south of Charleston and Millville now surged toward Contention City in a more furious flow due to the release of the waters that the dam had held back. "The rainy season has set in hereabouts and the rains for a week have been copious. The grass is growing finely and stockraisers and ranchmen are visibly happy. The San Pedro is on a rampage, from a small creek it has grown to the dimensions of a river; it has been running bank full for several days, owing, however, more particularly to the breaking of the Gird dam at Charleston, which gave way on the morning of the 24th inst., and the water came down a roaring torrent. It was feared that the dam of the Upper San Pedro Ditch Co. would be swept away also, but our ditch owners were on the alert, headed by the indefatigable Mason, who sounded the alarm, and with men and material d--d the dam so effectually that it stood and still stands.

"Travel has not been interrupted, the crossings are all good and unless the rainy season is prolonged indefinitely the roads will continue [to be] passable.

"For a few days the Contention Mill has been idle for want of ore, not having a surplus on hand when the rains commenced. The large ore teams 'stuck,' but all is right again and the batteries are thumping and pounding away as usual.

"The contractors, Malter & Lind, have finished the grading for the Sunset mill and will, as soon as lumber arrives, commence erecting the mill.

"The next in order is the Head Center, which we understand will soon break ground for their mill and push it to completion. We will have right here, almost within speaking distance, three mills for the reduction of ore from three of the best paying mines on this continent. It is understood that the mill-sites sold by McDermott will have grading commenced on them very soon, and another mill-site adjoining these is being negotiated for and no doubt will be sold. With mills erected on these sites it will give us six mills within a distance of two miles."

Contention City would never reach this level of milling capacity, but with the Contention Mill adjacent to the downtown area of Contention, and with the Grand Central to its south, along with the Sunset Mill just to its north, Contention City had unparalleled milling capacity in the Tombstone District. "First-class mill-sites are not so numerous on the San Pedro as some persons imagine, and we advise mine owners to 'look a little out' or they will not find eligible sites for their mills." [125]

Another problem surfaced as a result of the abundant monsoon rains. "…we met Messrs. Wyatt and Virgil Earp, who reached Tombstone last night about 10 o'clock, from Tncson [sic], by private conveyance. These gentlemen inform us that heavy rains have carried away the repairs previously made on the line of the railroad, and the probabilities are that no mail will be received here before Tuesday night." [126]

THE GRASS IS ALWAYS GREENER

"Prospectors are preparing to take to the mountains. The prospects for water and grass are excellent, and the demand about here for horses, mules and jacks has cleaned out the market. Very soon there will be a scarcity of skilled labor for our mills: every one has an attack of a disease prevalent in Arizona, viz., prospecting fever, and it is liable to strike both old and young. Many who are not partial to hard work and not used to privations put up grub for others, and thus every one is interested in some way in prospecting our mountains.

"A fine discovery has been made in the Whetstone mountains within a few days. It assays up in the hundreds at a depth of 18 feet. Our old friend Sam Weis has got his foot into this discovery and we are glad of it. Sam is one of the original Arizonans. We met him in Tucson in 1862, and he has been here and over the border, we believe, since the war. Sam Weis is a good specimen of a Berks county, Pa., Dutchman, and of course will vote for Jackson.

"Quietly but surely are all the water courses in the Whetstones being taken up for stock ranches and stock placed there. Weis has a large number of hogs on his ranch and the range is said to be a fine one for porkers. I am of the opinion that no better 'lead' can be struck now than to locate and stock a good ranch.

"Our town is steadily improving; since my last we have added to our list of merchants and restaurants. Cowan & Brother have built a commodious store house directly oppo[s]ite McDermott's Exchange, and have opened out with a fine assortment of general merchandise. Mr. A. Cowan, the senior, has been Wells, Fargo & Co.'s agent at Contention since the establishment of the office, and is also agent for H.C. Walker & Co., and both offices are removed to the store of Cowan & Bro. Mr. C. Cowan, the junior, has just arrived from Kansas City, Mo. These young men are full of business energy and having a business training will enter the list for patronage with a fine prospect of success. [127] Our S. Marks has laid in a large stock of goods, to house which he has extended his store room many feet; in fact, he has duplicated his original store room, and has also built a commodious residence for his family. Marks keeps on hand every thing from a needle to a goose yoke. M.J. Gurindin, our third merchant, has just finished up his frame store room and added to his stock of general merchandise." [128]

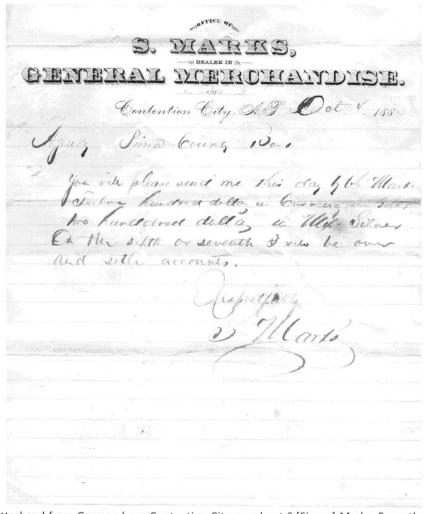

Original letterhead from German born Contention City merchant S.[Simon] Marks. From the collections of John D. Rose.

Marks would soon make his presence in Contention of a more permanent nature, investing heavily in the building and property that his store and home were already occupying. On August 18th, 1880, he purchased the property from his landlord, Tucson merchant Albert Steinfeld, for the princely sum of $1,000.00, not at all an insignificant amount at the time. It was market proof that Contention had already come a long way as a viable business community. Contention, as well as the rest of the Tombstone District, was still within the boundaries of Pima County, as Cochise County had yet to be created. Pima County officials did not have a plat map for Contention, and were forced to record the deed without benefit of block and lot number. It was another indication that although Contention was well on its way up, it would never be organized in the more official way that Tombstone was. Marks' purchase from Steinfeld was noted as "that certain lot piece or parcel of land situate lying and being in the County of Pima Territory of Arizona and bounded and described as…That certain lot piece or parcel of land situate lying and being in the Town of Contention more commonly known as, and called Contention City…" Such wording was really the result of not knowing officially how to identify the property, but Marks knew where he lived, and what he was buying, as did everyone else in Contention. It was more of a small village than the comparative metropolis that Tombstone was fast approaching. Marks' purchase was further described as follows: "…upon which said lot stands the double adobe House now occupied by said S. Marks as a store and Dwelling House, also the stable and corral and other improvements on said property." [129]

"The Delmonico Restaurant, after being closed for some months, has changed hands and has been re-furnished and opened in first-class style. They furnish meals at all hours, and cleanliness and abundance is the rule.

"We understand that the Western Hotel (Mason's) has been purchased by Mr. Smith, late of Monterey county, Cal., who will re-open it on the 1st of August. The Western has probably fed more people than all others in Contention combined, and no doubt under the new proprietors will take front rank. With good sleeping accommodations, Contention can provide for the comforts of all comers unsurpassed in Arizona." [130]

Mason's Hotel at Contention, sold to Mr. J.B. Smith of California, later Contention City Justice of the Peace. As well as serving as a Hotel, it was a popular Contention City eatery. Copy photo from the collections of John D. Rose.

84

"Just now we are lamenting our washout, or some other out, with the S.P.R.R. No arrivals for 48 hours. We understand, and are glad of it, that an opposition line is to be put on between Tombstone and Benson. The consolidation of Walker and Kinnear caused the fare to Tombstone [from Contention City] to go up fifty per cent. There was no good reason for charging 50 per cent…more after the consolidation; the people of Contention speak out plainly; most of the travel from here are working men who knock off a day to go to Tombstone to make purchases-$3 stage fare added to loss of one day's pay will not pay to go, and any one carrying at reasonable rates will get the travel, and express matter also." [131]

The public outcry against the rate hike caught the notice of Ingram & Co., who had been losing business to J.D. Kinnear on the Patagonia and Harshaw route. Seeing the opportunity, and also wanting to rid himself of Kinnear's Patagonia competition, Ingram hit Kinnear with a new line at a time when it was most beneficial to himself, and the worst possible time for Kinnear. "Oppositon to Benson. From Walter Coleman, agent, we learn that as soon as trains resume regular trips Ingram & Co. will put on an opposition stage line between Tombstone and Benson. Fare from Tombstone to Benson will be three dollars, from Benson to Tombstone three dollars and a half; all of which will be taken in dobies. It looks now as if it would soon be cheaper to ride on a stage than to go afoot." [132]

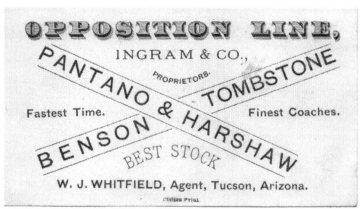

Ingram pushed J.D. Kinnear out competition for the Patagonia and Harshaw routes by briefly opening this competing line to Tombstone. He quickly folded when Kinnear agreed to his demands. Original trade card from the collections of John D. Rose.

THE IDEA IS TO KEEP THE STAGE COACH UPRIGHT AT ALL TIMES

It was not an easy start for Ingram and Co. "Opposition Stage. The opposition stage from Benson made its appearance yesterday a few minutes after the regular line. It brought in sixteen passengers. During the trip up, and near Contention, the wheels dropped into a mud hole, and the stage laid over on its side. No damage resulted to either coach or passengers. A return trip will be made to-day, starting from the office at 2 o'clock p.m." [133]

Suspecting some sabotage on the part of Kinnear for this accident, Ingram would respond by stealing away one of Kinnear's key employees. "New Agent. Mr. G.W. Chapman, formerly agent for Kinnear's Stage Line, succeeds Walter Coleman as agent for the opposition line in Tombstone. The selection is an excellent one, Chap's reputation as a rustler being second to none." [134]

The public outcry had been answered, it seemed, and now Kinnear would be forced to lower his prices. But Ingram never intended to permanently establish this new business leg. He printed up trade cards, opened a concession at Benson and Tombstone, and then quickly folded the entire enterprise as soon as Kinnear & Co. acquiesced to his demand that they withdraw from the Patagonia and Harshaw run. This left the travelers from Benson to Tombstone at the mercy of J.D. Kinnear & Co.'s growing hold on that market.

THE BOOM IS ON!

The booming summer of 1880 would bring more commerce and progress to the small, but rapidly growing settlement along the San Pedro. In fact, states outside of the Arizona Territory were taking notice. A passenger travelling from Tucson to Tombstone recorded his impressions as the modern advance of the railroad was still linked to the more primitive journey by stage coach. "Tucson is a very interesting and flourishing city, and about as cosmopolitan in its character as a frontier town can be…The business prospects of Tucson…never were better, the railroad going forward to Pantano…On entering the cars for Pantano the traveler at once sees evidences of rough frontier life in the appearance of his fellow passengers. The garb of civilization is generally discarded, and you see the majority of them wearing overalls, jumpers, cork hats, belts full of cartridges, immense revolvers, rifles, rolls of blankets, etc.…From Pantano the stages leave for New Mexico, Tombstone and Patagonia, and will do so until the new town of Benson is reached, which is promised by the railroad people on the 22d.…Upon the arrival of a train from Tucson the scene is one of great bustle and activity—stages loading mails and packages, and passengers securing seats…Then the hard part of the journey begins. After some hours whirling through dust and jolting over rut holes the first halting place is reached, which is Ohnesorgens, on the San Pedro river. This place is an old stage station, and for many years was used as a fort, where the settlers would flock for protection when rumors reached them that there were INDIANS IN THE VICINITY.

"It consists of a series of adobe building, formed in a square, with a court-yard in the center to hold stock. The new town of Benson…will soon assume an air of as much importance as any town in Southern Arizona. Leaving Ohnesorgens, the stage route runs south along the San Pedro river, which it crosses before reaching Contention City, to which place from Benson is about 17 miles. Contention City is simply the mill site for milling the ore from the Contention mine at Tombstone, and it ships $4,000 in bullion to Tucson daily. The mill has twenty stamps, and the owners are now putting in five more. From Contention City to Tombstone it is ten miles, over a good road, with the one exception of a steep grade in leaving the first-named place. About three miles from Tombstone a number of wells are reached. These supply Tombstone with water, which is hauled in carts and sold for half a cent per gallon." [135]

The Sacramento Daily Record-Union solicited advertising from Contention and other areas, and they made a point of covering the news there as well, sometimes sending reporters on the long trek to gain firsthand knowledge of the area. "The Weekly Union has a large and general circulation in Arizona Territory. The circulation is increasing and will continue to increase with the growth of the country. A thorough canvass of the entire Territory by competent agents resulted in large accessions to our lists at Pantano, Fort McDowell, Gila Bend, Maricopa, Camp Verde, Red Rock, Benson, Charleston, Contention City, Texas Hill, Alexandra, Monument, Casa Grande, Harsham [Harshaw], Tombstone, Prescott, Phoenix, Tucson and Yuma. The Weekly Union, therefore, possesses superior advantages as an advertising medium for all lines of business." [136]

The railroads had kept a keen eye on this developing area, so much so that in their annual report they noted that "Contention City has now about 200 inhabitants, but is growing rapidly, and must eventually become an important mill town. At present the two mills at Charleston and the one at Contention City consume about 150 tons of ore daily. The amount of freight now going daily to Tombstone alone from the terminus of the Southern Pacific is about seventy tons, and to Charleston, Huachuca, Patagonia and intermediate points, by wagons, is as much more; and the transportation is not sufficient for the wants of trade. The passenger travel over the Southern Pacific east from Tucson, going to the aforesaid points, is about 100 daily both ways; but the increase of passenger and freight traffic is so rapid that no approximate idea can now be formed of the status in these departments six months hence." [137] So reported James A. Zabriskie, as Secretary A. & M. R. R. & T. Co. Zabriskie had a long and respected relationship with the Arizona Territory as an attorney and prosecutor. In fact, when Wyatt Earp was asked by Curly Bill Brocius for the name of a good attorney after his shooting of Tombstone Marshall Fred White, Earp mentioned Zabriskie to him. Brocius declined, having been prosecuted by him in Texas.

Just under a month later more plans for Contention were news. "The Sunset Company have commenced grading for their 20-stamp mill. The Grand Central Company has secured a site just below the Sunset, and it is expected that grading for the Grand Central mill will begin about the 10th of August. The Boston and Arizona mill is located about three miles above Contention City. From present indications there will be from 100 to 130 stamps operating on Tombstone ore by the close of the present year. The building of the Tombstone railroad would be a godsend to the mills, as it would enable them to move their ore from the mines to the mills for about one half the price they now are paying. We trust that arrangements may be made in the east for capital to push this important enterprise through at an early day." [138]

It became clear that many who were thinking of relocating were thinking about Contention. The growth of Contention would be mixed with substantial structures of frame and adobe, as well as tents and other lesser dwellings. It would have proved helpful had Contention had a full-time surveyor living in town, as there were issues with straight lines. But it didn't appear to be a real concern to anyone-there was no stopping the tide.

"Contention City, A.T., August 18th, 1880…Since my last, Contention has more than duplicated its population, judging from the number of canvass shelters, tents, frame buildings, 'wickee-ups,' [a wickiup is an Apache dwelling made of grass and tree branches] of all sorts of architectural skill, adobe 'casas,' and, in fact, everything that will turn rain 'goes.' 'Evil communications corrupt,' etc., we have evidence of it right here. There is not a foot of ground in Contention that is not fenced in, that is to say, the [lot] jumpers have been around, (probably come from Tombstone), and the old townsite of Contention City is thoroughly staked off in lots varying from 20 feet front to 120, and as deep as they are wanted. If all these lots, 'corraled' with pine pegs, are built upon, we will have a town of magnificent dimensions if not, distances. Little regard has been observed for straight lines, in staking off lots, and roads are no impediment, neither are mill-sites exempt from the seekers after real estate.

"Every disease has its remedy and these things will cure themselves in time. The substantial improvements taking place daily are wonderful. Several good houses have been completed during the past week and are now occupied. Mr. Louis Goodman, lately with the large mercantile house of W. Zeckendorf, Tucson, has located here and already has housed a large stock of general merchandise. Mr. Goodman is young and full of energy, possessing fine business qualifications he will make a dash for the front rank in merchandising here. The stock of goods carried by several of our business men will compare favorably with your Tombstone merchants, and the time is past when our people will have to go elsewhere for an assortment and bed rock prices. Mr. Wm. Moore, from Ph[o]enix, has completed his building and tomorrow opens up the Shades with a fine stock of liquors, cigars, etc. We predict that the Shades will be a popular place. Mr. Walch, next neighbor to the Shades, we understand will soon add an addition to his saloon, his present limits being too contracted [constricted] for his increasing business. Hilford's wine rooms will be extended some forty feet. All these improvements indicate prosperity. McDermott's Bank Exchange, since the addition of a club room, is the center of trade, and everybody knows how Mack runs the Exchange. Directly opposite the Bank Exchange, and at the junction of the road leading to the Whetstones and Tucson by way of Kinnear's ranch, are two of our prominent mercantile houses, which makes this point a center.

"Grading for the Grand Central mill will commence as soon as carts can be delivered here, and we understand that every man that can be worked to advantage will be put on the grade to complete it. It is the intention of the contractors, Malter & Lind, to have the mill finished within ninety days after the grading is done.

"The Sunset mill is being built as fast as material can be had, and take it all in all things are lively at Contention.

"Mr. Burnham, late superintendent of the Contention mill, is in charge of the workmen on the Grand Central and Sunset mill sites, and will probably be retained as superintendent of one of them when reduction of ores commence." [139]

The travel between Tombstone and Contention would create yet another enterprise for hungry travelers. "One of the finest places to stop at in the vicinity of Tombstone, is the station kept by Mr. C. Mason, at the springs about six miles from town, on the Contention road. Here is to be found everything that is good to eat, and what is better, the genuine good treatment which everybody receives at the hands of the genial proprietor." [140]

THE SWITZERLAND OF ARIZONA

"A party of our citizens has just returned from the Huachucas, the Switzerland of Arizona, and speak of what they found there in high terms. The citizens of the Huachucas, amongst them Fatty Smith and Gus. Wardwell, were especially hospitable, and all vied to make the visit a pleasant one." [141] The colorful names of the area did not go unnoticed by the traveling public, either. "One of the first things to attract the attention of a stranger in regard to Arizona is the cheerful and pleasant suggestive names that everywhere confront him…a most astonishing array of cognomens, and all of this same mirthful, nay, almost hilarious, character. For instance, Tiger, Iconoclast, Vulture City, Contention, Lynk Creek, Bowie, Tombstone, Skull Valley, and finally Hell Canon…" [142] It only added to the mystique that the people of Arizona had a unique way of civilizing a frontier.

Photo of the Ramsey Canyon area of the Huachucas, by Stephanie Rose.

CHAPTER 7

TRAIN TRACKS ON THE HIGH DESERT

"…you are a thief. We have no use for you and hope you will emigrate as requested." –J. Landis

Not everyone who paid a visit to the San Pedro Valley appreciated is rugged aesthetic. One reporter from California made little effort to conceal his disdain for the area. "A Tombstone correspondent to the Colton Simi-Tropic gives…the following notes; In accordance with my promise [one that he appears to regret having made] I drop you a few lines to give your readers my impressions of this God-forsaken country of Arizona. To tell you the truth [as if he hadn't been candid enough already], I know by experience that a newspaper man wants nothing else. At Casa Grande we took the stage for Tucson, 75 miles distant, fare $15 and 8 cents a pound for all baggage over 40 pounds in weight. Tucson is a quaint old Mexican town, the buildings with very few exceptions are adobe, but will soon change to an American style of architecture…

"I left Tucson for this place on the 16th, and came through by daylight. Nice road and cheap fare-only $7-and delightful climate. Were out of the hot belt after leaving Tucson about 30 miles, and as you approach the Whetstone mountains. From the Whetstone summit to the San Pedro river is about 30 miles, with a nice road and all down grade. We strike the river at Contention City, where the Contention mine has its $93,000 mill ready for work. This mill will chew up from one to two hundred thousand tons of ore per month." [143]

The terrain wasn't the only thing that made the territory inhospitable. "Horse thieves have made it lively around here during the last week. R. Mason lost two of his best horses, and we pity the thieves if Mason overtakes them; he is on their trail now with his Henry [rifle] across his saddle. We hope these thieves may be caught and punished. Another horse was stolen on the same night from a traveler who had camped near town. News from the Dragoons [nearby mountain range] give big finds and some of our citizens have gone out to get their fingers into the silver pie." [144]

Further south of Contention and later Fairbank, was the Boston Mill, just north of Charleston. The mill's superintendent was C.W. Goodale, who wrote of the area. When referring to the types of communities which grew near the stamp mills along the San Pedro, he is resolute about the problems that Charleston had, but conspicuous by its absence is any mention that Contention struggled with the same issue. This is not to say that Contention was crime free, far from it, but it was nowhere near the level of shooting in the streets that Charleston had become accustomed to, and is still remembered for to this day. "Naturally small settlements sprang up in the vicinities of the several mills, located on the San Pedro River, 10 miles from Tombstone. Among them was Charleston, a community which soon acquired an unenviable notoriety for diversified viciousness. If anything good ever originated in Charleston it escaped the notice of those whose misfortune it was to be stationed in its vicinity. The two mills of the Tombstone

Milling & Mining Co. were built across the San Pedro within pistol shot of Charleston and the officials of the company found life full of unwelcome distractions." [145]

Crime news from Contention City was often mild. It became apparent one evening that two restaurant workers were in need of some improvement in their relationship. "A row occurred on Friday night at Contention City between a butcher and a waiter, names unknown, during the course of which the waiter made an attack on the butcher with an iron bar and was promptly knocked down with a club. No arrest to date." [146]

In spite of its reputation for law and order, Contention did have problems with the criminal element long before T. W. Ayles wrote of his frustrations with stock thieves in March of 1881. These thieves aided each other in the sale and transfer of stolen items out of the area. And there was also the lone criminal, an easier character to identify and prosecute. Charleston suffered from lawbreakers, and its citizens were publicly indignant about them, but some "lawmen" there dispensed justice primarily when it put money into their pockets. The Contention populace and Judge Rigg were less tolerant. A prime example is a letter from citizens in Contention, giving one thief public notice that he needed to find a new hunting ground.

DO YOU FEEL LUCKY…?

"NOTICE TO LEAVE. CONTENTION CITY, A.T., Oct. 12, 1880. To Hans. M. Christiansen, of San Pedro Valley. SIR:-You will take notice that we, the undersigned citizens and residents of the San Pedro valley, desire that you vacate the San Pedro valley within thirty days from this date. We don't want any more petty stealing, we don't want any more harness stolen, and we don't want any more houses burned. In short, we wish you to get yourself out of this community, and it will please us for you to not return. You have confessed in open court that you are a thief. We have no use for you and hope you will emigrate as requested. J. LANDIS, A.C. COWAN, D.T. SMITH, F.B. BICKLEMAN, Wm. F. BRADLEY, G.H. DREW, L.W. MEYERS, JOHN LOWENBRUNK, JOHN McDERMOTT, A.E. CARRILO, J.B. SMITH, W.R. PETTE, J.A. PEUGH, S. MARKS, A. JORDAN, Wm. T. GRIFFITH, D.N. CABLE, L. GOODMAN…" [147]

Contention would soon rise to take its place as the key milling center of the Tombstone District, eventually far surpassing the milling output of Millville near Charleston to the south. While reports of this progress were published, a controversy that could affect not only Contention but the entire Tombstone district was already underway. Wells Spicer is best remembered by Tombstone historians for his "Spicer Decision," which cleared Wyatt, Morgan, and Virgil Earp, and Doc Holliday of criminal charges after the gunfight near the O.K. Corral.

And Spicer involved himself in earlier controversies that weren't always to his advantage, making powerful enemies along the way. It only added to his rather curious persona. In January 1880, he would publish in the Tucson Star a false report that the Corbin mill, which hadn't even opened, was sold. It angered Frank Corbin as he was busy hiring talent and making contracts, and Spicer's false report could easily have shaken confidence in his business and jeopardized all that he was trying to achieve.

PASS THE SPICER

Just two months prior to the Corbin mill falsehood, Spicer questioned the validity of the founding of the Tombstone District, which included the milling towns on the San Pedro. In both cases his false charges were at the expense of the key owners of the Corbin and Gird mills, and their related mining operations, later known as the "Tombstone Milling and Mining Company." This was no small matter to those investing heavily into the district with their money, labor and lives.

Wells Spicer, whose hearing released the Earps and Doc Holliday, attempted to attain the District Recorder position. Courtesy of Roy B. Young.

Thomas Walker, an early insider in the formation of the Tombstone District and distant relation of Dick Gird's, would make the case against Spicer in the court of public opinion. "I notice in your last issue a communication relative to the establishment of a district…and also the election of a district recorder for Tombstone. This is the fourth or fifth time that the district recorder question has been agitated-ending without interest in Tombstone." An irritated Walker pointed out that many saw no need for the position that Spicer was advocating, and his purpose in pressing the dead issue appears to have been that he wanted such a role for himself. Spicer argued that without a district recorder, the Tombstone District did not legally exist, a stretch of an argument in Walker's eyes, as he noted: "Mr. Spicer says now in Tombstone we have no district; whether he makes this statement with a desire to misrepresent, or from ignorance of facts, I do not know. But I flatly contradict it, and reply that we have a district in Tombstone; properly established according to law, and the boundaries already defined. One year ago we signed a call; posted it; organized and adopted rules and regulations. Just as Mr. Pioneer Spicer recommended it be done today." Walker was chiding Spicer pointing out that he was not a part of the beginnings of the Tombstone District, as he himself had been. He also pointed out that the recording of mining claims at Tucson was still feasible, more so now than ever before. "…if miners and prospectors could afford to go to Tucson to have notices recorded at that time when there were no stages and no mails, why cannot they do so to-day?"

Walkers' position was that mining claims in the Tombstone District had to be taken to the county recorder's office, as this was the most official way to avoid unnecessary lawsuits in the future. "If a district recorder should fail to properly transmit a notice to the county recorder, to whom could the locator redress in case of subsequent notice (probably recorded in county records) being placed on his claim?" [148]

Spicer's approach seemed to be of two minds, arguing that the Tombstone District was not legally formed, but at the same time, advocating for a "district recorder" for the very district he claimed didn't exist, as if that would somehow legitimize it. The paperwork for the district had long since been filed at the recorder's office in Tucson, and this information was commonly known.

Walker wasn't the only one who stepped into the uproar that Spicer had initiated. U.S. Surveyor General John Wasson had been publicly mischaracterized by Spicer's letter, and he responded publicly as well. "…it is an error to suppose myself or this office has any information of which the general public is in ignorance." The Citizen weighed in, adding, "The 'District' question is agitated slightly by a correspondent [Spicer] of the Nugget…Tombstone is far too advanced to be returned to swaddling clothes. It looks as though somebody wanted the office of District Recorder very badly," as projections of Tombstone mining output in the next few years were known to be in the millions. [149]

The Citizen had moved to the heart of the matter - this was about creating a position that was of no use to anyone in the Tombstone District, with the notable exception of whoever held such a post, and with whomever he chose to share a bit of the related power and profits. The recorder's office in Tucson would continue to serve as the official location to record mining claims, property transfers, etc., until Tombstone would attain the political muscle to break away from Pima County and create Cochise County, which it did in 1881.

THE BIG FOUR ARE WATCHING

All of this occurred against the backdrop of a recent exploration through the area, one that could have a real impact on the district. Charles Crocker of the Southern Pacific Railroad sent associates on a trip through the San Pedro River Valley. Crocker wanted to know more of the area, to determine if he should consider extending south from Benson into the sprawling Tombstone District. "Judge H.B. Underhill and J.C. Clark left [Tucson] for a trip via Cienaga, San Pedro, Tombstone (taking in the mills), going south to the Sonora line and back by way of Camp Huachuca and the Empire ranche [sic] and they expect to get back to Tucson in about a week. The Judge goes partly out of curiosity, but primarily because President Crocker wanted him to personally inspect the country mentioned and its developments and their bearings upon the railway interest." [150]

The party finished their round trip in Tucson just over a week later, with the kind of enthusiasm that locals loved to hear of. "Judge Underhill and Messrs. Leatherwood and Clark returned today from a trip to [the] San Pedro, Mule Pass, Tombstone, Charleston and Huachuca. They also made a detour below the line [into Mexico], just to see the country. Engineer Hood joined the party at San Pedro and an examination of the valley towards Charleston was made with a view to future possibilities. It is putting it mildly to say that Judge Underhill was immensely pleased with the country and [its] outlook. His report must have a very cheerful effect upon the railroad company. He left for San Francisco by coach this afternoon." [151]

Within a short time, Judge Underhill would report his findings to Crocker. High hopes gave rise to grandiose rumors that the Southern Pacific railroad would soon be traversing all points in the Tombstone district, from Contention to Charleston to Tombstone. Whatever enthusiasm Underhill may have shared with Crocker, it didn't translate into S.P. laying ties and rail south of Benson. That would have to wait for other companies.

At the time of this trip, Charleston was a well-known and viable destination. Contention was little more than a mill. But by the time a railroad was ready to extend south, Contention City had become the most substantial milling town and bullion producer in the district.

THE RAILROAD CHOOSES CONTENTION

Contention had another advantage – it was the closest milling site to the railway connection at Benson, actually giving the railroads less incentive to build to Tombstone in the 1880's. The route from Benson to Contention was far less in mileage, and most of Tombstone's bullion was shipped from there anyway. This built-in disincentive may not have been obvious to town boosters in Tombstone, but it was clearly understood by the railroad executives of the day. Laying rail to Contention would eliminate the energy-expensive climb from the river to the higher elevation of Tombstone. Furthermore, travelers were quite willing to take a stage or another conveyance to Contention and board the train there. It was a shrewd business move on the part of the New Mexico and Arizona Railroad, aka the N.M. & A., the first to build into the area. It would bypass Tombstone and head southwest to Nogales, creating access from Benson all the way to the Mexican border, with travelers having the option of continuing into the Mexican interior. The N.M. & A. would reach Contention early in 1882, continue its progress south to Fairbank, then turn to the west near the Babacomari heading toward Nogales and points in between.

HIGH NOON AT TOMBSTONE

The Tucson press made mention of a doctor who was traveling around Arizona taking notes about his journeys. That in itself didn't merit a mention in the local paper, but when it was also known that he was writing as a traveling correspondent of the Chicago Tribune, it was hoped that he would give a good review of the area to readers elsewhere.

"Dr. A.H. [Adolphus Henry] Noon left to-day for Arivaca, Oro Blanco and other points south, and we may soon look for some bright letters from his ready pen. The Doctor was much pleased with Tucson and his notes about us to the Chicago Tribune we are sure will do us good. We commend Dr. Noon to the people in our mining districts as a gentleman of intelligence and culture, and one who seeks to do them and our territory good. A safe and pleasant tour to the Doctor, we say." [152]

Noon would later publish his thoughts of this journey in the Chicago Tribune, offering frank impressions of the area and its people. "To visit Tombstone, tha[t] new great mining-camp, of doleful cognomen but lively characteristics, is the recognized duty of every one exploring, investigating, or interested in Arizona, this new field of American enterprise; so of course I went to see and judge for myself…" But before judging Tombstone, Noon offered observations of the variety of people moving there. "…moneyed men and moneyless men; capitalists and confidence-men; mining men and mining bilks, whose cheek [is] greater than that of a government mule, is of bronze, but 'brass' they have none; 'busters' and 'busted' men…Some persons evidently imagine that all they have to do to become

Dr. A.H. Noon, witnessed the beginning of the Contention Mill on his way to Tombstone. Copy photo from the collections of John D. Rose.

rich is to reach Arizona, the new El Dorado. It is indeed a wide field for mining investment, and wise enterprise of kindred character; but soft snaps for merely professional men, bookkeepers, shopmen, and unskilled labor are scarce, and many new-comers may perhaps find the new road to Jordan a hard one to travel, for the country is yet rough and little improved; the landlord in many places has not yet built at all, and, where he has, the new-comer should be content to take things as he finds them…Tombstone is seventy-five miles in a southerly direction: At times it is dusty, and my fellow passengers' tobacco smoke—three of them inside the coach, smoking like steam-engines—is not delightful, but all are good-natured and full of information, and I live through it.

"Mark Macdonald (the Ursus-Major of the San Francisco Stock-Board), Senator Luttrell, and other lions are traveling to see those eccentrically-named mines; the Lucky Cuss, Tough Nut, Contention…Much of the road is over barren, uninviting country. The mountains in the distance everywhere are, however, all more or less mineral-bearing, but part of the road is through park-like country, oak and mesquite[e] trees, with miles of the finest kind of grass, extending to and up in the mountain-sides…There are no towns and few settlers en route, except a little Mormon affair [St. David] on the San Pedro River, the way-stations of the stages, and three little places between the rising village near the Contention mill-site and Tombstone…At the new mining [milling] camp called Contention City (and here be it observed that all mining villages containing two saloons and a restaurant are courteously called cities by the…custom of the country), we see the large framework and preparatory masonry of the Contention mill, which promises to be excellent and first-class in every respect. The machinery is calculated to work twenty stamps, with power to increase to forty. Every man around seems hopeful and cheerful, and full of confidence as to the future…We pass many dead soldiers on the road. For the benefit of the reader, I will explain that a dead soldier is an empty whisky-bottle; and their mournful remains are frequently visible under a tree or by the dusty roadside." [153]

Mark MacDonald was friends with Thos. Farish, who would play a significant role in Tombstone mining. It was hoped locally that MacDonald's connections with San Francisco banking and other entities would soon bring Tombstone its railroad. "Mark J. MacDonald, the well know stockbroker of San Francisco, who visited this camp [Tombstone] about one year ago, and at that time was determined a railroad should be built between this city and Benson, has been quiet so far as our citizens have known, since, but at the same time the project has been quietly worked and he now announces to his old friend, Thos. E. Farish, that all the arrangements have been perfected and the construction of the road will soon commence." [154]

The Epitaph was jubilant, and excitement was far ahead of the facts. "OH-BE-JOYFUL, When Y'er Hear the Racket of the Locomotive Look Out for the Cars. Baggage to be Checked Through from Virginia City to the Boss Camp [referring to Tombstone].

"A dispatch received by Superintendent Farish from Mark L. McDonald brings the glad tidings that Tombstone will ere long be connected with the Southern Pacific at Benson by rail. All the arrangements for its construction have been made, and the road is a fixed fact. Hip Hurrah! [A] broad-guage railroad to Tombstone." [155]

Whatever sway Mark McDonald had in the world of San Francisco stock brokering did not result in a railroad to Tombstone. In fact an article surfaced in September of 1881 which indicated that instead of heading to Tombstone, the new route would turn westward following the Babacomari toward Nogales. "The Railroad. A reliable gentleman yesterday informed an Epitaph reporter that contracts for the grading on the line of the Atchison, Topeka and Santa Fe Railroad [the parent company of the New Mexico and Arizona Railroad (N. M. & A.)] had been let from the Grand Central Mill up the Babacomari Valley, which settles the question of [the] route, if true. Also, that the graders from that point towards Benson are raising the roadbed three feet higher than originally intended, as a preventive against washouts." [156]

But railroad fever was still raging even at the dawn of 1882. "In a few weeks at most grading is to be commenced for the railroad from Contention to this city. There is every reason for encouragement in the outlook of the new year, and we predict for Tombstone and its adjacent camps a progressive era of prosperity." [157]

It had long been questioned as to whether or not the N.M. & A. was really coming to Tombstone. It was a debate that the railroad was in no hurry to clarify, leaving many in the Tombstone populace, especially those in business, to foster high hopes of such an arrival. The Epitaph continued to tell its readers that work would soon begin on the Tombstone branch of this line. In their case of "railroad fever," hope continued to spring eternal.

The press wasn't alone in ownership of this; in fact, they were being inspired by railroad employees, who either didn't know any better, or chose not to disclose the truth. Even as late as the summer of 1882 such myth was promoted as a coming reality. Tombstone was paid a visit by Henry Haus, agent of the A.T. & S.F. [aka, the N.M. &A.] railroad at Contention. Haus told the eager audience at the Epitaph office in July of 1882 that he had the expectation of becoming the agent at Tombstone once the railroad arrived. [158]

Railroad construction in the Arizona Territory, from the collections of John D. Rose.

MORE MILL NEWS

Meanwhile, construction of the mills continued to excite the inhabitants along the San Pedro River and interest the press. Enough progress had taken place on the Sunset Mill that its superintendent had moved to the site. "Mr. Moriarity, superintendent of the Sunset, has removed his residence to the new mill, at Contention City, which is expected to be in running order by the first proximo." [159]

"The grading on the Grand Central mill-site is completed and the masons began work on the 13th. A new road has been graded to Contention via the new mill, leaving the old road just below Waterville [Watervale], which is two miles nearer to Contention than by the old road." [160]

The Grand Central would be delayed while it was internally debated just how big this mill should be. "Mr. [E.B.] Gage informs us that the plans for the Grand Central mill have been changed to admit [the] erection of 80 stamps. This will delay the completion of the mill to the latter part of January next. However, the enlarged mill will more than make up for the loss of time." [161] Actually it didn't, as the plans would later be reduced to thirty five stamps, which still matched the entire combined output of the Gird and Corbin Mills at Millville. An eighty stamp mill would have been a remarkable achievement, but an unnecessarily expensive one.

There was also a report, albeit false, of great advances at Contention. "A new mill for the Contention, forty stamps capacity, is to be erected at Contention, which, with the twenty-five stamps now in operation, will give the Company sixty-five stamps to work their ore. It is certainly a favorable indication when the two most prominent mines of the camp, the Contention and Tough Nut, find it necessary to double their milling facilities." [162] Such reports would only boost local optimism, but the Contention Mine simply didn't have need of this much milling capacity, despite how productive it was.

There was enough prosperity even at satellite communities like Charleston and Contention that residents there were able to contribute to the construction of a building to house the "Church of Rome" in Tombstone, an effort led by Tombstone entrepreneur, Nellie Cashman. "I take this method of extending thanks to the citizens of Tombstone for their liberality in subscribing to the fund for the building of a catholic church in this city. Also, to many kind friends in Charleston and Contention City, who responded so generously to this most worthy cause. I can state that $700 has been raised, and all the bills for lumber and other building material being in, we know very nearly the exact cause [cost] of the construction of the church, say $1,000. It is proposed to give an entertainment soon, for the purpose of increasing our present fund...Again I extend my most heartfelt thanks to the public generally for their liberal support. Nellie Cashman. Tombstone, Oct. 6, 1880." [163]

As Contention flourished other matters came to the forefront, especially as election season neared. "An opinion seems to prevail that Contention City lies in this [Tombstone's] precinct and that in the selection of three justices of the peace for the precinct one should be given to that place. It will be seen by the published list of the precincts of the county that it was established as a separate one at the last meeting of the board of supervisors and hence the justices should be chosen from among our own citizens. It is more than probable that the business of this town alone will not require more than two justices." [164] The position of Justice of the Peace at Contention would later figure into the Earp controversies that were to follow.

On Christmas day, 1880, Clara Spalding Brown and her husband made note of Tombstone's "Christmas trees in the churches [that] made the little ones happy and proved enjoyable to the big folks as well…Christmas was observed as a general holiday, most of the mines stopping work, which is not the case on Sundays." Clara and her husband celebrated the holiday by taking a "thirty-mile horseback ride over the surrounding country, to take in the settlement of Charleston and Contention, and the Contention stamp mill, on the San Pedro river. This mill was running, and one who observes the action of its powerful machinery can but realize the importance of a mine that has paid $600,000 in dividends within seven months, whose stock is worth $80 per share." [165]

STATUS HAS ITS PRIVILEGES

Contention City king John McDermott was by no means a newcomer to the west, or to the Arizona Territory. He was popular throughout Arizona and Nevada, and was a player who knew how to insert himself into the game. McDermott was active in the politics of the time, and at Contention, sustaining a proven popularity. His Republican cohorts at the Epitaph were only too happy to build drama around the selection of a delegate to the upcoming convention. "CONTENTION CITY. Republicans Thoroughly Organized-John McDermott Elected Delegate to the Coming Convention. Contention, A.T., September 13, 1880…The Republicans of Pima County were willing to go into this election as a people and elect our best men to county offices, but were forced to organize by these zealous Democrats, stationed on the 'watch towers' of the Democratic battlements…At an election held at Contention, on Saturday last, for a delegate to the Republican County Convention, at Tucson, John McDermott received all the votes cast, and, of course, will represent the Republicans of Contention in the Convention. No better man could have been selected than McDermott. He is a thorough Republican, and has a back broad enough and a 'back-bone' to hold up his end of the Republican cable." [166]

Such an election in Republican circles would bring McDermott into close contact with many substantial figures in the Tombstone district. While McDermott represented Contention City, Dick Gird of the Tombstone Milling and Mining Company, E.B. Gage of the Grand Central Mine at Tombstone and mill at Contention, saloon keeper R.F. Hafford, teamster C.H. "Ham" Light (who would later witness a portion of the gunfight near the O.K. Corral), and firefighting as well as fire breathing L.F. [Leslie] Blackburn represented Tombstone. S. W. Wood represented Millville. [167]

As the pivotal election of 1880 approached, Rigg's Court House was listed as the place of voting, with E.A. Rigg as election inspector, and John McDermott and Chas. Conan as the election Judges. [168]

Much concern surrounded McDermott over a serious accident he suffered. "John McDermott, of Contention City, fell from his horse yesterday, causing injuries which it is thought will be fatal." [169]

"John McDermott, for several years engineer at [the] Curtis saw mill, Prescott, and well known throughout Arizona and Nevada, met with a severe accident near Contention City a few days ago. It appears that he was traveling from Harshaw to Bisbee, and when near the crossing of the San Pedro River his horse fell, and throwing Mr. McDermott violently to the ground, fractured his spinal column. As he was a heavy man, weighing 240 pounds, he may possibly have received other injuries. [170] John McDermott would survive this incident and live to fight a sharp attack of pneumonia over a decade later. [171]

TROUBLE FEEDS OFF OF SUCCESS

Many a man's labors built roadways, stamp mills, businesses, homes, and other things for the common good, and such progress inevitably brought with it the frontier parasites that preyed upon them. The area along the San Pedro was soon plagued by such types. "The stage from Tombstone to Benson was stopped last night by two men about half way between this place and Contention City. The express box was taken, but the mail and passengers were unmolested. The treasure in the box amounted to about $135. Deputy Marshal Carp [Earp] and a posse are after the robbers." [172]

THE SMITHSONIAN DIGS CONTENTION CITY

As more settlement and exploration continued in the area, an early historical find was noted by the press. "Capt. A.W. Chase, now excavating for the Smithsonian Institute near Contention, has discovered some fine relics of the Aztecs. One village has produced a number of pieces of pottery and stone implements. These underground ruins are near the Grand Central mill, and two other villages have been found between that mill and Contention City. Supt. Chase is an enthusiast in the work and we hope his efforts will give the world much needed knowledge of the early inhabitants of Arizona." [173]

"The Smithsonian Institute is represented here by a relative of the nations great financier, Judge Chase of Ohio. His nephew, Captain Chase, is here collecting bugs, spearing snakes, Gila monsters, and every other wonder for our National Museum at Washington, and if industry and zeal will get them Captain Chase will find them. There is not a monstrosity or bug, or any other curious thing, either in life or petrified, that this bug man don't pounce upon and capture. I really believe he would take Mexican or Indian decoction [174] of 'tis um' and forward it to the museum.

The Indian Department no doubt already has been supplied with samples of 'tis um' to judge from the blunders that department has committed in the last year.

"John B. Luding [John Baker Ludwig], late deputy Sheriff of Pima, has been appointed and qualified as deputy under our new Cachise Sheriff—a good appointment. He will continue to reside at Contention.

"All this day 'Old Boreas' has been on the rampage and has blown his horn in one uninterrupted blast from the north. Cold Iceland weather all day, and just now (12 o'clock midnight), it sleets, rains and freezes. For a hot climate, the mercury in our instrument tells a bad story. Every man, woman and child in our village, except our mill men, have hunted their blankets and I intend to go and do likewise." [175]

"NO ONE HAS DIED, BUT SOME OUGHT TO."

More from the above letter of March 1881 offered keen insight into life in Contention, a view of the town before tensions would arise over the shooting death of Bud Philpot, as well as the Earps' legal issues over the gunfight near the O.K. Corral which will have repercussions at Charleston and Contention.

"CRUMBS FROM CONTENTION. Our Regular Correspondent Sends the Usual Notes Regarding Railroads Saloons, Minerals, Mills, Mormons, Etc. Contention, March 14. EDITOR EPITAPH: -From the advent of railroads into Arizona, trials, tribulations, etc., have happened to our people. Our ancient saloon-keeper has sold out. Our first postmaster resigned in favor of 'some other feller,' who can afford to run an office of that class for $15 per month and find his own stationery. No one has died, but some ought to. One saloon has suddenly become quiet and dark from a visit of the new Sheriff of Cachise County. [This would be Johnny Behan, and it remains an open question as to why this Contention Saloon would be shut down following his visit there.] Our mill ships the usual amount of bullion weekly, and of a change, they add a brick or two.

"Our people are happy; morals are in 'statu quo;' whisky is sold at the same demoralizing prices and effects. The only exciting change in our community is that our school house is reopened through the enterprise and liberality of one of our School Commissioners and one of our prominent merchants. The school marm is here and ready for pupils. We in our 'sanctum sanctorum,' believe that enterprise of minds is good, and he who leads, to that end, is a public benefactor.

"Contention goes on in the quietness of law and order, but the school question here may cause trouble, because the pupils have been on the border so long that sometimes they are refractory and need chastising, which often results in resistance. We hope, however, that the enterprising Commissioner will see to it that order and di[s]cipline rules. Our Mormon friends below here, built a school house and petitioned for a division of funds, and it was granted to them: but now Cachise must look after her own schools. Where, Oh, where, are the school funds? I will say right here that our Mormons are as good as the best citizens in any county. They pursue the even tenor of their way in industry, sobriety and enterprise. They don't practice polygamy, but they do practice 'do unto others as you have them do unto you.' A better, more intelligent set of people we have not in this Cachise County.

"Mr. D.N. Cabie [Cable] and Mr. Robert Mason have fenced their ranches with a wire fence. If the grant men don't take it from them they have complied with the fence law; others will go and do likewise if they can get an undisputed title. I believe they can." [176]

Though the two may have agreed on fencing, Robert Mason sued Daniel Cables in 1883, and the court chose to pass on the case. This was the same Robert Mason who had taken a shot at William H. Drew. [177]

COMMUNICATION AT THE GRAND CENTRAL MILL

A new technology would soon be visited upon the Grand Central and Contention Mills, as well as their mining counterparts in Tombstone. This was an event of real importance, and Contention would become the first community along the San Pedro to receive such an advance. It was known as the "Telephone." "Tombstone's First Telephones. The contract has been let to Adams & Borner for furnishing and setting the poles for the telephone lines between the Grand Central and Contention mines and mills, and the work will be executed with speed, having commenced yesterday. The line is being built jointly by the two companies, and as it will furnish instantaneous communication between the offices of the Superintendents and their respective mills will prove of great convenience. These are the pioneer telephones of the [Tombstone] district." [178]

The phone at the Grand Central would later play a role in the near shooting of Mayor Clum. Tensions in Tombstone were at an all-time high following the gunfight near the O.K. Corral in October 1881. Subsequent court proceedings left Wyatt, Morgan and Virgil Earp, along with their close friend Doc Holliday, free men. A key supporter of the Earps in this case was Mayor John Clum, who under the auspices of his newspaper, the Tombstone Epitaph, had given key support to the Earps during their legal challenges.

Contention City was clearly hitting its economic stride, so much so that the Arizona Weekly Citizen sent Arthur Laing, a correspondent, to report the progress. "CONTENTION CITY. Its Industries and Population-The Quartz Mills for Tombstone Mines. Contention City, March 14. Editor Citizen: Before returning to Tucson I determined to stay a day at this place, so as to make my descriptions of the Tombstone mines and mills somewhat complete.

"This village or city, as it is called, has been brought into being by the erection of the Contention mill. It is situated ten miles from Tombstone on the San Pedro river, where there is planty [sic] of room for all mills Tombstone and surrounding districts may require for many a

102

long year, as there is lots of water. Wood costs about $7 to $8 per cord and is daily getting scarcer. The proposed railroad, however, will soon bring the necessary supply of coal to take its place. The population is, I should judge, about 150, and the city boasts three stores, several saloons of course, and an unpretending canvas-roofed eating house called the Contention House, where I had better meals than in many a more elegantly furnished hostelry. There is in course of erection a massive adobe hotel, that has been long in construction. It bids fair to be a convenient house of call for those visiting the neighborhood. There are three mills in the vicinity, viz: The Contention, the old Sunset mill, in the town, and the one recently erected by the Grand Central Company.

"The Contention mill, under the superintendency of J.D. Bousfield, has done much good work since it started. It has 25 stamps of 850 pounds each, 24 settling tanks one half the size of those of the Grand Central, 14 pans, 7 settlers, besides the other usual apparatus. They are at present working about 75 tons of ore daily, brought by teams from the mine at Tombstone at a cost of about $3 per ton. The engine of this and the Grand Central are similar, viz: 150 horse-power (nominal), ample power to do all that is at present required for it.

"The Sunset mill, lately bought by the Head Center Mining Company, of Tombstone, is at the north end of the town, and although the capacity is small, still all about it is good and in good order. It has ten 850-pound stamps, with room and power for an increase to 20 stamps, six pans and three settlers. During our visit the mill was not running, but it was expected soon to commence pounding away at Head Centre ore. The location is in my opinion not so favorable as either of the other mills, and the spot where the ore is deposited is at the top of a very steep ascent, which must be often an arduous task to drive a tired team of mules up, after their journey from the mine.

The Head Centre owned the Sunset Mill at Contention. From the collections of John D. Rose.

"The Grand Central Mill is about one and one-half miles on the Charleston side of the town, and is par excellence the mill of the Territory. I am not often given to superfluous adulation, but I must say that the substantial way in which this mill had been erected, gives great credit to the owners, designers and mill-wrights connected therewith. Every advantage has been taken of any and all late improvements, both in crushing and treatment of the ores, and taken all in all I feel sure the milling of one ton of ore here costs less than at any other mill. The facilities even for discharging the heavy ore wagons (there were four teams, of 16 mules each, waiting their turn when I visited the mill), must save a considerable sum per month over the method employed elsewhere. The rock-crusher and sizer too is another improvement on the usual mode, saving some labor on every ton of ore treated.

"There are 30 stamps (850 pounds each); 20 settling tanks, each 8x11x3; 16 amalgamating pans, 8 settlers, bullion furnaces, etc.

"The Eugine [Engine] (a counterpart of Contention mill), is of 150 horse-power, nominal, has a 20-inch cylinder and 42 stroke; also 4 steel boilers, 54 inches in diameter, 16 feet long with 46 3 ½ inch tubes.

"It was my good fortune to see the first four bars of bullion made at the mill. Of course they were just like other bard, but at some future day it may be something to have seen then.

"Mr. E.M. Crane is the Superintendent here, and I am informed that the cost of the mill inclusive was $130,000.

"And now one word for the firm that has built the three mills I have briefly described as well as the Boston Custom Mill, situated about seven miles from Contention. The firm is Malter, Lind & Co., of San Francisco, Mr. L. being a resident here. In all the mills they have erected, their work has been good and substantial; they have gone on improving in each mill they took in hand, until with the completion of their last masterpiece, the Grand Central, they seem to have attained as near perfection as possible. This is the largest silver mill in the Territory and the sixth mill built here by the same firm within the last year, the cost of the whole aggregating upwards of one-half million dollars. May they have the opportunity of erecting many more such on the San Pedro river!

"On the other side of the river, near the Grand Central, are some very old ruins. The Mexicans had a fort here which was an important place during their Indian wars and called Fort Santa Cruz, but Mr. Chase, a distinguished archeologist, who has given much time and attention to the subject, has found sundry pieces of pottery, etc., showing the place, long before Mexican rule, had been inhabited by a portion of the Aztec race, a subject too engrossing and interesting for a newspaper article. I leave to-night for Tucson, and will see you, likely, before this is in print. Arthur Laing." [179]

Laing's insightful letter was written from Contention City on March fourteenth. By the time it was printed, the tragic murder of a well-liked stage driver would overshadow all other news of the area—Bud Philpot, mentioned in the Drew's Station chapter.

It was D.T. Smith who, along with John McDermott, began selling lots and organizing Contention City in its early stages. By the summer of 1881 Smith had moved to the "suburbs" of Contention. Instead of being in the press for pushing forward Contention's early economic strides, he was now seen in the press because four stray mules had walked into his yard. "Estray Notice. Smith's Ranch, Cochise County, Arizona May 15, 1881. I have this day taken up four stray mules, which the owner can have by proving properly and paying charges. Description: One large brown or very dark bay, thin in flesh: joint enlarged on right hind leg, wart on nose; one large brown mule, white hair on both sides of neck, part of neck quite raw, right shoulder imperfect; one small brown mule branded, 'A' on left thigh; one small bay mule branded 'A' on left thigh. For further particulars call at my ranch on the west side of the San Pedro river, four miles below Charleston, or address me by letter at Contention City, A.T. Also one small dark bay mare. D.T. Smith." [180] Given the condition of the mules, the owner may not have seen them as worth paying Smith for the cost of his feed and the notice ad.

CHAPTER 8

CONTENTION'S SOCIAL SIDE

"If there is any one set of people more than another that enjoy a good time, it is our Irish." -
Epitaph

Another revealing letter offered Tombstone readers more insight into life at Contention. It had become a place known for participating in the finer pursuits of society – a place for fine dining, a place to throw a ball. The letter also points to the relief brought by the belief that Curly Bill Brocius and Bill Leonard were away from the area for the time being. It also illustrates a harsh side to the pioneer life as bodies are carted into town in a wagon. There is also growing concern by settlers in the area who in good faith built on what they thought were public lands owned by the U.S. Government, only to find they were squatting illegally on privately owned land grants. Life in Contention was, to say the least, a consistent series of contrasts.

"From Contention City. CONTENTION, A.T., June 28, 1881. Editor Epitaph: Anno Domini has about spent one half of this year in utter do-nothingness. Since the advent here of Curly and his pard, Bill Leonard, and the migration of the wrestler and his pard, we have gone on in the even tenor of our way so that life in Contention becomes monotonous. The only change from daily habits and early retirements to court the god of sleep occurred on the 8th of June, when Sen. Francisco Agular called upon our justice of the peace to perform the rites of matrimony between him[self] and the Senorita Carmen Garcia."

Justice Rigg let news of the impending nuptials be known locally, as this was seen as a major event—it was said to be the first wedding in Contention's history. For a town used to hearing about this killing along the railroad, or that shooting during a stage robbery, much of the community turned out to see a happy celebration. "Our venerable justice let the 'cat out of the bag,' and when the hour for the ceremony came there were present a large number of our people to see the first marriage ceremony in Contention. The bride and groom were on hand promp[t]ly at the hour set, and the two were made man and wife. The usual congratulations were given when the guests were invited to partake of 'dulces' and liquids, and then the room was cleared of all useless chairs and furniture, and the guests were informed by Mr. J.M. Castenada and Gen. D.K. Wardwell, who seemed to be masters of ceremonies, that there was to be a dance. The accomplished wife of J. Gunidaini, one of our principal merchants, appeared with her harp and the dance went merrily on to the wee hours, when all left, having enjoyed a very delightful evening."

The unnamed Contention author of this letter conveys a close knit community, where an impromptu invitation could bring out many for an almost spontaneous celebration. "On the 15th of June a lively son of Erin, Peter Conner, sent out invitation to meet him at his resesidence [sic] on Main street, at 8 p.m. A large party assembled at the hour named, and wine and wit flowed 'ad libitum.' Songs, dances and speeches held high carnival. S[e]veral of our ladies were present and everything was lovely. If there is any one set of people more than another that enjoy a good time it is our Irish." [181]

THE BALL

"It had been talked of for some weeks that a ball would be given for the benefit of our public school June 24th. Our citizens subscribed liberally, and McDermott's Hall was selected for the event. The ball-room was elegantly decorated, and every preparation was made to make the ball a success. Mrs. W.F. Bradley, the teacher in the public school, was indefatigable in attending to all the preliminaries, as well as disposing of tickets for the school fund, and we are glad to say that not only was the ball a success but it netted a handsome profit.

"Amongst those present were, Mr. and Mrs. W.F. Bradley, Mrs. Marks and family, Mr. and Mrs. Grindama, Mr. and Mrs. G.W. Platt, Sen. and Senna. J. Venda, Sen. and Senna. Michelana, Mr. and Mrs. D.N. Cable, Monsieur Leon Lamuir and Wife, Miss Carrol, Mr. and Mrs. Gale, and a host of others that we could not name from the Contention [Milling and Mining Company]. From Tombstone, Mrs. Broderick and Mrs. M. Marks, Mr. Breckenridge…"

"To describe the dresses and toilets of the ladies would require another than an old bachelor to depict as they deserved. Suffice it to say that 'honiton lace' and all kinds of lace was the rule, and to sum it up, the ladies were all dressed in good taste, danced with exquisite grace and kept it up until the comet, with his fiery tail, admonished them that it was at least 4 a.m., June 23.

"At 12, midnight, the guests adjourned to the restaurant of Mr. Jennisson, where a bounteous supply was laid of all the delicacies of the season. Mr. Jennisson deserves much credit for the handsome and recherché manner in which he provided for his numerous guests.

"The peculiarity of this ball was that there were no distinction or cliques, all seemed and did meet as one family living together, and good will, good feeling characterised this assemblage as a family party.

"It is hoped we may soon have another for like purposes for the amusement of our people." [182]

FROM JOY TO SORROW

"Contention City, June 22.—Jesus Vasquez was killed in a quarrel with two Mexicans seven miles below here last night. The two Mexicans were badly wounded." [183]

"We had a murder in our midst. On the 22nd of June there came to Contention a wagon drawn by two mules. The driver stopped at J. Varder's blacksmith shop and reported to him that in the wagon was one man dead, one badly wounded, and asked what ought to be done.

"The wagon was driven by two Yaki [Yaqui] Indians. Mr. J. Varder reported the fact to the justice of the peace, E.A. Rigg, and [with] the deputy sheriff, J.B. Ludwig, they went immediately to the wagon and found one dead man, who had been killed fourteen hours before, and one wounded man who had been in camp with him…and two employees of the man who killed him. A coroner's jury was immediately summon[e]d and found a verdict that the man killed was named Jesus Vasquez and that the man who killed him was named Robles. The only witnesses who saw the killing were employees of Manuel Robles named Jesus Maria Ochoa and Manuel Estella; that the deceased, Jesus Vasqu[e]z, was a native of Mexico; that he was about 27 years of age; that he was killed by Manuel Robles, by cutting on the face and neck with an axe: and that he was justified in killing him. One juror, Richard Parks, dissenting from the verdict on the ground[s] that the evidence did not sustain the verdict. The body of the man killed was horribly cut on the neck and face. He was buried at Contention on the evening of the 22nd of June, about 6 p.m., it being impossible to keep the body out of the ground any longer-it was getting putrid. The acting coroner, E.A. Rigg, J.P. [Justice of the Peace], remanded the man, Robles, who did the killing for examination before the justice of the peace, and, when examined, committed him for the action of the grand jury, and bound over the two witnesses, Jesus Maria Ochoa and Manuel Estella, to appear when required either before the grand jury or the District Court. Thus a summary of events of the doings in the vicinity of Contention city closes…" [184]

"The hotel built on the new townsite, if in Tombstone, would be worth $30,000. [Tombstone hotels were of higher value, as they could generate greater revenues, regardless of the cost of their construction] It is built of adobe, two stories high, and on the first floor are nine rooms. The dining hall is 50 feet long by 30 feet wide. The bar-room is large and commodious. The building is plastered throughout, and has wood floors. A foot-bridge now crosses the San Pedro river to the west side, and soon a bridge for teams will be erected to connect with the Charleston and Tombstone road at their junction here.

"Prospects for additional reduction mills here are good, in fact, notwithstanding your Tombstone Water Works the San Pedro is the legitimate place for mills, and in a few years, you will find a string of mills from Charleston to and far below Contention, and don't you forget it." [185] This oft repeated claim that the San Pedro would be soon lined from Contention toward Benson, and then from Contention to the south at Millville, was typical of the kind of optimism that it took to achieve all that such settlers did on the challenging frontier of the San Pedro Valley, even if it wasn't always practical.

The following condolence referred to the fire that surged through a portion of Tombstone's commercial section on May 22nd, 1881, just six days before this letter was written. "Contention tenders to Tombstone her sincere sympathy for the late misfortune, but, like a Phoenix from its ashes, Tombstone will rise again more grand and glorious than before." [186]

INSIDE THE GRAND CENTRAL MILL AT CONTENTION CITY

The industrialization of Contention City, and the Arizona Territory for that matter, would continue reaching new heights with the construction of the Grand Central Mill. Calling this mill and its related mine at Tombstone "Grand" was no exaggeration. "GRAND CENTRAL MILL. This mill is situated upon the San Pedro river, two miles above Contention, where the bottom opens out into a beautiful meadow that is now green with the spring grass begotten of the late rains. The foundation for the mill was made by grading into the face of a broad point of the mesa that bounds the valley on the east. On Sunday last, in company with Mr. G.W. Mauk, United States Deputy Collector for Arizona, we paid this magnificent structure a visit. Calling at the office, which is a large adobe building, standing upon a low promontory jutting out from the mesa into the valley, we were met by Mr. J.E. Lawrence, Assayer, and E.M. Crane, Esq., Superintendent, who extended the hospitality of the place to the party, and showing everything of interest about the office and mill.

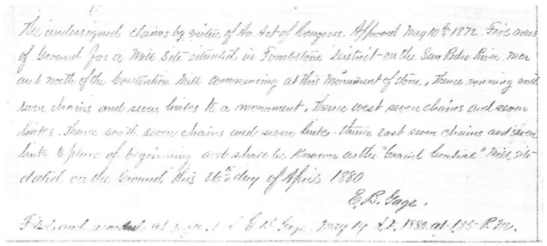

E.B Gage files the claim Grand Central Mill, showing the beginning of the Tombstone District's largest Mill. Gage is in error that the Grand Central was North of the Contention Mill, as it was to the south. Pima County Mill sites, Arizona Library and Archives.

"As before stated the office is an adobe building of dimensions to contain a broad corridor and four large, airy rooms. Two are fitted up and used for an assay department. The fitting is perfect, no expense having been spared to make it so, the work having been done under the personal supervision of Mr. Lawrence. On the opposite side of the corridor is the main office and another room. The doors and windows are all fitted with wire-screens to exclude insects and let in the air. It is by far the finest office of the kind anywhere around Tombstone. There is a thick growth of low mesquite trees around the place which gives it a homelike appearance.

"On another and higher bench are situated the boarding house, lodging house and stable. They are sufficiently removed from the mill to be out of harm's way in case of fire. The mill is the great feature, it being the largest in this part of the Territory, and probably combines more of the latest improvements than any on the river. There are 30 stamps, 16 pans, 8 settlers and 1 agitator through which passes all pulp that comes from the batteries, it first having run through the pans and then the settlers. The stamps crush 3 tons each in 24 hours, making 90 tons per day. The ore is delivered upon a platform on the top of the mesa, and goes thence down through trap doors over heavy iron screens into self-feeders, and thence under the stamps and out again in pulp into the settling tanks from whence it is taken for amalgamation. From the lower floor, where the amalgam comes out for straining and retorting, to the platform where the ore is delivered is 70 feet. It will be seen by this that gravity handles the ore from the time the wagons deposit it until the tailings are left to settle in the great reservoirs below the mill. The mill is driven by an engine of 140 horse power, fed with steam generated in four large boilers. There are 3 retorts and two melting furnaces. The quicksilver and amalgam is all handled automatically by pipes and pumps until it goes into the strainers, and the amalgam from thence into the retorts, when the quicksilver [mercury] is pumped back to the pan floor to be used over.

An inventory of Silver and Gold refined at the Grand Central Mill near Contention. Original Grand Central document from the collections of John D. Rose.

"The water supply is taken from the San Pedro and is brought in a…ditch that empties into a large well and is pumped by steam pumps up to the battery floor, 60 feet perpendicular into a tank holding 20,000 gallons or more.

"They have accumulated 800 tons of ore at the mill, so that in case of any stoppage in the daily deliver they will have a week's run ahead. Everything in and about the mill and premises is in the most perfect order, and reflects great credit upon Mr. Crane, the Superintendent, and Mr. Lawrence, Assayer. This month's run will probably exceed any yet made by the mill. The bullion averages 920 fine. Taken altogether, the mill is among the biggest of the big bonanzas of Tombstone." [187]

In sharp contrast to the openness of the Grand Central Mill, the Contention company, both mine and mill, had an adversarial role with the Epitaph. As the article above noted, the Grand Central Mill was very welcoming to the Epitaph reporter, in spite of the fact that he showed up with the United States Deputy tax collector for Arizona. But when it came to news from the Contention mine and mill, the Epitaph received a less than enthusiastic reception. "Contention. Where everything possible is withheld from reporters, it cannot be expected that much can be said even though it was about the biggest mine in the world. The Epitaph had ever done its best to keep the legitimate interests of every working mine before the public…In this matter is has not been met half-way by some of the mine managers who have large interest outside their paying mines. This has notably been the case with the Contention. Upon application at the office, or of the foreman, the universal answer is, 'we are not allowed to give any information.' This is not the fault of subordinates: they simply obey orders. From this time forward the Epitaph will not mention a mine…where the company is so discourteous as to refuse such information as will not injure them and might interest the thousands of readers throughout the United States who see these reports. The public will be left to draw its own conclusions about those properties that have heretofore been familiar through these columns, if the spirit of exclusion of legitimate news is withheld in the future." [188]

MYER IS BUYING UP CONTENTION

The most valuable real estate on either side of Contention City was the property nearest the N.M. & A. railroad depot, and the western side had been suggested as a new location for the town so that the Contention Mill could use the original town site as an ore dump. "Mr. H.B. Maxson, with a party of assistant engineers are now ingaged [sic] in surveying a new site for the town of Contention, across the river from the present location. This is made necessary for the reason that the mill of the Contention Mining company requires all the land on the east bank for tailing reservoirs and the erection of a new mill. The new site is preferable to the old, as it has a large scope of rich bottom land upon which to build and have room and soil to grow shade and ornamental trees, with fruits and flowers. Mr. Meyers has already a magnificent hotel nearly ready for occupancy. The building is 75 X 100 feet in dimensions and two stories high. It will be opened in about one month. The Contention Company, it is said, will assist largely in building

111

bridges across the river to facilitate the removal of the town to the new site. Mr. Maxson will be through with the work in about one week. In addition to this he has surveyed some Government land for the Mormons below Contention." [189]

The Epitaph was ahead of itself. It reported word of the hotel on June 11th, 1881, but it was only four days earlier that Myer had purchased the ground on which the hotel would be built. The Myers' House would face delays during construction, and not open until the following Christmas.

L.W. [Louis W.] and Charles Myer, also referred to as Myers, had purchased property from James G. Howard and his partner, famed western mining and real-estate magnate George Hearst. (The son of George Hearst was William Randolph Hearst, best remembered for offering the worst in newspaper publishing, as well as building "Hearst Castle" in California.) The date of the purchase was June 7th, 1881. For $300.00 Myer bought from Hearst "Block or parcel of land being part of the grant called San Juan de dos Boquillos Nogales…designated on the map and survey, made by J.B. [H.B] Maxson, surveyor, on the _day of June 1881 of the village plat of Contention, as Block. No (4) four being three hundred feet square…" [190] Myer had big plans for this property, and soon commenced a two story adobe Hotel on the site. [191]

A tracing of the Maxson map was made in 1935. The Maxson tracing does not identify any block numbers, including block number four, which Myer had purchased. According to the tracing his map makes note of the location of the railroad depot, a bend in the river, and an island. The island itself was a source of local gambling, with horsemen betting that they could jump from the east bank of the San Pedro to the island and from there to the west bank, without getting the hoofs of their horses wet. Maxson would later join the U.S. Survey, and often vacation with his family at the Hollenbeck Hotel in Los Angeles, owned by Albert Bilicke, who had owned the Cosmopolitan in Tombstone which housed the Earps during their final, tense times there.

Myer was planning for the future, as he did not want anyone building between his block and the San Pedro. The deed further states that he reserved a "parcel of land in front of said Block across the street Extending to the river as the same is designated upon said survey and map…"

LAND WITH A RIVERSIDE VIEW

More than just a view of the San Pedro, Myer wanted as much control of both sides of the river as possible, and he was willing to take a substantial risk to have it. Given the economies of such boomtowns are by nature fickle, Myer showed real faith in the long-term prospects for Contention, even accepting unfavorable conditions stipulated by Hearst and Howard that were not to his advantage. In addition to his purchase of block four priced at $300.00, on the same date he also invested an additional $500 for a controlling share of the western bank of the San Pedro, the second Contention City.   The property was described as "part of the grant Called and Known as San Juan de los Boquillas Nogales, and commencing at a point on the west bank of the

San Pedro River where the north boundary lines of first street…as surveyed by H.B. Maxson in June 1881…" The purchase contained just over fifty acres of land, and stipulated that "the right of way for a water ditch over said premises, also for a public road over the same along its front, and along the west bank of Said San Pedro River."

The water ditch and public roadway offered no disadvantage to Myer, but the following did. "…this deed is made also upon the condition that the said grantees… [Louis and Charles Myer] agree that they will not lay out or sell any townlots thereon for the next two years from this date." [192] This means that Myer had to hold the property without being able to gain any sales revenue until June 7th, 1883, a lifetime in the real estate market of a boomtown such as Contention. He would also pay the taxes on his investment while it idled.

Hearst and Howard had their own reasons for delaying Myer in selling lots at the western Contention site - they were planning on doing the same in the summer of 1882, giving them a year head start over Myer, as well as the luxury of having picked the area they preferred most, and selling Myer the alternative.

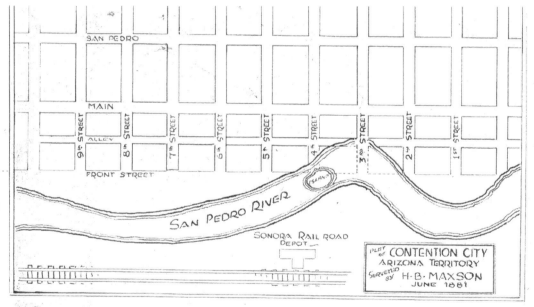

Map of the second Contention City, on the west side of the San Pedro River. The "Sonora Railroad Depot" is the N.M. & A., which was located on the east side of the river. Due to widening of the river, the blocks and island noted have been washed away. Courtesy AHS.

113

CONTENTION CITY MUST GO!

As the N.M. & A. prepared to build to the original Contention on the eastern bank, the rise of a second Contention City in the summer of 1881 was anticipated on the western bank opposite. It wasn't the first time that such settlements spanned both side of the river, but the Contention Mill wanted to evict the existing town of Contention on the east bank altogether. Josiah White, owner of the Contention mine at Tombstone and the mill at Contention, wanted to turn the town site into an ore dump for his mill. But the value of real estate was on the rise. "The reduction mills here, the Contention and Head Center, it is patent to any one are cramped for room for their tailings and cry for space. J.H. White, Superintendent of the Contention mine and mill, purchased 500 acres from the grant owners, and will probably proceed to eject all who will not willingly move off from the present site [east of the San Pedro] of Contention." [193] (The original deed for the Contention Mill states "five acres.")

This article did not have the effect of prompting Contention citizens to start packing. The moratorium on selling lots on the west side of the river would prevent anyone from moving to the new site; the irony was not lost on White. It was his mill that gave Contention its name, as well as its initial economic reason to exist, and now it was making his operations more challenging than he would have preferred. White would have been wise to purchase more of the east bank area when he had the chance. Now it was too late.

The local press would later report that Howard and Hearst themselves had plans for a town site of their own on the west bank of the Contention City area. "Mr. George Howard, one of the owners of the grant [The San Juan de Las Boquillas y Nogales] which covers all the land from the Barbacomari to and below St. David's Mormon Settlement has had a new survey of the grant, and has laid out a new townsite directly opposite on the west side of the San Pedro river from Contention and to be called New Contention." [194]

White would have to continue to operate his mill at Contention in cramped quarters, without the benefit of using the original Contention City site for his tailings. Losing this battle may have led White to rethink devoting all of his rich Contention Ore to his own mill at Contention. Once the Girard Mill opened at Tombstone in the spring of 1882, he had a fresh option to diversify the milling of his ore. "CONTENTION COMBINATION. This mine continues to yield as usual, keeping the men constantly employed and forwarding a surplus of about ten tons daily, which is being piled up at the mill, [at Contention City] in case of bad roads during the summer rains. Some 30 tons will hereafter be furnished the Girard mill daily, which will increase the bullion output of the mine." [195]

This move would reduce his limited storage space at Contention City for unprocessed ore, and the expense and intermittent difficulty of traversing the ore wagon roads that were often damaged if it rained. It also allowed him to boost bullion output, which only meant even more money flowing out of both mine and mill. The irony of the situation was that White, who already owned the Contention Mill, actually found it profitable to allow the Girard Mill to process a portion of his ore.

While the lords of the land debated the town location, the larger determinate would be the railroad itself. Town leaders did not have as much flexibility in this matter as they supposed. The planned route would bring the N.M. & A. south from Benson along the eastern side of the river to the original Contention, where the train depot would be located. It crossed the San Pedro a few miles to the south of Contention to avoid a substantial bend in the river. The power of the railroads in the late 19th century was such that settlements which wanted to prosper, or just survive, had no choice but to arrange themselves based on where the railroad located. Stamp mill locations had a similar economic draw on settlers and business investors. In the case of Contention, both factors combined to keep the east bank of Contention City the far more viable Contention location during its heyday.

TAX-PAYER'S NAME.	DESCRIPTION OF PROPERTY.	Lot.	Block.	Range.	No. of Acres.	Value of Land and Improvements.
817						
New Mexico & Arizona RR. Co.	Cochise County AT					
	35.40 miles Main Tram					1260452 5
	35.40 " Telegraph line					1416
	429.05 acres Right of way					513080
	Side Trams Benson 5 5/8 miles					11700
	" " Canister .38 "					760
	" " Contention .37 "					740
	" " Mile Post 16.18 "					360
	" " Fairbank 2.13 "					4260
	" " Brookline .39 "					780
	" " Huachuca .39					780
	Building. shop on Right way at all stations					20370
	Rolling Stock &c.					
	Tools, Fuel Furniture Machinery, supplies & Material					
818						

The N.M. & A. is shown with taxable assets for the year 1886, listing line to Contention and Fairbank. From the Cochise County Assessment and Tax Roll book, courtesy of Kevin Pyles, Cochise County Archives.

In 1882 Tucson diarist George Hand would pay Contention a visit, and note that some trouble makers had established themselves on the western bank in spite of the moratorium. They were either outside the boundaries of the land purchased by Myer, they were squatters, or Myer had violated the terms of the agreement. Regardless, Myer busied himself with the continuing construction of his hotel and the raising of funds via real estate speculation. On September 14th, 1881, he sold property to S. Marks. The $100.00 sale was for a Contention City property "upon which stands the adobe dwelling house situated between A.R. Park and G. Platte at Contention City Cochise County Arizona about 50 feet front to 100 deep." [196]

By Christmas of 1881 Myer had completed a local landmark. "The Myers House, at New Contention, will be dedicated by a grand holiday ball on the evening of December 26. The proprietors will spare no pains to make the occasion an enjoyable one, and a good time may be expected. Music will be furnished by Mendel Meyer's Tombstone band." [197]

Grand Holiday Ball !

—AT—

THE MEYERS HOUSE,

New Contention,

Monday Evening, Dec. 26.

THIS WILL BE THE FIRST BALL GIVEN by the proprietors at the new hotel, and no pains will be spared to make it a most enjoyable affair. A cordial invitation is extended to all.

Music by Mendel Meyer's Band of Tombstone.

Parties who may come by private conveyance are assured that their teams will be carefully attended to.

TICKETS (Admitting Gentleman and Ladies, including supper)............ ...$5 00

Referring to the planned eviction of the original Contention City town site, the Epitaph announced a farewell party at Contention. "There will be a farewell dance at McDermott's old place, to-morrow (Friday) night, just previous to the citizens being fired bodily (physically removed) across the river. An invitation is extended to the ladies and gentlemen of Tombstone." [198] (Rather than reporting the actual news in this case, the Epitaph was really promoting the agenda of Contention Mine owner White. When it came to the human impact of such a possibility at Contention, they were glib to say the least. In the end, residents of Contention had no intention of giving up their homes and businesses for the convenience of their nearby mill for which their town was named, and they didn't. It was but one more reason for those living in Contention to feel slighted by the Tombstone press.

NOW THAT HAS TO HURT

An unfortunate accident occurred near Contention that caused one man a broken leg when being kicked by a horse from a stage coach team. "Wm. McFarland, whose leg was broken near Contention recently by a kick of one of the stage horses, is getting along nicely, under the efficient care of his physicians. It was feared at one time that he would have to submit to amputation, it being a serious case of compound fracture. By unremitting attention this has fortunately been avoided." [199] (That the condition of the horse wasn't mentioned implies that the horse suffered no injuries from the incident, excepting of course the possibility of some angry words.

116

A BLESSING AND A CURSING

Although the railroad was on its way to Contention, commercial stage and horseback travel still navigated the same road that Bud Philpot had recently died on. The summer rains of 1881 pushed both the road and its travelers to their limits. "The road from here to Benson is in a terrible state. Many wagons have stuck in the mud, and the stage has twice capsized, seriously shaking up the passengers. I venture to say that more profanity has been indulged in on the Benson road, since the rains set in, than ever before since its construction. The ore teams, which were taken off for a short time, have been running for a week…Business people in Tombstone and Tucson, as well as other places, suffered severely from the non-arrival of the mail, and it was a matter of general rejoicing when, at last, it came through… A person visiting this part of the country at the present time has no idea how parched and arid it looks the greater part of the year. The plains are covered with shrubs of a vivid green, and grass is springing up with wonderful rapidity. It is really quite pleasant to look out upon it all, when we have been accustomed to see naught but dreariness. And we are unspeakably thankful to be rid of that disagreeable dust, which has tormented us so much of the time. [200]

But monsoon rains would not serve to dampen the excitement buzzing around Contention City—economic progress and news of the coming railroad kept the people optimistic. Building the road would take substantial quantities of men and material. The Atchison, Topeka and Santa Fe was ready to construct its first run south of Benson, penetrating into the Tombstone district. "EIGHTY WAGONS AND TEAMS Of this company arrived at Benson yesterday morning, and the work of grading the road up the San Pedro will commence this morning. It is believed the road will be completed in not to exceed forty days. The main line will run up the San Pedro river at all events to some where in the neighborhood of Contention. A branch will be built from the most available point on the San Pedro to Tombstone." [201] Of course everything but the Tombstone branch was constructed, a project that at the time was locally considered a forgone conclusion.

The summer rains of 1881 continued to make travel by stage in and around Contention problematic. "The stage upset a mile below Contention and Judge W. Earll of Tucson was so unfortunate as to have his right arm slightly fractured. It was set at Contention and the Judge came on to Tombstone. The cause of the disaster was the heavy rain that was falling at the time, which filled a deep rut with slush, completely obliterating the depth of the pit, which the driver strove to avoid, but the ground being soft the wheels slipped into it, upsetting the coach…No blame is attached to the driver."

These rains also caused injury to the bottom line of the major milling operations at Contention and Millville. The dirt roads bringing ore from mines at Tombstone to the mills on the river were now in substantial disrepair, and Gird's dam at Millville and water diversion ditches at Contention were not immune to flood damage either. "Much to the regret of every one the severity of the storms during the greater portion of the last half of July so obstructed the delivery of ore to the mills, besides carrying away the dams and injuring the ditches along the San Pedro that much valuable time was lost by the mills, which necessarily shortened the bullion output by about $75,000 what it was for June…had it not been for these unavoidable incidents the yield would have overrun that of June by nearly an equal amount." [202]

CHAPTER 9

KNIGHTS OF THE ROAD

"Be sure and get the old bald-headed son of a b----" -Epitaph

It was hard for any community to compete with Charleston for its reputed "diversified viciousness," but Contention was far from an insulated community in which trouble never visited its streets, or its outskirts. A rising border issue with American rustlers had moved from Mexico into the territory and was now infesting remote areas along the San Pedro, to Charleston and north toward Contention, and in some cases almost to Benson. Those living in Contention had to pay heed to news of the outlawry that could be displayed in and around it, often without warning.

"THE MURDERING COW-BOYS. More Depredations by the 'Rustlers'-An Attempt to Steal Cattle Frustrated-Three Mexicans Attacked and Robbed. News was brought to town [Tombstone] yesterday of further depredations by a party of five men, who are supposed to belong to the gang of outlaws infesting this county, calling themselves 'Rustlers.' They are principally from Western Texas and Lincoln county, New Mexico, from whence they have been driven by an outraged community, and now seem to have found the place they long have sought, where they can commit their depredations without fear of arrest. For a long time this gang have confined themselves and their operations to the east of Tombstone and along the line of Sonora, but seeing that no steps were taken for their arrest they have become emboldened to take up their haunts and perpetrate their depredations nearer the center of business and population. About half past three on Friday morning the son of Mr. Henning, who runs a milk ranch about three miles above Charleston, on the San Pedro, suspecting something wrong among the cows…aroused the two Mexican herders and a party of campers…and started down when they found a couple of cowboys gathering up the herd. Henning and his party frightened them off and saved the stock. About 10:30 that same day a party of four gentlemen who were coming to Tombstone, saw a couple of suspicious characters, who left the road when they saw the carriage and rode about forty rods towards the river, heading the up stream until they were a safe distance past the carriage, when they rode back to the travelled road again. Both were armed with rifles in leather cases and were well mounted. One large man on a powerful bay horse, and the other medium-sized man on a dark sorrel horse with a white face. Shortly after passing these men the party in the carriage met three Mexicans, who had a quantity of packages tied upon their saddles going up the San Pedro also. This party proved to be three of General Pesqueira's men from the Cananae, who had been to Tombstone and were taking out some supplies with them, as also $1000 in gold and Mexican silver for the General. When this latter party got above Hereford, and about half way to Ochoaville, they were set upon by a party of five cow-boys, who fired, mortally wounding one of the Mexicans and killing one of the horses. They took a rifle and one package of goods and it is supposed killed the one who had the money, as he had not up to last evening, been seen or heard from since the encounter. It is said that the Mexican who escaped, recognized one of the bandits having seen him in Tombstone the day before.

"Grown bold with the deeds of crime they have committed between here and Deming, and their merciless murders at Fronteras, [Mexico] these outlaws, having no fears of civil authorities, have taken up the San Pedro valley as their head-quarters, knowing that there is a large travel between Benson, Contention, Tombstone, Charleston and Bisbee, beside the Mexican travel from Sonora to these points. It will be seen from the foregoing that they have made a good beginning and unless immediate steps are taken by the citizens to rid the country of these outlaws there will be no more protection to life and property between Benson and the Sonora line than there has been in the San Simon and eastward for the last year. When the civil authorities are insufficient or unwilling to protect a community the people are justified in taking the law into their own hands and ridding themselves of the dangerous characters who make murder and robbery their business. It remains to be seen how much longer such damnable acts as the Fronteras massacre and the San Pedro murders shall go unpunished." [203]

Leopold Graff was a freighter who ran his team from Benson through Contention and onto Tombstone. Though news of the rustlers had just appeared in the local press, he felt safe enough turning his team lose to feed on the grasses that had been well watered that summer, at the east end of Tombstone. That night his stock was taken by two of the marauding cowboys; five mules and one horse were lost. [204]

HIGH SOCIETY AT CONTENTION

Contention City would continue to enjoy its social events, regardless of outlawry in the area, or in which direction the railroad was building. "A select party will be given at the new hotel at Contention City this evening, which will be attended by the best society of Tombstone. A happy time is anticipated." [205] The "select" party was considered a success, and the Epitaph gave it follow up coverage. The guest list may have been referred to as "select" partly due to the fact that one of the owners of the Epitaph also appeared on the list, John Clum. "The Party at Contention. An exceedingly pleasant entertainment was given evening before last at the new hotel, Contention City, on the occasion of the opening.

"A number of invited guests assembled at the residence of Mr. Chas. Glover, in Tombstone, and were conveyed from here in carriages. On arriving at the hotel the party was received by Messrs. Meyers & Son, the proprietors, who spared no effort to make it as comfortable for the guests as possible. The music, under the supervision of Mr. O'Connor, was excellent, and dancing was indulged in until 11 o'clock, at which hour the party repaired to the dining room, where an elegant supper was served; after which dancing was again indulged in for a short time. At 1 o'clock the party started for home, where they all arrived safely. The drive over the smooth, hard road was lovely, and every one agreed that they never had a better time before in their lives." [206]

"The Grand Central mill shipped nine bars of bullion from Contention City on Sunday, and Contention mill shipped six bars." [207] It was the kind of news that everyone invested in the future of Contention City hoped would never end. And the economic class of the reader had no bearing…whether you were a shopkeeper, a waiter in a Contention restaurant, a mill worker, or a RR executive, this is exactly why you came in the first place.

A REFRESHING STAGE RIDE TO CONTENTION WITHOUT A ROBBERY

A writer for Harper's Magazine took an Autumn stage ride to Tombstone and captured the tenor of the times, with a candid driver telling of his misadventures, inciting concerns for his safety. "A six-horse Concord coach carried us, not too speedily, over the twenty-five miles of dusty road to Tombstone. It was called the 'Grand Central,' after a prosperous mine. A rival line was the 'Sandy Bob,' from its proprietor, who preferred to be thus known…A guard got up with a Winchester rifle, and posted himself by the Wells-Fargo Express box. The driver began to relate robber stories. This stage had been stopped and 'gone through' twice within the past six months. The experience was enlivened on one occasion by a runaway and turnover, and on the other by the shooting and killing of the driver. Of this last feature his successor spoke with a disgust not unnatural. He would have the line drawn at drivers. He respected a person who took to the road and robbed those who could afford it. At least he considered it more honorable than borrowing money of a friend which you knew you could never repay, or gobbling up the earnings of the poor, received on deposit, like a certain large firm lately suspended in Pima County. But as to shooting a driver, even in mistake for somebody else, he had no words to express his sense of the meanness of it.

"He threw stones at his horses, as is done in Mexico, that is, at the leaders, which were beyond the reach of his long lash. A single stone was made to 'carom,' such was his skill, and served for both. Long teams of mules or of Texas steers, sixteen to a team, drawing ore wagons-three usually tackled together-were strung interminably along the road. The Mexican-looking drivers trudged beside them in the keep yellow dust, cracking huge 'black snakes' at the animals…We rode for a certain distance beside the branch railroad in course of construction between Benson and Tombstone…The route began to be up-hill. We changed horses and lunched at Contention City. One naturally expected a certain belligerency of such a place, but none appeared on the surface during our stay. There were plenty of saloons-the 'Dew-drop,' the 'Head-light,' and the like-and at the door of one of them a Spanish senorita smoked her cigarette and showed her white teeth.

"Contention was the seat of stamping mills for crushing ore brought to it from Tombstone, the latter place being without a water-power, though the defect has probably since been remedied. The stamps are rows of heavy beams dropping upon the mineral, on the mortar and pestle plan, with a continuous dull roar, by night as well as by day. The route grew steeper yet. On the few wayside fences were painted such announcements as, 'Go To Bangley and Schlagenstein's. They Are The Bosses, You Bet.' Then over the edge of bare hills appeared the outline of Tombstone itself." [208]

The Harper's writer may have enjoyed a safe ride, but stage robberies were still not uncommon. "$500 Reward. By resolution of the Board of Supervisors of Cochise County, the above reward will be paid for the arrest and conviction of the five men who robbed the stage between Benson and Contention, on Saturday, October 8th, or $100 for the arrest and conviction of any of them." [209]

As 1881 was coming to a close, the Contention Mill had an impressive performance to look back on. "The lack of water nearer the mines than the San Pedro river, compelled the owners of this property, like all others in the district, to locate thereon, and a selection of a site was so made that the haul would be all down grade, with the exception of crossing a few small ravines. The mill, like those we have described heretofore, is located in the face of the steep bluff where the mesa breaks abruptly down to the river bottom. The mill was built with room and power for 25 stamps, but had but 20 stamps for the first six months. At the end of that time 5 stamps were added, since when the output has been from 25 stamps…"

The Contention mill, from the start of its operations, "…and up to and including Dec. 31 [1880], it reduced 15,000 tons of ore, producing bullion to the value of $1,213,975.57, being an average of $80.93 per ton. From January 1, 1881, up to and including October 31, there has been mined and milled 20,016 tons of ore, producing $1,228,168.82, being an average of $61.10 per ton. This gives a total product from 35,016 tons of $2,437,144.39, being a general average for all the ore milled of $69.60 per ton. From the output has been paid the stockholders-who could, up to the time of the consolidation, be counted up the fingers of both hands-the munificent sum of $1,375,000, or over 50 per cent of the gross product of the mine, with a supplementary dividend to come of from $50,000 to $75,000, in the final winding up of the affairs of the Western Mining company." [210] This was all achieved in less than twenty months. Contention City's mill had more than proven it was a smart investment, and all prospects concluded that Contention would grow in the wake of its wealth.

But an unexpected turn of events sounded the death knell for the milling towns along the San Pedro; the days of silver mills at Millville and Contention had just begun to reach their economic prowess, and yet their very reason for existence on the San Pedro was about to vanish. In 1881, tunnels in the Sulphuret Mine hit water at 520 feet—such a large supply that milling could now be done in Tombstone, as soon as mills could be set up there. This also meant that the expense of freighting ore to the San Pedro could now be eliminated. There was an additional disadvantage: as Tombstone miners tunneled beneath the water table, the quality of the ore was reduced. Although the Contention mine would hit a rich strike below the water table, much of the best ore had already been mined above it. Reduction in freighting costs offered companies the chance of remaining profitable even with ore of lesser value. The change in the dynamic of the Tombstone District wasn't lost on the Epitaph.

"With the introduction of an ample water supply, which is now assured beyond a peradventure, the mills will be removed from the San Pedro to the mines, and other new and larger mills will be erected, whereby all ores returning $10 per ton can be mined and milled without loss. There is known to be millions of tons of ore thus far untouched that will yield in excess of that amount; therefore, the doubt as to the future is solved in favor of a long and prosperous one." [211] Good news if true, but the figure of "millions of tons of ore" would later be challenged by reality. As this was being written, the Girard Mill was already on its way to being built, and for the first time, a major mill would crush Tombstone ore at Tombstone.

This change wouldn't affect life in Contention immediately, and locals would find it easy to focus instead on a sign of tangible progress. "Judge Rigg, of Contention, paid us a visit yesterday. He reports that work has commenced on the depot buildings, and that cars will be running into Contention in three or four days." [212]

"The cars will commence running to Contention on or about the first of January. Then the stage ride will no longer be an event to be dreaded." [213] It was an event long awaited by Tombstone residents, but still not what they had hoped for, which was a direct railroad line to their city, and the complete elimination of all stage travel wherever possible. The cars referred to would travel from Benson to Contention to pick up passengers, mostly heading for Benson, then onto Tucson, and all points desired from there. This advent alone would change traveling habits for many, and it would end the viability of commercial stage traffic between Contention and Benson. If this had happened a year earlier, Bud Philpot would not have been driving a stage from Tombstone to Benson via Contention City that drove past Drew's Station, as the railroad would have already made such a route obsolete. Such was the rapidity with which the valley was changing.

JOHN CLUM'S MIDNIGHT WALK TO THE GRAND CENTRAL MILL

Not everyone in Tombstone was pleased with Mayor John Clum's open support of the Earps, and in the election that followed the gunfight and its legal aftermath, those in political power who were pro Earp were branded by Clum's competitors at the Tombstone Daily Nugget as the "Earp Ticket." Without exception they all lost office. But on the evening of December 14th, 1881, Clum came very near to losing something more than his office.

Mayor John Clum had boarded a stage heading from Tombstone, through Contention, and then onto Benson, but the trip would not go as planned. "The six-horse coach, driven by Jimmy Harrington, and the bullion wagon, driven by 'Whistling Dick,' had just left Malcom's water station, which is the last house on the road to Contention, and only about four miles from Tombstone, and were bowling along at a rapid gait, when the order to 'Halt!' was given from the roadside, and almost simultaneously a volley was fired into them. The off leader [the lead horse on the left] of the coach was struck in the neck, and all the horses became unmanageable. Dick was hit in the calf of the leg, receiving a painful flesh would, but kept his seat and his wagon right side up. The horses ran about half a mile, when the wounded horse weakened and fell from loss of blood.

"Mr. Clum, with the assistance of other passengers, cut the leaders loose, and on they went, it being the general impression that all the passengers were aboard. Mr. Clum had been riding on the inside, and he was missed, but it was supposed by his fellow-passengers that he had taken a seat on the outside, consequently his absence was not detected until the arrival of the coach at Contention. Upon learning this, Messrs. Behan and Reppy started for Tombstone, and upon arriving at the place where the attack was made, examined the locality carefully, but no trace of the missing man was found. In the meantime, THE SECOND PARTY, which had left Tombstone about 4 a.m., upon arriving at Malcolm's Station, learned that two teamsters in camp with their wagons at that point, had not only heard the noise of their shooting, but could distinctly see the flash, the attack having been made about the apex of the first rise beyond. Continuing down the road about a half mile beyond the attacking point, by the light of a match, two large pools of blood were found on the right, where the off leader had given out, and after wandering several hundred rods to the right of the road, marking his trail by his ebbing life, had already fallen a prey to the skulking coyote.

"Not being able to discover any trail, the party proceeded on to Contention, where from Mr. Dunham it was learned that after assisting in releasing the wounded leader, it was supposed by the passengers that Mr. Clum had either taken a seat with the driver or on the bullion wagon…his absence was not ascertained until arriving at Contention…teamsters at Malcom's and Mr. Dunham both state that the flashes seemed to come from both sides of the road, and as the wound received by the bullion driver, as well as the death-shot to a faithful leader that had done service ever since the establishment of the line, were made by revolvers, it does not, to say the least, have the semblance of an organized intent to rob the stage, as no rifle cartridge shells could be found on the ground, and all parties claim that there were from fifteen to twenty shots fired in quick succession.

"From Mr. O'Brien, one of the teamsters, it was learned that the would-be murderers had probably taken up the gulch to the northeast, just above Malcom's as about one hundred yards from the road there is evidence of the repeated hitching of horses in the…thick brush, and shortly after the shooting the sound of flying hoofs came from that direction. [214]

Clum's competition at the Nugget would report on the event, and couldn't resist ending their article with a quip at the pedestrian Mayor's expense. "The stage which left Tombstone last night at 8 o'clock for Benson, when about three miles from town, was jumped by robbers, who were concealed in the brush by the roadside. The robbers ordered the driver to halt, but he put [his] whip to the horses, disregarding the order. The bandits then opened fire, a shot striking one of the lead horses and another taking effect in the leg of 'Whistling Dick,' the driver. The driver continued to urge his team forward until when about a mile had been covered the wounded horse dropped. The driver then jumped down and cut loose the fallen animal and then drove on down to Contention.

"Hon. John P. Clum, our worthy Mayor, was a passenger on the ill-fated vehicle, and at the first fire jumped out, since which time, although at this writing, 2 a.m., several hours have elapsed, no tidings have been received of him. The prevailing opinion is that he is still running." [215] Actually Clum recalled trying to save the wounded horse's life, and assisting Whistling Dick with his wound. "Dick's wound was not serious. We rendered first aid by wrapping a couple of handkerchiefs around his leg, covering the wound…I had stepped fifty paces into the darkness to look and listen for sight or sound of horsemen. As I looked at the coach with its sidelights [lanterns on the side of stage coaches for night travel], I realized that my presence in the coach only jeopardized the other passengers. I was much better off with my feet on the ground and no sidelights. I struck off through the mesquite and cactus on foot. After a precarious trek, in and out of ravines, I arrived at the Grand Central quartz mill about one o'clock a.m. The mill superintendent was a friend and I told him my story. He telephoned Tombstone that I was safe…I slept there for two hours, borrowed a horse, and at 3 a.m. was again in route…it was nearly eight o'clock in the morning when I reached Benson." [216]

Rather than the "precarious trek, in and out of ravines," it is more likely that Clum simply walked the ore wagon road to the Grand Central, which was an off-shoot of the Tombstone to Benson stage road. After surveying the remaining routes that were available to Clum that evening, this author believes that this is the most feasible way for him to have reached the mill. A newspaper report echoes this finding: "Just after leaving Mr. Dunham it was stated that Mr. C. had been heard of at the Grand Central mill, whither the party proceeded, and learned that the mayor had taken the ore road to the mill, from whence, after resting, he had gone by saddle to Benson, arriving between 7 and 8 o'clock." [217] It is still debated whether or not John Clum's midnight stroll to the Grand Central was really based on an attack meant for him, and in direct relation to his support of the Earps. But there is no debate that just over two weeks later Earp opponents would attempt to assassinate Virgil Earp in Tombstone, and the following March they would succeed in murdering Morgan Earp.

Grand Central Mill worker J.Jameson is paid $14.00 for his efforts at the Grand Central Mill. Original Grand Central paycheck from the collections of John D. Rose.

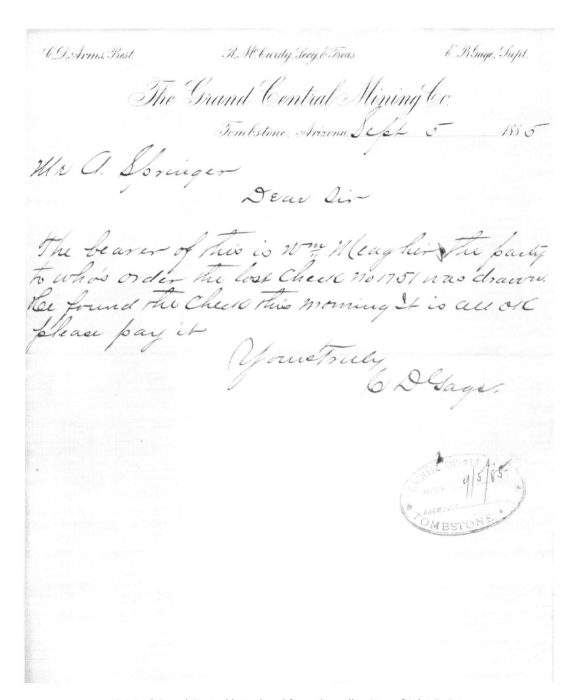

C. D. Arms, Pres't.   R. McCurdy, Sec'y & Treas.   E. B. Gage, Sup't.

The Grand Central Mining Co.

Tombstone, Arizona Sept 5 1885

Mr A. Springer

Dear Sir

The bearer of this is Wm Meagher the party to who's order the lost Check No 1751 was drawn. He found the Check this morning It is all OK please pay it

Yours Truly
C D Gage

Original Grand Central letterhead from the collections of John D. Rose.

126

To the Nugget this was a Clum-manufactured farce worthy of public ridicule, adding that it was an error that "our Mayor abandoned the vehicle to its fate at the first fire of the ambushed miscreants. Not he. He valiantly maintained his position in the bottom of the coach…until a halt was compelled by the falling of the wounding animal at a distance of about one mile from the scene of the ambuscade. Then, in company with the driver and other passengers, he descended to the ground to assist in cutting out the fallen horse. But now, like an inspiration, the whole diabolical plot of the would-be assassins was revealed to the mind of our city's ruler…It was a scheme to assassinate him, or mayhap abduct and hold him for ranson [sic]." [218]

The Epitaph made the case against the Nugget's assertion. "For a journal to make sport of, and publish articles intended to be funny on such an affair as the attempted assassination of the mayor of a city, is truly an outrage upon decency, and an insult to the intelligence of the community…It is well known that no bullion goes out in the wagon on that day; neither does Kinnear's light stage carry mail or express. In fact, it was well known that the stage that night had no treasure or valuables on board. Why, then, the attempt to stop it that night; and that, too, so near to town? The fact of firing fifteen shots into the stage, and the exclamation which two of the passengers heard them make of, 'Be sure and get the old bald-headed son of a b----,' explains it all!" [219]

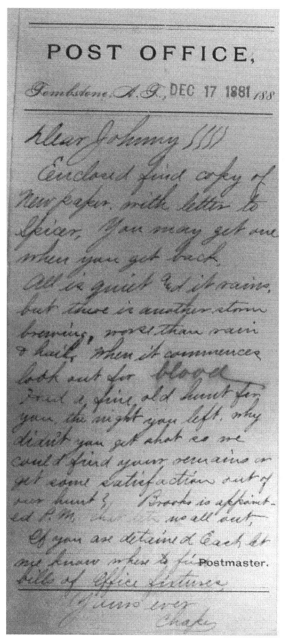

Seward Chapin writes Clum with gallows humor and a warning after his near assassination. Courtesy of U of A Special Collections.

127

Still wishing to weigh further in on the matter, the Nugget sought to blame Clum's own friends, possibly the Earps by implication. "Our view of the case is, that those who arrested the stage coach were friends of the departing mayor, and what is reported as an attack with the bloodthirsty purpose…was only intended as a send-off—a complimentary feu de joie." [220] It is doubtful that Whistling Dick would have had the same opinion.

Also from John Clum's personal scrapbook, a letter of concern from Thomas Hopkins regarding Clum's near brush with death. Courtesy of U of A Special Collections.

At the close of 1881, the turmoil that had been unleashed in Tombstone with repercussions of the gunfight near the O.K. Corral had, for a time, bypassed Contention. News coming in was comparatively of a stable nature. "Contention Chat. Result of the holidays: One man committed to the county jail in default of paying revenue to the county.

"One man found drowned in the San Pedro river; Coroner Mathews [was] telegraphed for, and in his absence Justice Rigg held a coroner's inquisition. Verdict of the coroner's jury-That the said Martin Flannigan, identified as foreman [for] Ward & Courtney, contractors on the A.T. & S.F. [N.M. & A.] Railroad, came to his death from accidental drowning. The funeral took place yesterday." [221] It was also pointed out that across the Tombstone district, remarkable economic strides had been made, and it was noted that "the next week or two will place Tombstone within easy distance of RAILROAD COMMUNICATION at Contention City. Who, even one year ago, [would] venture the prediction that we would so soon be given a railroad…" The Grand Central mine was now shipping to its Contention Mill "between 2,100 and 2,200 tons monthly." Of the Contention Mill, the structure that was the cradle of the industrialization and creation of Contention City, it was noted that "In the twenty months included between March 8 1880, and November 8, 1881…the latter produced bullion aggregating $2,431,511, and out of which it disbursed dividends amounting to $1,475,000."

Even Contention City's junior mill, the Head Center, which paced far behind its neighbors to the south, had made progress. "Despite the fact that this property has to date, dispensed no dividends, it must not be classed among the least productive concerns of the district. It has, however, under its present local management lately progressed very satisfactorily, and in view of the extensive developments, now being carried forward in the mine, it is not too much to say that a more prosperous future is opening for it.

"In February, 1881, its then superintendent, Mr. Thomas E. Farrish, purchased the Sunset ten stamp mill. This soon after was started on an experimental run in Head Center ore. The results accruing from the small parcel then put through the battery, [stamps of the mill] proving satisfactory, permanent milling operation were inaugurated on the 15th of April, 1881. From this date to December 31, 1881, embracing a period of eight months and thirteen days, bullion to the value of $206,853.88 has been produced." [222]

1882 OPENS WITH OPTIMISM

If those living in and nearby Contention had hopes that the troubles of 1881 would remain behind them, they would see changes that would make that impossible. Contention would lose a key founder and keeper of the peace; violence would follow the construction of the railroad, tempering the good news of its arrival, but linking Contention by rail to the rest of the nation; and the Earp troubles would spill out of Tombstone's city limits and to the doors of Contention as well. The small railroad settlement of Benson, the largest community to its north, shared in some of the trouble.

But '82 would begin more optimistically. "The Meyers House, a large, airy and pleasant new building at Contention, is said by travelers to be a comfortable and homelike hotel. It is kept by Meyers and son, who take pride in providing the best of fare, with plenty of pure milk and fresh butter, eggs and vegetables in the truly hospitable style of an Eastern farming community. Their rooms and accommodations are equal, if not superior, to the best in the Territory." [223]

THE IRON HORSE IS ON ITS WAY

The new year saw Tombstone brimming with confidence at its many recent achievements. Dick Gird was constructing a pipeline bringing spring water from the Huachuca Mountains to Tombstone, twenty six miles distant. "Within the next few months the cold streams of the Huachucas will be running through our streets." [224] If water could be piped across the San Pedro River Valley to Tombstone, how could a railroad be far behind? Much to the chagrin of the Tombstone press, the Arizona Daily Star noted that the railroad depot under construction at Contention City is "175 feet long. This would indicate that the road was not going to Tombstone.-Daily Star." [225]

"The Star is decidedly off its 'cabeza' when it thinks the Atchison, Topeka & Santa Fe road is not coming to Tombstone. The main line from Deming is located directly through the northern limits of the city, and Mr. Earl, the locating engineer, assured us upon the completion of the survey, that it would be built over this route, which will be as short as the Southern Pacific from Deming to Benson, and will make nearly an air line through to Calabasas, where it turns south into Sonora. The company cannot afford to leave out of its connections the most important mining district in the territory and a town that is destined in the near future to have the largest population of any place in Arizona. If it don't come this year it will next, and we can await patiently the building. As a matter of fact, the sooner it comes the better it will suit our people and the larger will be the company's profits. These are matters that the company will not be likely to overlook in their reaching out for the mastery of the trade of the Pacific coast. [226]

"In a few weeks at most grading is to be commenced to this [Tombstone] city. There is every reason for encouragement in the outlook of the new year, and we predict for Tombstone and its adjacent camps a progressive era of prosperity." But in the same issue the paper conceded "that grading has been stopped on the branch leading from Contention up to Tombstone." [227] Local optimism aside, Tombstone would not see its railroad coming in the near future, or in the same century for that matter.

ROBBING WELLS FARGO'S TOP DETECTIVE NEAR CONTENTION

While Tombstone awaited a railroad that was not forthcoming, travelers still had to contend with the "Knights of the Road," the stage robbers. The Sandy Bob Stage line was making a routine run from Benson to Contention, and then onto Tombstone, but after leaving Contention, the journey became anything but uneventful. "Robbers Reap a Light Harvest-Wells, Fargo & Co's Chief Detective Stood Up with the Rest. From Mr. Sheldon, driver of Sandy Bob's line, we learn that his coach, on the way up from Benson, was stopped just this side of the arroya, about half way between this city [Tombstone] and Contention at 1 o'clock this morning. There

130

were nine passengers, all males, eight of whom were inside and one on the boot with the driver. The driver was peremptorily ordered to halt by two men, and compelled to get down and hold his leaders while they went through the passengers. The outside passenger, on coming down, was relieved of a fine six-shooter, which one of the robbers remarked he needed in his business. Among the inside passengers was Mr. Hume, chief detective of Wells, Fargo & Co., who had on his person two fine revolvers. Instead of making use of them on the robbers, he stepped out with the rest and gracefully surrendered them on demand. It is not probable that the robbers secured more than enough booty to repay them for their trouble-the risk not being worth taking into consideration.

"The robbers did not take time to make a thorough search. There were from $1,200 to $1,500 among the passengers, but only about $75 and three revolvers were secured.

"Various expedients were resorted to by the passengers to secure their valuables; one hid his pocketbook under the cushions, but it was secured by one of the robbers, who neglected to take a valuable watch lying beside it." [228] (It had to be a low point in the career of veteran Wells Fargo detective J.B. Hume, who had fallen asleep during what had been up to that point, a trip without incident. It may have been an experience that informed his opinion of those living at and around Tombstone, as he once stated the following of Tombstone: "Six thousand population. Five thousand are bad. One thousand of these are known outlaws." [229]

Of the robbery that caught a sleeping Hume by surprise, he and three other passengers paid a visit to the office of the Tombstone Epitaph and offered this account. Hume appeared to feel the need to explain why he made no resistance to the robbers, as this was, to say the least, an embarrassing incident for a man of his considerable reputation. "Mr. Hume and most of the passengers were asleep when the driver pulled up [stopped the stage]. Mr. Hume was on the back seat, and before he was sufficiently awakened to take in the situation the driver was holding the leaders and the outside passenger was standing near the wheelers. These two appeared in the dim moonlight to belong to the robber party, there thus appearing to be four of them instead of two. One of the robbers held a shot gun at the window on the inside passengers and forbade any one of them to stir on pain of instant death. Mr. Hume says that to attempt to use his revolvers under the circumstances and being also under the impression that there were four robbers— would inevitably involve a sacrifice of the lives of several of the passengers, and as there was none of his employers' treasure on board, he considered he would be acting the part of wisdom to refrain from violent measures.

"The road agents first demanded that Wells-Fargo's box should be handed out, and were evidently disappointed when the driver responded there was no treasure on board.

"Both the…robbers were disguised with black cloth masks. One of them, a tall man, had a tight-fitting suit, like that used by the 'leg-maniacs' in the Christian pantomimes. The other, a shorter man, wore a gunny-sack over his other clothes, with holes cut for his head and arms. Both of them had powerful voices, and made no apparent attempt to conceal them.

"The inside passengers were ordered to hold up their hands, and come out, which order they obeyed with as much alacrity as their sleepy condition permitted, particularly as the order was backed by a determined looking man with a shot-gun.

"After they had filed out one by one they were ranged in line on the roadway, still holding their hands up, and rapidly gone through with by one of the thieves, while the other kept them constantly under cover with his weapon. In most instances only one pocket was searched, which accounts for the small pecuniary loss suffered. Watches and valuables other than money were not disturbed, the thieves evidently fearing future identification by means of such property.

"After this hasty search the passengers were allowed to re-enter the coach, and the driver to resume his journey. No shot was fired during the transaction.

"The robbers, though firm in their demands, were polite in their language and were evidently no novices at the business. They could not, however, have been so well posted regarding the prospects of the 'haul' as their confreres have heretofore shown themselves to be, or they would have reaped a bigger bonanza from their nocturnal raid. Marshall Williams, Wells, Fargo & Co.'s agent here, authorizes us to say that, notwithstanding the firm suffered no loss by the robbery, they will pay a reward of $300 for the capture of the robbers."

The robbers were polite to a degree, but voiced their frustration as to the low return of their criminal escapade. Driver Jack Sheldon added that "The robbers proceeded in a systematic manner to relieve the passengers of what surplus valuables they had about them, but after examining the contents of the pockets of several of them exclaimed, 'What kind of layout is this? It's the poorest crowd I ever struck.'" [230]

Wyatt and Morgan Earp, Fred Dodge and Charlie Smith would search for these robbers on the western slope of the Huachucas, ending up in Charleston, where they believed they had found those responsible, but were without enough proof to make an arrest.

Such news on the route from Contention to Tombstone didn't impede the use of the road for stages, as they really had no choice but to continue using the roadway, hoping to miss such misfortune, accepted as part of life in the area.

The Tombstone Nugget weighed in on the matter, making light of yet another example of lawlessness. It was a peculiar trait for the paper, which would work tirelessly to hang the Earps for murder following the gunfight near the O.K. Corral, and yet seem to offer tacit approval of other dangerous encounters, such as armed stage coach robberies. What is of interest in the Nugget account is that it does name, albeit jokingly, a known local as a possible suspect, while ridiculing its victim, J.B. Hume. Alex Arnold would later surface claiming to have taken shots at

Wyatt Earp during the Iron Spring fight, adding that "Earp was wearing a white shirt which made a splendid target." [231]

"Alex. Arnold, you are wanted! It is said you helped to rob the Benson and Tombstone stage on the 8th of January. That would not have made so much difference, but you were impertinent enough to deprive the valiant and garrulous [J.B.] Hume, high muck-a-much detective for Wells, Fargo & Co., of his two Smith & Wesson pistols. This was very naughty on your part, and he has been abusing the people of this section ever since. He says you are about 5 feet 8 or 10 inches high, weigh about 150, and have a small mustache, small eyes, deep set, and are about 33 years of age. You will observe, Aleck, that he was cool enough to note this, but all the same, you have those two pistols, and as he is getting old and peevish you had better send them back, so the boys will quit joshing him." [232]

WELLS, FARGO & CO'S EXPRESS.

REPORT OF ROBBERY.

_____

_____

☞ Agents will leave these two lines blank. ☜

_____ Office, _____ 18____.

Assistant Sup't,
SAN FRANCISCO:

Dear Sir :

The Stage bound from _____

_to _____ was robbed, about _____ o'clock ___ M., _____ instant,_

_____ miles from _____ in _____ County, by _____ men._

They were disguised as follows : _____

_____

and armed with _____

DESCRIPTION OF THE ROBBERS: _____

_____

_____

_____

Amount of Money taken, $ _____ . _Value of Packages taken, $_ _____ .

Name of Driver of the Stage, _____

The Mail was _____ _robbed, and letters were_ _____

The following are names, residences and losses of Passengers on board :

Mr. _____ of _____ Robbed of _____

" _____ " _____ " " _____

" _____ " _____ " " _____

" _____ " _____ " " _____

" _____ " _____ " " _____

" _____ " _____ " " _____

LIST OF WAY-BILLS IN TREASURE BOX TAKEN.

NO.	DATE.	FROM	TO	NO.	DATE.	FROM.	TO

STEPS TAKEN FOR CAPTURING THE ROBBERS: _____

Original Wells Fargo "Report of Robbery" form from the collections of John D. Rose. Such paperwork was routine when Wells Fargo suffered losses from theft.

CHAPTER 10

THE EARPS AT CONTENTION

"We come here for law, but we will fight—if we have to!" –William Herring

Death would soon visit Contention, though not through violent means, but rather, a bout of pneumonia. It was the end of a long life of the west, a man whose last years had been spent as Justice of the Peace during Contention's earliest days. In sharp contrast to his counterpart at Charleston, Jim Burnett, Justice Edwin Rigg had given Contention an early tradition of even-handed justice, whereas Burnett was simply a crook with a title. It can be argued that the difference between these two men would equal at least in part, the difference between the two communities over which they presided, and the safety of its citizenry. Rigg's death would also open the opportunity for a political change for the office he had held at Contention. Rigg was a republican, but the Cochise County Board of Supervisors was led by Democrat Chairman Milt Joyce. This meant that Joyce, and not the voters, would preside over the meeting which would choose his successor. Of course a democrat would be chosen, and it was of little surprise to Wyatt Earp and his supporters when this appointee used his new-found authority to aid Ike Clanton in hauling the Earps into court in Contention, over charges from which they had already been released in Tombstone. In the wake of Rigg's death, one of the earliest decisions of his replacement, J.B. Smith, would be to bring the Earp drama directly into the Contention City courtroom, the same courtroom where Judge Rigg had presided, gaining the admiration of many. "Death of Col. Rigg. The unwelcome news came in town yesterday morning of the death of Col. Edwin A. [Augustus] Rigg, at Contention City, on Friday night about 10 o'clock.

"Edwin A. Rigg was a native of Burk county, Penn., and was about 60 years of age. He was a pioneer to California, engaging at that time in mercantile pursuits. In 1856 he was captain of the law and order company against the vigilance committee in San Francisco. At the breaking out of the war of the rebellion, Rigg joined the California volunteers as major and was afterward promoted to the rank of colonel, serving in that state and afterward coming to this territory. He also served in the Mexican war. Some years later, going to New York, the Colonel was reinstated in the army. Shortly after coming to Arizona, Col. Rigg was married to a Miss Cooper, of El Paso, Texas. His wife and daughter are now residing in New York. Of late his residence has been in Contention, where he has been a justice of the peace for a long time. Col. Rigg was a very pleasant, social gentleman, and the news of his death will be sadly received by his many friends." [233]

Contention. Cochise County,
37" Precinct.
May 13" 1881.

To Clerk of the Board of Supervisors
Cochise County.
Tombstone.

Dear Sir.
Herein please find the following accounts
due me as Justice of the Peace 37 Precinct.
Territory of Arizona vs. Leonard Carney. Complaint Criminal
"   "   "   " George White.
"   "   "   " Henry Miller
"   "   " vs. John Doe & Richard Roe.
Amounting to $15,70. which please present to the board
of Supervisors for their disposal. When warrant
issue please forward to
Yours truly.
E. A. Rigg, J. P.
Contention, A. T.

Less than a year before his death, Contention City Judge Edwin Augustus Rigg, bills Cochise County for unpaid expenses. Courtesy AHS.

Contention City was facing the loss of not one, but two well thought of citizens, and their combined funerals on the same day brought out almost the entire population. "'William Riley Petty, born in Missouri, aged 42 years,' was the simple inscription on the coffin plate of our lamented friend. He died on January 27, of pneumonia, after a short illness of a week. He received every care that kind friends could bestow, up to the time of his death. Mr. Petty owned a ranch a few miles from this place, Contention City, A.T. After he was first stricken down he was removed from his home to town, and cared for by kind and devoted friends, Mr. and Mrs. U.F. Bradley, and his equally kind and attached friend and physician, Dr. J.G. Barney, by whom he was most closely attended. But that most dreaded of all diseases incident to this climate had too great a hold on his really delicate frame, and death claimed him as its own. The funeral, which took place on the 28th instant, was a double one, as another old citizen, Col. E.A. Rigg, died on the same day and of the same disease. The funeral drew out almost the entire population of town, and many people from Tombstone. The Rev. Mr. Tuttle preached the funeral sermon at the house and read the burial service at the grave, and as he repeated the mournful and sadly familiar refrain of 'Dust to dust, ashes to ashes,' one could but hope that in our friend Petty's case his spirit was, in the words of the hymn sung at his grave—nearer his God. For Mr. Petty, although we believe not a member of any church, was yet a firm believer in those grand mysteries of life and death, a supreme God and the immortality of the soul. Mr. Petty had a large circle of warmly attached friends. He was a man of great social qualities; ever gay and light–hearted, he was the life of all companies he mingled with. While no one enjoyed more keenly than Mr. Petty a ball or social gathering, he was ever ready and prompt in his business engagements, and also as ready and prompt to relieve with sympathy and purse any of the less fortunate of his fellow men. Mr. Petty was a bachelor, but we believe has relatives living near Leavenworth, Kansas, and a brother living in Placerville, Cal. To those relatives the friends of Mr. Petty here desire to offer their heartfelt sympathy and regrets, and wish them to know that in this far-off land their dear one had many friends gained by his worth, who dropped many a tear over his grave. Farewell, kind heart, and rest in peace. A.W.C." [234]

A DIARIST PAYS CONTENTION A VISIT

Tucson diarist George Hand would soon visit Rigg's grave, remembering him well. He may have also remembered this entry that he wrote about Rigg twenty years earlier: Lieut. Col. E.A. Rigg, formerly Major, is not as well liked as some others. His short name is 'Blue Wing.' He has done well so far but loves whiskey in too large quantities. That, however, is a fault of very many smart men. He has always been in command of responsible posts while Major. I have never heard of anything bad brought against him except his love of rum. He has very many friends in the First Regiment and none hesitate to say that he is superior to any of the Field Officers of the 5th. I have no fault with him and am pleased with his promotion. Carleton, West and Rigg have all seen service and stood the fire of the enemy." [235]

George Hand, from the collections of John D. Rose.

ANOTHER DEATH AT CONTENTION, ILLNESS, AND A BROKEN HEART

Less than a week later, Contention would again be hit with a loss of one of its own, the wife of Contention Hotel owner L.W. Meyers, a much loved member of the community. "Died at Contention City, A.T., Jan. 29, 1882, Mrs. L.W. Myers.

"Mrs. Myers was born in Wales, Great Britain, and came to the United States at an early age. She has living in the East a father, mother and sisters, to whose tender care all that was mortal of the lady was sent for interment. Her pure spirit, we well know, has its reward in heaven for her good and self-denying life here."

A CRIME CONSIDERED CRUEL BY EVEN CHARLESTON STANDARDS

"Mrs. Myers came to Arizona to join her husband and son, from whom she had been separated a year, in 1881. Her desire to see these dear ones overcame her natural reluctance in leaving a comfortable and refined home in the East, where she was surrounded by relatives and friends, to brave the discomforts of Arizona life. Mrs. Myer was a woman of superior culture, possessing great sympathy for others. Her kindness even extended to the brute creation. We remember one instance: She owned a little colt; its mother having died, Mrs. Myers raised the colt by hand, feeding it herself on milk; when half grown it was a great pet. About two weeks before Mrs. Myers' death some inhuman wretch stabbed the unoffending animal and killed it;

138

this affected Mrs. Myers' sensitive nature very keenly, and she wept for days afterwards, and the mention of the subject would bring tears to her eyes."

"We can well imagine the poignant and deep-felt grief nigh hopeless that filled the breasts of husband and son in losing such a warm hearted wife and mother.

"Mrs. Myers was taken ill about Jan. 23. Her disease was one of long standing, and of such a nature that little could be done to alleviate her sufferings, although closely watched by her physician, Dr. J.G. Barney, and also by many kind friends, ladies of this town. She died in comparative freedom from pain, we believe and hope, in expectation of a crown hereafter. She was a member of the Episcopal church…In concluding this short obituary of one so dearly loved by her relatives and so universally liked and respected by her many friends, East, at this place and at Tombstone, we are requested to say in behalf of her husband and son that they desire to give to the ladies of Contention their most sincere and grateful thanks for their kindness to her while yet living and rendering the last sad offices for their wife and mother. A.W.C." [236]

Along with the sadness of the death of Mrs. Myers, Contention continued to see progress as a transportation hub, offering connections between the stage coach of old, and the railroad of the new. Sandy Bob Crouch was a substantial player in the stage business, and adjusted his schedule for the benefit of the Tombstone traveler, and the railroad. "The following is the time on which the stages of Sandy Bob's popular line, carrying the U.S. mails, will hereafter run between this city and Contention: Leave for the East…5:30 a.m. Leave for the West…12:30 p.m. Arrive from the East at…7:30 p.m. Arrive from the West at…11:30 a.m." [237]

In part, the story of Mrs. Myers' devotion to the care of the colt which had lost its mother, only to see it stabbed to death in a hateful act of violence, showed the best and worst that Contention City had to offer. And in between those two extremes, Contention played host to advanced milling engineers, laborers and shopkeepers, honest ranchers and ruthless cattle thieves. Its new designation as a railroad terminus brought workers to build and later operate the train, and travelers seeking Tombstone or Guaymas in Mexico as their destinations. This would give Contention City a continuing series of remarkable contrasts, unusual for a settlement of less than 500 souls contained in its boundary at its peak. The intermittent clash of these varied groups, as well as in other cases, their assimilation as a community, gave Contention its fascinating persona, and a short lived, but powerful prosperity.

A Tombstone freighter and corral owner had reason to look forward to the upcoming year of 1882. "The contract for hauling Grand Central and Contention ore for the coming year has been awarded to J.E. Durkee." [238]

THE EARP STORY HEATS UP AGAIN, SOON HEADS TO CONTENTION

On January 30th, 1882, Ike and Phin Clanton were summoned to the Tombstone district court of Judge Stillwell, having been "accused of assault to commit murder, the specific offense being the waylaying and shooting of Virgil Earp some weeks ago. This warrant of arrest had been placed in the hands of J. H. Jackson, who was not deputized either as Deputy Marshal or Deputy Sheriff, and consequently it was held by the defense that he had no right to take or hold any one in custody. Judge Alexander Campbell moved for the dismissal of the accused…" [239]

Wyatt Earp's attorney, William Herring, argued against the Clantons in the case, and when the subject of bail arose, he pressed the judge for a large amount. As the day's arguments came to a close, the judge stated, "'They will be admitted to bail. What sum do you want fixed?' Mr. Herring: 'The offense is a grave one. The party alleged to have been assailed by these parties is lying dangerously i[l]l—so dangerous that death may ensue….We think under the circumstances that the bail should be at least five thousand dollars.'"

Arguing for Clanton, attorney Campbell countered that "It is higher bail than usual. I do not think it is a reasonable sum. We would like to see the affidavit." Judge Stillwell responded that "The affidavit is at Chambers," to which Campbell replied, "It is made by Wyatt Earp. Is it made on information or of his direct knowledge, because that makes a difference. It is hardly supposable that he saw this event [the shooting of Virgil on December 28th, 1881]…" Stillwell responded with a bail of $1,500. Campbell, pressing the advantage gained added, "I suppose these gentlemen [can] go into the custody of the Sheriff. He is the only officer that I know of that is authorized to retain them." [240] And with that, Ike and Phin Clanton were turned over to Sheriff Behan, whom the Earps and their supporters saw as sympathetic toward them and others of the cowboy gang.

Attorney William Herring, who represented the Earps and Doc Holliday at the Contention City hearing. Courtesy of Roy B. Young.

Wyatt Earp claimed that Judge Stillwell urged him to pursue other than legal means in dealing with the ongoing feud. "Wyatt, the next time don't bring in any prisoners alive!" [241]

Above and below, photos of Judge William H. Stilwell, whom Wyatt Earp claimed had advised him to not "bring in any prisoners alive!" Both images courtesy of Roy B. Young.

THE EARPS ARRIVE AT CONTENTION

The gunfight had taken place October 26th, 1881, and the Spicer hearing which followed soon after left the Earps free men, though still close to trouble as long as they remained in the area. The December 14th, 1881 near shooting of John Clum was then followed by a serious wounding of Virgil Earp on December 28th, 1881. The tensions never dissipated, but rather continued to escalate.

By February 3rd, 1882, Ike and Phin Clanton were free men once again. "The Clantons and their friend took their departure from the city yesterday, having been honorably acquitted of the charges against them." [242] With his new-found liberty, Ike would soon travel to Contention City. It was now his turn to draw the Earps into court. If Wyatt could force the Clantons to come before a judge in Tombstone, Ike would force Wyatt, Morgan, and Doc Holliday to appear before a judge in Contention, the Earp drama now arriving at its doors.

At Clanton's request, Justice J.B. Smith issued an arrest warrant against the Earps and Doc Holliday for the deaths of Billy Clanton, along with Frank and Tom McLaury. It was a case that had already been tried before Judge Spicer in Tombstone, and the local Grand Jury had chosen not to take it up, effectively freeing the Earps and Holliday from their legal woes following the fight, at least for a time. James Bennett Smith traveled back and forth between Contention City, and after Fairbank was formed, he would reside as a Justice of the Peace there as well. Smith was fifty five years old in 1882, and he was about to play host to an unusual court proceeding, even by the standards set in the old west.

Image of Ike Clanton, whose legal filing brought the Earps to a Contention City Courtroom. Courtesy of the Wild West History Assocation.

The court filing by Ike Clanton, and Smith's subsequent arrest warrant for the Earps and Doc Holliday, constituted a legal occasion which had little chance of success. Speculation at the time and since has asserted that the real motive was to lure the Earps out onto the stage road that ran between Tombstone and Contention, which clearly offered many fine locations for possible ambush. "Wyatt Earp, Morgan Earp, and Doc Holliday were arrested yesterday on a warrant sworn out at Contention before Justice Smith, at the instance of Joseph Isaac Clanton. The

142

charge upon which they were arrested, we are informed, was but a renewal of the one under which they were arrested last fall for the shooting affray in Fremont street. They were taken before Court Commissioner Drum last night to effect their release on a writ of habeas corpus, and the matter taken under further advisement until this morning. If it is a fact that this warrant has been allowed to issue without new evidence to warrant it, the code of right that protects all alike has been violently infringed. Cleared by a lengthy examination before a magistrate and then by a grand jury, it is only in the province of another grand jury to take up the case, unless new evidence is brought forward before the issuance of a warrant." [243]

Instead of arguing against Smith's arrest warrant, Earp attorney Herring would argue that Justice Smith of Contention was not officially an office holder, and therefore had no authority to make such a decision. The Nugget covered this event. "WRIT OF HABEAS CORPUS DENIED. The Earps and Doc Holliday Examination to be Held Before Justice Smith at Contention. The application of Morgan Earp, Virgil Earp, Wyatt Earp and J.H. Holliday for a writ of habeas corpus was heard before Probate Judge J.H. Lucas yesterday morning, at 10 o'clock, in the District Court, Messrs. Robinson and Ben Goodrich appearing for the prosecution, and Wm. Herring on behalf of the applicants. In order to do away with unnecessary argument and time, it was agreed among counsel that it should be stipulated that the merits of the case should be decided upon the question, as put forward by Mr. Herring, whether or not J.B. Smith, the Justice of the Peace of Charleston [Contention], who issued the warrants for the arrest of the applicants, was legally constituted and duly authorized Justice of the Peace. After hearing lengthy arguments on both sides the Judge decided that he was a duly authorized Justice of the Peace, having received his appointment from the Board of Supervisors, February 1, and within ten days after his appointment had filed his official bond and taken the oath of office, and in view of these facts the Court Commissioner denied the return of the writ and remanded the prisoners to the custody of the Sheriff, and their examination on the charge of the murder of Wm. Clanton will be commenced at 12 [p.] m. to-day, at Contention, before Justice J.B. Smith." [244]

A CONTENTION COURT ROOM THAT RESEMBLES AN ARSENAL

The Earps and Doc Holliday traveled with their attorney to Contention and argue their case before Smith. Based on her conversations with Wyatt Earp, Forrestine Hooker reported this version of the proceedings in the Contention Courtroom. "A vacancy occurred through the death of the Justice of Peace at Contention, Cochise County, tem [ten] miles from Tombstone. This position had to be filled by the Supervisors, and a man named [Milt] Joyce, at that time one of the Supervisors, was not over friendly toward Wyatt Earp. The appointment of the new Justice of Peace was largely a matter of Joyce's selection. So it was no surprise to Earp and his friends when the newly appointed Justice of Peace caused the re-arrest of Wyatt Earp on the very same charge of which he had just been acquitted in Tombstone. The new case was called for trial in Contention…Knowing the character of the Clanton followers, there was real ground to believe that this new move was merely a ruse. An attack, or shot from ambush would settle the matter out of court on the way to Contention.

"Sheriff Behan was to escort Earp to Contention. Behan made an effort to have Earp give up his arms, but Earp flatly refused to part with them. Behan did not persist. Then Behan discovered that twelve reputable citizens, all armed with Winchesters, had formed an escort for Wyatt Earp during the ten-mile drive to Contention. Judge Herring, [whose] gun was ready to be used, sat in his buggy and beside him sat his sixteen-year old daughter, who was her father's chum on all occasions. In her hands was gripped her own gun. She had refused to remain behind, and said she could follow alone, if he did not take her with him. He knew she would do it, too. Each bush and bit of rock was scanned sharply, and if there were any concealed enemies of Earp's, the armed escort caused ignominious failure of their plans. When the cavalcade reached the embryonic town, the Sheriff of the County presented the incongruous spectacle of marching into the Court room with a fully armed Deputy United States Marshall, as prisoner, and behind the prisoner filed twelve reputable citizens of the County seat, among them the daughter of a Judge, each and everyone carried a Winchester which was carefully set against the wall of the Court room before the astonished eyes of the newly-appointed Justice of [the] Peace.

"Then that Justice of [the] Peace was confronted by a famous attorney, Judge Herring, who had presided over higher tribunals than mere Justice Courts. Judge Herring stood looking steadily into the face of the presiding Justice. There was not a whisper in the room. Spectators leaned forward tensely as Judge Herring's voice cut the silence.

'Your Honor, (was there a tinge of sarcasm on that word?) 'We come here for law, but we will fight—if we have to!'

"With those preliminary words Judge Herring began an impassioned protest against the unnecessary trip away from the County seat, [Tombstone] the place where the alleged violation of law had occurred, and the inconvenience of being compelled to remain an indefinite time in Contention with Tombstone only a few miles distant. At the end of Judge Herring's address, the Justice, with a comprehensive glance at the faces of the Earp escort, and an apprehensive look at the grim array of Winchesters along the wall, decided astutely, 'I will transfer the case to Tombstone for trial.'" [245]

JUDGE SMITH AT CONTENTION GOT MORE THAN HE BARGAINED FOR

Now Smith was sending back to Tombstone what he had begun at Contention. "Back again rode Sheriff Behan, Wyatt Earp and the twelve armed men, and in their midst was a buggy driven by Judge Herring while his plucky little daughter sat alertly beside him. In Tombstone a writ of habeas corpus had already been secured and the prompt release of Wyatt Earp followed, much to the delight of those who had stood loyally by him in his determination to do his duty."[246]

"Yesterday was a lively day in the Earp-Holliday case. Judge Smith came up from Contention, and opened court at 10 a.m., when the case was taken up on a technical point and ably argued by William Herring, Esq., for the defendants and Judge Robinson for the

144

prosecution. At the close of the arguments Judge Smith took the matter under advisement until 4 o'clock, to which hour he adjourned court. In the mean time a writ of habeas corpus was issued by J.H. Lucas, Esq., probate judge, returnable forthwith. The points upon which the writ was issued were argued by Mr. Herring and against Ben Goodrich, Esq. Upon mature deliberation Judge Lucas sustained the writ. The full text of the decision will be found in another column, and will be read with interest by the entire community. It is an able document and settles, we trust, for all time in this county, the question as to how many times a person may be arrested on the same charge." [247]

As Parsons wrote, "Yesterday Earps were taken to Contention to be tried for the killing of Clanton. Quite a posse went out. Many of Earp's friends accompanied armed to the teeth. They came back later in the day, the good people below [Contention City] beseeching them to leave and try case here. A bad time is expected in town [Tombstone] at any time. Earps on one side of street with their friends and Ike Clanton and Ringo with theirs' on the other side-watching each other. Blood will surely come. Hope no innocents will be killed. [248]

Legal attempts against the Earps and Holliday had failed for the last time, and soon the ambush tactic used against Virgil Earp would be visited upon brothers Wyatt and Morgan, the latter suffering the ultimate price for this ongoing feud.

WAS WYATT EARP CORRECT ABOUT THE APPOINTMENT OF JUDGE SMITH?

The timing of Justice Smith's appointment did not serve the Earps and Doc Holliday well, as Smith had only held this office a scant nine days when he issued the arrest warrant on behalf of Ike Clanton. It was on February 1st, 1882, that the Cochise County Board of Supervisors had appointed Smith to this position, and he very quickly inserted himself into the Earp controversies. It has been implied that Smith's appointment pleased Milt Joyce, an open Earp opponent. Smith could have turned down Ike Clanton's request, a request that was quickly dismissed by another court in Tombstone, but chose not to. The Smith appointment also signaled a change in the party of the Justice of the Peace at Contention. Smith was appointed in the wake of the death of Justice Rigg, who was not a democrat. "Among the visitors in town [Tombstone] yesterday we noticed Mr. George McKenny and his father; also Col. E. Riggs, of Contention. The Colonel is an ardent Republican, and predicts a rousing majority for his party…" [249]

Wyatt Earp believed that much of the trouble between himself and Milt Joyce stemmed from his friendship with Doc Holliday, by no means the most popular person in Tombstone, or the Arizona Territory for that matter. Referring to Democrat Johnny Behan and others against him, Earp later added that "whenever they got a chance to hurt me over Holliday's shoulders they would do it…on one occasion he got into some trouble with part of the combination that was against me, Joyce, and his partner, and he shot Joyce in the hand and the other fellow in the foot and of course that made them pretty sore against Holliday. But they knew that I was Holliday's friend and they tried to injure me every way they could." [250]

The Nugget reported on this incident which occurred on Sunday evening, October 10, 1880. Wyatt's close associate Doc Holliday got into a row in the Oriental Saloon, an incident that Milt Joyce would not forget. "Sunday night a dispute arose in the Oriental Saloon between John Tyley and Doc Holliday, two well-known sports, and a scene of bloodshed was imminent. Mutual friends, however, separated and disarmed both, and Tyler went away, Holliday remaining at the saloon. M.E. Joyce, one of the proprietors, remonstrated with Holliday about creating a disturbance in the saloon and the conversation resulted in Holliday being bodily fired out by Joyce. The former came in and demanded his pistol from behind the bar, where it had been placed by the officer who disarmed him. It was not given him and he went out, but in a short time…returned and walked toward Joyce, who was just coming from behind the bar, and with a remark that wouldn't look well in print, turned loose with a self-cocker. Joyce was not more than ten feet away and jumped for his assailant and struck him over the head with a six-shooter, felling him to the floor and lighting on top of him. Officers White and Bennett were near at hand and separated them, taking the pistols from each. Just how many shots were fired none present seem about to tell but in casting up accounts Joyce was found to be shot through the hand, his partner, Mr. Parker, who was behind the bar, shot through the big toe of the left foot, and Holliday with a-blow of the pistol in Joyce's hands…All the parties directly implicated are still in bed and no direct arrests have been made, although a complaint has been entered against Holliday and he will be brought before Justice Reilly as soom[n] as he is able to appear, probably to-day." [251]

The Republicans at the Epitaph were quick to point out the larger issue as to the appointments made by Joyce while in office. "Mr. Joyce has a political future before him. But we tell him very frankly that he is making a very bad start. He is favoring his personal friends in opposition to the general sentiment of the public, and he is furthering his own material interests to the detriment of the county's interest." [252]

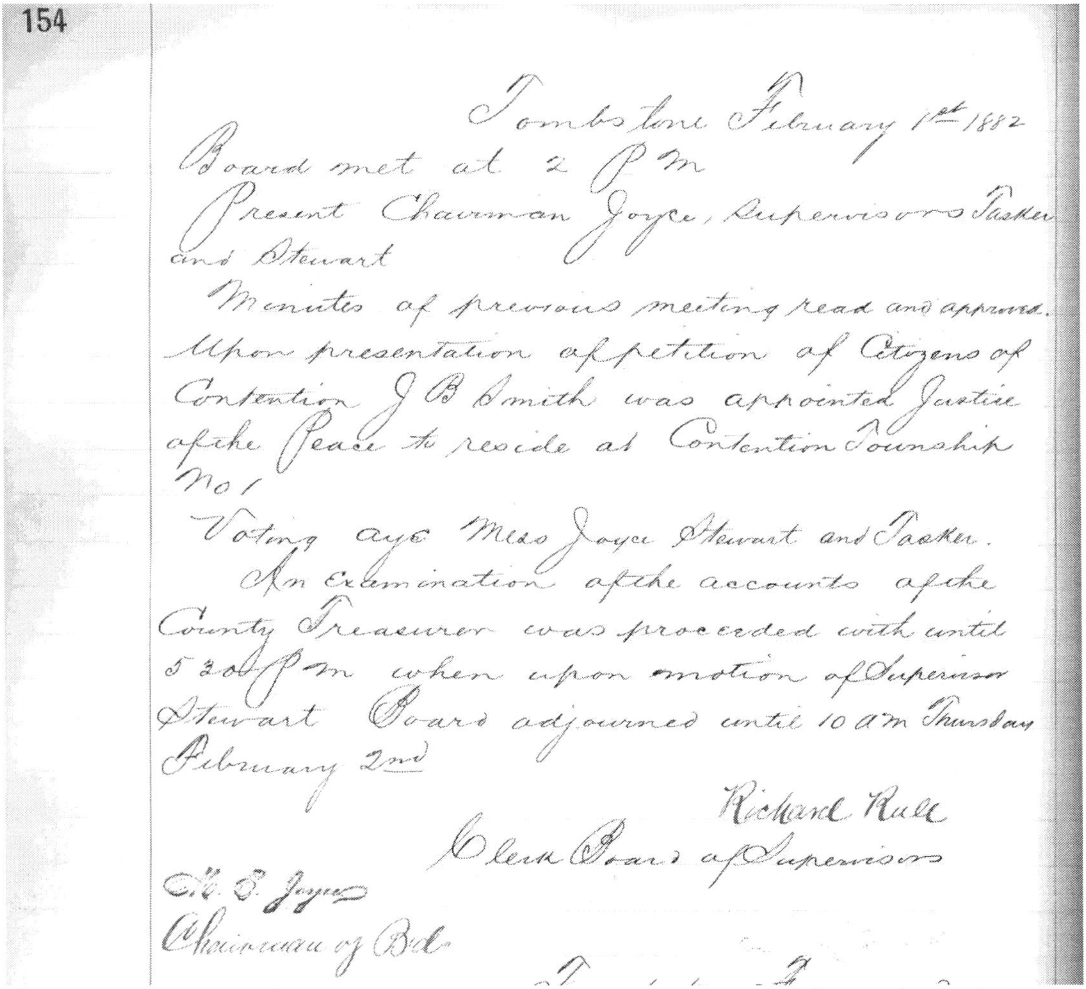

Tombstone February 1st 1882

Board met at 2 P m

Present Chairman Joyce, Supervisors Tasker and Stewart

Minutes of previous meeting read and approved.

Upon presentation of petition of Citizens of Contention J B Smith was appointed Justice of the Peace to reside at Contention Township No 1

Voting aye Mess Joyce Stewart and Tasker.

An examination of the accounts of the County Treasurer was proceeded with until 5 30 P m when upon motion of Supervisor Stewart Board adjourned until 10 a m Thursday February 2nd

Richard Rule
Clerk Board of Supervisors

M. S. Joyce
Chairman of Bd

The actual appointment of J.B. Smith as Justice of the Peace at Contention, following the death of Judge Rigg. One of Smith's first acts in his new role was to issue the arrest warrants for the Earps and Doc Holliday. Courtesy of the Cochise County Archives.

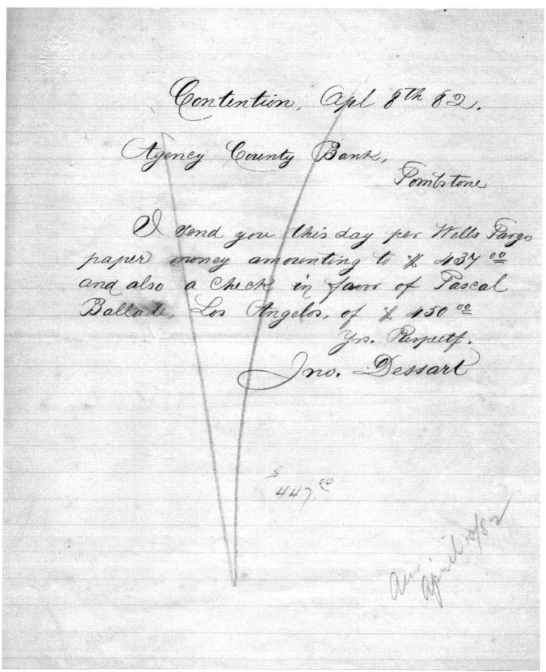

Contention, Apl 8th 82.

Agency County Bank,
　　　　　　　Tombstone

I send you this day per Wells Fargo paper money amounting to $ 437 00 and also a check in favor of Pascal Ballade, Los Angeles, of $ 150 00
　　　　　　Yrs. Respectfy.
　　　　　Jno. Dessart

$ 447 00

Ans April 10/82

Original 1882 letter from Contention City from the collections John D. Rose.

No. 898   TOMBSTONE. A. T., Jany 25 1883.

I, J. H. BEHAN, *Ex-Sheriff and ex-officio Tax-Collector of the County of Cochise, Territory of Arizona, do hereby certify, that by virtue of an Act entitled "An Act Amendatory to Chapter XXXIII of Compiled Laws of Arizona Territory, to provide revenue for the Territory of Arizona, and the several counties thereof, approved April 12th, 1875," approved March 10th, 1881, I have this day sold for taxes to*

Territory of Arizona   *for the sum of*

3.25 *Dollars,*

the following described property House at Contention

$50 Laundry Tools $25

Said property was assessed to Sing Wah

on the Assessment Roll of Cochise County, A. T., for the year 1882, in the sum of

$ 75 *, the taxes and costs on which amount to $* 3.25 .

And the said property is subject to redemption in six months, pursuant to the Statute in such cases made and provided; and that the said

Territory of Arizona *is entitled to a deed for said property on the* 25 *day of* July , 1883.

J H Behan

Ex-Sheriff and Ex-officio Tax-Collector, Cochise County, A. T.

416

Though no longer Sheriff, John Behan was still collecting delinquent for his ten percent fee. This bill is for a Laundry House owned by Sing Wah. All tax certificates of sales that follow are courtesy of the Cochise County Archives.

No 343   Tombstone, A. T. Jany 25 1883

I, J. H. BEHAN, *Ex-Sheriff and ex-officio Tax-Collector of the County of Cochise, Territory of Arizona, do hereby certify, that by virtue of an Act entitled "An Act Amendatory to Chapter XXXIII of Compiled Laws of Arizona Territory, to provide revenue for the Territory of Arizona, and the several counties thereof, approved April 12th, 1875," approved March 10th, 1881, I have this day sold for taxes to* Territory of Arizona *for the sum of* $160 **DOLLARS,** *the following described property:* House Main St Contention $30

Said property was assessed to Jno Solstein *on the Assessment Roll of Cochise County, A. T., for the year 1882, in the sum of $* 20 *, the taxes and costs on which amount to $* 160

And the said property is subject to redemption in six months, pursuant to the Statute in such cases made and provided; and that the said Territory of Arizona *is entitled to a deed for said property on the* 25 *day of* July *, 1883.*

J H Behan

Ex-Sheriff and Ex-officio Tax-Collector Cochise County, A. T.

342

A delinquent tax bill for a house on Contention's Main Street.

No 323   Tombstone, A. T., Jany 25   1883

I, J. H. BEHAN, *Ex-Sheriff and ex-officio Tax-Collector of the County of Cochise, Territory of Arizona, do hereby certify, that by virtue of an Act entitled "An Act Amendatory to Chapter XXXIII of Compiled Laws of Arizona Territory, to provide revenue for the Territory of Arizona, and the several counties thereof, approved April 12th, 1875," approved March 10th, 1881, I have this day sold for taxes to* Territory of Arizona, *for the sum of* 38,52 *DOLLARS.*

the following described property: House N. side Main St. Contention $200 Household Furniture $50 Mdse $1000

Said property was assessed to M. Kaufman

on the Assessment Roll of Cochise County, A. T., for the year 1882, in the sum of $ 1250 *, the taxes and costs on which amount to $* 38,52

And the said property is subject to redemption in six months, pursuant to the Statute in such cases made and provided; and that the said Territory of Arizona *is entitled to a deed for said property on the* 25 *day of* July *, 1883.*

J. H. Behan

Ex-Sheriff and Ex-officio Tax-Collector Cochise County, A. T.

323

No. 478   Tombstone, A. T. Jany 25   1883

I, J. H. BEHAN, *Ex-Sheriff and ex-officio Tax-Collector of the County of*
Cochise, Territory of Arizona, do hereby certify, that by virtue of an Act entitled "An
Act Amendatory to Chapter XXXIII of Compiled Laws of Arizona Territory, to pro-
vide revenue for the Territory of Arizona, and the several counties thereof, approved
April 12th, 1875," approved March 10th, 1881, I have this day sold for taxes to
Territory of Arizona _____ *for the sum of*
                                    $75,31 _____ DOLLARS,
the following described property: House and Lot Contention
$200 Mdse $2000 2Horses $200 Wagon and
Harness $75 _____

Said property was assessed to E. E. Rapert & Co
_____ *on the Assessment Roll of Cochise County, A. T., for the year 1882, in the sum*
of $ 2475 *, the taxes and costs on which amount to $* 75,31

And the said property is subject to redemption in six months, pursuant to the
Statute in such cases made and provided; and that the said _____
Territory of Arizona _____ *is entitled to a deed for said*
property on the 25 *day of* July _____, 1883.

                                    J H Behan
        Ex-Sheriff and Ex-officio Tax-Collector Cochise County, A. T.

                    476

A delinquent tax bill for a house and lot in Contention, as well as two horses, a wagon and harness.

152

No 5   Tombstone, A. T., January 25 1883

I, J. H. BEHAN, *Ex-Sheriff and ex-officio Tax-Collector of the County of Cochise, Territory of Arizona, do hereby certify, that by virtue of an Act entitled "An Act Amendatory to Chapter XXXIII of Compiled Laws of Arizona Territory, to provide revenue for the Territory of Arizona, and the several counties thereof, approved April 12th, 1875," approved March 10th, 1881, I have this day sold for taxes to* Territory of Arizona *for the sum of* Five and 20/100 DOLLARS.

the following described property:

House, tent and lot Main St. Contention — also Stock of Liquors and fixtures

Said property was assessed to Juan Alatorre *on the Assessment Roll of Cochise County, A. T., for the year 1882, in the sum of $* 140, *the taxes and costs on which amount to $* 5 20/100

And the said property is subject to redemption in six months, pursuant to the Statute in such cases made and provided; and that the said Territory of Arizona *is entitled to a deed for said property on the* 26th *day of* July *, 1883.*

J H Behan

Ex-Sheriff and Ex-officio Tax-Collector Cochise County, A. T.

5

A tax delinquent bill for a tent, house, and liquor sales on the Contention Main Street.

No 4   Tombstone, A. T. January 25 1883

I, J. H. BEHAN, *Ex-Sheriff and ex-officio Tax-Collector of the County of Cochise, Territory of Arizona, do hereby certify, that by virtue of an Act entitled "An Act Amendatory to Chapter XXXIII of Compiled Laws of Arizona Territory, to provide revenue for the Territory of Arizona, and the several counties thereof, approved April 12th, 1875," approved March 10th, 1881, I have this day sold for taxes to* Territory of Arizona *for the sum of* Eleven and 50/100 *DOLLARS,*

the following described property: House West side of Main Street Household Furniture and Merchandise L. Alexander Contention

Said property was assessed to L. Alexander *on the Assessment Roll of Cochise County, A. T., for the year 1882, in the sum of $* 350 *, the taxes and costs on which amount to $* 11 50

And the said property is subject to redemption in six months, pursuant to the Statute in such cases made and provided; and that the said Territory of Arizona *is entitled to a deed for said property on the* 25th *day of* July *, 1883.*

Jf. H. Behan

Ex-Sheriff and Ex-officio Tax-Collector Cochise County, A. T.

4

A delinquent tax bill for a house on the west side of Contention's Main Street.

154

No 104   Tombstone, A. T., January 25th 1883

I, J. H. BEHAN, *Ex-Sheriff and ex-officio Tax-Collector of the County of Cochise, Territory of Arizona, do hereby certify, that by virtue of an Act entitled "An Act Amendatory to Chapter XXXIII of Compiled Laws of Arizona Territory, to provide revenue for the Territory of Arizona, and the several counties thereof, approved April 12th, 1875," approved March 10th, 1881, I have this day sold for taxes to* Territory of Arizona *for the sum of* Seventeen 61/100 DOLLARS.

the following described property: House El Lot Contention 75 House hold furniture 10 4 Horses 200 Cow 20 2 Wagons Harness 40 Plow 10

Said property was assessed to E Clifford

on the Assessment Roll of Cochise County, A. T., for the year 1882, in the sum of $ 555.00 *, the taxes and costs on which amount to $* 17 61/100

And the said property is subject to redemption in six months, pursuant to the Statute in such cases made and provided; and that the said Territory of Arizona *is entitled to a deed for said property on the* 25th *day of* July *, 1883.*

J H Behan

Ex-Sheriff and Ex-officio Tax-Collector Cochise County, A. T.

104

155

No 386   Tombstone, A. T. Jany 25 ___ 1883

I, J. H. BEHAN, *Ex-Sheriff and ex-officio Tax-Collector of the County of Cochise, Territory of Arizona, do hereby certify, that by virtue of an Act entitled "An Act Amendatory to Chapter XXXIII of Compiled Laws of Arizona Territory, to provide revenue for the Territory of Arizona, and the several counties thereof, approved April 12th, 1875," approved March 10th, 1881, I have this day sold for taxes to* Territory of Arizona *for the sum of* $147.08 *DOLLARS, the following described property* Hotel, Lands & Imps 160 acres Contention $4000 Liquors & Bar Fixtures $300 Horse $50 Harness $5 Hotel and Restaurant Furniture 500

Said property was assessed to L. Meyers & Son *on the Assessment Roll of Cochise County, A. T., for the year 1882, in the sum of* $ 4865 *, the taxes and costs on which amount to* $ 147.08

And the said property is subject to redemption in six months, pursuant to the Statute in such cases made and provided; and that the said Territory of Arizona *is entitled to a deed for said property on the* 25 *day of* July *, 1883.*

J H Behan

Ex-Sheriff and Ex-officio Tax-Collector Cochise County, A. T.

384

Meyer's [Myer's] Hotel, as noted above, was a key social spot at Contention City, with many dances running through the night until dawn.

156

No 138   Tombstone, A. T., Jany 25 1883

I, J. H. BEHAN, *Ex-Sheriff and ex-officio Tax-Collector of the County of Cochise, Territory of Arizona, do hereby certify, that by virtue of an Act entitled "An Act Amendatory to Chapter XXXIII of Compiled Laws of Arizona Territory, to provide revenue for the Territory of Arizona, and the several counties thereof, approved April 12th, 1875," approved March 10th, 1881, I have this day sold for taxes to* Territory of Arizona *for the sum of* $3,03 *DOLLARS.*

the following described property: Mortg on Lot 8 Blk 47 Tombstone

Said property was assessed to R. Crouch *on the Assessment Roll of Cochise County, A. T., for the year 1882, in the sum of $, the taxes and costs on which amount to $* 3,03

And the said property is subject to redemption in six months, pursuant to the Statute in such cases made and provided; and that the said Territory of Arizona *is entitled to a deed for said property on the* 25 *day of* July *, 1883.*

J H Behan

Ex-Sheriff and Ex-officio Tax-Collector Cochise County, A. T.

138

Robert "Sandy Bob" Crouch was a key stage coach operator on routes to Tombstone, and is shown here delinquent on taxable property for a mortgage that he holds.

157

Sheriff John Behan, copy photo from the collections of John D. Rose.

Wyatt Earp, years before Tombstone. Copy photo from the collections of John D. Rose.

Virgil Earp, as appeared during his Tombstone years, according to John Clum. Copy photo from the collections of John D. Rose.

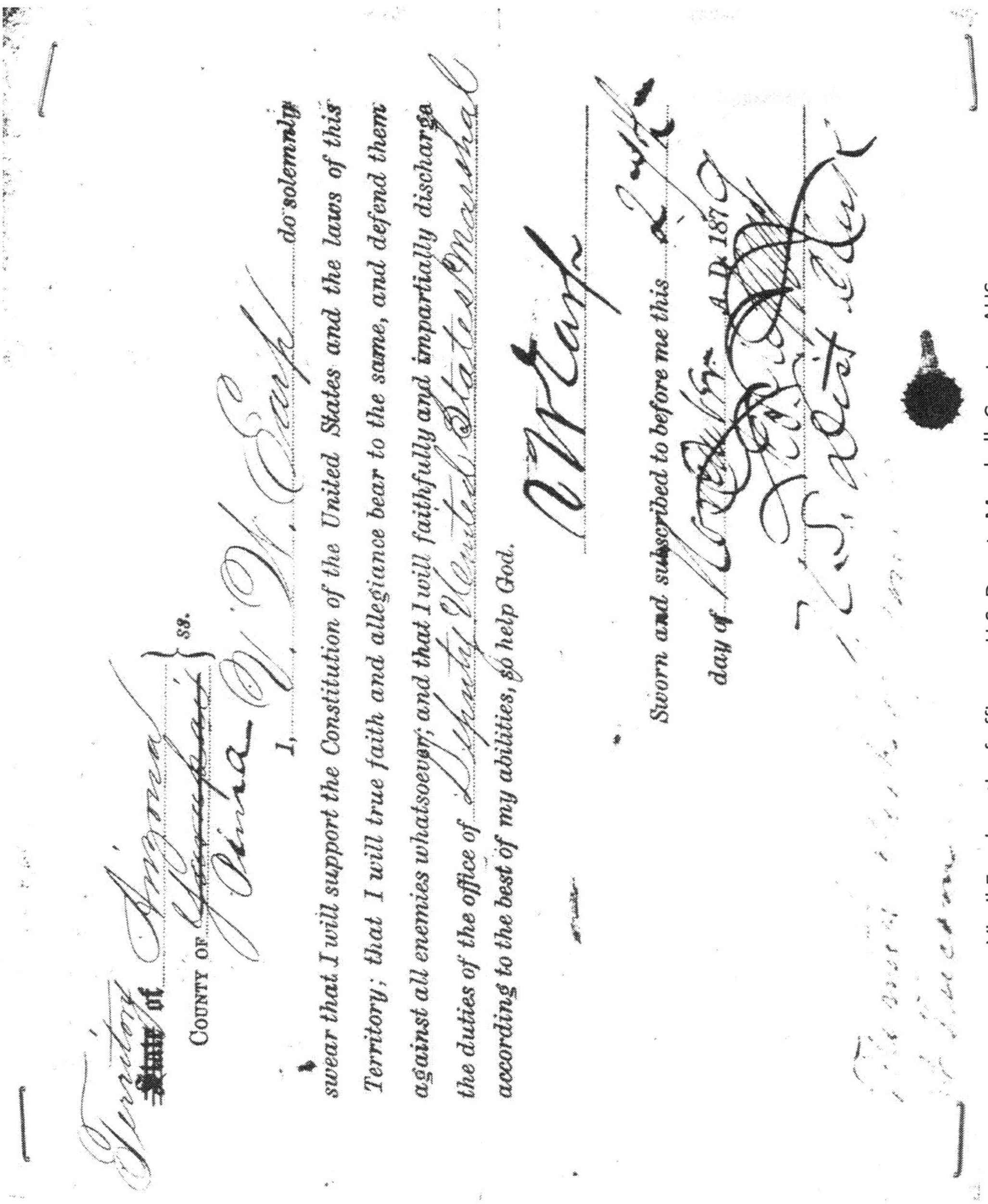

Territory of Arizona } ss.

County of _____

I, _____ A. V. W. Earp _____ do solemnly swear that I will support the Constitution of the United States and the laws of this Territory; that I will true faith and allegiance bear to the same, and defend them against all enemies whatsoever; and that I will faithfully and impartially discharge the duties of the office of Deputy United States Marshal according to the best of my abilities, so help God.

V. W. Earp

Sworn and subscribed to before me this _____ day of _____ A. D. 187___

Virgil Earp's oath of office, as U.S. Deputy Marshall. Courtesy AHS.

161

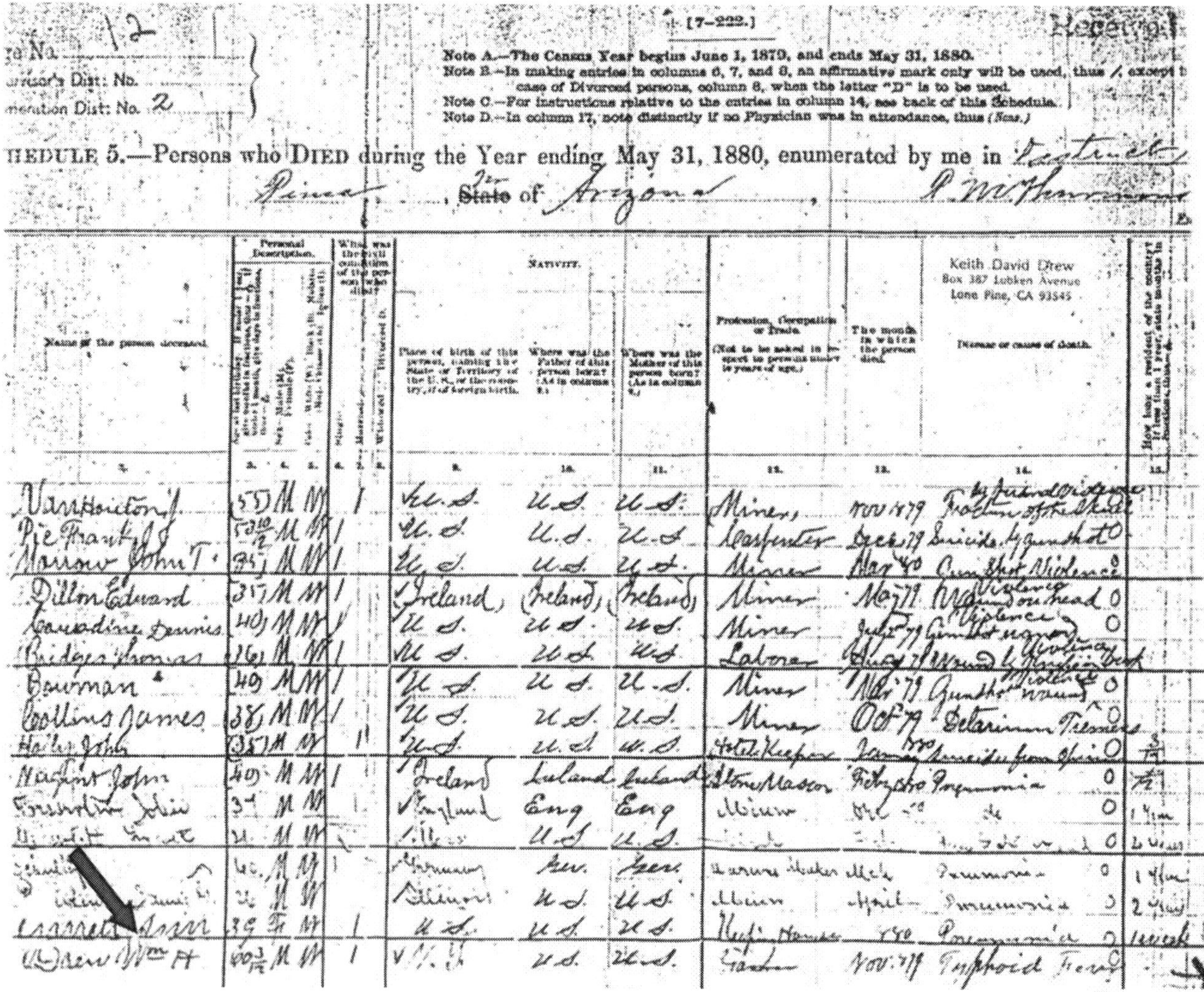

Keith David Drew
Box 387 Lubken Avenue
Lone Pine, CA 93545

SCHEDULE 5.—Persons who DIED during the Year ending May 31, 1880, enumerated by me in ____
State of Arizona

Note A.—The Census Year begins June 1, 1879, and ends May 31, 1880.
Note B.—In making entries in columns 6, 7, and 8, an affirmative mark only will be used, thus /, except in
case of Divorced persons, column 8, when the letter "D" is to be used.
Note C.—For instructions relative to the entries in column 14, see back of this Schedule.
Note D.—In column 17, note distinctly if no Physician was in attendance, thus (None.)

The final entry records the death of Wm. H. Drew. Courtesy of the Drew Family Archive.

162

Robert "Sandy Bob" Crouch is pictured along with his team mates at the bottom right. Copy photo from the collections of John D. Rose.

163

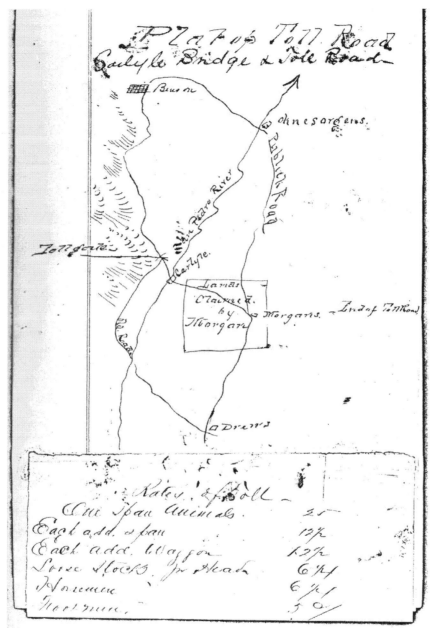

In November, 1880, William Carlyle proposes a toll road and bridge near Drew's Ranch. Note the site north of Drew's known as "Lands claimed by Morgan." This is the area of the TTR/Sosa and BLM site. Copy from the collections of John D. Rose.

CROUCH'S TOMBSTONE AND BENSON ACCOMMODATION LINE.

From......................... to .... 188....., ... Driver

NO.	NAME.	WHERE FROM.	DESTINATION.	FARE.	BY WHOM RECEIVED.
1					
2					
3					
4					
5					
6					
7					
8					
9					
10					
11					
12					
13					
14					
15					
16					
17					
18					
19					
20					

PACKAGES.

NO.	ARTICLE.	LBS.	NAME.	WHERE FROM.	DESTINATION.	$	Cts.	BY WHOM RECEIVED.
1								
2								
3								
4								
5								
6								
7								
8								
9								
10								

Original waybill for Sandy Bob Crouch's Tombstone to Benson Stage Line. From the collections of John D. Rose.

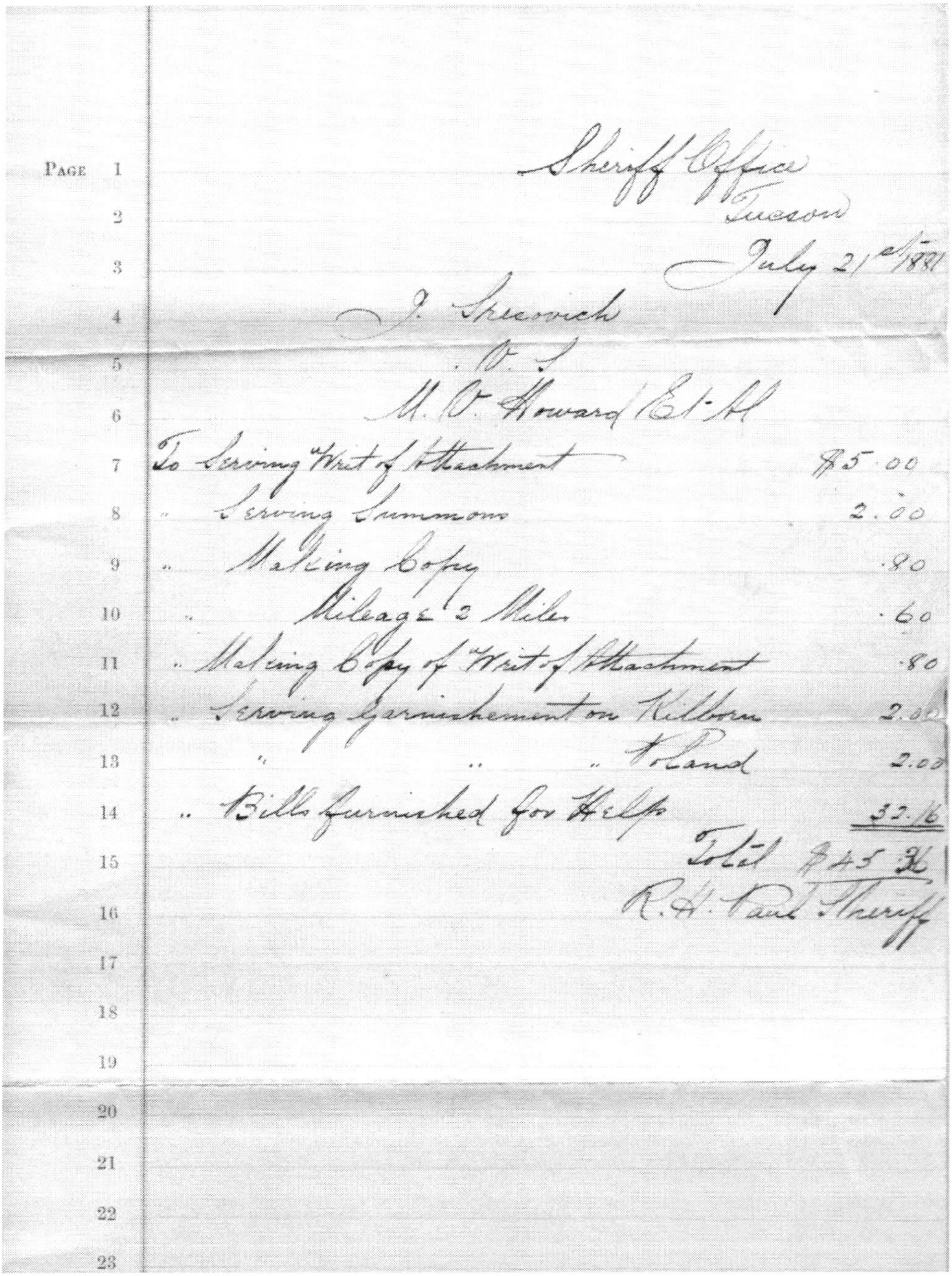

Sheriff Office
Tucson
July 21st 1881

J. Sresovich
v. J.
M. O. Howard Et Al

To Serving Writ of Attachment $5.00
" Serving Summons   2.00
" Making Copy   .80
" Mileage 3 Miles   .60
" Making Copy of Writ of Attachment   .80
" Serving Garnishement on Killborn   2.00
" " " " Rand   2.00
" Bills furnished for Help   32.16

Total $45 36

R. H. Paul Sheriff

Sheriff Bob Paul signs this expense form, just over four months after nearly being shot while riding next to Bud Philpot. From the collections John D. Rose.

166

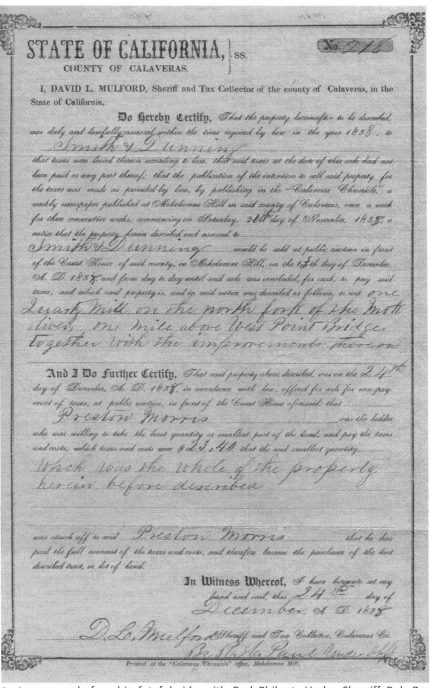

STATE OF CALIFORNIA, } ss.
COUNTY OF CALAVERAS.

No. 218

I, DAVID L. MULFORD, Sheriff and Tax Collector of the county of Calaveras, in the State of California,

Do Hereby Certify, *That the property hereinafter to be described, was duly and lawfully assessed within the time required by law in the year 1858, to Smith & Dunning that taxes were levied thereon according to law, that said taxes at the date of this sale had not been paid or any part thereof; that the publication of the intention to sell said property, for the taxes was made as provided by law, by publishing in the "Calaveras Chronicle," a weekly newspaper published at Mokelumne Hill in said county of Calaveras, once a week for three consecutive weeks, commencing on Saturday, 20th day of November, 1858, a notice that the property herein described and assessed to Smith & Dunning would be sold at public auction in front of the Court House of said county, in Mokelumne Hill, on the 14th day of December, A.D. 1858 and from day to day until said sale was concluded, for cash, to pay said taxes, and which said property is, and in said notice was described as follows, to wit* One Quartz Mill on the north fork of the Mok river, one mile above West Point Bridge together with the improvements thereon

And I Do Further Certify, *That said property above described, was on the 24th day of December, A.D. 1858 in accordance with law, offered for sale for non-payment of taxes, at public auction, in front of the Court House aforesaid; that* Preston Morris *was the bidder who was willing to take the least quantity or smallest part of the land, and pay the taxes and costs, which taxes and costs were* $23.40 *that the said smallest quantity,* Which was the whole of the property herein before described

was struck off to said Preston Morris *that he has paid the full amount of the taxes and costs, and therefore became the purchaser of the last described tract, or lot of land.*

In Witness Whereof, *I have hereunto set my hand and seal, this* 24th *day of* December A.D. 1858

D.L. Mulford Sheriff and Tax Collector, Calaveras Co.
By Robt. H. Paul Under Sheriff

Printed at the "Calaveras Chronicle" office, Mokelumne Hill.

Over twenty two years before his fateful ride with Bud Philpot, Under Sheriff Bob Paul sign this certificate of tax sale on December 24th, 1858. From the collections of John D. Rose.

167

The N.M. & A. Depot at Benson. The next stop for south bound travelers from this building was Contention City. Copy photo from the collections of John D. Rose.

CHAPTER 11

THE IRON HORSE – BLAZING A TRAIL THROUGH TROUBLE

"The railroad is steadily furnishing a supply of invalids to the County hospital." -Nugget

Both Contention City and Fairbank would benefit from the first railroad to penetrate the San Pedro River Valley south of Benson. This amplified their importance in the eyes of the Tombstone populace, which would continue to use these two cities as their access to the rail systems that were now expanding across the west. "The First Passenger Train to Contention. On Wednesday last, the first passenger car ran over the road from Benson to Contention. The occupants of the car were officials of the road who came up on a tour of observation. The regular trains will commence running on the 1st of February. The depot at Contention is nearly completed. It is a building 15 X 175 feet, two stories in height, and substantially built. The water tank is ready for its aqueous contents, and the steam pump has arrived and will be put in place immediately. The foundation for a large residence is now being laid. Several of the residents of old Contention are making preparations to remove across to the new town, and it is only a question of time when the whole of the town will be abandoned and a flourishing village [will] spring up around the station.

"The members of the party were Judge Messick, Col. Harry I. Thornton. Mark L. McDonald, Dock Dey, Louis Janin, I.L. Moody, Charles Leach and H.B. Maxson. Upon arrival of the party at Benson, Mr. Scott, master of construction of the road, very kindly furnished them with a special coach and sent them over the road in fine style. Arriving at Contention, mine host of the Meyers house treated them to an elegant dinner, after which they were taken in carriages and brought to this [Tombstone] city." [253]

Even at this late date, Epitaph reporters cite the railroad station as being located on the west bank of the river. The railroad line clearly runs on the east side at Contention, as shown by period maps done in the late 1880's—the same side as the Contention Mill. The depot was constructed on the east side as well.

Railroad construction toward the Mexican border promised a uniquely diverse traveling public that even Tombstone would rarely see. "THE GAUYMAS ROAD. 'Track laying is now progressing on the above-named road at the rate of a mile or over a day, and as the grade is nearly completed to Magdalena, it will not be long before the locomotive will be blowing its whistle at the 'out walls' of that 'ancient pueblo.' The distance from Magdalena to Contention City is but little more than one hundred and fifty miles, and as work will progress from both ends it will require but a short time to close up the gap." [254] This dusty little milling camp had gone from nothing to a small settlement built in the shadow of the mills which created it, and now it had moved into the arena of international trade and passenger routes. For a location not even four years old, Contention City had made remarkable strides, that at the time, almost seemed irreversible.

169

The optimism was shared by many. Speculators and those dreaming of an opportunity wanted to stake their claim to the pocket change of those who worked in the mills and those who came through Contention on their way to other destinations. "Mr. S.B. Wise, one of the old, old Arizonans, who has a fine ranch at the eastern base of the Whetstone mountains, was in town yesterday. At present he runs a milk-ranch two miles out of Contention. Mr. Wise thinks Contention the coming City." [255]

MORE MURDERS NEAR CONTENTION

As the N.M. & A. continued laying track south of Contention, trouble was awaiting its arrival thirty five miles to the southwest. "The grading of the New Mexico and Arizona railroad will be completed up to the Barbocomari creek, in about six weeks, a distance thirty-five miles from its junction with the San Pedro, near the Grand Central mill. At the junction, a turning track for engines, to be called the Calabasas Y, is now being constructed. Considerable hindrance to the progress of the line has been caused by the question of right of way. At one point near the mouth of the Barbocomari, on Friday last, a party of armed men compelled both pile drivers and graders to stop work, and are still holding the ground till the company arranges for the right of way." [256]

HELL ON WHEELS

The railroad camps that gave temporary shelter to their workers were never easy places to be, or even that safe to begin with. The term "Hell on Wheels" originated from such camps, as the saloon, brothels and other businesses were built on flatbed wagons, thus able to move about on wheels. This mobility allowed them to follow the road as it progressed, supplying the wishes of those workmen with cash in their pockets and indulgence in their minds. This gave them a recreational release and something to do other than pounding rail road spikes into stiff wooden ties. With such camps also came an occasional murder.

"A man was brought to the city [Tombstone] yesterday from the railroad camp on the San Pedro. He had eight gunshot wounds in his body, but how they were received or what his name was it was impossible to ascertain. He was in a semi-unconscious condition, and was taken to the county hospital." [257] Barely a week passed before another such incident occurred, with unfortunate results.

"J.F. Garner, who was employed at Ward & Courtney's railroad camp, on the upper Babacomari, was shot by a man named Kellogg last Sunday, and the wounded man was brought to this city yesterday and placed in the hospital. His body was pierced by four bullets, and he is in critical condition. The attack is said to have been unprovoked, and the assassin escaped, of course. Dr. J.B. [James G.] Barney, of Contention, was sent for, and promptly ministered to the wants of Mr. Garner. The men were fellow-laborers on the railroad, and up to the time of the shooting had had no difficulty." [258]

"The party named Gardiner, who was shot by a fellow workman named Kellogg at a railroad camp on the Babacomari, on the 2d instant, died to-day at the County Hospital, where he was taken the day after the shooting." [259]

Making light of bad situation, the Nugget quipped that "The railroad is steadily furnishing a supply of invalids to the County hospital." [260] Gallows humor aside, the progress of the railroad would not come without a human price, far beyond the hard labor and harsh working conditions. Acts of wanton violence had become accepted as part of the enterprise. No less disconcerting was the fact that men were losing their lives due to a fatal lack of safety procedures. "Railroad Accident. The mangled remains of two railroad employes were brought in from the Babacomari yesterday afternoon and consigned to the morgue. As far as we can ascertain the cause of the accident is unknown….The two men were working in a cut by themselves, and while preparing a blast an explosion occurred; one of them was precipitated [thrown] a distance of nearly one hundred feet, tearing his body to pieces; the other was frightfully mangled and disabled beyond recognition. Their names are Simon Consterdine and Thomas Kearnen. A coroner's jury was summoned by Dr. Matthews, but the examination wa[s] postponed till 11 o'clock this morning." [261]

The coroner's jury would quickly rule that "the case of the two railroad employees, who were blown up on the Babacomari, found a verdict of 'accidental death from a premature explosion.'" Death would also result from other than violent causes, an almost strangely pleasant change of pace. "Mr. R. Petty, a well known rancher on the San Pedro, above Contention, died at the latter place yesterday of pneumonia. He was a gentleman highly regarded by his friends and his place in the community will long remain unfilled." [262]

PROBLEMS AND PROGRESS

"On Thursday, an employe[e] of the New Mexico and Arizona Railroad, while loading a hole for a blast, had both eyes put out by the powder exploding prematurely." [263] Some light was shed on the rising incidence of violence that plagued the N.M. & A., but offered little in the way of answers. "There is a gang of thugs and thieves following the advance of guard of the constructionists who scruple at nothing and regard murder and robbery as their legitimate vocation. A party of these roughs while passing the camp of the O'Donnell brothers, contractors, the other evening, fired a volley into the camp without any provocation whatever. One shot took effect on Mrs. O'Donnell, an aged lady, the mother of the brothers, producing a dangerous wound. She has been sent to Tucson for medical treatment. Within the past week a Frenchman living near the Huachucas and a Mexican rancher on the Barbocomari, have been murdered, circumstances indicating that both deeds were committed through pure, unadulterated fiendishness. Robbery is of almost daily occurrence, and the wayfarer, if he would avoid being 'stood up,' must go thoroughly 'heeled.'" [264]

While bad news surfaced on the continuing construction of the N.M. & A. past Contention, the railroad was not the cause of violence in Contention City proper; it was providing jobs. "One hundred carpenters are at work on the new depot buildings at Contention." Also of note was that Judge Rigg of Contention was in the city for two days, attending the session of the board of supervisors. [265]

The railroad that would offer so much to Contention was now well past it and heading for Mexico, and it was an extensive project. "Over a thousand men are at work upon the New Mexico and Arizona railroad between the Santa Ritas and Contention. Last Monday Joe Hampson, one of the heaviest contractors on the road, started in with seventy-five teams and scrapers upon one cut and fill at the upper Babacomari." [266]

"George C. Marks, late proprietor of the Maison Doree, left to-day for Contention, where he will take charge of his father's business." [267]

The Earp controversies aside, a threat of a wider nature now emerged along the San Pedro River, and it was of concern to everyone who owned, traded, or relied on horses and cattle, which meant the entire populations of Contention, Charleston and Benson. "It is reported that a mysterious disease is at present prevailing among the cattle and horses along the San Pedro….Mr. McVeigh lost all his horses, five in number, and others have lost many cattle." It was thought that the substantial amount of stock coming up from Mexico may have brought plague to the area. "The disease is supposed to have been contracted from passing herds on their way from Sonora to San Carlos and other points of demand." [268] If true it would be yet another price paid by honest ranchers whose stock was now threatened by the import of unhealthy Mexican herds, many of them stolen by American rustlers raiding into Mexico.

A local joke regarding rustling and the use of fencing surfaced in the wake of the increase of these crimes that affected many along the San Pedro, in and around Contention and Charleston. "San Pedro farmer: Yes; barbed wire fence is expensive, but the hired man does not stop and rest five minutes on the top of it every time he has to climb it." [269]

PISTOL PLAY AND THE DEATH OF AN INNOCENT

As the railroad progressed toward Junction City (later to be known as Fairbank), news of yet another death surfaced. "Shot to Death by Accident. A melancholy accident resulting from the careless use of fire arms, occurred Sunday, at a railroad camp near the mouth of the Babacomari creek, about ten miles from this city, by which Daniel Hennesy came to his death. The circumstances are as follows: A boy named Carr, seventeen or eighteen years of age was employed carrying water and doing other work about the camp. He was the possessor of a small pocket pistol, which he was handling in a careless manner, when it was accidentally discharged, the ball entering the right side of Hennesy, who happened to be standing near. The unfortunate fell and expired almost instantly. Coroner Mathews held an inquest over the remains, and a verdict was returned in accordance with [the] facts as given above. The body was brought to this city [Tombstone] and the funeral took place yesterday. Deceased was a native of Ireland and about thirty-five years of age." [270]

THAT WRETCHED LITTLE HIVE KNOWN AS BENSON

Train yard at Benson, Arizona Territory, a town created by the railroad. Copy photo from the collections of John D. Rose.

Contention's new neighbor to the north, Benson, was acquiring a hard reputation, being victimized by the same ilk of predator that accompanies a boom town. But citizens there were loath to put up with their antics, as were their neighbors in Contention.

"SLUGGED AND SHOT. Brutal Assault and Robbery of a Wells-Fargo Messenger at Benson. Night before last John Brent, one of Wells-Fargo's oldest messengers (having been in their employ for sixteen years) was slugged, shot and robbed in Benson by some parties unknown. In company with James Harrington he was walking up the street when Harrington stepped into a house, leaving Brent on the street, he intending to follow Harrington in. But a few moments had elapsed when Harrington heard a pistol shot, but upon going out could see no one, not even Brent, who had been struck with a slung-shot or some blunt instrument, and, when

173

probably in the act of drawing his pistol, was shot and afterwards robbed of $75. Upon coming to, Brent staggered into a tent occupied by a negro, who built a fire and did the best he could for the wounded man. Mr. Brent was brought to Tombstone by yesterday's coach and placed in comfortable quarters at the Cosmopolitan hotel. Dr. Goodfellow attended him and extracted the ball, which had entered about four inches below the left nipple, and either passed around the ribs or went straight through the body, lodging just under the skin, two inches from the backbone. The wound is a dangerous one, but recovery is not impossible. If the perpetrators of this outrage should be discovered a necktie party should hang them at once and throw their bodies to the coyotes." [271]

"…The bustling little burg of Benson, down on the San Pedro…bears a rather unsavory reputation. It was for a long time known far and wide as the chosen haunt of a disreputable crowd of 'sure thing' sharpers, called the 'top and bottom gang,' among whom were the 'Off Wheeler,' 'Big Burns' and other congenial spirits of like kidney. At last the respectable portion of the citizens became weary of the 'work' being done by the 'top and bottom' gentry, and the result was that one fine day last summer the latter were incontinently 'fired out' of the town, which soon settled down into the quiet peacefulness of a country crossroads." [272]

"J.E. McComas, Justice of the Peace at Benson, and a very efficient officer, by the way, was in the city [Tombstone] yesterday. The judge reported that Benson was "orderly quiet since the exodus of the bunko sharps," to which the Epitaph quipped, "Their loss is our gain." [273]

Further south, Contention's advance continued. "Ten bars of bullion were shipped by the Grand Central mill yesterday at Contention by Well[s], Fargo & Co.'s express…Dunbar & Behan have established a corral in Contention, situated directly opposite the depot, where they will be pleased to see their friends and customers." Stage coach operators such as Sandy Bob Crouch had adjusted their schedules to the running of the railroad from Contention. It hadn't been a full year since Bob Paul had shot it out with the attackers near Drew's Station, telling them "I hold for no one!" Now commercial stage travel from Contention City north to Benson had become recent history. "Sandy Bob's accommodation line to Contention leaves Tombstone daily. Stages to connect with the east bound train leave at 5:30 a.m. Stages to connect with the west bound train leave at 12:30 p.m. Stages for Contention leave at 4 p.m. Office on Allen street, opposite the Cosmopolitan hotel." [274]

Readers must have chuckled at this sarcastic blurb: "It was just like the lunk headed stupidity of a San Pedro hired man to put the cow in the stall under the shed, and tie that measly backed old mule behind the wood-house. And the farmer never knew anything about it till he went out before daylight to milk, and got kicked clear across the yard and stopped against a barbed wire fence. He did not raise the man's wages, but he raised the man about four feet into the air." [275]

174

Contention City never gained the amount of press in Tombstone that Charleston did, due in part to the fact that it maintained some self-restraint, versus Charleston, the epicenter of calamity along the San Pedro. By early 1882, the most important building in Contention, to the Tombstone perspective, was the N.M. & A. train depot. This key structure was again misidentified as being on the west side of the San Pedro, and a report on roadways to the Cochise County Board of Supervisors echoed the error. "The viewers appointed by the Board of Supervisors to select the site for a road from this place [Tombstone] to Contention have filed their report. They suggest the present road until it reaches a point near Contention, where the road leads to the mills, from thence to run directly across the river to the New Mexico and Arizona Railroad depot." [276] Maps of the day contradict this. The fact that the board had asked for a road study shows the importance of access to Contention, but the fact that the report is in error shows that Tombstone knew very little of this riverside community to which it owed so much.

ONE MORE IN THE NAME OF LOVE

Contention experienced an accident of a tragic nature. When a fire got out of control, John R. Gibbon and Malvina Lopez, reportedly a prostitute, died in the cabin they shared at Contention. The couple had gone to bed with a pan of coal burning in their room, likely for warmth on a winter night. "This was the unhappy pair who climbed the golden stair on the fumes of a pan of charcoal Monday night. From the burned pants and the position of the unfortunate John, it would seem that he tried to repent the rash act, but was too far gone to get to the door and open it, so he crawled back to the bed where his body was found prone across the corpse of Malvina." [277] Clothing and a hat left near the burning pan caused the fire to spread. "The room was adobe and had neither window nor chimney, only one very tight fitting door…The walls of the room, the bed and clothes and the bodies were very much discolored by the smoke." Gibbon was a butcher at Contention, and it appears that by the time he awoke, he was already rendered incapable of saving himself by exiting through the door. "From the position of the man's body he must have made an effort to get out. He was found lying across the bed and the body of the woman." [278]

Ironically, this same home was the scene of a fight just one week earlier, which nearly one quarter of the entire population of Contention would witness, a scene that was more typical of Charleston than Contention. "About a week ago some Mexicans got into a fight in this same house and one of them, named Lonordo Moreno was shot and killed. The two men that did the shooting mounted their horses and rode out of town, firing their revolvers in the air. Three cow boys mounted their horses and pursued them, and a very exciting running battle was witnessed by about one hundred citizens from atop Head Center Hill. About fifty shots were fired. The murderers were so closely pressed that they had to leave their horses and take to the brush. Night coming on, the cow boys secured the horses and came in. The murderers escaped and next morning were seen riding between Benson and Tres Alamos, having stolen two horses from the Mormons." [279]

175

While that tragedy was still fresh, a lighter bit of news took place at Contention. P.A. Duper had traveled from Tombstone to Contention, and while walking to the train depot he attempted to reload his pistol, when it went off. He was angry that he was arrested, and four charges filed against him. [280]

AN AFTERNOON RIDE FROM TOMBSTONE TO CONTENTION CITY

Tombstone's consummate diarist George Parsons would take an afternoon ride with friends to Contention City. For Parsons, the thought of seeing a locomotive was worth the trip, as it was one of the technological wonders of his day. Going along with friends only made the idea more appealing, that is, until an inexperienced rider drew his concern for her safety.

"Celebrated day by going to Contention City on horseback-quite a party of us for ride and to see the cars, it being a little more than two years since I had seen a steam engine – locomotive - cars and track. Mrs. Glover chaperoned party. She, Miss Bessie Brown [first operator of the Tombstone's Grand Hotel], Miss Herring [daughter of Earp attorney William Herring who traveled with the Earps to court with a gun in her lap], Miss Thomas, Miss Locker and Miss Moses were the ladies and Jimmy Eccleston, Herring, Frank Earle, Casey Clum and I were the gentlemen. We were joined on the road by Ross and Strong, who were not very cordially welcomed by the ladies." Parsons soon learned that not all the ladies on the trip were well experienced on horseback.

"The poor girl-Miss L[Locker] - had never ridden horseback outside of a yard before and was bold enough to venture on a 25 mile ride, not knowing any better. Result was I had to look after her very closely and had a hard day's work of it and no pleasure to speak of, being afraid all of the time that something would happen…good lunch at Myer's new hotel [at] Contention…" Parsons was concerned that Miss Locker couldn't safely make the return trip to Tombstone on horseback, but when offered a wagon ride home, she refused, so the party began the return trip. It wasn't going well. A wagon happened along while they were returning to Tombstone, and Parsons and others finally were able to "put her in one [a wagon] though on the road." Miss Locker's luck had not improved with this precaution, and Parsons and the others concerned would have been wise to take a better look at the type of passenger already in the wagon before placing her in it. Only after they had done so did they notice "a manacled prisoner in behind and that the driver and another were armed….Escorted her a few miles and then she rode again, not caring to go into town, of course, with a prisoner." Miss Lock's luck remained unchanged, and Parsons fared no better. "Had a hard chase after her horse which got away from us. Chased him over rocks and gullies some distance. My horse was a good one – Epitaph - and finally caught the beast. Great time all around. I seemed to have much sympathy. Am glad all had a good time even though I did not." [281]

The Tombstone District would see the birth of yet another community. Junction City as it was originally known, developed late in the area. Had the site been key to the mining and milling that was Tombstone's lifeblood, it would have seen its rise over two years before. But this was created by the demands of the railroad. "The new town on the San Pedro river now being surveyed by [Tombstone] city surveyor Kelleher, is to be named Junction City. It is situated on the east bank of the San Pedro, about 1 ½ miles south from the Grand Central mill, on the land of the Peck Brothers, and at the junction of the Benson branch with the main line of the A.T. & S.F. railroad [The N.M. & A.]. Extensive preparations are being made for the erection of [the] depot and freight buildings, and also for the erection of commission houses and other buildings." [282]

Shipping of all kinds of goods became a supplement to the economy of Contention City. "The furniture for the Grand hotel is all at Contention, and is expected up tomorrow. It was all purchased by Mr. [Archie] McBride at the manufactory in St. Louis, Missouri, and is of late designs and workmanship. The freight bill amount[s] to about $3,000, sufficient of itself to furnish a pretty good house." [283] The Grand Hotel and all of its contents would later be destroyed in a disastrous fire on May 26th, 1882 in Tombstone. The owner would not rebuild. A building put up later on that site would be a one-story structure.

A couple of news bites may not have contributed to Contention's sense of well-being. "A case of small-pox is reported at the county hospital. The patient was sent up from Contention and admitted before the nature of the disease was known. He will be removed to the pest house where there will be no danger of the contagion spreading. There is no reason for any alarm as all reasonable precautions will be taken by the authorities." [284] This news from a Contention City restaurant: "A Man, who was a native of Portugal, died of heart disease in Long's restaurant, at Contention, yesterday." [285]

EAST IS EAST AND WEST IS WEST AND BOTH ARE THE SAME TO ONE REPORTER AT CONTENTION

But news of an undeniable importance would soon come from Contention, and the Tombstone press was quick to acknowledge the significance. "An Epitaph reporter took a flying trip yesterday through Contention and the embryo town of Junction City, and thus records his impressions of what he saw. An effort is being made to remove the town of Contention to the western bank of the San Pedro. There are two reasons for this—the railroad being on that side[east] of the river, and the Contention mill being on that side of the river, and the Contention mill being in need of a greater area for its tailings. The mud dam around this pond has already been erected to as great a height as safety permits, and a portion of the structure recently gave way, without, however, doing any damage. If more space cannot be obtained, it will be necessary to surround the tailings with a high stone or concrete wall at great expense. Already a considerable town is springing up on the western [eastern] bank, the most conspicuous buildings of which are Meyers' hotel and the railroad depot. The former building was erected nearly a year ago, the proprietor having the foresight to see that the town would eventually tend in that direction. THE NEW RAILROAD DEPOT is probably the most commodious and elegant structure of the kind in Arizona. The main building is two stories, containing below a large ticket and telegraph office and two passenger rooms. These rooms are elegantly finished in narrow panels of light and dark woods. In the second story are elegant offices for the use of the railroad officials. From the main building a one story addition for freight purposes extends for over one hundred feet, and beyond this are suitable out buildings. These buildings all have projecting roofs, are quite ornate in their architecture, neatly finished in every detail, are painted in a rich, dark color, and all surrounded with a wide platform. The depot buildings are built between the main and side tracks [the N. M. &A. laid track on the east side of the river], and the platform is of great length, affording ample accommodations to passengers and freight. Opposite the depot the leading merchant of Contention, L. Marks, is building a large store for the accommodation of his wholesale business, and a number of other structures are going up, giving the place quite an air of activity. The river is spanned at this point only by a foot-bridge, but is intended at once to build a substantial structure for teams, a step which the large freighting business from the depot to Tombstone will render necessary. From this point the railroad keeps UP THE RIVER for about four miles, passing from the west to the east bank [from Benson, the railroad passes from the west bank to the east bank north of Contention and continues south on the east bank to Junction City]. About 2 ½ miles south of Contention the Grand Central mill is passed [also on the eastern bank]. This is one of the best appointed mills of the district, and the clatter of its 30 stamps affords a cheerful contrast to the quietness of the surrounding country." [286]

Myer's hand at business would later take an unfortunate turn. Judge Reilly was a combative Irish attorney and part time judge, and full time in the thick of trouble. He once was arrested by Wyatt Earp in his own court room. Reilly produced evidence that convinced Judge Felter that he was the trustee of creditors who were unhappy with Myer's declining returns. After the trial "Judge Reilly then concluded to shut the shanty and sell out the furniture and household utensils…" [287]

A QUIET AFTERNOON AT A MOUNTAIN SPRING

On the morning of March 24th, 1882, Wyatt Earp and his posse were busy breaking camp near the San Pedro River, between Contention City and Drew's Ranch. They were about to head toward a spring in the Whetstones that Wyatt referred to as "Iron Spring," and it was to be a meeting point for badly needed funds. During the previous evening, March 23rd, Wyatt was conversing with a man at his undisclosed camp. "'Tell Gage that I need a thousand dollars,' Earp had said to Charles Smith, his emissary in time of need, the night before. 'Have him split it up into tens and twenties if he can, with a couple of fifties.' 'Meet us at Iron Springs, and don't lose any time; we'll be waiting there.'" Gage had helped Wyatt Earp financially before, and would do so yet again. As head of the Grand Central mine at Tombstone and mill at Contention City, he had already contributed to the Earps' and Holliday's second round of bail money during the Spicer hearing, and now he was aiding during Wyatt's "Vendetta Ride."

As Earp and the rest of his posse broke camp on the morning of March 24th, they headed westerly toward Iron Spring. The remote location would offer a safe place to receive E.B. Gage's critical funds, and allow their horses a much needed drink of water. As Doc Holliday later recalled, "…about 3 o'clock on a warm day after a long and dry ride from the San Pedro river, we approached a spring which was situated in a hollow…" [288] The area was long known, especially for travelers on horseback riding from Contention City to Tucson, as a short cut through the pass in the Whetstones where this spring is located. As Earp's posse approached the area of the spring, they surprised a party which had earlier arrived on the scene – a contingent of the cowboy gang. In the following fray, Earp claimed to have killed Curly Bill Brocius, a subject of Earp-related debate to this day. [289]

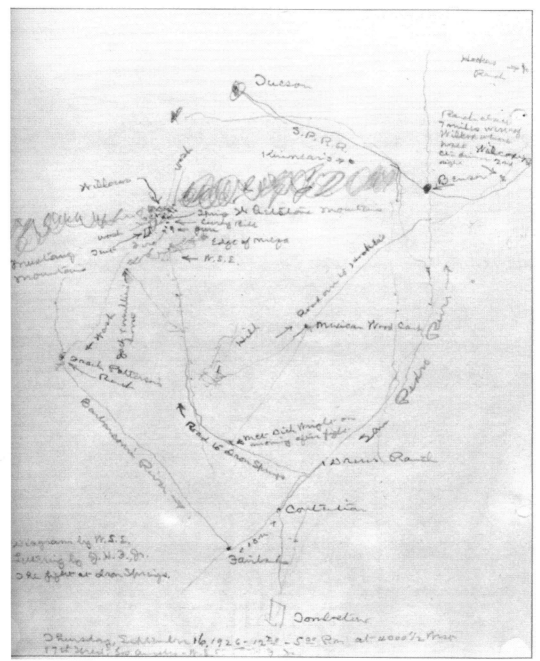

Depicting his version of the event, this is the map that Wyatt Earp drew and John Flood labeled regarding the Iron Spring shootout. Courtesy of the United States Marshals Foundation, Inc.

CHAPTER 12

LIFE AND DEATH ON A MEXICAN LAND GRANT

"And I thanked God I was takin' Virge away livin' and breathin' beside me." –Allie Earp

Contention and the future town of Fairbank had to contend with a land use issue of international implications. Both sites, along with Charleston and Millville to the south, were located atop the San Juan de las Boquillas y Nogales land grant. Honoring the rights of the actual owner of this grant was a stipulation of the Gadsden Purchase of 1854, which transferred ownership of a portion of Mexico to within the borders of the United States. This occurred more than two decades before Ed Schieffelin's rich silver discoveries would lead to the formation of stamp mills along the San Pedro, and nearby towns to supply the many needs of those working there.

The key for any American wishing to own a piece of this choice San Pedro property was to legally buy from the rightful heirs in Mexico, or buy from someone who had purchased the land from them. George Hill Howard had been making legal attempts to gain control of the grant, and by 1880, was successful. Although there were legal questions regarding some of his purchases with the rightful heirs, progress with the heirs as well as the American courts had now made him the owner of the grant. He signed a portion of the grant over to his wife, and a portion to George Hearst. Now the two were in position to take advantage of the boom that had already begun in earnest. [290]

It was an issue that would arise early as Contention City, Charleston and Millville, and later Fairbank were sitting atop these grants, together with ranches and settlements along the Babocomari (spelled a variety of ways in accounts of the day). "Land Grants on the Barbocomari and the San Pedro. Contention City, March 20. Editor Nugget-One of the important features of your valuable paper has been your 'Answers to Correspondents,' which we have read with great interest, and been furnished much valuable information. We have no hesitancy in asking you questions. Our ranchmen are on the alert and mean to know where they stand. You have facilities for knowing which we have not. For instance:-Messrs. Petty & Kimble arrived at Fort Huachuca February 23d, 1880. The commanding officer, Major Whitside, advised them to follow down to the Barbacomori and there locate. They did so, and located on the land now known as the Petty & Kimble tract. The cloud as to title recently lowering over them creates in them a feeling of insecurity. Mr. Barnes also located on the Barbacomari. Mr. Landers, Mr. [Daniel N.] Cable, and others, on the San Pedro, have likewise located ranches. All these people are pioneers, and during their time Apaches have been the principal crop. If you as a journalist, can give information as to the boundaries of these so-called grants, publish it, that these settlers may know where they stand. If the inevitable comes, and these grants are good, then let all compromise on such a liberal basis as to save contention and extra costs to innocent settlers." [291]

Concerns arose that some ranchers in the Contention area thought they had settled in good faith on public lands, but soon learned that they may have in fact located on the privately owned Boquillas land grant. If they had not purchased their lands from Howard and Hearst or the rightful heirs of the other grants, their ownership was in question.

"The sooner the titles to all the grants in Arizona are settled the better for our people. We have along the San Pedro river a number of ranches, the settlers on which are bona fide, and settled here years ago when no one claimed the lands, and they thought it was public land of the United States, and now, after years of toil and personal risk, find they are trespassers on private property. These people are the least grumblers, and would to-day or tomorrow, or on any day, willingly pay to the owners of the grant a fair sum to retain the homes they have made and where their children have been born. We hope that this grant question will be settled promptly." [292]

As the issue of the true ownership and use of these lands moved through federal channels, it became local news to those living in the area. "Mr. G. Hill Howard, the attorney for the following named Mexican land grants in Arizona, 'San Juan de Los Boquillos y Nogales.,' 'San Jose de Sonoita,' 'San Rafael del Valle' and 'Los Nogales de Elias,' who obtained a favorable report and decision thereon from the U.S. Surveyor-General of Arizona, has, at the present session of congress, succeeded in obtaining a favorable report from the committee on private land claims recommending congress to sustain the report and decision of the Surveyor-General in these land claims and recommends their confirmation by congress.

"The 'San Juan do Los Boquillos y Nogales' grant is situated in Cochise county and lies along the San Pedro, with a width on either side of the river of a mile and a half, its northern boundary being at about the stone house of the Mormon settlement [St. David], about six miles northerly from Contention, and its southern boundary is the northern boundary of the 'San Rafael del Valle' grant, about two and a half miles southerly from Charleston—five and a half Mexican leagues in length by one width.

"The 'San Rafael del Valle' grant is also in Cochise county and lies along the San Pedro, four Mexican leagues in length by one width, its northern boundary being the Boquillos y Nogales grant and its southern boundary at or near Hereford. The Contention, Grand Central and Tombstone Mill and Mining companies have purchased their mill sites on the Boquillos y Nogales grant, through and from Messrs. Howard and [George] Hearst.

"Messrs. Howard and Hearst, claimants of the grant, have laid out a town on the same, across the river and opposite Contention mill. They will also lay out a town at or about Kendall, or the junction of the San Pedro and Babocomari streams." [293] This would give rise to the second Contention City site, on the western side of the San Pedro, of which a map tracing still survives to this day.

The climax of the Cowboy Vendetta against the Earps took place on the evening of March 18th, 1882, at the Campbell and Hatch Saloon in Tombstone. Wyatt was observing his

brother Morgan and Bob Hatch at a game of billiards when shots rang from the back of the saloon. Though mortally wounded, Morgan Earp was still alive, and family members quickly came to say goodbye. "His brother, Wyatt, Tipton and McMasters rushed to the side of the wounded man and tenderly picked him up and moved him some ten feet away, near the door of the card room, where Drs Matthews , Goodfellow and Millar, who were called, examined him, and after a brief consultation pronounced the would mortal. He was then moved into the card room and placed on the lounge where in a few brief moments he breathed his last surrounded by his brothers Wyatt, Virgil, James and Warren, with the wives of Virgil and James and a few of his most intimate friends. Notwithstanding the intensity of his mortal agony, not a word of complaint escaped his lips…His body was placed in a casket, and sent to his parents at Colton, Cal., for burial, being guarded to Contention by his brothers and two or three of his most intimate friends. The funeral cortege started away from the Cosmopolitan hotel about 12:30 yesterday [March 19, 1882], with the fire bell tolling out its solemn peals of 'Earth to earth, dust to dust.'"[294]

Above Morgan Earp image and below original Campbell & Hatch token from the collections of John D. Rose.

183

"Already, James Earp, the oldest of the five brothers, had left the day before, with the body of Morgan, for their home at Colton, California. 'Virgil, you and your wife will have to go home to California,' Wyatt said, 'I can't look after you here and run down Morgan's assassins too.'

"And Virgil consented to go: not graciously, not without a protest; almost a quarrel. There was a score or two he wished to settle before he left.

"'But all those fellows will have left the country before you get on your feet again,' argued his brother. 'And besides, I can't look after you and round them up.' 'They're not going to prove any more alibies on me!' 'I tell you Virg, it's the only sensible thing, and you've got to go!' And Virgil Earp said he would go. With his wife and the driver beside him on the seat, the vehicle and its team of bays turned into the highway that led down to Contention, early in the morning of a wonderful Spring day, before the sun had climbed the mountain peaks.

"Hardly had they left the outskirts of the town when four riders appeared on the road behind. Earp had made up his mind that there would be no more ambush and no more alibies, and he and Holliday and McMasters and Johnson followed at a distance in the rear that threatened disaster to any who might have planned an attack.

"Leaving the saddle horses at a livery upon their arrival at Contention, the driver of the buckboard and the team were returned to the County seat, [Tombstone] while Virgil Earp and his wife and the four riders boarded the train for Tucson." [295]

Virgil, whose wife Allie was more than eager to leave, acquiesced. As they left for the safety of California, Wyatt and posse would soon gun down Frank Stilwell, Indian Charlie, and Curly Bill Brocius.

On March 20th, local building contractor John Hanlon saw Virgil and Allie along with their protection on their final, tense trip from Tombstone to Contention. "When about half way between Tombstone and Contention, [Hanlon] saw the Earp party. Some were on horseback and some were in a buggy. Also saw the same party at Contention. There were Wyatt Earp, Warren Earp, Doc. Holliday, McMasters, an unknown party, and Virgil Earp and [a] lady; all had rifles and shot guns except Virgil Earp who had a pistol. McMasters is a small man." That Virgil would be the only one with a pistol rather than the more lethal shotgun makes sense given that one of his arms was now useless.

Of that journey, Virgil's wife Allie had a vivid recollection years later: "And I thanked God I was takin' Virge away livin' and breathin' beside me. We got in a wagon to start for the railroad junction [at Contention City]. Wyatt, Warren, Doc Holliday and some other men rode on horses beside us to form a guard. Just before we left, Albert Billicke whose father Chris owned the hotel came out and gave me a present of a six-shooter." [296]

ALLIE EARP SEES THE CONTENTION CITY DEPOT FOR THE LAST TIME

The New Mexico and Arizona Railroad Depot at Contention City, which was a point of civic pride at Contention, would take center stage as the Earp saga continued to unfold. A resident of Ash Canyon in the Huachuca Mountains shared the train ride from Contention City that Allie Earp spoke of. Nathan W. Waite, who had also worked in Bisbee as a saloonkeeper, noticed the Earps and was apparently close enough to them on the train to hear some of their conversation, as he later recalled, "…Virgil Earp and his wife, Warren Earp, Wyatt Earp, Doc Holliday and McMasters: [he] joined them at Contention; McMasters said that they would leave the train at Benson but afterwards changed their minds and came to Tucson to see Virgil Earp and his wife on their way to California. On the train McMasters particularly inquired as to the arrival and departure of trains at the Tucson depot. All had guns and McMasters had two belts of cartridges." [297]

After boarding the train at Contention, they traveled from there to Benson, and then "At dusk we got to the railroad station at Tucson and had some supper. Wyatt and Doc Holliday were nervous and kept whisperin' and clutchin' their guns." [298]

Z.T. Vail was the conductor on the train that would take the Earp party onto Tucson from Benson. He recalled that "…a lot of men got on the train, five or six of whom had guns." As conductor, Vail had insight to the traveling plans of the Earp party, given the tickets they had. "Two only had through tickets to Colton. They were Virgil Earp and wife." Upon their arrival at Tucson, Vail noted that "one man with two guns followed me into the freight house and there left them, [I] think that three or four had belts with cartridges." This was Doc Holliday, as Deputy U.S. Marshall J.W. Evans stated that he saw "Doc. Holliday get off the cars, with a shotgun in each hand, and walk towards the railroad office. Shortly afterwards saw him returning without any guns…Afterwards met Wyatt Earp at Porter's Hotel, and while talking to him Virgil Earp came out of the hotel and shook hands with him." [299]

THE HUNTER BECOMES THE PREY

At about 7:15 on the evening of March 20th, Frank Stilwell was "coincidentally" present at the Tucson depot as Virgil and Allie were about to board the train for California. Speculation exists that he was there to exact more revenge upon the Earps. "J. W. Evans was at the railroad depot when the train came in from the east…Saw Frank Stilwell at the depot when the train came in, and from the way his coat protruded thought he might have a pistol. Also saw Ike Clanton there.

"David Gibson was at the depot with checks for passengers baggage. Met the train news boy who said 'I guess there will be hell here to-night,' and when asked why said that 'the Earps and Holliday were aboard and were going to stop here as they had told him that the man who killed Morgan Earp was in Tucson.'"

S.A Bateman was a witness at the Tucson depot and noticed a man walking up and down by the side of the train with a Winchester rifle. Bateman found out that "the man in question was one of the Earps guarding a party that were going through to California; shortly afterwards saw a man and lady come out of the hotel, the man carrying one arm in a sling; two men carrying Winchester rifles walked between them. They got on the cars, the one outside still keeping guard and apparently looking everywhere. Afterwards saw one of them walking down the track and in about five minutes heard two shots which were quickly followed by five or six others; heard some cheering in the direction in which the shots were fired." [300] Frank Stilwell was dead. This was Wyatt's opening salvo in his Vendetta against those he believed had wounded Virgil and murdered Morgan.

VIRGIL AND ALLIE EARP FLEE THE PERFECT ARIZONA STORM

As Virgil and Allie finally made it across the Arizona border and then further into the interior of California, a feeling of relief swept over her. "Finally we reached the Colorado River and crossed the bridge into where we could see trees and green grass and all. I heaved a sigh of relief. 'The land that God made!'

"A man who had got on the train after us turned around and said, 'I see you folks are from Arizona too. Don't you reckon He [God] made Arizona too?'

"'Maybe so,' I said, 'but He must of forgotten all about it right afterward.' And that was how I felt then about Tombstone." [301]

Virgil and Allie were now safely across the border, but things in Tombstone were not settling down. "WOULD NOT BE ARRESTED," The Nugget told its readers. "The Earp Party Refuse to be Arrested by Sheriff Behan, and Leave The City. Sheriff Behan yesterday received a telegram from the authorities at Tucson, requesting him to arrest Wyatt Earp, Doc. Holliday, Sherman McMasters and one Johnson, and hold them until further advices. Shortly after the receipt of the telegram, Sheriff Behan went to the Cosmopolitan Hotel, where he found the two Earp brothers, Wyatt and Warren, Holliday, Texas Jack, Johnson and McMasters. The Sheriff informed the party of his mission, when, in an instant, each one leveled a sixshooter at the officer, and peremptorily refused to submit to arrest. The Sheriff retired, and immediately took measures to raise a posse to enable him to accomplish his duty. SCORES OF VOLUNTEERS proffered their services to aid…and arms for a sufficient number were quickly obtained from the store of P.W. Smith & Co. Immediately upon the enforced retirement of the Sherriff from the hotel, the Earp party, six in number, also left the premises, all heavily armed, and betook themselves to the corral, corner of Allen and Third streets, where their horses were, ready saddled, and quickly mounting, they rode rapidly out of town, in the direction of Contention." [302] This report along

186

with other rumors swirling about town now brought the focus of the drama back to Contention City.

GEORGE HAND AT CONTENTION CITY, AND THE EARP VENDETTA

On Thursday morning, March 23rd, Tucson saloon keeper and diarist George Hand was preparing for a trip to Contention to visit an old civil war pal who had been in the California Column, Billy Bradley, a Contention City Saloon keeper whose wife was helping to start a school there. Circumstances on the ground at Contention had changed rapidly just before Hand arrived for his visit. The Earps had delivered Morgan's body to Contention just four days earlier. In response to his own anger and grief, Wyatt Earp would take matters into his own hands to settle those scores, starting with Frank Stilwell in Tucson. George Hand journeyed to Contention in the very middle of the unfolding turmoil. After a light breakfast and gathering his trunk and his dog Rip, Hand headed for the Tucson train depot and the journey began. "We had a pleasant ride to Benson, only stopping a moment at Pantano. Jerry Barton, who had just been discharged by the court for killing a Mexican some time ago, was also a passenger. This is my first visit to the town of Benson. I was surprised to the extent of it. The change here to the Atchison & Topeka [N.M. & A] which takes us to Contention City being accomplished, we were off and arrived 11 A.M…"

Friday the 24th was Hand's first full day at Contention. What may have appeared as the start of a routine morning began "with a good breakfast but the papers did not arrive from Tombstone and we were obliged to wait until 11 A.M. for a morning paper (Star) from Tucson. The cow boys, twenty or more, have been prowling around all the morning. They are well mounted, well armed and seem intent on biz. They are in search for the Earp party who took breakfast 2 miles above here this morning." Hand saw the same group later that afternoon. "3 P.M. –they again came from Tombstone, watered their horses here and started again at the double quick for Kinnear's ranch."

On March 25th Hand wrote, "The dept. sheriff and posse arrived here this evening. Raining so hard they put their horses in stable…Report says four cow boys encamped at a spring met the Earp party and had a fight. Texas Charley had his horse killed and W. Earp was shot. A man came in town 10:30 this evening to get candles, says he saw the Earp party at Drew's ranch a few miles from [north of] here. Closed house 11 o'clock…" (Wyatt Earp left this fight unscathed, and Texas Jack Vermillion did indeed lose his horse at this engagement. Flood manuscript, page 301) "A man came in town [Contention] 10:30 this evening to get candles, says he saw the Earp party at Drew's ranch [a] few miles from here." [303]

Garbled reports from Contention soon reached the Tombstone press. "The first dispatch from Contention was received at 8 p.m., and is as follows: Behan and posse just arrived. Four of the posse were encountered by the Earps, yesterday, while at dinner. Several shots were exchanged. The Earps fled, except Wyatt, who dismounted and emptied his shotgun. Texas Jack's horse was killed. Wyatt is supposed to be wounded. The posse were unhurt.

"The latest from Contention was received at 1 a.m. this morning…The Earps were within thirty yards of the camp when the fight commenced. The shooting occurred in the Whetstones, twelve miles distant. Wyatt, without a doubt, is wounded. Sheriff Behan is here [Contention City]. He states that four men engaged in the fight had no connection with his posse. There is much excitement here, but the report of the killing of Curly Bill is not credited. The Earp party were seen from the train, three miles below here, this afternoon." [304] Though these incomplete reports were less than accurate, it was clearly the talk of the town at Contention, creating a buzz of rumors ranging from the partially accurate to the ridiculous. Wyatt Earp's whereabouts during his Vendetta ride were subject to a great deal of local speculation.

And again from Hand, Sunday March 26th, 1882. "Cold, windy…The sheriff party left, struck the trail of the Earp party a few miles below town, returning toward Tombstone and followed it. Sheriff Paul of Pima Co. still at Tombstone. Waite & McClusky arrived from Tucson, brought some papers & other articles for me…Jack Schwartz was here yesterday….Last evening a man named Peal was killed in Charleston [Millville] by two masked men. [Sheriff Bob] Paul passed here from Tombstone this afternoon…No more news from the Seat of War in Cochise Co…" [305]

"The town has been full of reports for the last two or three days as to the whereabouts of the Earp party, and their probable movements. No sooner had one report got well under way before another was started that contradicted it. There has been marching and countermarching by the sheriff and his possee [sic] until the community has become so used to the ring of spurs and clank of steel that comparatively little attention is paid to the appearance of large bodies of horsemen in the streets. Yesterday afternoon the sheriff with a large force started down the road toward Contention, possibly to follow up the report that the party had been seen in the Whetstone mountains, west of the San Pedro river…"

The Earps had already evacuated more family from the now inflamed Tombstone area. It would mean another wagon ride to Contention of a solemn nature. "Mrs. James Earp and Mrs. Wyatt Earp left to-day for Colton, California, the residence of their husbands' parents. These ladies have the sympathy of all who know them, and for that matter the entire community. Their trials for the last six months have been of the most severe nature." As the two Earp wives left the area, the drama between Wyatt Earp and his pursuers continued. "Sheriff Behan, with a posse of twelve men, left town at 12:45, going towards Contention." Those in Contention who had wished for a cessation of the drama had yet to see relief from it. [306]

IT DOESN'T PAY TO BE RICH

News south of Contention only added to wave of violence which was now dominating the headlines on a regular basis…" An Old Man Murdered near St. Davids. After the EPITAPH

188

went to press last evening, word was brought from Contention of the murder of an old man who lived across the San Pedro, opposite St. Davids, the Mormon settlement about six or seven miles below Contention. The name of the man was McMenomy. He owned a sheep ranch, upon which he was living alone at the time of his death. He was shot through the head and must have died instantly. It was supposed that he had money, and robbery was the probable cause of the damnable deed. Justice Smith of Benson, was notified of the murder and proceeded to the spot to hold an inquest, the result of which has not been learned." [307]

The Nugget echoed the Epitaph's coverage, with a few minor differences, placing it in context of the killings that had occurred in the entire area. "MURDER MOST FOUL. Another Unppovoked [sic] Assassination Near Contention. Late yesterday evening intelligence reached here of another murder near Contention. A Nugget reporter was detailed to investigate the matter, and ascertain if there was any truthful foundation for the rumor…another foul assassination had added one more dark stain to the fair fame of Cochise county. The circumstances of the murder, as far as ascertained, characterize it as one of the most fiendish and cold-blooded of the SERIES OF DEVILISH ATROCITIES which have been committed within our county's borders during the past ten days. The victim was an old man named McMenomy, who owned a sheep ranch opposite the Mormon settlement, about five miles from Contention. He was a quiet, inoffensive man, and believed by some to have quite a sum of money in his cabin, where he resided alone, and it is now thought that it was the hope of gain that furnished a motive for the perpetrators of the crime. The intelligence was brought to Benson yesterday afternoon, and Justice J.B. Smith, acting Coroner, hastily impanelled a jury and departed for the scene of the murder. As yet no clew is known to have been obtained to the murderers…" [308] Three men had arrived at Contention on March 29th, and reported the murder.

"A DISPATCH from Contention reports the murder of Patrick McMenomen [sic], known in his neighborhood as 'Old Sheep,' at his ranch five miles north of that place, last night. Robbery is assigned as the cause. On the 16th instant [the] deceased was in Tucson and made the final proof at the Land Office for the south half of section 20, and the north half of section 29, township 18 south, range 21 east. He is said to have been possessed of considerable means." [309]

Billy Ohnesorgan had known McMenomy, and recalled that he lived in a stone house. McMenomy had "located a lot of land and herded sheep. He used to carry a sack around with him and gather mesquite beans. Had a whole shack full. One day he was found dead-was found in the back of the room with a bullet hole through him. The Mormons brought suit for title to his land and got it." [310]

The same day that the McMenomy tragedy hit the presses more information surfaced on a recent killing to the south of Contention, at the railroad camp along the Babacomari. It would fall to Justice J.B. Smith of Contention to lead the inquest into the death of Peter Smith. "Inquest on the Body of Peter Smith, Before Justice B. Smith at Contention. Information having been laid before me, J.B. Smith, a justice of the peace in and for township No. 1, County of Cochise, that a man, whose name is unknown to me at the time, was dead at a railroad camp on the Babacomari creek, and it was supposed that he came to his death by foul murder. I immediately started on the construction train…accompanied by Dr. J. G. Barney [a physician at Contention] and department Sheriff John B Ludwig, arriving at the camp, where the body lay, and an inquest was held on the body, after a coroner's jury had been summoned. Several witnesses were sworn and testified, and also, Dr. Barney, who made an autopsy of the body. After deliberation the jury rendered the following verdict: We, the undersigned coroner's jury empaneled to determine the cause of Peter Smith's death, do find that he was a native of Germany, about 23 years of age, and that he came to his death from a blow on the back of the head inflicted by a blunt instrument in the hands of Thos. Doland, on the night of the 21st of March, 1882." [311]

The Tombstone Epitaph made light of an otherwise serious situation, chiding that at least this killing hadn't happened at Tombstone. "A man named Peter Doland killed a young German named Peter Smith, with a poker, in Cochise County on the 21st inst., and so our neighbor keeps ahead of us." [312]

On March 25th, 1882, Hand wrote that "The dept. sheriff and J.P. [Justice of the Peace J.B. Smith] have gone to a railroad camp to hold an inquest on a man [Peter Smith] who died yesterday from the blow on the head [he had received] several days ago. Dept. sheriff & J.P. returned, wet & cold, found the man dead as stated before." [313]

YET ANOTHER CONTENTION MILL BEGINS

But not all news from Contention was bad. More construction was in the works which would further add to Contention's dominance as the top producing site of the entire Tombstone District for silver bullion. "Mr. C. Lind is in town again from Contention City, and informs us that his firm (Malter & Lind) have commenced grading for the new Sunset mill, which will be erected about a quarter of a mile below the Contention. It is to have 10 stamps, with a capacity for 15, and the reputation of the builders is a guarantee that it will be a good one. It will probably be finished sometime in October. The Boston Mill is somewhat delayed by the scarcity of lumber, but Mr. Lind thinks that by September it will be ready for business. Malter & Lind have also taken a contract to build a 10 stamp dry crushing mill in New Mexico, not far from Silver City."[314]

Contention City continued to report a steady prosperity in April of '82. "Mr. George Marks, late of the Maison Doree, of this city, was up from Contention to-day. He says they have established a branch store, with a warehouse, at the depot." Referring to the new Contention City which was being promoted on the west bank of the San Pedro by George Hearst, the Epitaph added that "Not much building is being done across the river, owing to a reluctance on the part of the people to leave their old quarters…" [315] More than that, a substantial railroad depot was now located on the east bank, giving the old Contention City site new life, flanked by stamp mills to its north and south. Simply put, the eastern bank of the San Pedro was the best investment for those living in Contention in 1882.

LOCAL HUMOR IN THE AMERICAN ETHNIC MELTING POT

Of the countless stage coach rides from Tombstone to Contention, and back again, little is known of what the conversation, or lack of was actually like. This article is more of an example of the humor of the day rather than a part of the historical record. "STAGE TALK. The Result of a Free and Easy American Habit. There was a stage full going to Contention, and, as usual on such occasions, the conversation soon became general. One of the passengers said: 'Probably there isn't a man in the coach that knows the name of the other, and yet we are all chatting as if we had been acquainted for years. This is one of the remarkable features of this great American Republic. In fact, it might almost be termed a national peculiarity, for no other people will exchange ideas without the formality of an introduction. Now, an Englishman would almost see another man drown before he would assist him without an introduction. A Frenchman would think a stranger who spoke to him a garroter; a Spaniard, a sharper, or one lacking the essentials of good breeding; a German would think it was queer, but they are more liberal in their views in this respect than any other people except ourselves. You see we are all good judges of human nature and not easily taken in.' 'If that's the case, said the sick passenger on the back, 'what do you think of Bill Slickum?' Now Bill WAS HIS BROTHER and he thought he was a pretty good fellow, and when the other would say he was one of the nicest men in the country, he would spring his relationship on him and stand in with him on general principles; but he was slightly astonished, for the talker said: 'Think of Bill Slickum? Why, I think he's the biggest stiff in the country.' 'Un vot you dink oof Peter Grout, vot lives 'tween de brewery, mit Allen street?' 'What, that old lager-beer stinker? Why he'd steal sourkraut from his blind grand-mother, and sell her wooden shoes for cord-wood.' By this time the sick passenger had straightened up, and hit the talker on the head with a whiskey bottle. The German lit on to him, because Peter was his uncle, and he beat him over the head with a paper bag of turkey eggs which he was taking home, and in less than half a minute that advocate of free conversational intercourse looked like a rum armelette or a well mixed whisky punch, and he believes now that any man who will address another without knowing him is a sneak thief or a prize fighter in disguise." [316]

IT TOOK ALL KINDS…

Contention was its own melting pot of sorts. If one could walk through its dusty streets, the amount of spoken accents would be surprising. The west was full of towns filled with immigrants whose origins spanned much of the globe, and Contention was by no means an exception. Voting records of 1882 offer but a sample of Contention's populace, as the vote excluded women and some minorities. It was unfortunate for them and us, as it makes it harder to follow up on their personal stories. Exclusion from voting rights in many cases also meant exclusion from the historical record.

Residing in Contention in 1882 was German born Leopold Alexander, who at the age of 27 worked as a Contention merchant. Irish born Edward Armstrong Spence, 26 years old, worked in one of Contention's mills. Alphonse Ayala, a native of Panama, was 35 in 1882 and worked as a laborer in Contention, and Canadian Frank Ballom was 32 years old working in a local mill. Dr. James G. Barney, who had comforted Mrs. Myers during her final moments of life, was born in the U.S. and was 44 years old in 1882; an Englishman named Milton Barret endured the physically demanding conditions of working in a stamp mill at the age of 43. Robert Joseph Barry was born in the U.S., and worked as a laborer at the age of 27. Gustav Bengston was far from home having been born in Sweden, and endured the hard work of a Contention stamp mill at the age of 42. Older yet for such work was U.S. born John Berry, also a mill man. William Franklin Bradley, who was a signer of the petition warning local thief, Hans Christiansen, that he had better move onto other more tolerant hunting grounds, was born in the U.S. and worked as a clerk, age 44. A twenty three year old Anthony Breen hailed from the Emerald Isle, and labored in a Contention mill, as did a native of the U.S., Alexander Burk. At the ripe old age of 65, American born Israel F. Burdick was making and selling shoes at Contention. John Canble was a member of Contention's upper income class, working as an engineer, was born in the U.S., and Mexican born Jose Miguel Castenada was a Contention merchant. Swiss born Lien Paul Cavalli offered his blacksmith skills to the small community along the San Pedro.

GIVE ME YOUR TIRED, YOUR POOR, HUDDLED MASSES, AT LEAST 472

American born Alexander Wells Chase offered the community his services as a surveyor, but ironically, the map that has surfaced of the western side of Contention was made by Tombstone surveyor H.B. Maxson. Canadian Thomas Copeland was 35 years old when working in one of Contentions mills; Carter Oliver Crane ranched near Contention; Milton Crane was a mill superintendent, both born in the U.S. Peter Burton Crane also ranched near Contention, and was 31 in 1882. Charles Dearwater was but 21 while working a Contention mill in 1882, born in the U.S.

George Harrison Drew, brother of Cora, who helped to build a stage station and home known as Drew's Station, was a teamster living at Contention, just a year after Bud Philpot was murdered 1600 feet from his family's home. He was 25 in 1882. John R. Dunn, born in Ireland, kept a saloon in Contention, and would have seen its seedy side on a regular basis. Henry Clay Echols was a miner late in life. U.S. born Curtis Smith Fitzpatrick was fifty years old working as a blacksmith at Contention. Edmond Waller Gale worked as a bookkeeper; Carson Alexander Gale - a miner, and Henry Patrick Gale - a teamster. Frenchman John Galin was a cook, probably in one of Contention's restaurants, and U.S. born Henry Grant was a carpenter, likely benefiting from its early construction boom. U.S.-born Charles Carrol Griswold would labor at a Contention mill, as did 28 year old Robert Emmett. Asa Hampton was 39 and a Contention laborer, and Silas Harnes was a Contention rancher, both born in the U.S. German-born Frank Harter was 32 and labored in a Contention mill in 1882, while Henry Kinney Hause had an occupation of a less physical nature, working as a Contention City clerk.

Patrick Healy was born in Ireland, and at the age of 33, labored in a mill, while U.S.-born Samuel Howell operated as a merchant. James Munroe Johnson was well into his career as an engineer at Contention, at the age of 55. Prussian born Isadore and Henry Kaufman, ages 29 and 35 respectively, were both merchants at Contention, an environment that may have seemed a different world from their origins. All totaled, the Great Register of 1882 listed seventy-two voters, out of an overall population of 472. [317] In both cases the numbers may have been low, as it was a challenge to count everyone in such remote locations, and a high percentage of the population was transitory. But what this limited sampling illustrates is a Contention City filled with different cultures from near and far-away lands, with customs that built a diverse, culturally enriched community on many levels. In this respect Contention, as with other locales in the district, had an international aspect too often forgotten in the study of the American West. It was a microcosm of an America that had already taken shape, where a dreamer from any corner of the globe could come and stake his or her claim to a peace of the dream, and in the process, add their talents, ambition, and culture to the American ideal and the American reality. In the case of Contention, they staked their claims in the shadow of the stamp mills pounding their way into prosperity day and night, and perhaps bought a piece of land in view of a lazy river, bordered by a railroad that would only add to their optimism about the future. Some may have believed that one day their children and grandchildren would own and operate businesses at Contention that they were now starting. Such was not to be the case, but it was their present reality, and they shared their dream with so many other places in the West.

CHAPTER 13

GEORGE HAND REPORTS MORE FROM CONTENTION CITY

"...the savages were almost at our doors...rivers of blood would mark their meandering." – Captain Hurst

Monday, March 27th, 1882. Stage arrived from Tombstone-no papers today. Train in 11 sharp. Gov. Tritle passed here for Tombstone. Very lonesome all day, no news & nothing to read..."

Tuesday, March 28th, 1882. Cold morning, clear & very pleasant. Stage from Tombstone for the paper-we have to wait till 2 P.M. Train from Benson on time. Mr. & Mrs. B. sent to the depot and rode up to the turn table."

Wednesday, March 29th, 1882. "News from Tombstone says two men killed at milk ranch [Jack Chandlers] above Tombstone..." This fight would square Billy Breakenridge against Zwing Hunt and Billy Grounds, assassins of Martin Peel at Millville. Grounds would die shortly after the fight, and much to the surprise of everyone, Hunt would recover, and worse yet, escape. Hand continued "Train in on time. Cap. Jeffords [known for his rapport with the late Apache Chief Cochise] & others arrived...Bradley & I inspected the Contention Mill this morning. Report of a dead man [McMenomy] at a sheep ranch 8 miles below here caused the J.P. to summon a coroner's jury to investigate. They brought the body here late in the evening and adjourned until morning."

Thursday, March 30th, 1882. "Fine morning-cool. The murdered man proved to be [McMenomy] and was found by two men traveling who went to the house for some food. They immediately reported the case. Jury met [at] 10 A.M but for lack of evidence adjourned sine die [without assigning a day for a further meeting or hearing]....No clue to the murderers yet...Funeral of McM...this afternoon. Meeting of the property holders this evening. Resolutions [were] passed and two men ordered to leave town. They left."

March 31st, 1882. "Very dull. Nothing of importance occurred today. Soldiers from [Fort] Huachuca arrived en route to Cal. & Washington Ty. [Territory] No one killed today."

Saturday April 1st, 1882. "...Soldiers left on cars. [railroad cars]

Following two uneventful days, on Tuesday April 4th, Hand recorded, "Man arrested this morning for stealing two pigs 1 day old. He was tried & sentenced but got away."

Wednesday, April 5th, 1882. "Cold. Constable found the pig thief early. Judge Smith took him to Tombstone. John Ludwig returned today and proceeded to get tight [drunk]."

Other highlights from Hand's Contention Diary include...

Friday, April 7th, 1882. Eastern Train arrived 11 A.M…Genl. W.T.S. [William Tecumseh Sherman]…arrived on the 5 P.M. train-remained only long enough for a few hand shakes and left for Tombstone." General Sherman was on a visit to Tombstone to assess and then advise President Chester Arthur as to whether or not he should declare martial law in the area; the President opted for the use of the bully pulpit, rather than more dramatic steps. [318]

Ike Isaacs used General Sherman's visit to promote his Keno Game in Tombstone. Preserved by the Isaacs scrapbook.

breakfast while they were in Tombstone.'" [319]

Sherman's colorful arrival at Tombstone befitted the areas growing reputation for wild west antics. His first encounter at Tombstone was "when the carriage he was in was within a few hundred yards of the town a cowboyish looking individual rode up and asked if General Sherman was there. Being answered in the affirmative, he pulled a pistol and fired two shots in rapid succession. That was the signal for a volley, and for a few minutes the air vibrated with the sharp reports of pistol shots, bursting of anvils and Chinese bombs. He said that Tombstone was a decidedly live town…The ladies of the party were also much pleased with the lively mining camp. Miss Poe naively remarked that she was expecting that at least there would be two or three men killed every day, and to her great disappointment, she added, in the suggestive language of the West, 'they hadn't a man for

195

While General Sherman continued his "march" to Tombstone, George Hand continued to record history at Contention.

Sunday April 9th, 1882, Easter. "…Vigilance committee had a meeting this evening-Bradley did not go."

Wednesday, April 12th, 1882. "Got a little full [drunk] toward evening. Took a walk into Sonora [likely the Mexican quarter of Contention] for the first time since my arrival here. Saw Dona Mercedes McCarty. She gave me a very cold reception…" [320]

The Contention road saw travelers from all walks of life. Prisoner Zwing Hunt, who shot M. R. Peel down in cold blood at Millville on March 25th 1882, was spotted on it after his escape from the law. "Zwing Hunt and his abductors (?) are said to have staid Thursday night at a chicken ranch about two miles below town, on the Contention road. It is believed that this report is true, as Harry Jones, who lives there, is said to have told it in town yesterday. Quien Sabe." [321]

CROSSING A LINE THAT SHOULD NEVER HAVE BEEN CROSSED AT CONTENTION

In April of 1882 Contention had a local trouble maker to contend with. A town drunk known as "Big Jake" had on more than one occasion been disarmed by Deputy Sheriff John Baker Ludwig for going about town drunk and intimidating people with his pistol. But when he threatened to harm a child living in Contention, he had crossed a line that even most outlaws in the wildest of the west knew never to cross. Under the title of "Served Him Right," the Epitaph told its readers that "On the 13th inst. (yesterday) Deputy Sheriff J.B. Ludwig, of Contention, arrested Jacob Fisher, alias 'Big Jake,' for being drunk and disorderly, and took him before the justice where he was convicted and sentenced to thirty days in the county jail. Mr. Ludwig delivered him safely at the county hotel [jail] this forenoon and turned him over to mine host, Mr. [William Henry] Soule. The circumstances are briefly these. For a long time, now, this fellow has been accustomed to getting drunk and flourishing his pistol around promiscuously to the great danger of the lives of respectable people. The deputy sheriff has upon several occasions disarmed him to prevent danger. Yesterday he heard a child screaming in great fright, and went out and saw Big Jake holding up one about six or seven years old, flourishing a big knife threatening to cut off the child's ear. He arrested the fellow with the after results above related. Mr. Ludwig is to be commended as a faithful officer for bringing this fellow to a just and deserved punishment." [322]

In a surprisingly callous reaction, diarist George Hand was sympathetic to "Big Jake." Thursday, April 13th, 1882. "Big Jake,'Dutch,' arrested for frightening a child. He was sent up for 30 days-a very heavy punishment for such a trifling offense."

George Hand continues: Monday May 1st, 1882. "Windy & dull, very quiet. Dr. Barney, in returning from visiting patients down river, saw some Indians. He reports that they shot at him. He was scared but emptied his six shooter at them and put on the whip for town. The news made quite a sensation. The ladies of Contention were scared and the men were parading with guns & pistols, expecting the Indians in town every moment. They did not come. We slept on our arms [guns] and awoke safe in the morning."

Tuesday, May 2nd, 1882. Fine morning. No Indians. The story of the Dr. was true but the Indians were Papagoes. They did not fire at him nor did they know that he was shooting at them. Capt. Harris of Camp [Fort] Huachuca with 10 men was in town-went below [town, meaning to the south of Contention City], found the Indians. No trouble is anticipated. The Dr. feels very sore [likely embarrassed given Papagoes were nothing like the warrior Apache tribe] over his fight. O.A. Hyatt arrived in town this evening, hunting for cattle." [323]

INDIANS! WELL, MAYBE

What Hand is referring to came to be known as "THE CONTENTION SCARE. The following dispatches explain themselves, and only serve to show the material of which rumors are made. CONTENTION, May4.--Captain Hurst, Tombstone: A Mexican by the name of Serapia Peralta brought the news of Indians. He left here at daylight this morning with a wagon to haul wood about four miles north of here. He saw fresh Indian tracks, and half a mile away saw a band of Indians numbering not less than one hundred. They were well armed, and were on foot, making for the Whetstones. The Mexican came here as soon as possible, with empty wagon, and reported what he had seen. The Mexican is truthful. He has no reason for making false reports. [Despite knowing the name of the man who first reported the Indians in the area, it's an indicator of the racial climate that he was repeatedly referred to as the "Mexican."]

"Captain Hurst immediately telegraphed for confirmation of the report, and while awaiting an answer made all necessary preparations to forward troops to that point if necessary. The following is the answer:

"CONTENTION, 2 p.m.--Captain Hurst: From the best information I can gather the bands of Indians that passed four miles north of this place are Papagoes. There has been a number of them down the river, about four miles below Contention, making ollas. No doubt but they are the Indians seen. J.B. Smith." [324]

The assumption was that Apaches were raiding the area, but before this was disavowed, a near frenzy had broken out in Tombstone and Contention, and an army officer who should have known better than to represent local rumor as official military report was at the heart of the problem. A chronic fear in the Tombstone district was of an Indian outbreak. If Apaches left San Carlos reservation, they would often kill whomever they encountered as they didn't want witnesses alive who could betray their last known location. Apaches never chose to fight on disadvantaged ground, and they were careful at picking their targets. So the idea that they would attack heavily armed and populated towns like Contention and Tombstone, was impractical and unlikely.

197

"Hostiles at Contention. Last night the startling intelligence was...around town that the Indians had attacked Contention, and that life and property was in jeopardy. Diligent inquiry on the part of an Epitaph reporter was unable to get a detailed account of the transaction. The telegraph account office at Contention being closed, we were unable to wire for further particulars. The following telephone message was received, which is authentic: 'Indians appeared near town this evening in force. Fired on Dr. Girbis about a half mile below the mill. The doctor returned the fire, killing one Indian. Send rifles and ammunition to the mill as soon as possible.' The above dispatch was received by the acting superintendent of the Contention mine. The required aid was sent.

"Later.—Messrs. Rice and Goodale, of the Contention mine, with a posse of eight men, went to Contention in answer to a telephone message. They returned at 2:30 this morning and report all quiet at Contention. There were no Indians visible and the excitement had about subsided."

While Contention was busy not finding hostile Apaches, Tombstone had whipped itself into a fervor. "The Apaches Must Go-Blood versus Bacon and Blankets-Volunteers to the Front, An enthusiastic Meeting Yesterday. Yesterday morning hand bills were flying about the streets, calling the people to a public meeting on Allen street fronting the Grand Hotel, at 10 o'clock. About 11 a.m. an immense multitude of people had assembled. The Tombstone Brass Band distributed strains of martial music from the hotel porch, and excited citizens discussed the situation in vigorous language on the street." Judge Southward soon called the meeting to order and introduced Don Miguel M. Corrella of Sonora Mexico. Corrella spoke on behalf of Col. Ahumada who was the commandant of the Mexican forces on their frontier, just south of the boundary with the U.S. Corrella was told by Col. Ahumada to "inform the citizens of Tombstone that he would co-operate with any troops on this side engaged in crushing the marauding Apaches." [325]

AN ARMY OFFICER WHO SPOKE BEFORE KNOWING THE FACTS

Captain Hurst of the U.S. Army, who had once pursued stolen government mules to the ranch of Frank and Tom McLaury, only made matters worse telling the crowd that "the savages were almost at our doors, and were getting bolder and bolder, rivers of blood would mark their meandering." Hurst was by no means performing a public service by making such over-blown claims, and was self-aggrandizing when telling the frenzied crowd that "as far as he was concerned he had done everything in his power; he had put three companies of troops in the field; had sent a courier to Fort Huachuca with orders for the commanding officer to march to the aid of the settlers; he paid the courier out of his own pocket, five dollars per hour, and it took him fourteen hours to complete the twenty miles intervening between Tombstone and [Fort] Huachuca." [326] This behavior is was unbecoming conduct for an officer, and offered little rational thinking in response to reports that Indians could have been in the area.

Hurst also told the press that the "Indians who did the killing at Helm's ranch, and those who made the attack near the Contention mill, are probably of the same party."

But of Captain Hurst's frantic reports to both the citizenry and his military superiors, it was soon learned that he "was deceived by false reports brought him by citizens, and sent telegrams based thereon to the various commanders. It now turns out that there was no killing at Helm's ranch, no murders in the Dragoon mountains, no outrages in the Sulphur Springs valley, and in fact that there have never been any hostiles this side [west] of the Chiricahua mountains. This false intelligence has operated very injuriously in drawing the troops away from the possible trail of the savages, and in spreading unnecessary alarm throughout the country….It is now the general opinion that the hostiles have crossed into Sonora and are safe from the vengeance of the United States army. There may be a few stragglers in the Chiricahua mountains, but if so they will shortly follow the main body. As the Indians captured a large quantity of stock, the country many be considered safe until they want another grub-stake." [327]

NO INDIANS AT HELM'S RANCH

Even Chas. Helm himself gave a contrary report. "Chas. Helm and Alfred Schultz came in [to Tombstone] last evening from Helm's ranch, and declare everything quiet in that direction. Mr. Schultz declares that the first indication they had of Indians being in their vicinity was when they were so informed by the troops. No serious fear is apprehended of an incursion by the Indians…" [328]

But Helm did offer the embarrassed officer public thanks for attempting to help when he believed it was needed, even though it wasn't. It was a gentlemanly thing to do-Helm ended up coming to the aid of Captain Hurst in the court of public opinion, whereas Hurst had thought he was coming to the aid of Helm on the battlefield. "Tombstone, A.T.: Sir- I desire to return thanks to you for your very prompt and energetic action in causing to be sent to Helm's ranch, at Cochise's stronghold in the Dragoon mountains, the body of infantry and troop of cavalry, U.S. army, on May 2d, for the assistance of A.B. Schultz and myself who, as reported to you, were surrounded and defending ourselves against a great number of hostile Indians…While it is true that their presence was not needed (as there were no Indians there, nor had there been any in that part of the country, the report on which you acted, and given you by Henry Niven being wholly without foundation), the promptness of the troops is none the less appreciated by us…" [329]

MORE FROM GEORGE HAND'S DIARY

Saturday, May 6th, 1882. "Cold and cloudy, very dusty and disagreeable. Trains on time. John Ludwig took a young man to Tombstone for petty larceny. Stegman passed here en route to Tucson. The Tombstone people are very much excited over the President's proclamation declaring Cochise Co. [County] in a stage of lawlessness. They talk of an indignation meeting. If Ches. [U.S. President Chester Arthur] finds that true he will feel very bad, as it will be sure to defeat him for another term." It's hard to imagine today, or even then, a scenario where Cochise County could decide a presidential election.

Friday, May 12th, 1882. "Fine morning. Bradley away all day decorating the school house for the installation of the officers of the Druids. The ceremony closed with a grand ball. 3 ladies present. 1st lady was dressed in black with a big gold chain on her neck. 2nd lady also in black with a pinafore under her chin. 3rd lady [wore a] brown frock and white sacque with a straw hat on her head. 4th lady in black also, straw hat on with rose decorations and a brass chain round her neck. Nuts & raisins on the table, lemonade in the back room. The ball closed early and they all chassed [sashayed] home. No one hurt."

Wednesday, May 17th, 1882. "…Took a ride with Dr. Barney. Went to the Boston Mill…Had a pleasant time, barring dust….Dance this evening at Myer's Hotel. Mr. Rupert gives the dance. Several ladies present. They were all dressed [up]. I have forgotten the names of the different articles of ladies apparel. Some had black frocks & blue shawls on, others had red Morocco shoes. They had hard work to get Bradley to go. He went and they had a good time, danced till 4 tomorrow morning. Myers made a hit this time."

Friday, May 19th, 1882. "Fine morning. John Ludwig returned from Tombstone. [I] took a ride with Dr. Barney to Kendall's Station 'picnic ground.' Had a pleasant time. Returned 11 A.M. Jack Schwartz of Charleston was here with his youngest boy…Bill went to the Druid Lodge this eve…"

Sunday, May 21st. 1882. Fine morning. No church today. Took bath, changed clothes…Picnic today at Kendall's Station. Quite a no. [number of people] from Tombstone [were there]. Ludwig returned with prisoner. [I spent] all the evening looking for the comet-failed to find it. Young man from the country, drunk, with a six shooter, looking for someone to kill, got arrested. He was incarcerated in Bill's saloon…"

Monday, May 22nd, 1882. "Fine morning. Train in on time. Judge Smith gave the watch man [possibly a watch thief] 90 days and the shooting fellow [the young man to whom Hand referred on the previous day's entry] [a] $15.00 fine." The idea that Judge Smith would give the more harsh punishment to a petty thief, and the minor fine to a man who was a danger to others is indeed remarkable.

Tuesday, May 23rd, 1882. "Fine morning. Sam Latta fell and hung himself on a meat hook at LaRue's butcher shop. The hook went in about six inches from the navel…Sam Latta is not as badly hurt as at first supposed…We spent the evening looking for the comet, [but] did not find it."

Monday, May 29th, 1882. "Fine morning….11A.M. commenced blowing like fury. Mrs. B sent a box of wild flowers from Huachuca for Decoration Day. Martin of Kendall's Station sent a basket of roses & fern leaves, laurel & other grasses….Gen. Wardwell left with Sheriff Behan & Mike Grey for Tombstone to attend Decoration Day. Some visiting young fellows without brains, at a late hour of night commenced firing pistols in the main street for their own amusement, to the discomfort of families & other persons. And having an Indian scare this afternoon, it did not suit people very well. But as they were running the town, they kept it up. After being remonstrated with & in return insulting a lady, they, getting out of ammunition, left for their home on the west side of the river."

Tuesday, May 30th, 1882. "Fine morning. Considerable excitement about the disturbance last night. A complaint was made and the dept. [deputy] sheriff, John Ludwig, with a warrant arrested Mr.Chas. Meyer & Ed Severance. On appearance [before the judge] they pled not guilty, but on second thought they concluded best to plead guilty, pay fines and stop proceedings…went with a big basket of flowers to the cemetery to decorate graves of the late Col. E.A Rigg & Wm. Petty…" [330]

YOU'RE SURE YOU SAW AN INDIAN?

What Contention City feared the most, a visit from Apaches. Original cabinet card from the collections John D. Rose.

It wasn't long before another Indian scare rocked Contention, and those who traveled to and from it on a regular basis. This scare had even less foundation than the last one. It's reasonable to say that the residents of Contention wasted far more time worrying about Indians than they ever did encountering them. But George Hand recorded the commotion it caused in town. Saturday, June 10th, 1882. "…great excitement caused by man riding in town with report that Indians had fired on them and taken 8 mules from the lumber teams on the northern road toward Drew's ranch. Several men mounted and left in pursuit. The stage passed down but saw nothing of it. Guns & pistols are being cleaned all over town in anticipation of an attack by Indians, Fifteen mounted & armed men went out…"[331]

"INDIAN EXCITEMENT. How a Lively Imagination can Excite a Community. About two o'clock yesterday afternoon the following dispatch was received at this office from the editor of the Epitaph, who was in Contention at the time: CONTENTION, June 10.—Indians jumped a six mule team between here and Tombstone, taking ten mules. They shot at the driver. An armed force went from here. Find out particulars. [Sam] Purdy.

"About the same time that the above arrived, Mr. Wade, of the Contention mine, received a dispatch by telegraph from the mill to the same effect. There was some talk of throwing up entrenchments around the town, and eager inquiries were made as to whether there was any cannon or Gatling guns in case of a siege. Philanthropists insisted that a public meeting should be held to devise means of securing safety to women children and non-combatants, and the warrior element dusted off their Winchesters and carefully examined their side arms. Just then some skeptic observed that it might be a good idea to throw out a few skirmishers and ascertain the location and extent of the hostile force. Mr. L.W. Blinn, accompanied by two friends and an Epitaph reporter, decided to make sacrifices of themselves, so far as to proceed to Contention and investigate the facts. Mr. Blinn had two teams on the road and he was apprehensive for the safety of his drivers and mules. A carriage was hitched up, three Winchesters, a double-barreled shotgun and two hundred rounds of ammunition stored in, and the quartette departed on their perilous errand. A few miles from town [Contention City], to the astonishment of the occupants of the buggy, the two teamsters were found jogging comfortably along. The foremost teamster, whose name is L.E. Dole, was asked if he was dead or alive, and answered that he was alive. Whe[n] asked to tell his little story, he said that about half past twelve, when he was three miles from Contention, and was about to steer his team through a deep washout, he immagined [sic] he saw an Indian pop up his head in front of him. He immediately put on the brakes, and just as the team stopped a bullet whizzed by him. He dismounted rapidly on the other side and run [ran] for dear life. He heard no more shooting but did not stop until he reached Contention and gave the alarm. That patriotic town had nearly her entire population armed and on horseback immediately, and several scouting parties departed in quest of the savages. The driver said he was pretty sure it was Indians he saw, but was not certain of it. On repairing to the scene, the team was discovered just as they were abandoned by the driver. Nothing was touched or disturbed. The mules were all

202

there waiting patiently for their driver. The driver states that he saw two men, and that one of the 'Contention scouts' saw the tracks of two men, one wearing moc[c]asins and the other boots. That is all the foundation there was for the wild rumor. Some men were doubtless shooting rabbits or other game in the vicinity, and the timid driver took fright and in turn conveyed the contagion to two communities. Let us have peace." [332]

The driver soon responded to the Epitaph's sarcasm, and appeared to be defending his ability to discern between an Indian and a rabbit hunter. "Editor Epitaph. Dear Sir: In regard to L.W. Blinn's team being stopped on the road between here and Contention, I being the driver of said team, have been in the habit of leaving here before daylight, in the morning and have seen Jackass rabbits in all their glory at sunrise, but never have I anticipated any trouble on the road. I know full well from where this Jackass business came from. They are of the stripe that cover up their head with a blanket when in bed, afraid of the dark. If any of them think I am a rag baby, under the bed, and won't dance at any racket they can make, give me an equal show, and see. I was shot at, wholly unarmed. Hoping you will give this a place in your paper, I am Yours truly, E.L. Dole." [333]

In spite of the report being false, the June 11th article did show that Contention was a civic minded community. When it was believed that Apaches were raiding in the area, many from Contention, aided by some from Tombstone, armed themselves and went out into the night to face down the greatest guerilla fighters in human history. When faced with such a threat, they were willing to risk life and limb to protect Contention. Further calling the account into question, the Epitaph noted that of his six mule team, somehow ten were taken.

HELM AVOIDED APACHES ONLY TO DIE AT THE HANDS OF A PROSPECTOR

In enduring irony, which was not atypical of life in the valley, Helm would soon suffer a serious gunshot wound, not at the hands of the Apache, but courtesy of another settler. This case speaks to the myth that has grown up in the San Pedro river valley, as well as other parts of the west, as to countless settlers dying at the hands of merciless raiding Apaches, when in truth, far more settlers died at the hands of their own neighbors. "Seriously Wounded. Information reached town yesterday of a shooting affray about twelve miles north of Summit station. The participants were Charles Helm, proprietor of Helm's ranch, and Wm McCauley, a prospector well known in these parts. Helm was seriously wounded, being shot in the right breast, the bullet passing through the body, and his recovery is considered doubtful. It is probable the wounded man will be brought to town [Tombstone] to-day. The difficulty is said to have originated in a drunken growl, there having been no previous ill-feeling between the men from which so deplorable a result might have been expected." [334]

Unfortunately, reports of the seriousness of Helm's condition were not exaggerated. "Death of Charles Helm. Charles Helm, an account of whose shooting by Wm. McCauley we published a few days ago, died yesterday at the Palace lodging house on Fifth street [in

Tombstone], where he had been under the care of Dr. Blackwood. Helm was about thirty-four years old, and was one of the pioneers of Cochise county. He came here in the infancy of Tombstone and took up a fine tract of land in the valleys of the Dragoon Mountains, and went to raising horses. At the time of his death he was a partner with the Schultz boys in 10,000 acres of land under barbed wirefence, and had all the water rights in his vicinity. He is spoken of by those who knew him best, as an honest, industrious man, and was never known to be in any trouble, though possessed of a high temper. A warrant was sworn out yesterday for the arrest of William W. McCauley his murderer, but as he fled the country, the Sheriff will doubtless experience some trouble in making the arrest. Helm and McCauley were warm personal friends, and how the tragedy came to be enacted is a marvel to those who knew them both." [335]

While Contention City, its mills, and Tombstone remained safe from the Apaches, and less so from its drunken inhabitants, saloon keeping alcoholic George Hand finished his entries from Contention.

Saturday, June 17th, 1882. "…Got some milk from Dr. Wise for pups. They take to it like old dogs. Stage went up full of passengers….Mercury 12 [P] M.-86. R.R. [railroad] pay car went to the front today [the end of the railroad near which the workers camped], returned 3:30. Horse & wagon on the track. Engineer blew the alarm whistle. Man ran to drive across but too late. The horse's harness & pole of the wagon thrown 60 feet. Killed the man—sat on the seat scared nearly out of his wits. Stage came down, crossed the river above the P.O. [Post Office], but did not take the mail…Concert 8 o'clock sharp. Singing by the ladies and 2 gentlemen came in with the basso profundo and spoiled the whole thing. Dessert after the concert consisted of cordials in the shape of rock & rye, soda & whisk., lemonade & slop beer. Fruits-cherries & apricots-no nuts nor raisins. Took a drink."

Monday June 19th, 1882. "…Wallace's sister arrived this morning from Tombstone…Went over to see the engineer & fireman. Took them a small flask of rye. Theatre in the evening. I had the honor of dong the grand in escorting Mrs. Bradley & Mrs. Kaufman, after which the dance was commenced. Some singing. I danced only 1 time with Mrs. B. Returned 1:20. Slept well."

Wednesday, June 21st, 1882. "…Dick Durand arrived from Tombstone, drunk as usual. He managed to get over to the cars & I reckon he got away. Everybody drunk tonight except Mrs. B. & Mrs. K."

Thursday, June 22nd, 1882. "…Up early. Had a wash-cold water-nearly froze. Took an aesthetic walk and a ride with Dr. Barney to the Grand Central [Mill] & other places. Mrs. B. has been very busy today making dresses for some children friends of hers at Huachuca…"

Friday, June 23rd. 1882. "…Had a fine ride on engine 256 with Bailey. Went to the front [of the railroad construction] beyond Crittenden…"

Saturday, June 24th, 1882. "San Juan day. The usual drinking, horseback riding & singing in the street. Mrs. B. & two other ladies went up the river swimming. Very little fighting today. Man found drunk behind the stage stable. Thompson & Andrew McDermott took $13.00 from him." San Juan's day was always a day of great celebration, not only in Mexico, but also in communities in the southwest with large Hispanic populations.

Monday, June 26th, 1882. "…Bill & Mrs. B. went to Tombstone. Lodging house in Tombstone burned last night. Mr. & Mrs. B. returned this evening."

Tuesday, June 27th, 1882. "…Capt. Madden & Cap. Jeffords arrived from Charleston, stayed all night. Everyone tight."

Wednesday, June 28th, 1882. "…Capt. Madden & Mrs. B. left for Fort Huachuca. Jeff. [Tom Jeffords] went to Tombstone….Tiers & Alexander fighting. Judge Smith fined Alexander and let the other go free, all of which was wrong. In my opinion he should have fined both."

Friday, June 30th, 1882. "…Packed my trunk in readiness for my intended trip home tomorrow…We sat and talked on the stoop until a late hour [before] we stirred. Supposed to be my last night in Contention. Slept soundly."

George Hand would return to Tucson, and later gain employment outside of the saloon keeping fraternity, as he was later hired by Bob Paul as custodian at the Pima County Courthouse later that summer. His time in Contention and related writings are important not only because they captured some of the tensions during the Earp Vendetta and their interactions with Contention City, but of equal significance, he offers us insights into the day to day life in Contention, written as it happened. [336]

CHAPTER 14

MORE OF CONTENTION IN THE PRESS

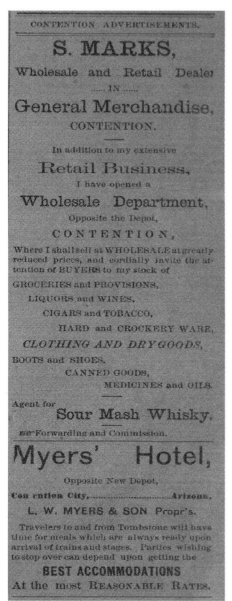

Original Commercial Advertiser, April 29, 1882, from the collections of John D. Rose.

"The Mexicans, maddened with drink, said the claimant was a liar, and fortified their positions by pulling their pistols." –Weekly Citizen

A Tombstone livery partnership that was expanded to Contention City had now come to an end. "We are informed that the partnership heretofore existing between John O. Dunbar and John H. Behan, in the livery stable business, has been dissolved by the former purchasing the entire interest of the latter." [337] Although Dunbar had ended his partnership with Behan, Dunbar's wife would continue an affair with Behan for years to come. Thus, a Dunbar/Behan "partnership" of sorts would endure.

A shortage of the right kind of laborer took place in the spring of 1882. Substantial rains had turned the valley green, giving area ranching near Contention and along the San Pedro a boost. "Ranch men on the San Pedro river are short handed. There are plenty of idle men in that neighborhood, but they are said to turn pale if work is offered within forty miles of them." [338]

"Doings at Contention…Our town is still getting along finely. The mill still keeps on furnishing its regular supply of bullion.

"We still keep our name of giving the pleasantest parties in the Territory. For real joy you should come to one of our dances.

"Last Wednesday night, at Meyer's Hotel, Mr. E.E. Rupert gave a farewell party to the people of Contention and surrounding points. His invitation to his friends was very unique. He had posters put up around town which read as follows: 'To each, and everybody: Fatty Rupert invites you all to the grand ball at Meyer's Hotel to-night.' So everyone was on hand, and they all had a right royal good time. Mine host Meyer put up one of his elegant suppers, which was well appreciated. We all danced till morning. Before Mr. Rupert's departure for his home in Pennsylvania his friends presented him with an elegant pair of gold quartz sleeve buttons. He has been our express and postoffice [sic] agent here, and as such has formed a host of friends, who wish him good speed on his journey.

"The Nugget is still the boss paper here in Contention. It is newsy and full of life, and is read by one and all." Actually the Nugget had ignored Contention City for most of its existence, and its status as being "full of life" was closer to "one foot in the newspaper grave," since it was to go out of business later in the month. [339]

Shipments of bullion reaffirmed the promise that many believed Contention City held. "Bullion shipped from Contention for the week ending July 8th: Grand Central, 13 bars: Contention Mill, 11 bars." [340]

This prosperity could even afford a change in the tax code that would elevate Contention's mills, which continued on unabated by the hindrance. "Bullion, once taxed in its net production, is now taxed in gross." The Epitaph further protested by telling its readers that "The present law taxing mining property, weights down both rich and poor, if its terms are fully carried out. The law should be changed, and its substitute will require deep and patient thought." Locally, that parting wish was viewed as fanciful, that lawmakers would utilize "deep and patient thought." [341]

A HORSE WITH A DIGNIFIED PALLET

A touch of class was added to the town with a French Restaurant that was run by a native of France, Leon Larrieu. Larrieu, who also kept a hotel at Contention, was paid a visit at his restaurant by a stray horse. Perhaps the unique aroma of authentic French cuisine wafting in the Contention breeze was too much for the animal, and it was led astray. "Estray. CAME TO MY STABLE, A HORSE branded SW on left him, also branded on left shoulder W. Any one owning such a horse can have the same by paying costs and proving prop[e]rty, L. LARRIEU French Restaurant, Contention." [342]

Horse related news of a different sort would emerge from Contention in July of 1882. Horse theft in and around Contention city yet proved alive and well. What was unusual about this case was the boldness, or outright stupidity, of the perpetrator, who stole the horse at a ranch near Contention, sold the horse at Benson, and then returned to Contention as if he had nothing to worry about. Which may have been correct, until the new owner of the stolen horse road from Benson, to of all places, Contention. "Horse Stealing at Contention. Yesterday morning a Mexican named Pedro Gorgiola was arrested near Contention by Deputy Sheriff Ludlow, charged with stealing a horse from Juan Navarro, a well known and respectable citizen of Contention. It seems, Mr. Navarro had the horse at the ranch a few miles from town and Gargiola, went there in the dead of night and stole the animal rode to Benson, sold the horse and boldly returned to Contention. In a few days the man who purchased the horse rode into Contention, and

207

Mr. Navarro recovered his property on a writ on replevin. The deluded man, in walking around town discovered Gargiolo, and had him arrested. He was arraigned before a Justice yesterday, and will be awarded an examination today. There is a dead case against him, and the occupants of the Cou[n]ty jail will doubtless be re-enforced in a few days." [343]

It may have been an indicator of the racial climate of the day, or the fact that desperadoes from south of the border were perpetrating crimes in the area of Contention, that the Epitaph made a point of stating that Navarro was "a well known and respectable citizen of Contention." Had the victim not been of Latin heritage, the Epitaph may not have felt the need to qualify and vouch for him.

ARE YOU SURE YOU WANT TO PULL THAT GUN?

As railroad construction continued to progress from Contention, it would repeatedly attract a rough element. The summer of 1882 would see another outbreak of violence, this time on the railroad between Contention and Calabasas. The station at which the affray took place was known as Crittenden, named in honor of an old army post nearby. "From the accounts received it seem[s] that two Mexicans, named Manuel Lopez and Ramon Monteverde, rode into town on spirited chargers, one of them leading a crippled mare. They halted in front of a whisky shop, dismounted, hitched the steeds, entered the shop and proceeded to fill themselves with the material that both cheers and inebriates. When a sufficient quantity was punished, the caballeros became boisterous, mounted their horses and rode furiously through the town. A number of railroad employees were present and did not seem inclined to allow the boys to have their fun out. They were, however, deterred from interfering by the wiser counsel of some friends who were present, but were still very far from being in love with the proceedings. Things would doubtless have gone on all right had not the Mexicans gone a little beyond the bo[u]nds of reason. They reined in their steeds in front of the railroaders, called them damned gringos and other pet names, threatened to ride over them, and in other offensive ways helped to irritate the feeling of the crowd, and bring to a climax the brewing broil.

"Just as things were beginning to get serious a long bearded citizen made his appearance on the scene, and asked the Mexicans which of them claimed the lame mare. He was informed that she was the property of both of them jointly, and that she was the 'damned best mare in Arizona.' This, though explicit, was not satisfactory, as the bearded citizen claimed the mare as his property, and said she was stolen from his ranch on the Babocamari, some two weeks before. The Mexicans, maddened with drink, said the claimant was a liar, and fortified their positions by pulling their pistols. Almost instantaneously a dozen pistols were pulled, and without unnecessary delay, as many shots were fired, and the Mexicans fell of their horses pierced by several bullets. When the smoke cleared away, the Mexicans were picked up and their injuries investigated. It was found that Lopez was shot through the right arm in two places, and had two flesh wounds in the upper portion of his body. Monteverde had one serious would on his left breast, the bullet having apparently passed through his lungs. Peace was then proclaimed, the wounded men were taken into the saloon and tenderly cared for by those whose fingers touched off the deadly missiles that wounded them. Dr. Peters, of Calabasas, was summoned, and succeeded in extracting all the bullets, save that which passed through Monteverde's lung. He declared both men not necessarily fatally wounded, but still in a very precarious condition. The bearded man took the disputed mare to his ranch on the Babocomari."

While the bad news at Crittenden reached Contention City, familiar news also reached the press. "The following bullion was shipped from Contention during the last two weeks ending August 20th: Grand Central seventeen bars, Head Center eight bars, Contention Mill twenty-six bars." It was news of the successes of Contention City's milling operations that kept payrolls flooding the Contention area with a rising prosperity. [344]

INDIANS!

Confirmed as well as unconfirmed reports of Indian sightings were still important to the local press, and the populace reacted to them quickly. New Troubles at Crittenden would reach Contention City just over two weeks later, and this time it was to the benefit of those selling guns and ammunition at Contention. Word of an Indian scare was out. Though many miles away from Contention, this news put the locals on edge, especially due to the fact that if the Indians were proven to be Apaches, their ability to move across valleys with lightning speed and stealth was even then legendary. "September 2.—A man from Crittenden station yesterday afternoon told me that the Indians had crossed into the southern spur of the Santa Rita mountains, after killing fourteen men, women and children on the east slope of the Patagonia mountains and the foot-hills. They number about two hundred warriors and are said to be taking things clean as they go. At the little town of Santa Cruz fourteen miles southeast of our camp (Babocomari Mining Company's) they marched boldly into the town and opened up a scene of butchery and destruction that is said to have been fearful. The mission of this band, it seems, is more for blood than booty, and their outrages are more horrible than usual…On Tuesday a troop of fifty-two soldiers left [Fort] Huachuca to pursue them but no one has as yet learned of any engagements between the soldiers and the Indians…The settlers expect but little from the soldiers.

"A scarcity of arms and ammunition is causing a great deal of anxiety. We received in our camp a short supply of cartridges, but we have only two guns…We have our guards out every night and keep a sharp lookout during the day…Since writing you this morning I have learned…that a large party of Indians are to-day depredating and fighting about ten miles southeast of this place (Simpson's camp)…The people in this vicinity are greatly alarmed, and many are seeking safety in flight, in fact, most all who can conveniently leave are getting out.

"John Thompson, a member of our camp and formerly a scout under Hatch, left for Contention to-day for arms, and expects to return by to-morrow." Although the exodus was understandable when hearing such reports, those who left inadvertently left those who remained feeling even less secure. "Unfortunately for us, those who are leaving this section are in most instances those who are best armed and equipped. Most of those in the vicinity of our camp who cannot leave are moving to the railroad station [at] Sonoita, which they consider a safer place."[345]

News from Simpson's Camp echoed that of Crittenden. "Sept. 3, 1882...It is believed that a large portion of the band which has been committing outrages along the Santa Cruz and Sonoita valleys has either gone into the Mule or Dragoon mountains. But it is feared that small bands are still infesting the Patagonia and Santa Rita mountains and foot-hills with the intention of raiding scattered ranches and camps. Many camps along the Sonoita are abandoned and those of the ranchers who can leave sought safety in flight. Most of the ranches and camps along the Sonoita are small with but very few men, and this fact precludes the possibility of organization for anything like a formidable defense." [346]

One of Dr. Barney's saloon keeping competitors at Contention would play host to a different event just a week later. "A Tough Customer in Jail. A fellow named Jack Sharp was brought to the county jail by Deputy Sheriff Ludwig, of Contention, Thursday night. He was one of the parties, his companion being Bill Davies, who 'held up' Mr. Walsh, a Contention saloon keeper, a few nights ago, and divested him of everything around the house that they had any need of. Since then the Sheriff's office have been on the alert to catch the thieves, and learning that parties answering their description were loitering around the Barbacomari valley, Sheriff Behan, Deputy Ludwig, and Walsh went there Thursday morning, and found Sharp asleep in a barn with his rifle by his side. He was taken into custody, and as stated above, lodged in the county jail. The Sheriff is still on Davies' track." [347]

Democrats at Contention organized and elected officers for themselves at Barney's saloon: Henry K. Hause as president, S. Marks as vice president, Pedro Michelano secretary, and E. M. Severance treasurer. [348] "Our ticket as it stands is well liked on the river and will be elected by a large majority if the river sentiment can be taken as a criterion." [349]

ROMANCE AT CONTENTION

1882 had started out with shootings to the north and south of Contention, the Earps in and out of court, posses' hot pursuits, and industrial progress with successful mills and railroad construction. September brought news that gave Contention an event of a more romantic nature. "Contention-A Romantic Wedding-General Notes....Thinking a line or two from our town would be acceptable and interesting to some of your many readers, I drop you this. The mills are all working steadily and yielding the usual amount of bullion. Business is also about as usual.

"We had a quite a romantic wedding in our town last night, the parties to the contract being Mr. Ed.S. Armstrong and Miss Sarah Spence. They were youthful admi[r]ers in Old Ireland twelve years ago, when Edward left for America. Miss Spence arrived in Contention three days ago, and so last night, after twelve long years the happy couple were made one by our genial Judge, J.B. Smith. Pete Ruffiey and Chas. H. Taylor acted as managers during the evening and by their untiring efforts made things pass pleasantly to all present[.] About nine o'clock Mr. Armstrong's friends, headed by the music marched to his residence and serenaded them. The boys were all invited inside and after music and drinking to the health of the bride departed. The happy pair were the recipients of many useful presents."

J.B. Ludwig, Deputy Sheriff at Contention, had been a part of many the most colorful events to take place there, and he decided to leave the position. "J.B. Ludwig, who has been officiating as Deputy Sheriff at Contention since the organization of Cochise county, has resigned that position in order to engage in other business." [350]

A RAILROAD COACH WITH A VIEW

Just over a month later news came of the successful completion of the last leg of the N.M. & A. It was a challenging project from the engineering and labor stand point, as well as a significant advance for the San Pedro and other valleys through which it traversed. Its construction was also occasioned by the intermittent wanton act of violence, and cold blooded killings. Still, it was a milestone that could not go unnoticed, regardless of any related price that was paid in the process. "This road, which has just been completed and will soon be opened for business, extends from Benson, on the line of the Southern Pacific, to the boundary of Sonora [Mexico] a distance of 88 miles. At the Sonora line it connects with the Sonora (Limited) which extends to Guaymas, a distance of 260 miles, making the entire length of this new line 348 miles."

"The New Mexico & Arizona passes from Benson up the San Pedro Valley to Contention, going within ten miles of the famous mining camp, Tombstone, and placing the mills on the San Pedro right on the line of the railroad. It passes through the Barbocomari into the Sonoita [valley] and down the Sonoita to Calabasas at the junction with the Santa Cruz and then south to the line [International boundary between the U.S. and Mexico]. It passes through some of the richest land and finest scenery in the country. The San Pedro Valley is being cultivated and is filling in with settlers, and the Sonoita [area] is proverbial for its fertility. Many portions of it are finely wooded and travelers who pass through will hardly think Arizona the desert it is pictured to be. It traverses some of the finest stock ranges in the world and from the car windows fine herds of cattle can be seen grazing on the Empire, Crittenden and Calabasas ranges…The road is substantially built. The company…has made the road bed solid and substantial so that the water which rushes down through the valleys during the rainy seasons will not be likely to disturb it. To do this and keep out of the beds of the streams many expensive cuts had to be made, but it will prove wise economy in the end." [351] In spite of their best efforts, mistakes in the layout of the N.M. & A. would haunt the line almost from its inception. In the area along the San Pedro from Benson to Contention to Fairbank, the line was located much too close to the bank of the river, and was plagued by wash outs and widening of the river throughout its use.

211

Judge Smith would soon have a courtroom session that required an interpreter. "An amusing scene occurred in Judge Smith's court at Contention, not long since. A Chinaman had been brought in, charged with larceny of some spoons, knives, etc. The services of an interpreter were necessary, and a fellow celestial was called up and interrogated as to his knowledge of English, nature of an oath, etc. The heathen 'heap sabe em' all. To make assurances doubly sure, the Judge finally asked him if he knew what a Justice's court was. 'You bet, belly good,' was the reply. 'Well, what's it?' said his honor. 'Alle same one man he steal'em spoons, alle same Justice court he catch'em spoons.' He was sworn in as interpreter." [352]

"A party of Contention gentlemen who own some mining claims in this vicinity are preparing to put a large force of miners at work at an early day. Our beautiful weather hangs on with commendable tenacity and miners rejoice thereat.

"A party of amateur hunters at Contention are making preparations for an organized raid on the game in the hills near here. Just now cinnamon and black bear seem to be most plentiful, and it is hoped that those amateurs will come down before bruin 'holes up'-we want to see some fun.

"Through the kindness of conductors Sparks and Hafer of the N.M. & A.R.R. and the postmasters at Contention and Benson we now get our mail matter with some degree of regularity." [353]

CONTENTION TRAINS RUN ON TIME

For Contention City, the arrival of the railroad had already been of great benefit. Gone were the days when a dusty stage ride from Benson began their final leg of the journey to Tombstone. Gone were the days when local merchants were limited to only what could be supplied in their stores via wagon train—now they had access to all that the railroad could offer from the outside world. At the same time, that was only the beginning. The railroad had never seen Contention City as its final destination, but as a stopping point along the route, and that route led to Mexico. It was a disappointment to Tombstone, but Contention saw its travelling population increase. "On Monday regular passenger trains began running in the N.M. and A. R.R. from Benson through Guaymas, Mexico. The passenger traffic is very large and seems to increase daily. The fare to the Mexico line is ten cents a mile and three cents a mile in Mexico. So much for anti-monopoly laws.

"The first shipment of oysters from Guaymas over the N.M. and A. R.R. passed up this week and consisted of one car load. The oysters were in the shell and were loaded loose, in a box car. They were fine large ones and were consigned to parties in Silver City, New Mexico.

"Harry Turner, formerly of this camp has become one of the proprietors of a wet and dry grocery establishment in the bustling city of Contention. Harry is the ingenious British subject who while here was sent into the hills to look for some stray oxen and was discovered some

212

hours afterward busily engaged in a canyon dipping up water and sand with a yeast powder can. When interrogated as to the object of being thus employed he blandly replied that he was washing the sand to see if he could discover any cattle tracks. A man with such brains as he seems to possess ought to succeed in any business, and we would not be surprised to learn any day that he had bought the Grand Central mill, or the Bird Cage Academy of Music in Tombstone. However, Harry is a jolly good fellow and everybody here wishes him success. Express service has been put on the N.M. and A. R.R. between Benson and Guaymas and our old friend Billy Smith was the first messenger to make the trip." [354]

Harry Turner wasn't the only unique individual living in Contention, as a woman who was thought to have a mental illness was found wandering the desert nearby. "The woman Carmen Losa, who left her home in the Barrio Libre during a fit of insanity on the 22nd instant, has at last been found wondering on the mesa near the San Pedro river several miles from Contention City. When discovered she was pretty badly used up and although she appeared to have recovered her reason was unconscious of her whereabouts, and made inquiry of her finder as to where she was. She was taken to Contention and is now there with relatives." [355]

In the winter of 1883, veteran freight magnate Julius Emmons Durkee would set a local record. "An ore team consisting of three wagons, belonging to J.E. Durkee, of Tombstone, hauled a load of ore weighing 56,000 pounds from the Contention mine to the mill a few days ago. This is said to be the largest load ever hauled in the district." [356]

One of the more bizarre events from the Grand Central Mining Company didn't take place at Contention, but rather at the mine itself in Tombstone. "Rowell, the man who fell down a 65 foot incline in the Grand Central mine, about two months ago, is convalescing, and can now go about on crutches, although still partially paralyzed. His escape from death is miraculous." [357]

The mills at Contention and Millville were of surprising reliability, but when one of the engines of the mill went into repair, all progress and production of bullion ground to a halt. "The Contention mill, which has been so faithful during the past three years, has met with an accident that will require about three weeks to repair and put in running order." A portion of one of the mill's engines had broken in two, and given it kept running after the first break, this only led to additional damage before it could be shut down for lengthy repairs. Still, this mill had proven itself and would continue to be of great profit to its owner. [358]

November of 1883 would again show the Contention, among the other mills nearby, producing bullion. "The following bullion was shipped from Contention during the week ending Oct. 27: Tombstone M. & M. Co., 2 bars; Custom mill, 1 bar; Grand Central, 5 bars; Contention, 6 bars; total 13 bars." The fact that the Tombstone Mill and Mining Company shipped its bars out of Contention shows the shipping advantage and savings made by the mills at Contention, versus the Gird and Corbin Mills owned by the Tombstone Mill and Mining Company at Millville. They had to pay the expense of freighting their bullion to Contention City via wagon, the greater burden being the possibility of robbery on the isolated roadway that ran alongside the San Pedro between those two points. [359]

TOMBSTONE DISTRICTS WANES; BISBEE AND FAIRBANK RISE UP

In 1908 versions of the story of Bisbee's founding began to surface as its rising success in the copper and gold mining industry fueled interest in its humble beginnings. "According to Judge Duncan of this [Tombstone] city, who is [the] authority on pioneer history of Cochise county, thirty years ago this month, George Warren discovered the Wade Hampton and other claims at Bisbee, constituting the beginning of the great Copper Queen system. The year before, '77, Jack Dunn and Major Rucker had made some locations in the same district." [360]

The name George Warren and story of Bisbee, Arizona are inseparable. Though he could have been one of the great success stories of western mining, Warren was later reduced to conning Bisbee locals out of free drinks. "Even old George Warren, the discoverer of Bisbee's famous mineral deposits, worked the late Judge Chisholm and a few associates for innumerable drinks a few years prior to his death by walking his gullible victims about the rocky reaches of upper Brewery Gulch searching for the ledge from which he had secured a fabulously rich specimen-perhaps; also maybe." [361]

The discoveries that would lead to Tombstone and Bisbee both occurred near each other in the historical record, but what followed in the wake of those discoveries was a developing story of very different

Photo of early Bisbee prospecting pioneer George Warren. Copy photo from the collections of John D. Rose.

natures. Tombstone would eclipse Bisbee and instantaneously rise to one of the most promising mining camps in the west. Bisbee was comparatively just a small mining upstart, with a population of 366 in 1882, versus the "metropolis" of Tombstone with 5300 plus souls. Decades later Bisbee would become the truly advanced city that Tombstone founders had once dreamed of, but never quite attained.

But even as early as 1882, the shipping of mining materials and commercial goods to Bisbee via Fairbank would show small signs of economic advantage to both locations. By the end of 1882, Fairbank was officially on the N. M. & A. route before the track swung southwest to Nogales. Shipments were brought by railroad to Fairbank, then taken by wagon to Bisbee. A lengthy journey to be sure, but far better than shipments that had in earlier times come by wagon from Benson, and before that Tucson. That too would change in dramatic fashion when the Phelps Dodge Company in Bisbee decided to construct a railroad to Fairbank at the end of the 1880's. They named it the Arizona Southeastern. Tombstone citizens must have been astonished that once again, the railroad had passed them by. But before Fairbank had its railroad connection, shipments to Bisbee came from Contention.

"SEALED PROPOSALS IN DUPLICATE will be received at Bisbee, AT., until 12 o'clock [p] m. on the 14th day of March, 1882, for hauling for the Copper queen Mining Company all their lumber, machinery, merchandise, coke, etc, from Contention City to Bisbee and return with copper bullion…The contractor must provide at Contention City, A.T., a suitable building adapted to the storage of at least 400 tons of coke, and such storage shall be free of charge to the company…COPPER QUEEN MINING CO., By Ben Williams, Superintendent. Bisbee, March 6, 1882." [362]

FAIRBANK, THE LEAST LIKELY TO SUCCEED, DOES JUST THAT

While Charleston and Contention got most of the notice along the San Pedro, a location in between those two points that was of little consequence in 1882 had begun to take shape. Whereas Charleston and Contention would not see the dawn of the 20th century as living town sites, Junction City, Kendall's Camp, and Kendall would all combine and eventually turn into Fairbank, and it would far outlive its sister locations nearby on the San Pedro.

"About four miles south of Contention, the railroad makes an abrupt turn, crosses the river and climbs the western bank, on its way up the Babacomari valley to Calabasas and Sonora. At the point where this divergence is made some enterprising citizens, not connected with the railroad, have surveyed and located a town site, and called it JUNCTION CITY, anticipating that the freighting business to Tombstone and other places south and east will hereafter be carried on from this point. It is not probable, however, that the railroad magnates have given them any assurances on this point. Contention town boosters, on the contrary, argue that the erection of so large a depot at that point is conclusive of the intention of the railroad to make that the shipping point until the main line shall have been built from Deming [New Mexico], via Tombstone, to connect with the Mexico line at Junction City…the building of ample side-tracks at Junction City indicate their intention to do a considerable freighting business at this point. The only freight thus far discharged there are the pipes of the Huachuca Water Company. Great piles of these are strewn along the side track for hundreds of yards, and Mexican teamsters are loading them up for various points along the pipe line.

"The improvements at this place consist of a store, saloon and several dwelling houses, all substantial structures. Junction City is about eight miles from Tombstone, or two miles nearer than Contention." [363] During the construction of the N.M. & A., a railroad camp would become the beginnings of Fairbank. "Division Engineer Kendell has a camp about half way between Tombstone and Contention, [not a correct estimation of this location] ostensibly for the purpose of estimating the cost of a road between the 'Y,' about two miles from Contention…" [364]

The parallels of Bisbee and Fairbank are noteworthy. Early on both locations appeared secondary in nature to their area counterparts. Fairbank seemed of little importance located near the confluence of the Babocomari and San Pedro Rivers, in between the boom towns of Contention City to the north, and Charleston and Millville to its south. Likewise, early indications in Bisbee showed promise for the future, but little to suggest that it would one day far surpass the mineral wealth of Tombstone, just as Fairbank would surprisingly long outlive both Contention City and Charleston. Both Bisbee and Fairbank would advance well into the 20th century, leaving their contemporaries far behind.

Long believed locally is that Fairbank was named for N.K. Fairbank, a Chicago man of great wealth, who invested in Tombstone's Grand Central Mine which only added to his substantial fortune. Having started out in the trades, Fairbank wanted all to know that years of success had not softened him. "N.K. Fairbank boasts that he can lay a brick now as well as in his youth, when he worked as a mason." [365]

A RIVERSIDE PARTY SPOT AT KENDALL'S LAKE

A central location for recreation along the San Pedro had become known as Kendall's lake. It offered easy access for picnickers from Tombstone, and closer yet, for those at Contention. It was very close to where the town of Fairbank would soon be established. "The picnic at Kendall's yesterday was a complete success in every sense, more than 200 being in attendance. Parties from this city [Tombstone] who attended report a most agreeable time." [366]

"There will be another grand picnic, at Kimbal's [Kendall's] Lake and Grove, three miles from Contention, and on Sunday next. The one held at the same place last Sunday was a success in every particular, and in view of the varied attractions, it is likely that a large crowd will be in attendance on Sunday next. The fare for round trip is only $1.50, covered wagons leaving for the grounds at 10 o'clock a.m." [367]

One of the two Tombstone fire companies soon got into the rush to host a party at Kendall's. "The picnic to come off at Kendall's grove on the twenty-eighth, under the auspices of Engine Company No.1, will undoubtedly be an exceedingly pleasant affair. Extensive preparations are being made in the way of entertainment, and the utmost good order will be preserved. The company will appear in full uniform. There will be dancing, foot-racing, target-shooting, base ball, races for ladies, and all kinds of hilarious enjoyment." [368]

The firefighters of Tombstone Engine Company No. 1 catered the event which went "off like regular clockwork: there was not a hitch or pull in the whole arrangement. The grove is admirably situated for picnic purposes. The greenest of green swards, trees in full leafy verdure, inviting the breezes; and cool, pure water. There is no more choice spot in Arizona for rustic recreation." The majority of the picnickers arrived by 1 o'clock, and the band consisted of two violins, a clarionet, a guitar and base viol. While dancers enjoyed a tree-shaded pavilion, gambling began as the athletic competition took shape. "The first was a foot dash of forty yards, Sheriff John H. Behan and Mr. Isaac Jacobs being the contestants. Pools were sold on the race and several hundred dollars changed hands. Behan was the choice from the start, though we understand that Mr. Jacobs informed his friends that it would be safe to bet their money on him, as he was perfectly satisfied of his ability to win the race. The track was cleared, pistol fired off and the contestants started Behan jumped the winning line exactly twenty-four feet ahead of his competitor, and the friends of Jacobs were in high dudgeon [angry] because they took his advice and bet according to his directions. The next race was for the grand badge, presented by the company for the best 100 yards runner in the fire department. There were three entries—Messrs. Osbourne, Pope and Barron. Osborne was the fattest and heaviest, Barron the smallest and Pope the tallest…Mr. Osbourne astonished everybody with his fleetness, and made a nice pile of money for those of his friends who bet on him." After the boys raced, young Albert Behan challenged the two winners and got away with them in good shape. "The dancing match was perhaps the most entertaining feature of the day's amusements. There were five judges chosen, Messrs. Purdy, McCarthy, Aaron, Smith and Spangenberg…" A baseball game was held, and then many of the group headed just down the road to Contention City for a ball at Meyers Hotel. "Young & Kellogg furnished the music and a first class time was enjoyed by all. The dance was fairly well attended and good order prevailed. A supper fit for the gods was furnished about ten o'clock, to which the hungry picnic[k]ers did complete and ample justice. The dance was kept up until the light of morning was beginning to appear over the eastern hills, and all are unanimous in wishing Meyers to try his hand again at the ball business, when a majority of his guests would not be handicapped and exhausted by a picnic." [369]

LOW STAKES FOR A HIGHWAYMAN; LET'S GET A DRINK

Misadventures along the San Pedro occasionally took a humorous turn. "Twice Held Up. Last Sunday evening a well known prospector named Ed. Parker started from Charleston to Kendell to transact some business. He had not proceeded more than half way when a man rose up in front of him on the road and in thunder tones commanded him to throw up his hands and disgorge his pockets. Mr. Parker hastened to obey, and said cheerfully that he was never in better condition for a robber, as he had not a cent and had not seen a dollar except at a distance for more than six months. This seemed to cool the ardor of the knight of the road and a conversation ensued. They inquired each other's name and business, related anecdotes and became like old friends in a few minutes. Parker said that he was going to Kendell and suggested that the highwayman accompany him, as a fellow at that point would take jawbone for the drinks. That of course was sufficient inducement to walk a couple of miles. The conversation was continued during the walk and by the time they reached the "Y" were firm friends. Several drinks were disposed of, Parker transacted his business and they retraced their steps toward Charleston. About the same place where they encountered each other, two other men sprung up and had the drop on the travelers instantly. They were ordered to throw up their hands, notwithstanding the protestations of one of them that he was in the same line of business. One of the robbers kept two guns unpleasantly near their faces, while the other one went through their pockets…the job bore no fruit for the thieves. Recriminations ensued. One of the robbers rebuked them for not having something to defray the expense of so much labor. Parker who was in excellent humor…related the circumstances of the first meeting with his companion. This made the party good natured, and Parker asserted that a drink was all that was necessary to make things lovely all round. At this the strangers almost simultaneously produced a pair of bottles; the party sat down on the roadside and a good drinking bout began. The festivities did not end until the last drop of whisky was gone…" [370]

THE BISBEE MASSACRE AND CONTENTION

On December 8th, 1883, a robbery turned bad in Bisbee would lead to a manhunt that would catch the attention of the press beyond the borders of the Arizona Territory. The robbers would leave the store owned by A.A. Castenada and Joe Goldwater, opening fire on innocent passers-by on the main street in Bisbee. This tragic affair is known as the "Bisbee Massacre." The Sacramento Daily Record-Union would send their own reporter to cover the manhunt of those believed responsible, and Contention City and Fairbank would become part of the story. "Tombstone, December 21st. –For the past two days this community has been in a feverish state of excitement, in expectation of the return of Sheriff Ward from Clifton with 'Tex' and 'Red,' the Bisbee murderers, recently arrested near Clifton. Rumors were rife and threats openly made that they should not live to enter the jail here. Upon the arrival of the regular stage last night there were fully 300 men in and about it, it having been noised about that the Sheriff would arrive with them. It was well known that since the departure of Ward for Clifton a party of men from Bisbee had been at Fairbanks. Their only object could have been the lynching of the prisoners. Under the circumstances it looked as if their threats would be carried out. The most prominent citizens in the camp favored a smmary [summary] disposal of the fiends as just and economical. About noon to-day word was received by Under Sheriff Wallace from Ward, at Contention, that he had left the train there, and was en route for Tombstone. Wallace quietly selected fifteen men known for coolness and bravery, and by his instructions they got into the Sheriff's office unnoticed, where they were armed and made ready for any attempted rescue. Sheriff Ward's plan was well taken. By leaving the train at Contention he would have quite a little start of [over] the vigilantes, who were known to be at Fairbanks, the point where the stage connects for Tombstone. Your correspondent was permitted to be with the party enrolled, and as the minutes rolled swiftly away the suspense got irksome. To add to it a horseman, with his animal reeking with foam, suddenly dashed past the Court-house from Contention, and was recognized as Joe Russell, of Bisbee, one of the gamest and most resolute men on the frontier. Charlie Smith, of the Sheriff's posse, remarked as Russell passed, 'We are in for it, boys. That

218

man can have but one object here, and you know what it is.' It was evident that the wretches at Fairbanks had found that Ward had given them the slip, and had started to overtake him, or else Russell had been at Contention, and was hurrying on to raise a crowd here in advance of the Sheriff's arrival. Fortunately the preparations had been made so secretly by Under Sheriff Wallace that beside the party directly interested no one knew that the prisoners were on the road. Not a lounger was to be seen about the Court-house. The anxiety was getting painful, when on the run up came a vehicle containing Sheriff Ward and deputies, and with them the prisoners, who, in the twinkle of an eye, almost, were out of the wagon and safe behind the bolts and bars, from which they will never emerge alive. Death is their certain portion, either by law or at the hands of Judge Lynch. ..Both prisoners looked haggard, but showed no signs of fear. Red is suffering from a wound received at the hands of some Mexicans in September last, which has not yet healed. Tex is a splendid specimen of manhood, and seemed to enjoy the attention he received as he passed down the corridor of the jail." [371]

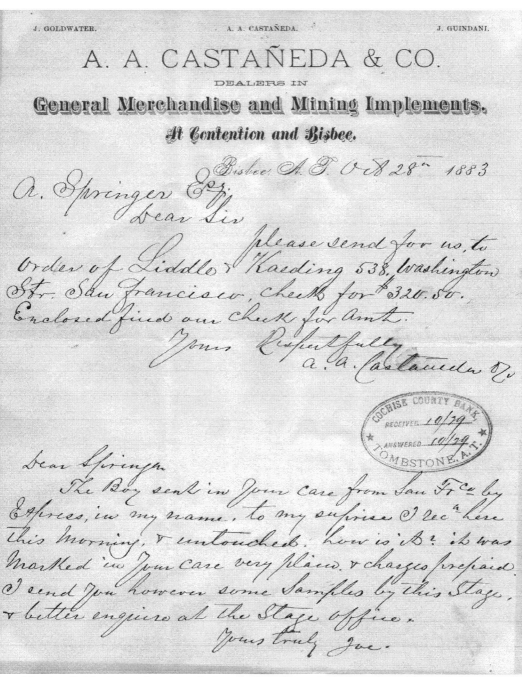

J. GOLDWATER.   A. A. CASTAÑEDA.   J. GUINDANI.

A. A. CASTAÑEDA & CO.

DEALERS IN

General Merchandise and Mining Implements,

At Contention and Bisbee.

Bisbee, A.T. Oct 28ᵗʰ 1883

A. Springer Esq.

Dear Sir

please send for us, to Order of Liddle & Kaeding 538 Washington Str. San Francisco, check for $320.50. Enclosed find our check for Amt.

Yours Respectfully

a. a. Castaneda &c.

Dear Springer,

The Box sent in Your care from San Fr Co by Express, in my name, to my surprise I rec'd here this morning, & untouched. how is it? it was marked in Your care very plain, & charges prepaid. I send You however some Samples by this Stage, & better enquire at the Stage office.

Yours truly Joe.

Signed by Joe Goldwater and partner Casteneda just six weeks before the robbery of this store that sparked the Bisbee Massacre. Original letter from the collections of John D. Rose.

John Heath, mastermind of the robbery that led to the Bisbee Massacre. Original Fly photo from the collections of John D. Rose.

Bisbee's Main Street, near the time of the Casteneda store robbery and the Bisbee Massacre. Copy photo from the collections of John D. Rose.

The author somewhere in the general area of where the Bisbee Massacre took place, but by no means an exact location of it. Photo by Aubrey Summer Rose.

223

CHAPTER 15

CONTENTION'S BEST DAYS ARE BEHIND IT

"Of one thing we feel assured…the great ore bodies below the water will not be permitted to remain undeveloped." -Epitaph

The declining fortunes of Tombstone would only spread out across the district that bore its name. In late 1881, the construction of the Girard Mill began, just across Tombstone Gulch to the south of Toughnut and Allen Streets. Milling at Tombstone meant the beginning of the end of milling on the river and the economies created for towns like Contention.

By 1885, Fairbank was still holding its own with the railroad, and Contention still had the same advantage, but the heart of its economy, its mills, was on a decline that was irreversible. For the next four years the Head Center Mill (formerly the Sunset Mill) would fuel Contention City's economy, but this too would change. Tombstone eagerly welcomed the moving of mills from the river, and there was little concern for the impact that such losses would have on river front towns such as Contention that were once part of its greatest successes.

In late 1888 Sterling Silver Mining Company was the new name for what had been the Vizina. There was optimism enough over the ability of Tombstone to produce valuable ore at even this late date, and their operations would impact Contention City. "Sterling Silver Mining Company…will be started up as soon as the diamond drill arrives, which will be about the 10th of January. This company have purchased the Head Center mill from the Contention Co., for $7,000 and will start to move it next week to the mill site about half a mile below town. It is the intention of the company to commence work on the Ground Hog soon after the 1st of the year." [372]

"In our own particular district [Tombstone District] some few changes for the better have taken place. The hitch in the removal of the Head Center mill from Contention to Tombstone has been overcome and the work will probably be begun this week and completed as soon as men and teams can do it." [373]

"There were several bids opened yesterday for the removal of the Head Center mill (formerly the Sunset Mill) from Contention to this [Tombstone] city. The lowest bid was from E. Rathburn, his bid was $2,250. The work will be commenced at once." [374]

As Tombstone struggled with the pumping issue that made continued mining more expensive, the unused ore lying around at the dumps was now of use. "Work will also be commenced on the Ground Hog and Vizina. The extensive dumps of the latter mine will pay to run through the mill, and will probably be so treated as soon as the stamps are ready to drop." [375]

ANOTHER HISTORIC LANDMARK FROM TOMBSTONE TO THE SCRAP HEAP

Eventually, the one last vestige of Tombstone's most successful mining enterprise, the Grand Central, would also disappear from the landscape. In a retrospective report, the Epitaph stated the events of the downfall of the Grand Central. "In the space of several days there will have been demolished and thrown into the scrap heap the famous old Cornish pump now standing on the property of the Tombstone Consolidated Mines Co, on what is known as the Grand Central mining claim, having been included in the three hundred tons of old scrap iron sold on Saturday to the Tucson foundry, and will be the passing of another of the historic and familiar landmarks of the Tombstone district.

"The mammoth pumping plant was erected in the year 1883 by the Grand Central Mining Company, and at the time was considered the largest of its kind in the entire southwest. After operating for about a year the plant was closed down on April 30, 1884, owing to a strike in the entire district of miners for higher wages…" In 1886 a "fire, which destroyed the old plant, which was at the time enclosed and covered by the wooden shaft and hoist house, was so fierce as to not [o]nly melt the bearing of the machinery, but to take the temper from the steel portions and warp and twist the balance of the iron structure, rendering the whole $300,000 plant fit for scrap only." [376]

The water issue had plagued Tombstone's progress for years. Back in the summer of 1886, Josiah White, owner of the Contention, was on a return trip to Tombstone. Even the knowledge of that was enough for the struggling town to read into his return a possibility that things were about to change. "The EPITAPH trusts that some plans will be formulated, whereby operations on the hill will be speedily resumed. Of one thing we feel assured, and that is that the great ore bodies below the water will not be permitted to remain undeveloped." [377]

But nothing would reverse the declining production of the Tombstone district. Citizens in Fairbank would read of the possibility of an additional railroad which could further enhance their position as a transportation hub, but the livelihood of the nearby river towns was gone.

"Ed Hewitt who has been visiting Tombstone tells the Citizen of Tucson that a Tombstone banker is in San Francisco raising money to build the road from Fairbank; that a meeting of the Contention and Grand Central companies will be held next month to fix the pumping project; that the Contention Mill is closed down, and that the mill at Fairbank is also closed down…all of which bring to memory the two lines from Hamlet: 'There is a divinity that shapes our end, Rough Hewitt as we will.'" [378] In the face of such setbacks, Tombstone was still hoping against known circumstances that the road from Fairbank, meaning the railroad, would finally be built and save the fading town from further decline. Another twelve years would pass before the big event finally took place.

The meeting to come "next month" was simply a repeat of one that had occurred three months prior in September, 1891. The issue that continued to divide was that of who would pay to pump out the water so that the mines at Tombstone could continue to follow the ore deeper into the earth. Pressing upon this issue was the fact that the ore resting beneath the lake (approx. 520 feet down) wasn't as rich as the ore that had already been mined above the water. This meant that it was critical that a cost sharing arrangement between the two richest mines, the Grand Central and the Contention, be reached. If only one mine is pumping, its neighbor might be getting their water removed for free. "…whether the Contention folks will do the pumping or the Grand Central people drain the mines on a contingent is not yet known even by the principals themselves…It is the belief of the Contention people that they can drain the basin with their present pumping machinery, at least if things fall their way they will try it. The Grand Central Co. are prepared to swing the pumping proposition if the task is imposed upon them." [379]

Along the river, ranching and farming were still viable occupations. Charleston had become a largely deserted village with transitory squatters living here and there in the area. Most of its buildings had been destabilized or destroyed by the 1887 earthquake. But the mettle of many who settled this area included an optimism that may not have always been realistic, but had served them well as they had endured many hardships in developing the San Pedro Valley. "A gentleman who does not wish his name mentioned, has deposited $25 with the Prospector that he wishes to wager on the propo-[s]ition that there will be 500 men at work at the mines and mills around Tombstone before Jan. 1st 1892. This includes… Grand Central and Contention mills." The Epitaph quipped with an unusual lack of its renowned optimism that "Here is a chance for a croaker to make an overcoat." [380]

THE DESTRUCTION OF THE CONTENTION MINE AT TOMBSTONE

1892 would bring bad news for the Contention Mine at Tombstone, and its owner. As Tombstone began to show promise, Josiah White made the purchase of a lifetime, buying the Contention Mine from the Schieffelin/Gird partnership for a paltry $10,000. Millions were made, and it allowed White a lifestyle few would ever know. When a fire demolished his buildings at the mine, it was a loss that White took in a personal way. He had already made his fortune from the mine, but on quite an emotional level, he was openly upset. "Mr. White went up to the Contention mine today…He was naturally affected by the scene of the ruins of a once magnificent property in which he took a pride other than entirely a mercenary one. When he returned down town some one asked him how long he would remain in Tombstone, to which he replied 'from what he had just seen he felt like running away at once.' From a letter received from San Francisco, the Prospector learns that the mill at Contention will be dismantled in case no arrangement is perfected for a combination for deep mining between the Grand Central and Contention companies."

White went to visit the Contention mill still at Contention City, and had planned on returning to Tombstone, but "after looking around the property he concluded that he would not return to Tombstone. He was so worked up over the loss of the Contention works by fire that he did not care to come back even for his valise, which he left at the San Jose House in this city

[Tombstone].” The Epitaph was conciliatory adding that “It was perfectly natural that he should feel sore over the loss. In conversation with him yesterday morning, the question was asked him how long he would remain here, to which he replied: ‘a few days.’ When he was questioned regarding what would be done during his stay here, he said nothing could be done now that the works were destroyed. He did not talk business during his stay being very much out of humor. He, no doubt, came with a desire to do something toward a resumption of work if an agreement could be reached. He so expressed himself on his journey to Tombstone. He even went so far as to say that now as his company and the Grand Central people were on the same level, something might be agreed upon.” [381]

In April of 1902 Tombstone was paid a visit by an acknowledged expert on milling. He reported on his work at the Contention Mill. “Mr. Nicolai Anderson who is operating the tailings of the Contention mill at Contention was a Tombstone visitor today. Mr. Anderson is handling 30 tons daily by the cyanide process and employs quite a force of men. He is an authority on cyanide matters and is one of the best posted men in the west on treatment of ores by the cyanide process.” [382]

A few months later brought an unwelcome milestone: “Mr. Peter Effrein, the Copper Queen foreman, who has charge of the work tearing down the old Contention mill at that place states that he will finish today. All the castings have been shipped to the company foundry at Bisbee where [the] same will be remodeled. Four boilers, the engines and pumps have been shipped to Douglas where they will be used on the well that is being sunk by the company there at that place. Pete says that considering the long usage and then the time the machinery has lain idle, it is most remarkable how well preserved the shafts and spindles are, which goes to show that the man who had charge of the construction and care of same knew his business.” [383]

With the milling equipment gone, the land itself would be sold off four years later. No longer a site for industry, it would now become part of one of the great ranches of Arizona history, owned by the Hearst family. “According to a deed placed on file in the county recorder’s office the Tombstone Consolidated Company has sold to the Boquillas Land and Cattle Co, the old Contention mill site, containing five acres, near Benson. The land was formerly a part of the grant and was purchased by the mining company from the grant people 25 years ago. It will now be fenced and put under cultivation with the balance of the grant[.]” [384] Such was the final tribute to the mill that had named the city which would play host to it for over two decades. All that was left of the labors of so many had been dismantled, making way for cattle to graze in its wake.

CYANIDE DOES NOT ENHANCE ONE’S HEALTH

The milling of silver was always a risky business, and working with the related chemicals could lead one to the undertaker. The use of cyanide, though an effective milling component, was clearly unsafe. Although the cause of his death was reported as pneumonia, it was commonly known that chemical workers simply didn’t live as long as other laborers in the mill, thus their pay was twofold higher. But less than eight months after he paid the office of the Tombstone Epitaph a visit, Nicolai Anderson would die like so many before him.

"Mining Man Dies. Nicolai Anderson died at Fairbank Tuesday morning about 10 o'clock after a brief illness from pneumonia. Mr. Anderson was a well known cyaniding expert, having had charge of the large cyaniding plant at Mammoth and was operating the Contention mill tailings at the time of his demise. His illness was brief. The remains of the deceased will be shipped to Tucson for interment. He leaves a wife to whom general sympathy is extended." [385]

THE RAILROAD GETS TO TOMBSTONE, AT LAST!

"TOMBSTONE CELEBRATION…Tombstone has not seen such a day as it did Sunday for twenty years. Fully 1,500 outsiders were there to help celebrate the advent of the new railroad from Fairbank. The Tombstone people deserve great credit for their hospitality.

"The Tombstone celebration was a grand success. Bisbee, Tucson, Naco, Fairbank, Douglas and Pearce each contributed their quota toward a crowd that numbered not less than 1,500 people.

"The approach of the long excursion train to Tombstone was the signal for a salute of dynamite bonmbs [sic] on top of Comstock hill. From there to the old Vizna [sic] shaft the visitors were given an ovation." This new railroad was called the El Paso and Southwestern.

"When the train had unloaded its burden the Huachuca band, stationed near the new depot, played inspiring airs. From there the crowd marched up town, many of them heading for the barbecue grounds.

"Tombstone was in gala attire. The principal buildings were decorated inside and out with bunting and flags. Each resident of the city made himself a committee of one, and saw that the visitors enjoyed themselves.

"When the train pulled out of Tombstone on its return toward Bisbee, it was with sincere regret that the people left off their day's outing in Arizona's most historic town. Some of them remained over night.

"Many of the old abandoned mines near the city, which have made several men wealthy, were visited during the day. Without an inspection of them, it is impossible to comprehend the due-time exten[t] of the camp.

"The railroad into Tombstone from Fairbank is one that will not permit engines to haul heavy loads. The Tombstone end is a rapid rise, and Sunday the excursion train had to stop on one of the hills and steam up. In nine miles there is a rise of about 700 feet.

228

"The main event of the day was the hose race. The principal street of the city was used as a race course. Both sidewalks were lined with people eager to see the winning team. Several deputies were kept busy forcing the crowd back."

Festivities were enjoyed by all, but even such gleeful events could turn Tombstone to its cantankerous side. The row began over the hose pulling contest, and ill will soon got the best of what was otherwise a fine day of celebration. "The attitude of some of the Tombstone people has stirred the boys of this city [Bisbee], who believe that an effort was made to give them a trifle the worst of the deal. Yesterday the following statement was handed in for publication: 'It is strange that the ill feeling Tombstone has against Bisbee does not die out as the years roll by. It was plain to see on Sunday that the Tombstone fire department wanted to give Bisbee the worst of it at every turn.

"'First they refused to loan their nozzle, which they had already proposed to do, and it was not until the Tucson team had generously volunteered to loan Bisbee theirs that Tombstone dug up their nozzle, which had been hidden.'" [386] Tombstone at the very least has to be given credit for consistency as a place where even the mundane is anything but.

The arrival of the train to Tombstone, so anxiously awaited by residents and businesses alike, signaled that the last vestige of frontier travel to Tombstone was now forever gone. Those former residents who could now visit Tombstone by train had to grasp the momentous changes they had witnessed since the discovery of that place 25 years prior. Memories of Drew's Station, Contention City, and the mayhem that ensued as posses took to the field in pursuit of murderers, robbers, and the Earps must have seemed a lifetime ago to them. But had the railroad arrived in 1881 as had been hoped for, it's hard to say how much of Tombstone's history, some of which has passed from the historical to legend, may have been altered. But at its core, it was always held together by those who believed in it the most, and in many ways such can be said of the place today. Its constant stream of controversies just went with the territory. They always have, and likely always will. But then again, who ever thought of going to Tombstone for long-term peace and quiet?

Although Tombstone finally received the railroad that was the dream of every town booster since its inception, it too would soon fade as a viable mining operation, and begin down the long path into history, legend, and popular culture, not because of the earnest labors of so many who had made it all possible, but from subsequent generations of Americans who became more compelled by the mystique and romance of the west, rather than its reality.

City of Tombstone, Arizona.

Purported to be the first train arrival in Tombstone. Whether it is or not, clearly it is a major event, with many coming out to view the Iron Horse. Note that the roof to the building on the left, which was constructed to be the train depot, is not yet complete. Today this building remains and serves as the Tombstone City Library. The original is a bi fold picture postcard, from the collections of John D. Rose. On the page opposite the image has been enlarged and split into halves for more detailed viewing.

City of Tombstone, Arizona.

PICKING THROUGH THE LAST OF THE BEST

The Grand Central Mill still stood and was briefly noted on a small road project as a roadside marker, not as a bright spot in local industry. "John Somers was authorized to expend an amount not to exceed fifty dollars where needed on the S. David Road from Fairbank to the San Pedro River and on the River Road between Elij Clifford's ranch and the Grand Central Mill." [387]

The Grand Central exceeded the output of all the mills in the Tombstone District—its thirty five stamps alone equaled the combined milling capacity of both the Gird and Corbin Mills at Millville. With the advances in the cyanide process, speculators were eyeing the remains of the dump at the Grand Central Mill in hopes of a quick profit, regardless of the inherent dangers of dealing with cyanide. "Mr. W.H. Pomeroy is at Fairbank, testing the tailings at the old Grand Central mill with a view to buying them and extracting the values by cyanide process." [388]

Another part of the Grand Central Mill story closed at the word of the death of one of its former managers. "A.W. Howe this morning received a telegram announcing the death of his brother-in-law, E.W. [Edward] Perkins, at Johnsville, Cal., on yesterday. He had been ill for a week, suffering from stomach trouble. Mr. Perkins was well known in Cochise County by the early residents, having for a number of years had charge of the Grand Central Mill near Fairbank." During Tombstone's decline, E.B. Gage, who had led the company to great success, moved for a time to Congress, A.T., taking with him key personnel. Perkins had made the cut. "He afterward was located at Congress for some time with the Congress Gold Co. For the past seven years he has had charge of the mill at the Jamison Mining Company property in Plumas County, California." [389]

The Slimes Tailing Company specialized in taking old tailings and turning them into profits. "The Slimes Tailing Company, at the old Grand Central mill, near Fairbank, has let a contract for a well 8x10 feet, and expect to strike water within 50 feet. Four carpenters arrived this week, and were put to work arranging the foundation timbers for the big cyanide tanks, which are expected to arrive the coming week. Eighteen steel tanks and two wooden ones will be required to handle the tailings as the company propose." [390]

The Grand Central mill itself would see a similar fate to that of the Contention and Head Center mills. A massive pumping effort was attempted in 1905 to clear the Tombstone mines of water, and the mill was moved in pieces to Tombstone. "A number of carpenters are at work framing the big timbers for the various places where they will be used, and when the work of putting them in place is started there will be no delay. The cyanide tanks have arrived, and will be put together shortly. Several car loads of machinery and battery timbers arriv[e]d from Fairbank during the past week, and most of the material that is to be used from the old Grand Central mill is now on the ground." [391] It is a final irony that the Grand Central mill shipped so much bullion via railroad out of Contention City during its glory days, and now the mill itself was shipped in pieces via railroad, out of Contention City, to Tombstone.

But the tailings of that mill, left at Contention, attracted J.W. Dawson, "who has been conducting a series of cyanide experiments at the Grand Central mi[l]l tailings, near Fairbank..." Contention City was no longer a geographical location by which readers unfamiliar with the area could envision a site. Early settlers at the Fairbank area had boasted that they would one day eclipse the much larger location of Contention City. In the end, twenty five years later, they were proven right. "Mr. Dawson states arrangements are being made to resume work on the big tailings pit and extract the values by the cyanide process. The plant now on the ground which has a capacity of 200 tons daily will be partly utilized, as a different method of treatment adopted by the former company will be used. Mr. Dawson estim[a]tes there is fully 60,000 tons of tailings available for his plant and with the successful treatment of [the] same the plant will be in operation a number of years. The tailings [are] from Tombstone ores run through the Grand Central mill during the early days of the camp. The tailings are said to contain values from $3 to $10 per ton." [392]

Apparently Dawson's attempts did not finish the last of the tailings. A newcomer to the project, but by no means to Tombstone mining, would now take over the Grand Central tailings. "Bert Macia, the general foreman of the workings of the Tombstone Consolidated Mines company, who with W.W. Poindexter, has a lease on the tailing bed on the old Grand Central mill, about a mile below Fairbanks on the San Pedro, yesterday received a telegram from Mr. Poindexter to the effect that the sampling works in San Francisco had a way to successfully handle the tailings so that they could be worked at a profit."

For months Macia and Poindexter had searched without success for a way to process these tailings in a profitable manner. Although the tailings averaged about $3.80 in gold and silver, it was the seven percent copper content which consumed the cyanide, thus ensuring the failure of the process. According to the two partners, "The tailing bed at the Grand Central mill covers several acres, and there is over half a million of dollars in gold and silver in them that has been awaiting some process to take it out." It was noted that "A number of parties have taken leases on the tailings, but have never been able to get the values out that were known to be in them. Several years ago the Slimmes Tailing company of Utah invested several thousand dollars in erecting a cyanide plant at the [Grand Central] mill and erected a large number of tanks at a large cost, and after about a sixty days' run were compelled to give up the plan." [393] But Bert Macia never gave up on Tombstone. His descendants remain the last pioneer family there, operating the Rose Tree Museum and preserving the family's collection and their own share of Tombstone's history in the process.

CHAPTER 16

FAIRBANK – A SURVIVOR'S STORY

"He next attacked an old man who was sitting on the porch…striking him with a chair." –Daily Tombstone

It is interesting that a mythology was created regarding the sequence of events involved in the founding of Fairbank. Its inception would be related to the arrival of the railroad. On January 1st, 1935, the University of Arizona published General Bulletin No. 2, commonly known as "ARIZONA PLACE NAMES" by Will C. Barnes. Still sought after by collectors, in this early work of merit, Barnes is mistaken as to how Fairbank began. He referred to it as a "Station on the San Pedro river, established in 1882 on the E.P. & S.W. R. R. [El Paso and Southwestern Railroad] at [the] junction [of the] Tombstone branch." [394] Although Fairbank was very much in existence in 1882, the E.P. & S.W. wouldn't arrive for another 21 years. It was the N.M. & A. which had first brought rail service to the area which had been known as Junction City, Kendall's camp, then Kendall, and eventually Fairbank. In the 1888/1889 time frame, the Arizona & Southeastern would build from Fairbank to Bisbee, and finally in 1903, the El Paso and Southwestern would build through Fairbank and into Tombstone, finally giving Tombstone its railroad connection two decades after its greatest prosperity.

The grading for this line was well underway in 1902, and was encountering challenges from the elements. "Thursday seventy men were on the pay roll at both Sprague and Anderson's grading camps. The rain has somewhat retarded work and Friday quite a number of the employees drew their time. Work will not be in full blast until about September 1st, as now it is a difficult matter to keep the men on account of the extreme heat of the past ten days. However, when the balance of the contractors outfit arrives work will be pushed very rapidly toward Tombstone. Rex Waters, the popular E.P. & S.W. assistant engineer arrived from El Paso Thursday and was conveyed to the survey camp by the party's team. Rex is the much look[e]d for instrument man and his arrival is hailed with joy by the balance of the party. The survey party including Thursday's reinforcement is now seven strong." [395]

This road would be completed the following year in 1903. It was a milestone not without its ironies. What began with dusty roads departing from Tucson to Tres Alamos, to Drew's Station to Tombstone, and all points between, had given way to the most advanced form of travel of the day. Gone were the days when a pioneering wife like Allie Earp could say "The road wasn't hardly one at all. The wagons spread out one behind the other and tried to keep in the same tracks." [396] Such dusty caravans were fast becoming a thing of the past in a rapidly developing Arizona Territory. Almost forgotten were isolated places like Drew's Station that had offered travelers a bit of comfort and a family a livelihood with memories of stage coaches passing through. Like those key locations, the colorful characters that had visited them would also drift from the historical record and into folklore and legend, all in the lifetime of a little girl like Cora Drew whose favorite toy as a child was a discarded bottle.

THERE'S A REASON WHY IT'S CALLED A MONSTER

A longtime debate as to whether or not the bite of a Gila Monster was poisonous would soon be rekindled in Fairbank. "'The deadly Gila monster' is now the word. It has always been argued that this reptile did not bite and that it was perfectly harmless. Some people have even gone so far as to say that it was splendid eating when properly cooked, and that the Indians, especially, regarded it a delicacy. It turns out now that the bite of the Gila monster is fatal…COLONEL YAEGER, of Fairbanks, Cochise county, was bitten by one of these reptiles on the thumb, while attempting to open its mouth, and that death relieved him of his sufferings within a few hours after he had been bitten. The sad ending…settles the much debated question, as to whether, or not, the bite of a Gila monster is fatal." [397] But the debate was far from over.

Weighing in on the issue several years later, Dr. H.C. Yarrow from the far away Smithsonian Institute insisted that the bite of the Gila monster is not poisonous, based on a number of experiments he had run on rabbits and chickens. Commenting on the deaths of Yaeger and a Johnny Bostwick at Tip-Top who was bitten, he said, "the death of these two men is but another proof of the killing qualities of Arizona whisky." [398]

INDIANS, AGAIN!

The entire valley was again rocked by reports of Indians in the area. They had recently killed lawman Billy Daniels June 9th, 1885 outside of Bisbee, near Sandy Bob Crouch's ranch near the Mule mountains. Reports came in from all directions at an alarming rate. "This morning John Slaughter and J.J. Patton arrived in town [Tombstone] from the Swisshelms and reported the killing of four soldiers by Indians on Tuesday, at Gaudalupe canon…While the guard were engaged in eating dinner they were surprised by the Indians and four of their number were killed outright…Mr. Patton reports that on Monday night signal fires were displayed by the Indians in the Sulphur Spring valley and on the mountains…"

As of June 11th, reports from Tombstone stated that "The Indians are surrounding this vicinity in all directions. The trail of twelve Indians was seen between the Grand Central mill and Fairbank this morning and today a band of seven was seen heading for the Whetstone mountains by the mill hands at Contention mill…George Norton arrived from Bisbee this afternoon and reports the Indians [are] still in the Mule mountains…Mayor Thomas who took some men in wagons is at Dixie canon, where [Billy] Daniel[s] was killed, ready to take the field on foot…A.H. Emanuel, whose ranch is at the south end of the Huachuca mountains at Ash canon…reports that at about seven o'clock a.m. to-day, he saw with a glass apparently a large party of Indians between a body of citizens and soldiers, being pursued toward the line about a mile from it. The troops were heading them off from the San Jose mountains…To this added a confirmation by telephone, which comes from Huachuca via the private [phone] line of [L] W.

Blinn Lumber Co., at Fairbanks. The report says a courier arrived at Fort Huachuca this evening with the intelligence that the forces of citizens and soldiers had been fighting."

With Apaches in the area and people's nerves on edge, factual reports were hard to discern from the fictitious ones, and the same sensational account added, "All is excitement and confusion now." But there was a confirmed wounding of two men who were out to stop the raiding Apaches at all costs, and although the following incident was questionable, their bravery was not. "Tonight's stage from Bisbee brings messengers for doctors to dress the wounds of Thomas Jones and a barkeeper, both of whom were wounded by the accidental discharge of a gun sent from here among other arms, last night, in the hands of a careless volunteer, who supposed he had emptied its magazine. Jones was hit in the shoulder blade, and the wound is not reported serious." [399] This may well have been the only true combat involving local citizenry in the entire incident, but such news reports put Contention, Tombstone, Bisbee and everywhere in between on a fever pitch alert.

To lighten the mood, Fairbank experimented with a prank that had years before wreaked considerable havoc in the early days of Tombstone. Some of the 'old boys' amused themselves by tying tin cans to dogs' tails; the ensuing racket made as the canned dogs made the rounds around town attracted much attention and made for a humorous spectacle. The Tombstone press remarked that if the people of Fairbank noticed any extra curs running loose in their town they will charge them to the pound in Tombstone. [400]

ANOTHER WAY TO MAKE A LIVING

By the summer of 1885 the press addressed what was already well known, the era of milling along the San Pedro was in clear decline. The Epitaph sought to recast the image of the area, hoping to offer optimism amidst bad news. Those in Tombstone also knew that the moving of mills along the river would help Tombstone as it struggled to stay viable, at the expense of its satellites, which had once been such a part of its prosperity.

"AGRICULTURAL. A REVIEW OF THE VARIOUS RANCHES. The Land Adjoining the San Pedro from Fairbank to Reddington Blooming like a Rose-Cattle and Horses by the Score are to be seen. The agricultural industry of Cochise county are fast assuming immense proportions. It is a pleasing sight to see the acres of grain growing and maturing along the entire length of the splendid valley of the San Pedro, a few years ago it was generally conceded that if Arizona was not a success as a mining region, it was not fit for anything else with a possible exception of a home for the Apaches; but experience has demonstrated that the soil of Arizona will respond liberally to the demands of the man who will give it some of his attentions.

"The San Pedro Valley commencing about three miles north of Charleston, is in a high…of cultivation. The ranch owned and watered by the Boston mill company which consists of 160 acres of arable land surrounding their mill produces the finest crop of alfalfa we have ever beheld, and it could by proper management mode to be a very valuable ranch, the only serious drawback is evidently on the Tevis land grant. Traveling north from this place you first encounter the ranch of the Noyes Bros. who some five years ago came to this Territory from the State of Maine and located this place, and they have by frugal and industrious management succeeded in amassing a nice fortune. The sales of hay alone from their property for the past year has been some six thousand dollars…This productive valley from the city of Charleston to the ranch of H. Taylor which is something over one hundred miles down the river is one continuous garden, and any and all kinds of cereals are to be seen growing in abundance. The river is here and there dotted with prosperous little villages, the largest being the town of Benson which contains about 500 souls; it is situated on the west banks of the San Pedro, 30 miles from the city of Tombstone and is a thriving busy town and will some day in the near future become a large and prosperous town; it was called into existence by the Southern Pacific railroad and made the shipping point for Tombstone. The smelter at this place turns out nearly a million dollars worth of bullion annually, which adds very substantially to the growth of the place.

"Charleston, Fairbanks and Contention are all gradually clim[b]ing the scale of magnitude and all have their future which is an unquestionable good one, all having the advantage of splendid mining and agricultural surroundings."

"Tres Alamos, eight miles below Benson [downstream on the San Pedro River], signifies three cottonwood trees. The village contains some 300 good people principally Mexicans, but at the present writing is rapidly filling up with Americans anxious to avail themselves of the chances now to be had. Here we find the ranch of the Dunbar cattle company which occupies nine miles of the finest portion of the San Pedro river, and bears evidence of thrift and good management. Here in the olden town which in years gone by resounded to the songs of the murderous Apaches and now bears evidence of their cruelty…the waving fields of corn and barley, bear silent evidence to the fact that the days of the Apaches are fast fading away and over the graves of their numerous victims and the ashes of the long deserted wigwams are growing and thriving a prosperous and happy country.

"Leaving the village of Tres Alamos some four miles down the river is the newly located ranch property of Mr. White which gives promise at no distant day to rival the old place above of the Dunbar cattle company. Mr. White and the Oberfelder Bros. are leaving nothing undone to make their place both attractive and valuable, both of which they have succeeded in doing from the ranch of Mr. White passing down the river on the last but not the least ranch on the river is that of Z.H. Taylor who is raising some of the best blooded horses in the territory[.] Mr. Taylor is an old Tombstone business man who sold out his business in the city and hied himself away down the river to build a fortune for himself and his genial wife…he now has one of the best ranches to be found in Arizona with a fine large commodious residence and outbuildings corrals and etc., suitable for the business. He has now some 300 head of horses running on his range which will amount, he expect[s], to increase in the next two years to 1,000 head this making himself the largest horse raiser on the coast…The Tombstone wishes Mr. Taylor suc[c]ess as we know he is a worthy honorable gentleman and has labored like a trogan [sic] in the wilds of Arizona to build him up a home for those he loves." [401]

The foundation of the Boston Mill, north of Charleston and south of Fairbank. Photo by John Rose.

Fairbank would soon hear of a much hoped for economic asset— a smelter. "Another smelter will soon be erected in Cochise county, at Fairbanks." [402]

Fairbank's Hispanic population would soon celebrate honoring their homeland. "The Mexican residents of Fairbank and the San Pedro valley, will celebrate the anniversary of Mexico's Independence by a grand ball at Fairbank on the evening of September 16." [403]

Constable Letson of Fairbank was asked to aid in the recovery of some stolen horses from Tucson. The assumption was that the stolen animals would be smuggled down to Mexico, and the Fairbank area was one possible route for such contraband. Letson "received a telegram from Tomas Elias of Tucson, asking him to look out for some horses of his which were stolen. The officer kept a sharp lookout and on Sunday found them in possession of some Papagos. He recovered ten of the stolen animals and captured two of the Indians, two more of them having succeeded in escaping. He at once telegraphed Mr. Elias who arrived last night and identified his horses. Sheriff Paul was then telegraphed for and will probably take the prisoners to Tucson for trial." [404]

An outbreak of fever would strike Fairbank. At times referred to as "Guaymas fever," and other times as "San Pedro fever," it was a serious condition that plagued many living along the river. "Notwithstanding the fact that the weather has become cool, the fever still prevails at Fairbanks." [405]

UNRULY ELEMENTS AT FAIRBANK

Though its present sleepy demeanor belies little of its past, Fairbank was at one time far from the peaceful place that visitors see today. In fact, any town in the Tombstone District which sprang up and thrived attracted lawless elements, and Fairbank was no exception. Close to the summer of 1884, a shooting would take place and prompt some negative publicity in the Tombstone press. "J.R. Mason, was shot and instantly killed at Fairbanks on Sunday night by Williams Humphries. From the testimony at the coriner's [sic] inquest, it looks like an unprovoked murder. Humphries gave himself up and is now in custody. The killing is said to be the result of an old feud." [406]

Fairbank had a Charleston transplant join their ranks, although perhaps unwelcome. His reputation shadowed him, but lawmen had difficulty keeping him in prison. "...in almost every place in which he has resided for any length of time he has left a black record of diabolical crime behind him. In personal appearance, [Jerry] Barton is not altogether prepossessing. He is about 37 years of age, five feet and nine or ten inches in h[e]ight, wears brown hair and sand moustache and imperial [pointed beard]. He is stout built and will likely pull down nearly two hundred pounds. In conversation he is somewhat arrogant, but very insinuating at times. He has a slight impediment in his speech, and when he gets th[r]ough with the courts he will likely have a serious impediment in his neck—a fate he richly deserves." [407] Such was the local view of Barton in 1881, and years later he was still a free man, though he had been linked to a number of deaths in Charleston during his time there. "Territory vs. Jerry Barton; assault to kill.—A jury was secured in this case and the forenoon was occupied by the trial, and the jury brought in a verdict of simple assault. Sentence will be pronounced to-morrow." [408]

Mention of Barton also came in the form of unusually good publicity. "...a teamster, who is working for James Carr, missed a roll of bills amounting to $225...He made the matter known at Fairbank, and Frank Broad and Jerry Barton took the matter in hand and succeeded in recovering $117 of the amount this afternoon." [409] "Jerry Barton of Fairbank, came up from that burg this morning and was shaking hands with his numerous friends." [410]

But never away from trouble for long, Barton would again surface on a murder charge. The trouble began with a dispute of the settlement of a liquor bill. "Jerry Barton, who is said to have killed six other men, struck E.J. Swift several blows on the neck in two places causing almost instant death. Barton was arrested and is in jail." [411] What looked like a quick trip through a trial and then off to the gallows ran into a technical problem that, of course, would be of benefit to the neck breaking Barton. "In the District Court at Tombstone, the case of Jerry Barton, indicted for killing E.J. Swift at Fairbank, was, upon motion of defendant's counsel, contin[u]ed for the term, owing to the absence of one Crane, a material witness who could not be found." [412]

By 1900, Barton had moved on yet again, after a stint in the "Cross Bar Hotel." "Jerry Barton, who is one of the most extensively known men in Arizona, has opened a saloon at the Weaver mines," located in Yavapai county. "Jerry at one time kept a saloon at Fairbanks, [also at Charleston prior to that] and while intoxicated one day, in Tombstone…struck an old man on the head with his fist, dealing instantaneous death, which he was sentenced to the penitentiary for eight years." For all the confirmed and unconfirmed deaths that Barton may have been involved in, it finally appeared that Justice had come to it, though eight years hardly seemed like enough of a punishment. For Barton, it was more than he wanted to serve, and he wasn't alone. "He was afterwards pardoned by Gov. Hughes." [413]

News of other violence in the surrounding area would become known at Fairbank due to its now central location as a transportation hub. "A Mexican brought information to Fairbank of the finding of the body of an unknown white man hanging to a tree near Kinnear's ranch at the foot of the Whetstone mountains." [414]

THE JUDGE AT FAIRBANK IS BRUTALLY BEATEN WITH A STICK; THIS IS ONE HARD-HEADED MAGISTRATE

As the new year of 1886 began, the people of Fairbank knew that Geronimo was still on the loose in Mexico, and it was always an open question as to where the Apache leader would strike again. But a more immediate form of violence hit at Fairbank, and as was often the case, it proved that most of the dangers that befell western settlers occurred at the hands of their fellow settlers, especially when alcohol was involved. This time it was an assault on a local judge of a most startling nature.

"SHOOTING AT FAIRBANK. A serious shooting affray occurred at Fairbank last night. A man named Wilson, who keeps a saloon there, got drunk and struck a man on the head with a chair. He was brought before Justice J.B. Smith, who fined him $15 or 15 days. Not being able to pay the fine, he was brought to town [Tombstone] and confined in jail. Thompson, a barber, who has a chair in the saloon, was left in charge. He had been taking part in the altercation and afterwards got into a dispute with Justice Smith, the result of which was that Smith shot him in the chest. This happened between 7 and 8 o'clock…It was not expected that Thompson would recover…It is reported that Smith is also hurt." [415]

Details of the story continued to emerge. "Trouble at Fairbank. On Saturday afternoon last, a man, name unknown, and a Mr. Wilson, proprietor of a saloon at Fairbank, had a little scrapping match. The former gentleman claimed that Wilson struck him over the head with a chair. Constable Letson arrested Wilson and he was tried before Justice Smith, and fined $15 or fifteen days in the county jail, Wilson not paying the fine was brouget [brought] to Tombstone and placed in the county jail. Wilson before leaving Fairbank placed one Thompson in charge of

240

his saloon, who as near as a reporter of THE TOMBSTONE could learn, got drunk in the evening, and going down to the store of Paul DeMartini met Justice Smith and bruised him up pretty badly. Smith left the store, and went in the direction of his office, Thompson following him and continuing to beat him. Smith when in front of his office slipped in and seizing a shot gun, turned and fired it at Thompson, the contents entering his left arm. Word was immediately sent to Sheriff Hatch, who went down to the scene of the shooting. Shortly afterwards Dr. Dunn went to Fairbank and tended to the wounded men. Mr. Thompson was brought to this city [Tombstone] yesterday and placed in the county hospital. It is thought that the wounds are not serious." [416]

Word that Thompson's wounds were not of a serious nature was soon discounted. "It was found necessary, yesterday, to amputate the arm of Mr. Thompson, who was shot on Saturday evening, in Fairbank, by Justice Smith. The wounded man lies in a dangerous condition." [417]

But an eye witness would take issue with this account, and the original report that Thompson's wounds were not of a serious nature would be proven incorrect as well.

"Dear Sir:-- The report of the Tombstone papers as to the shooting in Fairbank on Saturday night last is not wholly correct…In the first place, Wilson got drunk on Saturday and commenced a difficulty with me, calling me all sorts of names and accusing me of assisting others in robbing him out of $800. In regard to the matter Mr. Fortlouis, of Tombstone, attached Wilson, and I served the papers. After Wilson calling me a son-of-a-b--, I knocked him down. He then went to his saloon and attacked a man named Mills, calling him a son-of-a-b--, and ordered him out of his saloon. He next attacked an old man who was sitting on the porch, saying to him, 'What are you doing here? You old son-of-a-b--,' and at the same time striking him with a chair. The man started to leave the house, when Wilson followed and struck at him with a chair. A warrant was issued for the arrest of Wilson, and I arrested him. The above statement was proven in court, Justice Smith fining him $15.00. Wilson, failing to pay the fine, was committed to the county jail for fifteen days. Had Wilson been sober at the time, I have no doubt he would have paid the fine. The man Thompson was left in charge of Wilson's saloon, and in the evening he got drunk, and meeting Justice Smith at the store of De Martine, commenced calling him names, and, without a moment's warning, struck him a heavy blow on the side of the head with a heavy stick, knocking him down, and as Smith attempted to regain his feet, Thompson again knocked him down with the stick, and continued it to the third or fourth time. It's only a wonder to me that the blows Smith received with such a club did not break his head. This latter assault I did not witness myself, but it was detailed to me by some five or six men who witnessed the whole pounding. These men tried to interfere, and Thompson knocked two of them down. As to the shooting, I know nothing, only that Thompson was severely wounded. The foregoing statement is correct, so far as I know of my own knowledge and what I learn from others who were witnesses. James Letson, Constable of Fairbank. Fairbank, Jan. 26." [418]

As for C.O Wilson, the Fairbank saloon keeper who kicked off the festivities, he chided Constable Letson saying that " he would like to make out that he is a John L. Sullivan," the latter being one of the best known bare knuckle boxers of the 19th Century. Wilson cared enough about how the incident was seen in the eyes of the public to write the following to the Daily Tombstone on February 2nd, 1886. "The statement of James Letson published on the 27th, I have but just seen, and I wish to state that it is not right and does me an injustice, and I can prove it. I had some words with Letson about the whisky, but I did not call him all sorts of names. He struck me but did not knock me down. He would like to make out that he is a John L. Sullivan. Thompson separated us. In regard to Mills I had no words with him, he wants to put himself in the case because I would not trust him for whisky. Letson called him that was on the porch. I seen him at my place some time ago, and I had not seen him again up to the day he came around. I lost some wine some time ago and a man said that he took it…I told him to stay away and get off the porch, and he drew a knife on me, and I raised a chair but did not strike him, and then they fined me one dollar and fourteen dollars [court] costs. The Thompson matter I cant say anything about, [as he was in custody at the time when it occurred] but I find that there are several different stories about it, all different from Letsons. Respectfully, C.O. Wilson. Fairbank, February 2, 1886." [419]

While Wilson complained about how unfairly he had been treated, the man who tended to his bar when he was arrested died at the hospital in Tombstone. Gangrene had set in his wounded arm, so his arm was amputated in a desperate attempt to save his life, but the gangrene had already moved past the point of amputation. "Thompson, the man who was shot by Justice Smith at Fairbank, last week, died in the hospital yesterday morning, gangrene having set in in his shoulder above the place where his arm was amputated." [420]

That series of incidents proved an ugly affair, and whether coincidental or not, this announcement appeared shortly thereafter: "Dissolution of Copartnership. The copartnership heretofore existing between A. F. Paredes and James Letson, in the saloon business at Fairbank, in Cochise county, Arizona, is this day, by mutual consent, dissolved, Mr. Letson retiring and Mr. Paredes assuming the payment of all outstanding debts." [421]

Thompson's attack on Justice Smith cost him his life, and the blows to the head that Justice Smith suffered may have precipitated his untimely death. "J.B. Smith, justice of the Peace at Fairbanks, while eating in the Pacific Chop House, on Allen Street, dropped dead suddenly from his chair. The cause of death is not known, but a postmortem examination will be held today. Deceased, who was a very popular man, came from Texas and had been J.P. at Fairbank and Contention for several years. He had a son, who is a Wells, Fargo's messenger between El Paso and the city of Mexico [Mexico City]." [422]

Unknown is whether the death of Smith at the Pacific Chop House prompted a change of plans for its owner, W.D. Coleman. Six months later, he sold out to William A. Anderson, with the promise that Anderson would "conduct the same in the future in the same manner as I have conducted in the past, and I desire all parties knowing themselves indebted to me to pay the same to him at their earliest convenience. W.D. Coleman. Tombstone, Oct. 30." [423]

APACHES

"From Constable Letson who arrived in this city about noon to-day, we learn that a courier passed through Fairbank last evening with the intelligence that there was a band of hostiles in Cochise stronghold in the Dragoon mountains. Mr. Letson states that one company of cavalry passed through Fairbank this morning about 3 o'clock for the Dragoons, and that another company arrived about 8 o'clock this morning and are now stationed below Fairbank in order to intercept the hostiles should they attempt to cross over to the Whetstone mountains." [424]

The intermittent Indian outbreaks would bring a troop of cavalry to Fairbank, who had just been scouting in the Dragoon Mountains near Tombstone. "A. Morris came in from Charleston at a late hour last night. He brought the news that Monday a band of 25 Indians surrounded the house on Courtney's ranch in the Whetstones, keeping the family corralled all night. At daybreak the Indians drove off 40 head of horses. A troop of cavalry who had come from the Dragoons, at once left Fairbanks with one of the Courtney boys to put them on the trail."[425]

COCHISE COUNTY TAXES - SAME STORY, DIFFERENT CENTURY

Another issue that was brought to the forefront of local Contention discourse was the amount of taxes being paid there. This had been a long running issue in Cochise County, and remains so even today. But at Contention, some felt especially singled out for higher rates. An exasperated taxpayer argued with passion that Contention was being over taxed. His writings are sincere, and the fact that the fortunes of Contention City, as well as much of the Tombstone District, were well along in their mutual decline prompted frustrated citizens to question the high rates. (Fairbank was the one noteworthy exception, given that its small economy had the advantage of international trade from Mexico, via the N.M. & A.)

"A TAX RIDDEN CITY. Contention Offers the School Trustees Some Hard Nuts to Crack…In Sunday's issue of your valuable paper the school trustees published the financial condition of the district in their charge. In their statement, it appears that the expense of conducting the schools, for the five months ending January 31st, was $3,482.86. Will the gentlemen now please tell us why the schools cannot be maintained another five months for another $3,482.86? And if such a feat is possible, why do they ask an over-burdened people to vote them $8,000 to do in the next five months what $3,482.86 has accomplished in the five months just ended? Rule or ruin, eight thousand or nothing is the motto of our heaven-sent school guardians, and they are sparing no effort to win the fight which they have so unwisely precipitated between themselves and the taxpayers.

"In proof of this assertion, witness the summary closing of the public schools. In the littleness off their hearts and the fullness of their spleen, these gentlemen regard that act as a perfect masterpiece of strategy, although many who have the courage to differ with them unhesitatingly pronounce it the most rascally piece of intimidation every perpetrated upon a school going, school loving, school supporting community. It was unnecessary and is unjustifiable: it was entirely uncalled for and was done to force parents into voting for the new tax, extravagant though it be.

"Personally, I want the schools open, whether it cost eight or eighty thousand to maintain them; but when the trustees, injudiciously publish that less than four thousand will run the school for five months I, in common with most other taxpayers of this town, object to furnishing them with a sum more than twice as large as they need.

"Here, let me say, that this is the most tax ridden community in the territory. The levies the past year were unusually heavy, and occasioned more suffering than was ever before experienced in this city. We have scarcely recovered from paying those assessments before we are met with a demand for special school tax of 1 per cent. more, and I learned to-day that an extra municipal tax will be arbitrarily collected early in March to meet the deficiency in the interest on the City Hall bonds. No wonder the taxpayer cries, 'How long, Oh, Lord, how long?'

"So long as the people stand fleecing, just so long will some one ply the sheers: and I, for one, think the time has come when the sheep should call for a new lot of shepherds." [426]

Just south at Contention the decline would continue to make news. Even S. Marks, a longtime Contention success story, made the delinquent tax roll in 1885. "Marks, S. Contention, store and building on Fairbank road, value $500 tax $17.50, penalty, $2.87, collector's fee 51 cents…" [427]

CHINESE LAUNDRY TURNS POLITICAL

From the time that settlers began taming the San Pedro valley, Chinese immigrants arrived, opening laundries and restaurants, growing crops, laboring when allowed to, but they were not welcomed by the majority of the population. Settlers of European descent must have forgotten that they, too, were transplants from other places. Discrimination issues were exacerbated given the ability of many Chinese to work hard and well for long periods of time, and their willingness to work for lower pay than many others would accept. Discrimination often took center stage in race relations, sometimes with violent and tragic results. [428]

The anti-Chinese movement would come and go, and in 1886, a concerted effort would be made to run the "celestials," as they were sometimes referred to, out of the San Pedro valley once and for all. There had always been intermittent outbreaks of subtle as well as open bigotry against them, but this time an economic approach was suggested. With the decline of Tombstone, the nearby communities would face harder times as well, especially Charleston and

Contention. All of these communities had their own Chinese populations, and stereotypical as it seemed, they did often run the laundries there. Now hope surfaced in Tombstone that a new mine might generate enough funds to bring in advanced laundry facilities, thus depriving the Chinese of a living.

"That Steam Laundry. Since our last issue giving figures as to...amount of money paid out by our citizens to the Chinese, and the advantage that Tombstone would reap by the establishment of a steam laundry, our citizens have manifested a great deal of interest in the matter...If a new mine starts up in this camp and puts 50 men to work our merchants and citizens generally all brighten up, and feel that times are going to get better. Now this steam laundry will employ 75 or 100 people on [the] start, whose wages will circulate among our merchants. Carpenters and masons will be employed...in the building of the works...and best of all, if the people of this city will abstain from patronizing the Chinese, the institution will be self-supporting from the start. Agencies can be established at Bisbee, Charleston, Fairbank, Contention and Willcox, and the washing of those cities can be done here, and those towns will be rid of their Chinese populations." [429] The fact that transporting the valley's laundry to be cleaned in Tombstone and shipped back over dusty roads with transportation expenses didn't deter this half-baked idea from reaching the press.

The effort to remove Chinese from Tombstone ended up pushing some of them to Fairbank, to the advantage of those who enjoyed their cuisine. "The restaurants and bakeries in Fairbank are run by Mongolians, who have been compelled to leave Tombstone." [430]

This obviously racial post was presented to its audience a couple of years earlier as an actual story, when in reality it was a fictitious incident intended to further bias. "Among the occupants of the stage from Fairbanks to Tombstone on New Year's day were an old lady of Milesian extraction, and a Chinaman. It was a bitterly raw day and many of the passengers were complaining. After the rest were all through the Chinaman ventured to remark in his pagan English, 'Belly cold to-day.' The old lady looked at him with an air of contempt and remarked: 'If you'd put your shirt inside your pants like a Christian, you haythun blackguard, your belly wouldn't be cowld.'" [431]

FIST SWINGING JUDGE

Sam Katzenstein had been a long-time Charleston merchant, eventually becoming the judge, and was known for throwing a punch due to "too much nose paint" when the occasion struck. Now he had become of one Charleston's economic refugees and was building in Fairbank, taking as a partner one of the Rogers brothers of Benson. "Messrs. Katzenstein and Rogers, of Fairbank, have under construction a large adobe warehouse, the dimensions of which are 100 x 50 feet. This building, when completed, will be one of the finest structures of the kind in this Territory. Both of these gentlemen are old-timers and are thorough business men. We are confident that they will be very successful in their new venture. They have on hand at present a very large stock of goods, which they are selling at reasonable prices, but when this new house is completed, they will enlarge their present business." [432]

Two months prior, before beginning substantial operations in Fairbank, Katzenstein was mentioned in a case of contraband. "Samuel Katzenstein, of Charleston, made another haul of a lot of contraband goods near Fairbanks, yesterday. They were consigned to Joe Goldwater." The goods were the property of an unnamed Charleston resident. "This capture, no doubt, will aid to suppress smuggling to some extent. Mr. Wilson, collector of customs at Tombstone, was duly notified and promptly responded. He took charge of the goods, wagon, animals and smugglers and marched them to Tombstone." [433]

SANDY BOB WON'T BACK DOWN

The advent of the railroad had effectively ended the commercial stage coach travel from Benson to Fairbank, but up until 1903, the route from Fairbank to Tombstone was still open to stage operators competing for every trip. "Tim Taft says that he runs the only legitimate opposition line from this city [Tombstone] to Fairbank, and that he will continue to run the same if it takes all summer to get there. Fare 25 cts. Book yourselves at Harry Stevenson's Willows Saloon." [434]

But Sandy Bob Crouch, a Tombstone stage operating veteran who had outlasted Ohnesorgen & Walker, J.D. Kinnear, and other comers had no intention of allowing his grip on the remaining stage travel from Fairbank to Tombstone to wane. The Fairbank economy was expanding, and increased business meant additional travel to and from Fairbank. A fare war would break out at the ironic time when passengers could actually afford to pay a bit more than they could years earlier when J. D. Kinnear monopolized the roads. "Fairbanks is one of the liveliest towns on the N.M. & A. R.R., north of Nogales. Katzenstein & Rogers, the largest wholesale house there, is reaching out in all directions for trade and by liberal advertising, are reaping a big harvest. Their business had grown so large in the last few months, that they are compelled to add to [t]heir already large store, another building 50 X 100 feet, which is in [the] course of construction. Sandy Bob, the biggest man of his size, in his line in Cochise county, now has competition in the stage business from Fairbank to Tombstone, by a new line just started, and fares have gone down. A small railroad war is likely to ensue. The new line cut the rate from the former price of $1.50 to $1.00, and Sandy Bob saw the cut and went one better, and now he hauls passengers without money and without prices and if the war continues, he will doubtless throw in a chromo of Geronimo." [435] The chromo referred to was short for an image made by the chromolithography process, popular at the time for reproducing photographic images in mass.

Fairbank would soon count among its number an early explorer of Arizona to its population. "Old Uncle Sam Wise, who guided a company of Dragoons through this Territory in 1856, and who is known to almost every man, woman and child in Arizona, has settled down in

246

Fairbank and opened one of the neatest saloons in the Territory, where he will be pleased to meet all who may visit his town." [436]

Judge Mills would take over the position of Justice at Fairbank, following the untimely demise of Justice Smith, who died not long after blows to the head at the hands of a raging Thompson. "It was then ordered that Joseph L. Mills be appointed a Justice of the Peace for Fairbank, upon filing the necessary bonds with the Chairman of the [Cochise County] Board of Supervisors." [437]

Judge Mills was referred to as "a jovial fellow and an old settler in this Territory, and the man he don't know must certainly be a tenderfoot. He is among the Mexicans to-day and is doing good work. He speaks the language well and to hear him talk to them and tell them the necessity of registering one would think he was a regular politician. He was asked at the fort [Huachuca] which ticket he was running for, and he replied that he was an officer appointed by the county to register the legal voters and could not work for any ticket just yet; that the American was a free man and could use his own judgment, but the Mexicans needed a little talking to, which I think he is doing satisfactorily." [438]

Fairbank citizens, as much as their counterparts in Contention and Charleston, found time to enjoy social events. "DANCE AT FAIRBANK. The Young People of Fairbank and Surrounding Country Indulge in a Sec al Dance. "Last evening Roger's warehouse, at Fairbank, was the scene of dazzling beauty, consisting of handsome women and brave men. The dance was gotten up by the young people of Fairbank, who had extended invitations to their friends in Charleston, Contention and Tombstone, and was attended by many who availed themselves of this invitation. Among those present a reporter of THE TOMBSTONE noticed the following ladies and gentlemen:

"Fairbank—P. Demartini and wife, William Gordon and Miss Burnett, William Lyons and wife, H.B. Addington and wife, A. Wentworth and Mrs. P. Martin, Mrs. Barton and daughter, and Harry Goldwater.

"Contention—Harry Lewis, L. Larcen and daughters.

"St. David—J.C. Rilley and Miss Wilds.

"Tombstone—Joe McPherson and Miss Maxon, Jas. Hennessey and sisters, W.D. G[u]nzhorn.

"Charleston—H. Brooks and Miss McClaren.

"Grand Central Mill—H.G. Brown and wife, Miss E. Bostelli…Jas. A. Geary, P. Lawson, D.W. Martin and wife.

"Benson—W.E. Walsh.

"Good music was furnished to which the dancers tripped off, waltzes, polkas, mazourkas [aka Mazurka, a polish dance], quadrilles, etc., until the light in the west warned all that the commencement of another day had begun, and that the night of mirth and glee had come to an end when all left for their homes, firm in their convictions that the people of Fairbank knew just how to get up a pleasant social dance." [439]

The N.M. & A. was of key importance to Fairbank as well as Tombstone. The status of their manager of the operations at Fairbank was enough to gain a small mention in the Tombstone press. "J.C. Riley the general operator of the N.M. & A. railroad company at Fairbank, has returned from a visit to the old folks at home." [440]

Fairbank would bring through its doors travelers of all kinds, as the railroad always created a different dynamic wherever it went. It made small remote places more worldly. It allowed merchants to purchase items from far away suppliers and gave an air of sophistication to an otherwise unremarkable locale. The railroad would also aid in the escape of killers. Under the dramatic heading of "The Fairbank Murderer Captured at Nogales", the Daily Tombstone in the spring of 1887 told its readers that "Carmen Mandibles, the man who murdered Tomas Salcido, at Fa[i]rbank, was captured here today by James Speedy, deputy sheriff of this place. The fellow was evidently making for Sonora, and had just arrived in Nogales, at which place he had some Mexican friends. He is a sullen evil looking individual and is very much exercised at his being taken. He maintains his inosence [sic] and claims that he does not know any person in Fairbank and has not been in the place for seven months, but parties here know better as is quite well known in this town. James Speedy, arrested the murderer close to the line [border between the U.S. and Mexico] for which place he was making rapid pace. He will be brought to Tombstone to morrow and turned over to Sheriff Slaughter." [441]

It was John Slaughter who had telegraphed Deputy Speedy to be on the lookout for Mandibles, as he had already jailed the three accomplices of the accused killer, after Coroner Koska held his inquest and determined that these four men where the guilty parties. [442]

"Fairbank has a lady barber. Much of the Tombstone shaving is being done in that little town at the present time. The matter needs investigation." [443]

The affections of a young Fairbank maiden may have been at the root of another unfortunate death. "Thomas Salicido, a Mexican boy, was killed at Fairbank with a dirk knife. It is supposed by a rival for the favors of a certain signerita [sic]." [444]

THE GREAT EARTHQUAKE OF 1887

All of the San Pedro Valley would be rocked by an earthquake, which damaged the north wall of Schieffelin Hall in Tombstone, where a newspaper reporter pulled out his pocket watch and clocked over 30 seconds of intense shaking. Charleston, which was already well on its decline, would suffer greatly. A manmade reservoir known as "Kimball's Lake" near Fairbank, as well as the townsite itself, would not go unscathed. "From Bob Darragh it was learned that Kimballs Lake near Fairbank was completely dried up in twenty minutes after yesterdays shock. He also states that the embankments along the railroad were moved in many instances as much as twelve inches from their former positions. At Fairbank, the shock was very severe and many houses were greatly damaged." [445] The claim that the epicenter of this quake was Fairbank is false- it was actually Bavispe in Mexico. Had it been Fairbank the town would have been completely razed.

The repercussions of the quake continued to be reported as news came in from all over the valley detailing individual experiences. And yet, most aspects of life seemed to carry on as usual, as seen in print.

The Tribolet brothers were well-known and somewhat renowned in the San Pedro valley and Fort Huachuca for their business ventures. Charley Tribolet was responsible for prompting Geronimo to renege on his surrender to General Crook in 1886. One of the brothers appeared in the news a short time later. "We, the undersigned members of the Rescue Hose Company, respectfully request that a special meeting of this company be held…to take action in reference to the departure of chief Tribolet, with the badge of the fire department…

"It was whispered about the city [Tombstone] last evening, that the 'firemen' had held an impromptu meeting at Fairbank yesterday, and superinduced by Jerry Barton's 'bracer' proceeded to make Chief Tribolet a present of the firemans badge." [446]

The hope of Justice for a Chinaman who was robbed near Fairbank came to no avail when the case went into court, leaving the victim to wonder what rights he could count on in the future. "The Mexicans arrested some days since on a charge of robbing a chinaman near Fairbank were arranged [arraigned] yesterday before justice Shearer and upon motion of the District Attorney were discharged, the evidence not being deemed sufficient to warrant their further detention." [447]

Fairbank merchants had an advantage over those in Tombstone due to their location directly adjacent to the railroad tracks of the N. M. & A. They wouldn't have to pay for hauling their goods by wagon as did Tombstone merchants. One shop owner wanted his customers to know that he would compete with the merchants in Fairbank, railroad or not. "Paul Bahn is offering to the people of Tombstone and the county in general, some of the best bargains in groceries and liquors ever offered in this county. His stock is new fresh and desirable canned goods, wines, candles, in fact every thing sold in a first class grocery store is being sold by him at Fairbank prices." [448]

Another benefit of Fairbank's location was a set of performances by the 4-Paw's Monster United Railroad Circus that traveled from town to town via the "iron horse." Fairbank itself would not be enough of a draw for such entertainment, unless there was a larger customer base just down the wagon road, such as Tombstone. Stage coach operator Bob Darragh took advantage of the opportunity. "ANOTHER CHEAP EXCURSION. On Tuesday, December 13th, I will carry passengers from Tombstone to Fairbank and return, to 4-Paw's circus, for $2.00 the round trip, including a ticket into the circus. Tickets will be placed on sale at the stage office on Friday afternoon, December 9th. Stages will leave the stage office at 9:15 a.m. and at 2.30 p.m."[449]

As a fair amount of crime was casting a shadow over Fairbank, it was also developing a reputation as a place for rigged gambling, and the Tombstone press was quick to point out that such practices were not tolerated in Tombstone. "The usual haul of suckers was taken in by the shell games at Fairbank, last Tuesday. Chief of Police Oaks very properly refused to allow the crossroaders to work the gullible Tombstone public. And yet, if men are such fools as to bet against the game, they don't deserve much sympathy. It is as sure a thing as bunco or four aces, that a person who goes against it loses his money." [450]

J. H. Ja...ro, one of the members of the Kern County Cattle company, of Califo n..., will be here on or about the 1th ins...nt for the purpose of going over an inspecting the Boquillas land gant on the San Pedro river, which t'ev have purchased from the Hearst estate. This grant takes in all that strip of country lying between St. David, on the north, to above old Charleston, on the s...h, a distance of about twelve miles. The intention of the compay is to fence this tract in and use it for pasturing cattle. A very serious proposition now confronts the people living on this tract of land, the title to which was recently firmed by the land court, sitting at Tucson, and they now have to make terms with the Kern County Co. or be ispossessed of the homes which many of them have spent the best years of their lives in building up and improving, and which will entail heavy loss to a number of our best citizens.

On March 5th, 1899, the Bisbee Daily Orb. reports that unresolved land grant issues still plague settlers on the river, even at the dawn of the 20th Century.

Paul Bahn Warnekros, the Tombstone merchant who sold at "Fairbank prices." Original   Fly from the collections of John D. Rose.

CHAPTER 17

STRANGE BEDFELLOWS AND SHADY DEALS

"It required the forcible argument of a Colt's self-cocker to persuade Levi to release his hold." –
Weekly Citizen

"TILL DEATH (AND YOUR NEW BOYFRIEND) DO US PART"

While Fairbank was anticipating the arrival of a second railroad, crime in the area was still making headlines. "AMBUSHED." A Runaway Wife and Her Escort Waylay and Kill the Pursuing Husband. The killing of A.J. Martyn last Monday, by Charles Williams and the wife of the deceased, on the San Pedro river, about fifteen miles from Tombstone, is a remarkable tale of blood, the particulars of which were yesterday graphically narrated at the inquest held by Justice Shearer in this city, and are now published for the first time. The last heard from our vigilant Sheriff and his posse, they were still on the trail of the murderers, leading toward the Gila [river]."

One of the first to testify was Edward F. Foster, a miner who lived in Nacosari Sonora, Mexico. As he told the inquest, "On the morning of the 27th of February, A.J. Martyn, Wm. Davidson and myself left Hill's ranch, on the San Pedro, and went to Somers' ranch, and learned that Charley Williams and the woman known as Tommy Martin, had taken supper there the night before, after which they went through Somers' field and crossed the San Pedro river. We followed their tracks for three or four miles west of Somers' ranch, and about 11 o'clock we left the trail and rode up on the mesa towards some little hills where the sign was quite fresh, when we got down and left our horses and started ahead on foot. We arrived within fifty yards of a canyon running down from the hills, when I saw the horses that Williams and the woman had been riding, and called to [the] deceased and Davidson. They came towards me. I went below deceased, to his right down the mesa, and kept looking towards the horses, and again all three of us started towards the canyon. Deceased was about twenty yards ahead of me and probably about ten yards from the bank of the canyon, when I heard four or five shots fired almost simultaneously. I saw deceased stagger back, turn around and fall on his face. Davidson went up to him, turned him over on his back and spoke to him. Deceased groaned once, but uttered no word, and died almost instantly.

"A few moments after we heard a shot down the canyon, where we afterwards found a dead dog; which had belonged to Martyn and had followed the woman from Sonora. A hat and coat were afterwards found near the scene of the killing, which I identified as belonging to Williams; also some clothing was found belonging to the woman. We remained there a few minutes talking the matter over to find out what we had better do, when Davidson and I went to Somers' ranch and from there to Fairbank, and reported the killing. At Contention we met Sheriff Slaughter and went with him to the place where [the] deceased met with his death. We followed the trail of Williams and the woman on foot till sundown and then rode into Benson. Next day we came back up the river where we learned that the fugitives had stolen a horse from

Orson Elliott at Reed's ranch the morning of the 28th. The Sheriff's posse then went down the river, where it was learned that Williams had been at Etz & Everhardy's ranch, about 8 o'clock on the morning of the 28th and had got some food and an old hat. Elliott, Slaughter, Bill Showers and George Boyle went out and found their sign [tracks] leading towards Willcox. The three latter took the trail and the balance of us went down to Apadoco's. From there we started east through the hills, and then south. When east of Etz & Everhardy's we saw the track of the horse that Williams was riding and saw the Sherriff's posse were following. We then came back to Tombstone. Martyn, George Boyles, Wm. Davidson and myself left Nacosari on the 23 inst. for the purpose of overtaking Williams and Martyn's wife, for the reason that Martyn had reported to us that Williams and Tommy had taken $3530 in greenbacks belonging to him, also his horse and saddle. Williams rode Boyle's grey mare and the woman rode a dun horse belonging to Martyn. I saw these horses on the 27th inst. about 75 yards from the place where Martyn was killed. It was the trail of these two horses and a dog that we had followed. None of our party fired a shot, although all were armed. Williams had a 45 caliber pistol, but [I] don't know whether the woman had any arms or not. I heard deceased say that he wanted to kill Williams on sight. He had a rifle in his hand when shot. I cannot say whether there was one or more persons shooting at deceased. When we returned with Sheriff Slaughter to the place where Martyn was killed we found the camp, some blankets, an old quilt, coat and pants worn by the woman while living in Nacosari. All the shots were fired before Martyn fell, except the one heard down the canyon.

"Wm. Davidson testified to the facts above stated." It didn't take long for the jury to render their verdict. A.J. Martyn, at the age of 39, had been shot down in cold blood by Charles Williams and his own wife, Tommy Martyn. [451]

News in the summer of 1888 would confirm Fairbank's viability as a town, while Contention City and Charleston were fading into memory. "The Board of Supervisors have passed a resolution making eight judicial districts in this county, in each of which will be elected a justice of the peace and constable. They are divided as follows: Tombstone, Bisbee, Fairbank, Soldier Holes, Bowie, Wilcox, Benson and St. Davids." [452]

Someone who may not have been a fan of Fairbank's saloon fraternity decided upon a graphic display to discourage drinking. "The stomach of a whisky drinker was on exhibition in Fairbank recently, and it did more for the cause of temperance that a hundred lectures by weeping orators. It resembled a boot-leg which had put in about twenty years in an alley.-Prospector." [453] It's unlikely that the viewing of anyone's stomach was a delight to the eye, whisky drinker or not. And in the end, there was no record of all the Fairbank saloons closing in the wake of this display, as it's hard to keep a drinker from drinking.

JOE GOLDWATER, A RASCAL WITH A BUSINESS CARD

Joe Goldwater would later relocate from Bisbee to Fairbank. Due to the rise of Barry Goldwater in Arizona politics in the 20th Century, Joe, Barry's great uncle, has become one of Fairbank's most celebrated former residents. Mike Goldwater was Barry Goldwater's grandfather whose brother Joe would cut a colorful path through the pages of Arizona's territorial history. [454] His antics in his own day made him the focus of angry San Francisco businessmen, who were willing to have him kidnapped and brought to California. "Joseph Goldwater. His Arrest at Yuma-a Plan for His Escape Thwarted-Vigilant Detectives Outwit Perfunctory Officials. A few weeks ago we gave our readers the particulars of the crooked business transactions of Jos. Goldwater, of Yuma, who obtained goods of San Francisco merchants to the amount of about $80,000, and turned them over to third parties to avoid paying therefor. At the time his irregularities first became known there was said to be no law which would reach his case, and therefore Goldwater took no pains to conceal his whereabouts. Nevertheless…preparations were made for his escape into Sonora should an attempt be made to arrest him; and as a further safeguard a writ of habeas corpus was already prepared for signature and service should the attempt to escape fail." A series of telegrams would soon lead Bob Paul and Captain Sam Deal, chief of the railroad to a private dinner at Yuma with an awkward ending.

"When every preparation had been completed the detectives went to the store of Mr. Isaac Lyons, the supposed confederate of Goldwater, and were told that the latter was at dinner at Lyon's house. Capt. Deal and Paul proceeded to the house and found in the dining room Goldwater, Lyons…and a Mr. Levi, who is Probate Judge and also clerk in Mr. Lyon's store. Mr. Paul informed Mr. Goldwater that he was a Deputy United States Marshal and had a warrant for his arrest. Goldwater said yes, he'd go, yet he made no movement in that direction, but gave a sign to Levi, who arose from the table and went out the back door. Lyons invited the officers to sit down and partake of dinner, which offer was refused. Goldwater was again reminded that his person was wanted, and that he must go. Again he said he would go, but made no motion to do so. Paul placed a hat on the prisoner's head, and with the assistance of Capt. Deal, took the resisting offender out of the house. Capt. Stone opened the gate for them, and Levi coming up asked them where they were taking Goldwater. Capt. Stone replied they were taking him aboard the train. Levi then said he was an officer, and that he would not permit them to kidnap Goldwater, and took hold of Capt. Stone as if to enforce his demand, and would not let go until Stone drew his revolver. On the steps of the car Levi again attempted to rescue the prisoner…It required the forcible argument of a Colt's self-cocker to persuade Levi to release his hold." [455]

Whatever consequences Goldwater endured as a result of his theft, they did not keep him away from Cochise County and his enterprises there. In a letter to Albert Springer of the Cochise County Bank of Tombstone, Goldwater requested, "do me a favor to make out a petition for privat[e] subscription for to build a good crossing for the San Pedro River here, which is very much needed, beneficial for here [Fairbank] as well for Tombstone. The county gives me $200.00 in Scrip, and we must raise at least $150.00 more. When you have the paper made, please head the same with $30.00 for our firm, mark it paid, and hand the paper to Mr. Stevens. By doing so you will oblige yours truly, J. Goldwater." [456]

A change of partnership would occur at Fairbank, involving Goldwater. "NOTICE IS HEREBY GIVEN that A.A. Castaneda, of the firm of J. Goldwater & Co., has sold all her right, title and interest in the said firm to Lemuel Goldwater, who will in the future be a full partner in all the firm's business houses. The present firm of J. Goldwater & Co. consists of J. Goldwater, A. Guindani and Lemuel Goldwater, who will collect all accounts due the late firm and who will pay all liabilities of said firm. J. Goldwater & Co. Dated Fairbank, Jan. 16, 1889." [457]

It may seem unusual in that day that a woman (Castaneda) was partner in a business enterprise with two other men. But the partnership required a drastic measure to get the business running. "This was a three-partner venture involving some of Arizona's most notorious credit risks. Joseph Guindani had failed in a store operation at Florence in Pinal County two years earlier. Jose Miguel Castaneda had a record of business failures as long as his arm, at La Paz, Ehrenberg, Signal, Phoenix, and points between.

"Because there was not a name among them that would entice a wholesaler to ship merchandise to them, they adopted one: 'A. A. Castaneda,' a name which happened to be that of Jose Miguel's wife, Amparo Arviso Castaneda.

"The subterfuge apparently worked beautifully, because they bought on credit, made money, and soon had a second store at Bisbee…" [458]

As an additional revenue stream, Joe Goldwater had been subletting space in his Fairbank store. "THE UNDERSIGNED HEREBY GIVES notice that Leo Korner, partner of late firm of Korner & Peterson, keeps his office as custom house broker at the store of J. Goldwater & Co., Fairbanks." [459]

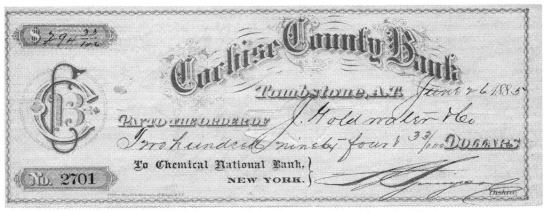

Original check in the name of J. [Joe] Goldwater, from the collections of John D. Rose.

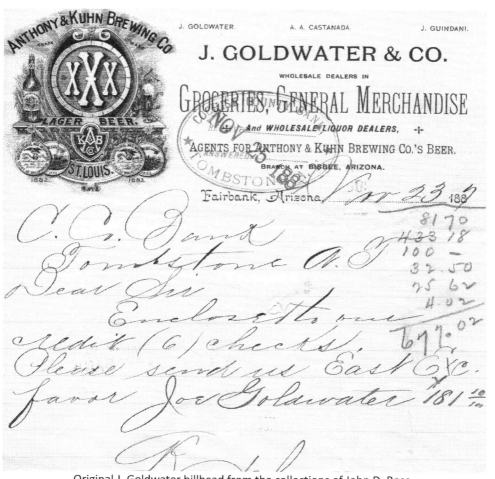

Original J. Goldwater billhead from the collections of John D. Rose.

COMPETING PLANS FOR A RAILROAD TO BISBEE?

The Atchison, Topeka & Sante Fe Railroad (parent company of the N. M. & A.) had an early opportunity to pioneer railroad service from Bisbee to Fairbank. But they were dismissive of such a project, perhaps not correctly gauging Bisbee's mining potential. In early 1885, talk surfaced that Phelps Dodge might fund the project itself. "House bill granting right of way for railroad from Fairbanks to Bisbee via Tombstone passed." [460] Now the A. T. & S. F. took notice. To discourage this plan, this article was posted in the paper: "There is strong talk at Bisbee and other points along the proposed route, upon the alleged intention of the Atchison, Topeka & Sante Fe railroad company to extend their road from Silver City to Bisbee, Tombstone and Fairbank and Tucson. The rumor is based upon an authoritative statement said to emanate from the company itself." [461] But nothing materialized outside of this rumor.

In 1887 the Bisbee mines were still dependent on wagons for shipping, and the invention of a "Steam Wagon" was deemed worth a try. "The steam wagon is now reported as doing good work, having made several trips from Bisbee to Fairbank and return within seven hours each way, hauling four loaded wagons and a water wagon. This is good work, and if the wagon continues to give satisfaction as at present six or seven more wagons will be ordered from England." [462] Unfortunately, the long-term performance of the steam wagon was not satisfactory, though its early performance had appeared promising. The machine itself worked well on hard ground, but when it traversed loose soils, it was deemed unfit for desert duty. Furthermore, men had to be sent from England to address repair issues. The failure of this experiment would prompt Phelps Dodge, under the leadership of Dr. James Douglas, to carry on with its plans to build its own railroad, known as the Arizona & Southeastern.

The steam wagon experiment which failed, leading Phelps Dodge to build the Arizona & Southeastern from Bisbee to Fairbank. Copy photo from the collections of John D. Rose.

Phelps Dodge made the project official by filing the necessary paperwork. "Articles of incorporation have been filed in Cochise County for the Arizona & Southeastern R.R. Co., for the construction of a railroad from Fairbank to Bisbee, about forty miles, the entire distance being in Cochise Co. Capital stock, $400,000." [463] This plan did not include a stopping point at Tombstone, as originally stated in the Sentinel's 1885 report.

Fairbank looked forward to its second railroad. James Douglas had long looked for alternatives to shipping by wagon. The plan that Douglas had settled upon was to run his track from Bisbee to Fairbank and connect his shipments from there with the New Mexico and Arizona line to Benson. Once they reached Benson they would connect with the main line tracks of the Southern Pacific, and from there shipping options abounded. "Work on the Bisbee and Fairbank railroad was to have been begun on Monday last by the contractors, Ward and Courtney." [464] "Fifty car loads of steel rails for the Bisbee railroad have been received at Fairbanks." [465]

In 1894 the Arizona Southeastern was looking to expand its operations. Douglas wanted to eliminate Phelps Dodge's dependence on the N. M. & A. to Benson. In order to construct a parallel line from Fairbank to Benson, they had to sue land owners in the area for a right of way. While listing the area over which they were suing, they referred to "a point near the old city of Contention…" [466] In less than fifteen years Contention City had gone from an untamed piece of cattle range along the San Pedro River to a key railroad stop and milling center, and almost back to its original state.

But with the progress of the railroad also came a more brazen type of highwayman, the train robber. Stage coaches had always made easier targets for would-be robbers - they were made out of wood and relatively slow, drivers were completely exposed and made easy targets, and shooting the lead horse made for a quick stop. Although they were by no means invulnerable, trains were more defensible, unless caught by surprise.

TRAIN ROBBERS GIVEN JUSTICE, JOHN SLAUGHTER STYLE

Sheriff John Slaughter would be drawn to the Fairbank area in June of '88 as he pursued three train robbers, with predictable results. "Sheriff Slaughter of Cochise county and his deputy had a fight with three Mexican train robbers on the 7th near Fairbanks; the three robbers were killed." [467] Many in the area were supportive of Slaughter's record of often bringing back his prisoner(s) dead, rather than alive. It saved the county the cost of incarceration during a trial, related legal expenses, and the risk of prisoner escape; and most felt that if they had the guts to fight it out with someone of Slaughter's formidable reputation, then it was just as well that they were dead.

The New Mexico and Arizona went from Fairbank to Nogales, with connections into the Mexican interior. Thus, the N.M. & A. would become known as the "Sonoran railroad," along with its affectionate nickname of the "Burro." The robbers referred to above decided to rob the train below the Mexican line, thinking they would not have to contend with American lawmen, namely legendary Sheriff Slaughter...that is, unless they made the mistake of entering Cochise County after the robbery to hide out.

The Silver Belt covered the story in more detail. "In the case of three of the Agua Zarca train robbers, vengeance has followed close upon the heels of the crime. Taylor has been delivered to the Mexican authorities, and his doom, therefore, is no longer in doubt. Two of his accomplices, Manuel Robles and Nieves Miranda, and a brother of the former, Guadalupe Robles, who was not implicated in the robbery it is said, were surprised in camp in the Whetstone mountains, twenty-five miles west of Tombstone, on Wednesday morning of last week, by Sheriff Slaughter and Deputy Alvord, and in the fight which followed the robbers' refusal to surrender, Guadalupe Robles was killed, and Manuel Robles and Nieves Miranda were badly wounded. Manuel Robles managed to escape, but was being closely followed and his capture is probable. Miranda was taken to Fairbanks and thence to Nogales to be turned over to the Mexican authorities. With the exception of Manuel Robles, whose wounds it is believed will prove fatal, even if he is not captured, there are only two of the gang not apprehended, and the Tombstone Prospector says it is only a question of time until they will be captured." [468] John Slaughter's Deputy, Burt Alvord, would again surface in the newspapers in relation to a train robbery, later time at Fairbank, though under very different circumstances.

TWO WEEKS OF RIOTING AT FAIRBANK

"The track of the Fairbank-Bisbee railroad is laid for a distance of 13 miles. When completed it will be about 40 miles in length." [469]

But with this welcome news came the inevitable turmoil brought by those who built the railroad. "The building of the Fairbank-Bisbee railroad has brought together a dangerous set of men. The Bisbee Democrat says: Fairbank for the past two weeks has been one continued scene of rioting, resulting all the way from skinned noses to homicide." [470]

Signs of economic decline would be seen in obvious ways, such as the dismantling of mills, but with lesser indicators as well. "For Sale Cheap. Eighteen yoke of cattle and six wagons All in good running order. Enquire of S. Friedman, Contention, A.T." [471]

FAIRBANK'S REPUTATION ONLY WORSENS

Slaughter's attention would again focus on Fairbank, over a vicious attack which left its victim but clinging to life. An ongoing drunk of more than two days was at the root of this horrible incident. "Sheriff Slaughter received notice this afternoon from his deputy at Fairbank that four men, Mexicans, had assaulted and beat[en] a countryman nearly to death with sixshooters and rocks about 9 o'clock this morning. Four warrants were sworn out against the men, whose names were unknown. The wounded man, Jose Mungie, is very low, his skull having been crushed in a horrible manner. The four men had been drinking for two or three days and wound up their spree by getting themselves in trouble, out of which they will not get until they have had a good long time to ruminate on the evils of intemperance." [472]

Perhaps Dr. Yarrow of the Smithsonian had been right when he implied that more damage is caused by "the killing qualities of Arizona whiskey" than the wildlife.

Amongst the visits by John Slaughter regarding wicked deeds of some, others at Fairbank found time to pursue matrimony. "George Thiel, of Fairbank, was married last Sunday evening to Miss Lydia Colburn, of Hannibal, Missouri, the ceremony taking place in that city…Mr. Thiel is well known to Tombstoneites, and is a successful business man of Fairbank. The newly mated couple arrived at their future home yesterday and were warmly congratulated by their many friends." [473]

W.A. Cuddy was a colorful character who would often appear on Arizona's frontier stage. He was formerly a hard drinker and Sergeant-at-Arms of the Lower House of the Arizona legislature, the thirteenth such body assembled in Arizona history, known then as the "Thieving Thirteenth." Cuddy would later leave Tombstone, and for a time, work in "Modesto, where I went to work for Bilicke, who formerly kept the Cosmopolitan Hotel in Tombstone. He was running a big hotel, and gave me full swing over the establishment, including the bar. The result was that I let whisky get the best of me, and made an ass of myself." Years later Cuddy returned to the Tombstone area a new man, an old west version of a "born again Christian." With his new purpose in life as an evangelist, he publicly proclaimed his intentions: "…as my life is given up entirely to doing good, I want to go among the people of Arizona." [474] "W.A. Cuddy will leave for Fairbank to-day to enlighten the heathen." [475]

INSURANCE FRAUD – AN OLD GAME

An arrest made in Fairbank was of national notoriety, and it showed that not every criminal at Fairbank had committed a crime locally, but used the area as a hideout. "Interest is revived in the Hillman insurance case, which has been in the Kansas courts since 1882, by the arrest of a man supposed to be J.W. Hillman…The case has gained wide notoriety, and the litigation thus far has cost $80,000. Hillman was insured with three companies for $35,000 and paid one premium on each policy. Shortly afterwards, in company with J.H. Brown, Hillman started from Lawrence on a trip through Southwestern Kansas. On March 5, 1879, they left Wichita, and a few days later Brown appeared in Lawrence and stated that he had accidentally killed Hillman, while attempting to draw a rifle out of a wagon, near Medicine Lodge.

"An investigation was instituted by the coroner at Medicine Lodge, the body declared to be that of Hillman and death to have been accidental. The insurance companies, not satisfied, had the body disinterred and taken to Lawrence where a second inquest was held which resulted in a verdict that the body was not that of Hillman. During this second inquest Brown, Hillman's companion on his travels, disappeared. Later he was reported at Wyandotte and is alleged to have made a confession to W.J. Buchanan in which he admitted that the body brought from

Medicine Lodge was not that of Hillman, but of a stranger known to him as 'Joe,' whom they had picked up at Wichita. When in camp on Elm creek, eighteen miles from Medicine Lodge, as Brown alleged, he was at the hind end of the wagon getting out food, he heard a gun go off, and turning around he saw the stranger had been shot and Hillman was drawing him away from the fire. Hillman…had previously changed clothes with the stranger, then transferred a diary from his pocket to the dead man's pocket, and started north. Armed with Brown's written statement Buchanan succeeded in inducing Mrs. Hillman to sign a release of the policies, but the policies themselves were in the possession of her attorneys who refused to give them up. The matter was taken into court. Brown's statement was put in evidence by the insurance companies and the plaintiff produced Brown who repudiated his statement. The companies contended that the body brought from Medicine Lodge was that of Fred Walters, from Fort Madison, Ia. Photographs of the body were identified by the father, brother and two sisters of Walters. The first and second trials of the case resulted in hung juries. On the third, a verdict was rendered for plaintiff, awarding about $37,000. An appeal was taken to the U.S. Supreme Court and there the matter rests. Mrs. Hillman has married since the second trial and is now the wife of a traveling salesman named J.C. Smith.

"Hillman's arrest as set forth in the press dispatches is said to be due to the persistent efforts of one J.W. Miller, a farmer, near Clyde, Kan., who has been on his track for years, and now claims to have found his man. The alleged captured Hillman is said to have been recognized by several who knew him in Kansas, but his positive identification is still a matter for the courts. The Hillman case is apparently good for some interesting reading in the near future." [476]

All that effort paid off in June of 1889 at Fairbank, as it was announced that "the departure for Lawrence, Ks., of detectives Miller and Franklin, having in custody the man supposed to be Hillman and who was arrested at Fairbank, Cochise county. It is said that the prisoner, while in jail at Tombstone, was positively identified as Hillman by several persons. A reward of $8,000 is offered for Hillman. Detective Miller has kept up the search for Hillman continuously for seven years, and believes he has found the right man at last." [477]

That some in Fairbank might have been in need of increased moral insights may have been partly due to a law enforcement policy in Tombstone, that is, export the problem to them. "Two youthful tramps, were given a night's lodging [in jail] by Chief Gage Thursday and yesterday morning were shown the road leading to Fairbank and given the same instructions as were given Lot's wife. They went to a bakery and fished up two-bits for bread and started down Fremont street. After going about two blocks they met a man and struck him for some money, which was given and they continued on Jordan's road." [478]

THE RIVER GIVETH, THE RIVER TAKETH AWAY

Fairbank was blessed being located near the confluence of two key waterways—the San Pedro and the Babacomari Rivers. Because the streams were often dry, the meeting of rivers in the high desert of southeastern Arizona had long provided passable routes for animal and man alike. Rivers lie at the lowest point in any given valley, and this is why many stage routes and railroads chose to locate in their general area; portions of these routes rarely exceeded three percent grades, ideal for the stage and Iron Horse alike. But with that advantage came the knowledge that such a location could, under the right conditions, flood at an appalling rate. What many in Fairbank had hoped would be a once in a lifetime event was quickly dubbed as "The Great Flood. The Body of One Man Found At Bisbee and Two Others Missing—Much Damage Done. Last Monday evening, about 4 o'clock, rain began falling and in a few minutes increased to a flood and continued about an hour and a half. Old-timers say that more water fell in that time than ever before in their recollection. The storm was a circular and seemed to revolve around Tombstone and vicinity. All the gulches were filled with raging torrents and no one ventured across the streets while the storm was at its height. All the bridges between here [Tombstone] and Fairbank were washed away and those living in the track of the waters suffered the loss of their gardens and fruit trees, in several instances three and four feet of sand being left on their cultivated land. Wells were filled up, reservoirs broken and much other damage done… Railroad bridges were washed away and it will be several days before the trains are running again.

"Fairbank was flooded to a depth of several feet and nearly all the houses partly filled with sand and mud. Considerable damage was done to property but no loss of life is reported. The San Pedro river was higher than ever before known, in many places flooding the valley several feet.

"The Grand Central mill, on the river, was compelled to shut down for a few days, but no damage was done…Tuesday evening another storm let go on the Huachuca and Mule mountains, which was more severe than the one the evening previous, but none of it reached Tombstone and very little fell at Bisbee. No damage of any consequence is reported except at Fairbank, where the flood washed down and completely wrecked the International Hotel. All the roads throughout the county visited by the storm are washed out and nearly impassable and it will be several weeks before they are in fair condition again.

"Serious washouts are reported along the S.P. railroad and the mails are very irregular, none arriving in this city last Thursday." [479]

This storm did not come at an opportune time, as telegraph service from Fairbank to Tombstone was already in need of repair, cutting both towns off from the outside world. "Owing to the telegraph lines between Tombstone and Fairbank being down the Prospector does not publish its usual dispatches to-day." [480]

262

In spite of the damage, the summer of 1890, Fairbank's role as a hub for transportation and commerce would continue. Its counterparts, Contention City and Drew's Station, were now gone, as was Charleston. "The mail now leaves Tombstone at 8:15 a.m. and arrives at about 4:30 p.m. There will be but one stage running out and one in until the railroad is repaired to Fairbank from both sides. The stage company run six horses to Fairbank, change there and make the trip to Hill's ranch, where the train from Benson arrives about 11 o'clock. Passengers are transferred across the break to the stage and upon arriving at Fairbank another change is made and six fresh horses carry the passengers to Tombstone. The enterprise shown by the stage company and the obliging disposition of the railroad company is a pleasing contrast with the wash-out days a few years ago, when no mail arrived in Tombstone for two weeks and passengers were obliged to camp until walking was good." [481]

The residents of Fairbank had lived through and survived a terrifying disaster, one that none of them present would ever forget. The only conciliation was that the shock of those events might become less of a trauma with the passing of time, unless of course, the worst was yet to come.

THE NIGHTMARE IS NOT OVER

"FAIRBANK GONE. The Flood Strikes the Town and Causes Great Damage. The Water Still Two Feet Deep and Loss Only Approximated. It was learned last night that Fairbank would suffer seriously from the flood and news received from there today proved the fears to have been well founded. James Dobson, who carried the mail down there on horse back this morning returned this afternoon and reported the town in a most dilapidated condition.

"Shortly after midnight a roar of rushing water was heard from the direction of Tombstone and was a warning to the people to get out of their houses and seek higher ground. In many instances but a few moments elapsed between the flight of the inhabitants and the coming of the water. The volume of the latter was variously estimated and was sufficient to sweep through houses four feet above ground and carry everything before it. At the same time the wind blew a hurricane, and the rain although not heavy added to the terror of the moment. Many persons rushed from their houses in a frantic condition and narrowly escaped being drowned.

"Most of the women and children sought refuge in the hay in the stage company's stables where bedding was brought and their rest made as comfortable as possible. Every house in the town with the exception of 2 or 3 were damaged.

"The heaviest loss will fall upon Guindani, whose building collapsed all in a heap, the roof falling till it reached the goods piled on the floor where it now rests. The water undermined the adobe walls and the crash followed.

"Several smaller houses were swept out of sight. The Montezuma hotel and Dr. Williams drug store escaped without any damage, being on higher ground.

"Paul Demartina's store is all right but the water went through it.

"The water was ten inches deep in McKay's saloon and this morning six inches of dirt covered the floor.

"The water was at 11 o'clock this morning two feet deep along the railroad track and the track or ties were not visible at Hill's ranch.

"The work done by the railroad company during the past week has been undone, although the track and the ties still hang across the river bed below.

"What has become of the track between Hill's and Benson is only a matter of conjecture.

"The stage road from Tombstone to Fairbank is obliterated, and no evidence of this once smooth driveway can be found. The damage can not be estimated with any accuracy, but is put at $15,000 by conservative figures."

What was surprising about the storm was its relatively humble beginnings, which only added to the shock of those who endured its wrath at Fairbank. "Yesterday was a day by itself, and was characterized by a lack of clouds and signs of rain. Up to 10 o'clock the sky was clear, but a black bank of clouds hung over the horizon in the southeast and the heavens in this particular direction were aglow with perpetual lightning. This cloud at 11 o'clock moved rapidly toward the northwest and at midnight reached Tombstone. The glare of lightning, which was accompanied by thunder, was incessant. The glare was blinding to one's eyes and the fact that no thunder was audible caused a feeling of wonderment.

"The wind blew furiously and rain fell in torrents. It was a terrible storm, and one that but few people care to ever witness again. Many persons dressed themselves and prepared for the worst. The streets were knee-deep with water. Many roofs were unable to carry off the water and overflowed the gutters into the rooms below." To make matter worse, the wind driven rains fell at a forty five degree angle allowing the water to do even greater damage as it found its way "into the most inaccessible places. After the first heavy fall was over there was a lull for a few minutes, after which another storm, accompanied by heavy thunder and lightning, but no wind, frightened many persons into the belief that the end was at hand. When the news shall have reached Tombstone from the surrounding country it is feared many cases of suffering and probable loss of life will be recorded."

Chinese farmers had also suffered in the area. They were locally referred to as "Chinese Gardens," the largest of the two being located near Fairbank, at nearly 100 acres, and other near the Boston Mill, which was north of Charleston, totally forty acres. It was no accident that they did not locate more closely to Charleston, given the brutality that had been shown some of them in its streets, and in broad daylight. This storm would bring suffering to all races in the area. "The rains this year have wrought sad havoc with the Chinese gardens on the river, of which there were two that supplied the Tombstone markets with vegetables. The one near the Boston Mill, which contained about forty acres of land, is completely covered with water and the house belonging to it washed away. At Fairbank the garden covered between eighty and 100 acres, all but four or five of which are submerged. This will result in great loss to the owners and a scarcity of vegetables for consumers.

"The Chinaman from the Fairbank gardens came to town yesterday and purchased some lumber to make a boat, in order to circulate around over his real estate, but last night's storm brought him to Tombstone at midnight with what few possessions remained to him packed on his horses." [482] Although the massive flooding would make a boat useful for a day or so, this water would soon drain away and the area would revert back to one that required no flotation devices.

The flooding so damaged the entire area that the N.M. & A. would be forced to make substantial repairs. "The N.M. & A. trains will cross the bridge at Hill's ranch tomorrow. Supt. Richards expects to reach Fairbank in three days by building around the washed out road." [483] It would also necessitate the re-routing of shipments in the area. "Three of [J.E.] Durkee's big wagons, rigged with pitch roofs of canvas, left for Fairbank this morning to bring up a lot of freight for Oso Negro, which has been lying there since before the washout, but which will have to be hauled now via Tombstone." [484]

Continued track issues would further add to mail disruptions to Tombstone. "The obstruction on the track of the N.M. & A. had not been removed yesterday in time to get to Fairbank before the stage started for Tombstone consequently no mail came in last night." [485]

There was finally good news in the wake of the disastrous storms of the summer of 1890. "Trains were running last Monday between Benson and Fairbanks, the breaks in the railroad having been repaired." [486]

But Fairbank would be plagued with this problem off and on in its continuing longevity. In 1894, newspapers reported yet another devastating flood. "From the Prospector we learn that a heavy rainstorm in Cochise county last Sunday wrought considerable damage at Fairbanks and in the vicinity of Tombstone. At the former place several houses and the stage company's corral were washed away and two horses drowned, one of them belonging to Rev. Downs. The Montezuma hotel was badly damaged, and many business houses flooded and merchandise ruined. Near Tombstone A. Morgan's house, windmill and fences were washed away; also Chris Robinson's windmill. Water ran in the gulches four to ten feet deep. Trees were uprooted and telegraph wires and poles prostrated."[487]

TOMBSTONE YOUTH LEAVE FAIRBANK WITH HANGOVERS

Given that Fairbank had a more open atmosphere to revelry in general, there were occasions when the youth of Tombstone would travel there for some unrestrained excitement.

"Quite a number of young bloods visited Fairbank yesterday, which accounts for the pale faces and headaches prevalent today among them." [488]

In spite of their local controversies, there was also a feeling of community while Contention City and Fairbank shared their individual portions of the eastern bank of the San Pedro along with the mills. The Grand Central was the closest mill to Fairbank of the three at Contention. A tragedy brought the remainder of both communities together. "Mr. J.A. Smith of the Grand Central mill wishes to return thanks to the people of Fairbank and Grand Central mill for their kindness and expressions of sympathy during the illness and after the death of his beloved wife." [489]

By 1890, the original telegraph line that ran along the San Pedro into Charleston and onto Tombstone needed to be replaced. It was a sign of the times that Fairbank was chosen as the pivot point for the replacement line, and not Charleston. Few people a decade before would have imagined it, as Charleston in 1880 was a far more important location than the area where Fairbank would later rise. "A new telegraph line is being constructed from Fairbank to Tombstone by the W.U.T. Co. [Western Union Telegraph Company] Nine men are at work placing poles. The old line via Charleston will be abandoned. The commencement of work started up a rumor that a railroad was to be built." [490] Though Fairbank was never a boomtown, its economy was more steady in nature, the railroad at its core. It provided needed transportation, supplied area ranchers and businesses, and served as a shipping point for cattle.

Natural disasters aside, a crisis of a different sort would befall one of Fairbank's most famous, or more accurately, infamous residents. Jerry Barton, the neck breaking saloon keeping brawler of Charleston fame had relocated to Fairbank due to Charleston's dramatic decline. Now his own financial difficulties were clearly on display. "SHERIFF'S SALE. By virtue of an execution issued out of the District court…in favor of A.C. Rogers, E.F. Rogers and H.A. Rogers, doing business under the firm name of Rogers Bros. and against Jerry Barton and S.A. Barton, his wife, wherein I am commanded to make the sum of $1950.00 damages with interest thereon from date of judgment at the rate of 18 per cent per annum until paid, together with accruing costs.

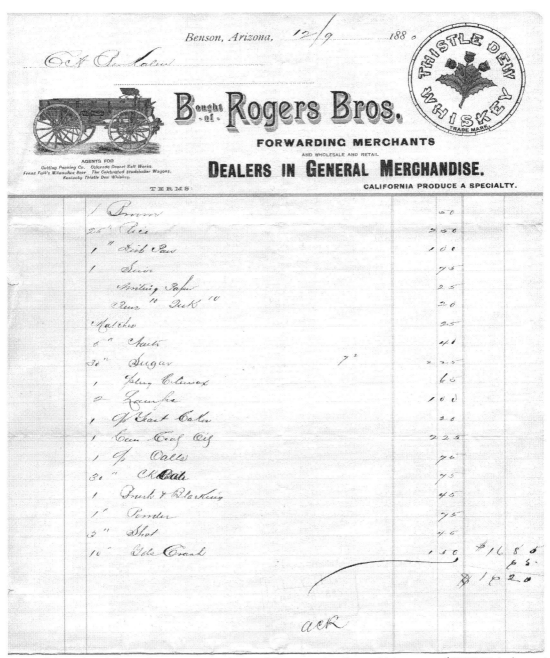

Benson, Arizona, 12/9 188 0

Bought of **Rogers Bros.**

FORWARDING MERCHANTS

AND WHOLESALE AND RETAIL

DEALERS IN GENERAL MERCHANDISE.

AGENTS FOR
Cutting Packing Co.   Colorado Desert Salt Works
Franz Falk's Milwaukee Beer   The Celebrated Studebaker Wagons.
Kentucky Thistle Dew Whiskey.

CALIFORNIA PRODUCE A SPECIALTY.

TERMS:

Original letterhead from the Rogers Brothers of Benson, the firm which won a $1950.00 judgment against Barton, forcing the Sherriff's sale of his assets. From the collections of John D. Rose.

"I have this day levied upon the following described property…Lot number ten (10) in block number five, 5, in the town of Fairbank said county of Cochise, together with tenements and improvements, also ninety eight (98) head of cattle branded thus: LL on right side, now running on the ranch in the Huachuca mountains [of] said county, together with the brand being recorded in book one of the marks and brands, page 265 Cochise records." [491] The auction was announced to take place on October 23rd 1890, under the authority of the Cochise County Sheriff, John Slaughter. Given all of the controversies that Barton had been in during his years at Charleston, and the men he had killed, fate may have wisely chosen John Slaughter as the ideal choice to confront Barton.

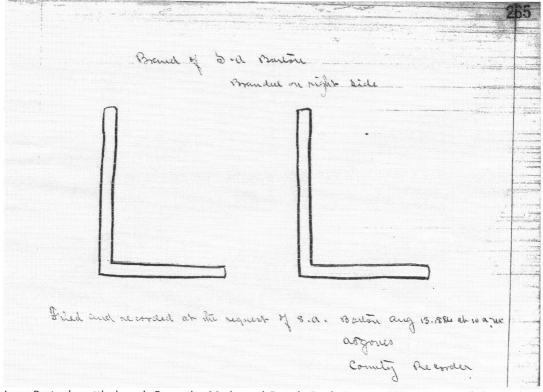

Jerry Barton's cattle brand. From the Marks and Brands Book 1, page 265, courtesy of the Cochise County Archives.

Jerry Barton's troubles aside, Fairbank could boast of its two railroads in the summer of 1890. In an evaluation of their status, the Territorial Board of Equalization valued the N.M. & A. at $6,473.00 in 1890, not at all a small amount when considering that the Southern Pacific was valued at $7,500.00. The Arizona & Southeastern was below that amount, but came in higher than it would have otherwise, owing to a penalty. "In the case of the Arizona & Southeastern, as there was no return made to the board by the company, the penalty of 30% was adopted as required by law, but which is included in the above valuation. The N.M. & A. runs from Benson to Nogales…the A. & S.E. runs from Fairbanks to Bisbee…" [492] It is surprising that the Arizona and Southeastern was errant in reporting to the board, especially when considering the very capable management of James Douglas of Phelps Dodge fame, who presided over the line he had built.

ON A FADING FRONTIER, FAIRBANK REMAINS AN OLD WEST OASIS

As the 19th Century came to a close great strides had been made turning a wild frontier into a place where towns and citizenry saw their surroundings continually improve. Geronimo had surrendered on September 4th, 1886, and though other Apaches would still on occasion leave the reservation, they were no longer considered the threat that they once had been. Although Tombstone had declined dramatically in the late 1880's and 90's, efforts continued to reopen mining there, which did occur, but milling operations were then done on site. So a number of economic refugees from Charleston and Contention City, such as Jerry Barton and Judge J.B. Smith, found new lives at Fairbank, which was now a station for two railroads. The prosperity that Bisbee was enjoying would only increase, and the Arizona and Southeastern Railroad which Phelps Dodge had built would share some of that prosperity with Fairbank as well. And more good news would appear on the horizon for Fairbank. The building of a railroad spur from Fairbank to Tombstone would become known as the El Paso and Southwestern [E.P. & S.W.], giving Fairbank a third railroad, an unusual feat for any town its size. It would also be Tombstone's only railroad, arriving in 1903.

CHAPTER 18

WATCH OUT, HE SHOOTS BACK!

"…get my six-shooter out of my bag and put it under my pillow. I'll feel better with it there." - Jeff Milton

But if anyone assumed that the dawn of the 20th Century meant the days of robberies had come to an end, they weren't reading the local news. A gang of train robbers was hiding out in the area; no one knew who they were, but on September 9th, 1899, they held up a train at Cochise, a small depot outside of Wilcox, Arizona. They secured from this heist between $2,000 and $3,000. The crime remained unsolved. The gang was not identified till over one year later, in the wake of their most famous robbery in Fairbank. [493] The New Mexico and Arizona railroad still came through the valley with regularity, moving passengers to and from Mexico, as well as massive shipments of cattle. Money moved on the railroad as well, making fine targets for bandits.

Jeff Milton, feared by outlaws, and remembered for the Fairbank shootout. Copy photo from the collections of John D. Rose.

An Arizona lawman and his wife were taking a ride in their car, traveling back to their ranch, when she dozed off for a nap. She suddenly was awakened. "We were driving up the last long mesa to our ranch near the Arizona border when I woke from a brief nap against my husband's shoulder to hear him say with a chuckle, 'They told me at the hospital that my left arm would never be anything but a useless lump of flesh, always in the way, but, by jolly, here I am driving my car with one hand and hugging my wife with the other.' And then I learned another chapter in the story of the battle in which he won that badge of courage, his crippled arm, and the longer and harder fought struggle he made to keep it." Though clearly written with the sentiment of a proud wife, her account describes Jeff Milton, a well-respected man of formidable reputation who had spent years on horseback chasing outlaws. A man of resolve and commitment, lawbreakers preferred to avoid him, while honest citizens were pleased to see him.

"At dawn of February 15th, 1900, five men broke camp in a canyon of the Dragoon Mountains and set out to ride, by different routes, down the long treeless slope to Fairbank, Arizona, in the valley of the San Pedro. Around their campfire, the night before, they arranged to meet at dusk in the river bottom near the point where, in the summer rains, Walnut gulch pours its sudden floods into the river. And they took [a] mutual oath before parting, pledging themselves to kill the first man of them who should show fear when they came to carry out the thing they had planned to do.

"Behind them, across the mountains in Wilcox and Pearce were Burt Alvord, deputy-sheriff of Cochise County, and Billy Stiles, constable, leaders of a gang of rustlers, train-robbers, and cold-blooded killers of unarmed men, for no man was allowed to live who might suspect them of complicity in the outbreak of crime in that section.

"When the gang decided to hold up the [N. M. & A.] train at Fairbank, it had been agreed it should be done on a day when Wells Fargo express messenger Jeff Milton was not on the train...none of the Stiles-Alvord gang wanted to tangle with him. It seemed a simple matter to arrange, for Styles and Jeff were old-time acquaintances. In fact, Jeff had brought Billy to Cochise County a few years earlier as one of a posse on a hunt for outlaws. Jeff says Billy was a pretty good fellow before he went broncho. [rough, wild]

"Jeff used to 'lay over' in Nogales a day or two after his run to Gu[a]ymas, Sonora, on the west coast of Mexico, before making his trip to Benson and back and when Billy came from Wilcox to Nogales for a day, Jeff was glad to see his old compadre. Billy said he wanted to introduce a mining man to Jeff and asked him to let him know in advance just when he would make his next run to Benson, so Billy could make the necessary arrangements." But the arrangements Stiles was really making were not to meet Milton with his imaginary "mining man," but rather to avoid Milton when Stiles and his gang planned to rob the train at Fairbank. A trusting Milton never saw through Stiles' plan. Milton's wife described him as having "warm, friendly eyes [that] registered everything they saw on Jeff's photographic memory." She also recalled someone once saying to her that Jeff had eyes "too kind for an officer..."

Styles would understandably think that this arrangement would keep himself and his gang safe from Milton at Fairbank, but an unanticipated situation would serve to change the course of events. "But when Jeff, coming up from Gu[a]ymas on his next trip, received orders to go on through, relieving a messenger who had been suddenly taken ill, he completely forgot his agreement with Styles." With the Stiles Alvord gang traveling in from the East, and Jeff Milton traveling along the N.M. & A. up from Nogales, the busy railroad stop of Fairbank was about to experience one of its most infamous incidents. "It was about dark that February afternoon, when the train...pulled into Fairbank. At that time Fairbank was a lively little community since it was the point where all mail, express, and freight to and from Tombstone was handled. The stage was waiting for passengers, and the usual crowd gathered on the station platform. As the train slowed down, Jeff threw open the door of the express car, greeted the Wells Fargo clerk, and began handing out packages. Suddenly a voice cried, 'Hands up.'

"'What's going on around here?' Jeff asked the clerk. 'Just a bunch of drunken cowboys having a little joke, I reckon,' was the reply. 'Poor kind of joke. Apt to get somebody killed sometime,' said Jeff, passing out another package. 'Throw up your hands and come out of there,' cried the voice. A shot sounded and Jeff's Stetson [hat] left his head.

"'If there's anything you want, come and get it,' shouted Jeff, reaching for the sawed-off, double-barreled shotgun which stood beside the door.

"Then from behind the by-standers whom they had lined up on the platform, five men, with high-powered 38.55 rifles, began pumping soft-nosed bullets at the white-shirted figure, a fine target with the light of the car at his back.

"Frightened by the noise, the stage horses were prancing, and the driver, [Ed Tarbell, see following account] who had left his high perch when the train came in, started to run toward them, but was menaced by a gun and ordered to stop. A rancher, nearly half a mile down the track, heard the fusillade and got up from the suppertable and went to his barn, thinking his horses were loose in their stalls and kicking.

"With his pistol at hand, Jeff might have jumped from the car and gone into the fray, but that weapon was on his desk in the rear of the car. His shot-gun would cut down friends as well as foes. So, with his shirt in ribbons, his left arm and side bleeding where they had been creased by bullets, Jeff stood helpless through those seconds which seemed like hours. Then a bullet shattered the upper bone in his left arm and, at its impact, the stalwart figure swung half-way round and crashed to the floor of the car.

"As he fell, the gang left shelter and rushed the car. But Jeff, who in boyhood had learned to shoot with one hand, was not yet out of the fight.

"One barrel from his gun and one bandit, eleven buckshot in his body, was down crying, 'Look out for that damned---. He's shootin' an' shootin' to kill.'

"A second bandit, with a buckshot warming the seat of his trousers, was leaving the fight and never stopped until safely across the line in Mexico.

"Half-fainting, Jeff pulled the door shut. Blood was spurting into his face from his wounded arm. He fixed his left hand in the handle of a trunk, and with his right, ripped what remained of his shirt sleeve up to his shoulder, and twisted it around his arm above the wounds. Then he fainted." In spite of the preceding moments, Milton was fortunate that he hadn't fainted seconds earlier. If so, he would have bled to death while unconscious.

With Milton unconscious, the robbers seized the opportunity, but not without caution. "Before they would risk entering the car, the three remaining bandits circled it, pouring round after round of ammunition into it. Even then, they sent the engineer of the train in ahead in case Jeff should be alive and still able to shoot. But Jeff was lying, apparently dead, between two heavy trunks, his dog whimpering over him.

"It was a fruitless victory. The bandits, who had not expected resistance, were unable to open the safe…" The robbers fled the scene of the crime. "In the riddled express car, Jeff came to consciousness to find his dog licking his face. 'Shuckins', he thought, 'I've never been this drunk before.'

"Then came the voice of Homer Pricket, conductor of the train, and as friends entered the car, the realization of what had happened came to him.

"Authority was received over the wire from Tucson to back the train to Benson where a special [train] met it and conveyed the wounded messenger to the hospital in Tucson.

"Next morning early, an eager posse was trailing the bandits up Walnut Gulch between Tombstone and the Dragoons. In the foot-hills at Buckshot Springs, they found Three Fingered Dunlap, abandoned by his companions and left to die. In extreme anguish, the terribly wounded man had begged them not to leave him, but they were determined to go on without him. Then he implored them to put him out of his misery, swearing he would give the gang's secret away if he were found alive. But they felt sure he had only a few minutes of life remaining and continued their flight.

"Three Fingered Jack lived for several days after being removed to Tombstone and made good his threat, implicating the two Owens boys, Bob Brown, and Bravo Juan, the man who had 'hightailed it' to Mexico, as well as Billy Styles and Burt Alvord, who, though not present, had planned the robbery.

"It was difficult, at first, for people to believe that these two men, respected in the community, could be concerned in the violence of the past months, but on Jack's testimony, the members of the gang were arrested and put in jail in Tombstone….Meanwhile, in Tucson, and later in San Francisco, Jeff was fighting to save his arm from amputation. Several inches of bone had been shattered and the doctors agreed he could not live unless the arm were removed at the shoulder, but Jeff felt he would rather be dead than to live with only one arm.

"One day his long-time friend, Frank King, was calling on him in the Tucson hospital. Jeff said, 'King, get my six-shooter out of my bag and put it under my pillow. I'll feel better with it there.'" [494] Milton's wounds would not heal, so his attending doctor, H. W. Fenner, sent him to the Southern Pacific Hospital in San Francisco. [495]

"When next the doctor, also an old friend, came in, Jeff explained that it wouldn't be safe for anyone to try to amputate his arm. He had been lying in the hospital in San Francisco for nearly eight months and had grown to be on good terms with the staff, when the head surgeon came into his room one day and sat down for a chat. They talked aimlessly for a time and then the doctor asked, 'Have you ever made your will, Milton?'" [496] By this time his arm was stinking and his left leg swollen the size of his body. [497]

'Why, no, Doc. Haven't anything to will anybody.' 'Oh, you must have a lot of little stuff in Arizona that you would like some of your friend to have; and everyone has some arrangements to make.'

"He hesitated a moment and then continued, 'A short time ago I got to thinking things over and made my will. Got everything straightened up. Something every man should do.'

"Jeff tried to show polite interest in what he felt did not concern him, but was startled into closest attention at the next words.

"'We've decided to take your arm off at the shoulder day after to-morrow. It wont be dangerous, but you will be here in the hospital quite long time.'

'See here, Doc…You remember when I first came I told you there'd be no arm taken off. Well, I'm still in the same frame of mind.' 'But if, by miracle you should recover without the operation, the arm would be just a dangling piece of flesh, always in the way.'

"At that Jeff rang the bell and when the nurse came in told her to have his bill made out.

"'What's that for?' asked the surgeon. 'I'm paying my bill and getting ou[t] of here today. That talk about wills doesn't sound good to me.'

"'But you can't do that', exclaimed the doctor, jumping up and approaching the bed. 'We can't permit you to leave, man. Think of the reputation of this hospital.'

"'It's my arm I'm thinking of, Doc,' retorted Jeff, pounding each word out on the side of the bed with his good hand. 'I'm quitting this place to-day and if anyone tries to stop me, he'll be carried out feet foremost. Nurse, get that bill and call a carriage.'

'There was, at that time in San Francisco, a celebrated surgeon whom Jeff had known well in Tombstone and Nogales, Dr. George Goodfellow. At one time he had said 'Milton, you're in [a] mighty dangerous business and some day you'll get pretty badly shot up. If you aren't killed outright and I can get to you, I'll save your life. Don't let anyone else touch you, but send for me and I'll come at once.'

"The morning after the hold-up in Fairbank, Dr. Goodfellow saw an account of the fight in the papers and wired Wells Fargo's office in Tucson. He learned Jeff had been operated on, the surgeons having cleaned the wound and attempted to reconstruct the missing framework from piano wire.

"Goodfellow was unreasonably hurt that Jeff had not sent for him, but Jeff was in no frame of mind for logical thinking nor for remembering Dr. Goodfellow's promise when he reached the hospital. Now, however, Jeff had one of his friends call Dr. Goodfellow on the 'phone, and then accompany him to the Lane Hospital where Goodfellow took over the case, saying, 'You and I will be down at Zincan's in a few weeks, Milt, having a champagne supper.'

"The surgeon made good on his word, and eventually Jeff returned to Nogales, but with his left arm hanging helpless, the fingers of the hand tightly clenched, and even Dr. Goodfellow holding out no hope that hand and arm would ever [be] useful again.

"A man living in Nogales at the time says Jeff's determination to regain the use of hand and arm, and the persistence of his efforts, together with the success which crowned them, will always be a lesson in the overcoming of handicaps. With several inches of the bone missing above the elbow joint, his arm had shortened. To his wrist Jeff tied a money sack filled with No. 8 shot. This hung just right to dangle against his closed fingers as he walked, and was a constant reminder to him to struggle with will and muscle to move the fingers and catch hold of the bag. The day came when his fingers made response, and in time they regained their normal strength and freedom of motion.

"Then, since the arm could not raise the hand, Jeff had to devise new ways of eating, tying his necktie, holding and driving a nail, shooting a rifle, and countless other activities. To-day he can do almost everything except 'throw up both hands.' It is problematic whether he would do that if he could."[498]

275

A FAIRBANK SHOOTOUT

"A HOLD UP The N.M. & A. Train Held Up at Fairbank

ONE ROBBER CAUGHT 'Three Fingered Jack' is Wounded and Run Down By the Posse.

Train depot at Fairbank. The sign at the front of the building identifies Fairbank as Fairbanks. Stages left from the side of the building shown, and the railroad arrived on the opposite side. Copy photo from the collections of John D. Rose.

MESSENGER MILTON SHOT"

"Fairbank was the scene of a hold up last night, three masked men armed to the teeth making a raid on the N.M. & A, train just as the north bound passenger train pulled into and stopped at the station.

The movements of the robbers and their methods would indicate that they were no novices in their work, exhibiting plenty of nerve and reckless courage and during their brief stay made things very exciting as a hold up usually is. The robbers secured but little booty for their trouble and although various reports are given out as to the amount of money secured it is authentically stated that but one package, containing $17 in Mexican money, which happened to be out of the safe in the express car is missing.

"The particulars as learned by the Prospector from several eye witnesses is to the effect that as soon as the train stopped and the agents and helpers were busy unloading and loading mail and express matter, three men were seen to emerge from the side of the depot platform. One of the three men went to the engine and the other two hurried to the express car, ordering everybody to throw up their hands and immediately began shooting by way of enforcing the order. The bystanders, with hands aloft, were somewhat scattered and the leader commanded all to 'bunch up' punctuating his remarks with comprehensive profanity. It is needless to say all hastened to obey. Presently the engineer and fireman came from their post and were marched to the crowd w[h]ere they were also commanded to remain with hands up. The first robber who stopped at the engine had marched the two railroaders to the crowd at the point of a pistol.

"Meanwhile a fussil[l]ade of shots was kept up and the mail and express car was perforated with shots. Express Messenger J.D. [Jeff] Milton appeared at the door of his car with a Winchester and began firing at the robbers. At the first fire from Milton one of the robbers was positively seen to fall to the ground. Whether he was wounded or not is not known but he returned the fire as did also the others, when suddenly Milton dropped having been shot in the right arm. At this exciting moment the horses on the Tombstone stage, who were nearby, became frightened from the shooting and started to run away. Driver Ed Tarbell, who was in the 'bunched' crowd started to head them off when one of the robbers sternly ordered him to halt, Ed wisely halted. Then the robber who had fallen to the ground as stated above, fired several shots at the fleeing animals, one bullet taking effect…and effectually stopped the runaway although at the probable cost of the horse which may die.

"When it was evident that Milton was helpless, one of the robbers climbed into the express car with a sack and hurriedly rummaged through papers, packages etc. The…safe was locked and but little value was found. Quite a number of things were overlooked in the hurry of the robber and no attempt was made to blow open or have the messenger unlock the iron box. It is said but one package containing $17 Mexican money is gone…

"The leader of the robbers then turned his attention to the depot and inquired of the 'crowd' where the agent was. Agent Gay was in the 'bunched crowd' but discretly [sic] kept silent and none of the others cared to impart…his whereabouts. With another voluminous outburst of profanity, the robber went to the door of the depot which was locked. He kicked down the door, walked in, found all the safes locked and came out empty handed. The three robbers walked off together going west of the depot where it is presumed they had horses ready in waiting.

277

"The train immediately backed to Benson for medical assistance for Messenger Milton. It is understood the bones in his arm are so shattered that amputation will be necessary. The injury to Milton is to be regretted. He was a brave and efficient officer and well know[n] here.

"A Sheriff's posse was organized last night in Tombstone and were at the scene as soon as possible. Trailing was impossible last night as no trails could be found. This morning more officers were sent out and notifications were dispatched in every direct ion to keep a sharp lookout. No clew whatever is had to the identity of the robbers thus far."

The case would break open quickly. "LATER. Just as we go to press Deputy Sheriff Geo [George] Bravin arrived with the information that one of the robbers was found and proved to be Three Fingered Jack, the notorious character who was recently released from the county jail here [Tombstone]. Jack was found shot in the abdomen being the wound he received from Messenger Milton during the hold up. " [499] One by one, the robbers were hunted down and brought to justice.

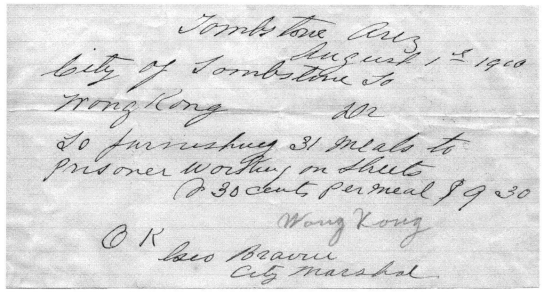

Deputy Sherriff George Bravin, who at gunpoint watched the Alvord Stiles gang break jail, signs this bill for 31 meals for prisoners doing street work in Tombstone. The meals were provided by Wong Kong. From the collections of John D. Rose.

278

"BRAVO JOHN"

"The strong Testimony Which Held Him to Answer"

"The examination of Thos Yoea, otherwise known as 'Bravo John' on U S charge of obstructing U.S. mail was had before Commissioner Emanuel this afternoon. 'Bravo John' had no attorney and did not care for one. 'Bravo John' is charged with being one of the five who held up the…train at Fairbank on Feb 15th. There were but three witnesses for the prosecution, Ed Tarbell whose testimony was to show that he witnessed the hold up. Deputy Sheriff Mullen one of the posse on the trail of the robbers told of the chase and running onto Three Fingered Jack lying wounded on the prairie. The deputy told of Three Fingered Jack's dying statement saying that the Owing Brothers, Bravo John, John Brown and himself had robbed the train. 'Bravo John' was identified as the man referred to by Three Fingered Jack.

"W N [William,aka, Billy] Stiles, the confessed train robber in the Cochise holdup, was also an important witness in this case. He stated that he [had] seen the five men just named, at a ranch in the valley and they informed him that the party proposed to hold up the train at Fairbank on the night that the robbery was committed. The Owing Brothers had told him that they just sold their cattle and proposed making a haul and get out of the country. 'Bravo John' was present and one of the number.

"When the prisoner was asked if he cared to question witnesses he replied no and also refused to make any statement. Court Commissioner Emanuel held the prisoner over to await the action of the grand jury under bond of $10,000.

"The cases of Owing Bros and Bravo John also Downing and Alvord under territorial charges of trainrobbery will come up tomorrow. [500]

"J.D. Milton, the fearless Wells Fargo messenger, who several weeks ago at Fairbanks sent one robber to the other side, was out yesterday from the hospital. Mr. Milton said that he still felt a pain in his left arm, the result of wounds inflicted by the robbers, and was otherwise better. The injured arm will be in plaster [of] paris for a long time and in the end it will be two inches shorter." [501]

NO HONOR AMONG THIEVES

"JAIL DELIVERY Wm Stiles, Who Turned States Evidence, the Liberator

DEPUTY BRAVIN WOUNDED

Burt Alvord, Bravo John and Stiles Get Away...Posse in Pursuit

OTHER PRISONERS STAY

Halderman Brothers and the others Choose to Remain-Calmness of the Deputy

THE PRISONERS KINDNESS"

Cochise County's train robbing lawman, Burt Alvord. Copy photo from the collections of John D. Rose.

"About 3 p m Tombstone was thrown into a fever of excitement, the like of which has not visited our city since the days of the hanging of [John] Heath by an indignant mob. The occasion for this was the news of a jail break at the county jail and the shooting of Deputy Sheriff Geo Bravin who was wounded in an attempt to block the break for liberty.

"Despite the most precautionary measures taken by the Sheriff's office to guard against any attack of friends of the prisoners in jail on [the] charge of train robbery to secure their release by force, as was feared, the expected happened, but from a source that was never suspicioned, the dastardly work being done by Wm Stiles, the self confessed train robber who turned states evidence against his pals, then further proved his treachery by attempting to help them escape from jail, even at the sacrifice of the lives of any who might stand in the way. Fortunately the brave Deputy Sheriff, Geo Bravin, was not killed though he had a most narrow escape.

"Last evening Matt Burts was brought over from the Tucson jail for his preliminary examination here for train robbery. Wm Stiles the principal witness who turned states evidence, also arrived to testify. It was deemed advisable by the authorities and prosecution not to place Burts in jail in company with the other prisoners on some charge for reasons that are obvious. As a consequence Burts was under guard of the two deputies. His trial was to be had today and was again to be taken to the Tucson jail tomorrow.

"While the guards were away from the jail with Burts, Deputy Sheriff Bravin was left alone in charge of the jail. Wm Stiles, who, up to this time had helped the officers in everyway to prosecute his pals, and who was believed to be the last man to even think of aiding in a jail break, suddenly pushed a six shooter at Deputy Bravin, while in the front jail room and commanded him to deliver the keys of the jail. Bravin was unarmed…Bravin…knocked at the pistol of his assailant. At the same time Stiles shot and the Deputy fell. Stiles in an instant secured the keys and opened the main cell doors inviting all the prisoners to make a break for liberty. Burt Alvord and 'Bravo John' both charged with train robbery came out and, rushing to the front with Stiles, took three Winchester rifles and two six shooters…and hurriedly left, the three going down Fremont street to the ranch of John Escapule below town where they stole two horses, grazing near, and rode off toward the Dragoons two of the men riding one horse.

"The opportunity to escape was offered to the entire 24 prisoners in jail. As the Halderman brothers came out, Deputy Bravin spoke to them saying kindly that they better not attempt escape as they would not have time to get away. Both of the condemned men said: 'all right George, we'll stay.' Wm Downing one of the accused train robbers refused to go at all as was also the case of the Owen brothers under the same charge: Sid Page also remained inside. Several of the other prisoners started to go and one prisoner named Griffith, at the request of the deputy, closed the iron door bars.

"The Halderman brothers seeing the wounded condition of the deputy, together with the other prisoners, carried him to a bed in the ante room and endeavored to relieve his pains.

"A few minutes after the escape several posses were in pursuit and are believed to be but a short distance behind the three fugitives. Many determined men offered their services and were sent out. The feeling runs high and should the escape[e]s be recaptured the probability for a lynching is exceedingly good.

"Bravin is shot through the calf of his leg the bullet passing below his knee, through the leg and taking off two toes on his other foot. He is resting easy at his home under the medical care of Dr. Walter. Up to this writing no news from the posses has been had." [502]

There would be no quick capture of this group. Nearly a month later a substantial reward was being offered. "A total reward of $1500 is now out on the heads of the Tombstone jail escape[e]s, Bert [Burt] Alvord, Wm. Stiles and Thos. Yoes, otherwise known as Bravo John." [503]

"Bob Brown charged with being one of the Fairbank train robbers, was brought to Tombstone yesterday from Texas, where he was arrested, and is now in the Tombstone jail. Brown made no resistance enroute and quietly came with the officer. He protests his innocence of the crime charged against him and expects to prove his case at the coming term of court." [504]

THE PLOT THICKENS

"A Confession of the Fairbank Train Robbery

"...there was a sensation in the district court at Tucson yesterday when George Owings confessed the charge of train robbery in which he was implicated with Brown and several others. It was during the trial of Brown, the man who is said to be the leader of the band...Owings took the step he did without solicitation, it was as much a surprise to the district attorney as to the crowd that assembled in the court room to witness the trial.

"The confession was complete, the story was told with graphic effect, every detail and circumstance of the Fairbank holdup, the days of planning, the craftiness of Burt Alvord in providing protection for the men who were to take part in the affair, the preparation for the first nefarious work of the band which was to be but a beginning of a series of holdups. It was a scene which might form the foundation for a yellow-back novel, and the story would be one of more, than ordinary interest in thrilling scenes and picturesque description.

"George Owings and Louis Owings were arrested along with Alvord, Stiles, Bravo Juan [aka, Bravo John], Downing, [Matt] Burts and Brown soon after the Fairbank hold-up. Very little was known of the Owings brothers and but for the confessions made by Three-Fingered Jack when he was found dying upon [the] trail of the fleeing bandits these men would probably not have been suspected...Owings told of the part taken by Alvord, how he organized the gang, commissioned Bravo Juan the captain of the crowd, and secured men in Wilcox who would give their testimony that the men were innocently playing cards in a saloon in some town or camp at the time of the hold-up. Every possible protection was made, every care of the successful consummation of the crime, and Alvord looked after the preparation to the last. But he remained behind and let the others do the work. Owings' confession left the defense of Brown in a precarious position, for Owings, too, was to be tried for interfering with the United States mail. When he was taken back to his cell he told his brother what he had done, and Louis this morning came into court and pleaded guilty along with George." [505]

By the following December Billy Stiles and Matt Burts were back in custody and testifying at the Downing hearing. It revealed a remarkable tail of outlawry, theft, treachery, and proof that this was not the happiest bunch of criminals, nor did they all get along with each other. Matt Burts admitted that "He would like to see Downing's neck broke." Stiles made light of his treachery to the authorities who had trusted him saying "...the whole matter of the Cochise county jail delivery was gone over." The Stiles Alvord gang would long be remembered less for their crimes, and more for the treachery of Billy Stiles, who betrayed his outlaw comrades by first testifying against them, gaining the trust of Deputy Sheriff Bravin, and then shooting him in favor of their escape. Jeff Milton would remain a lawman, later bringing to justice the perpetrator of a bank robbery in Tombstone.

While working as the historian in 1995/96 on the San Pedro and Southwestern, a tourist railroad that ran from Benson to the Charleston area, I met an elderly gentleman who told me that he had known Jeff Milton while working as a shoe shine boy at a Tucson Hotel. I had already grown leary of people making such claims of having known historical characters, but he had correct answers to every historical question that I asked him, so much so that I found him to be credible.

I asked him of his memories of Milton, whom he said was a gentlemen, well liked, and kindly toward children. He also noticed the respect that others paid the aged lawman, almost a reverence as well as a bit of celebrity. I eventually asked him if Milton ever mentioned the Earps. Without hesitation he told me of this conversation: "You know those Earp boys they're always going on about?" "Yes," said the boy. "Not one of them was ever half the man that I am."

On petition of the lawful number of Electors of Fairbank Precinct, J. C. Burnette was appointed Justice of Peace of said Precinct, resident at Ft. Huachuca,

On April 7th, 1892, Jim Burnett becomes J.P at Fairbank. From the Cochise County Archives.

Jim Burnett. Copy photo from collections of John D. Rose.

A stage coach leaving Fairbank for Tombstone. Copy photo from the collections of John D. Rose.

Original bill for shipping cattle from Nogales via the N.M. & A. Note Fairbank in the circular stamp. Original bill from the collections of John D. Rose.

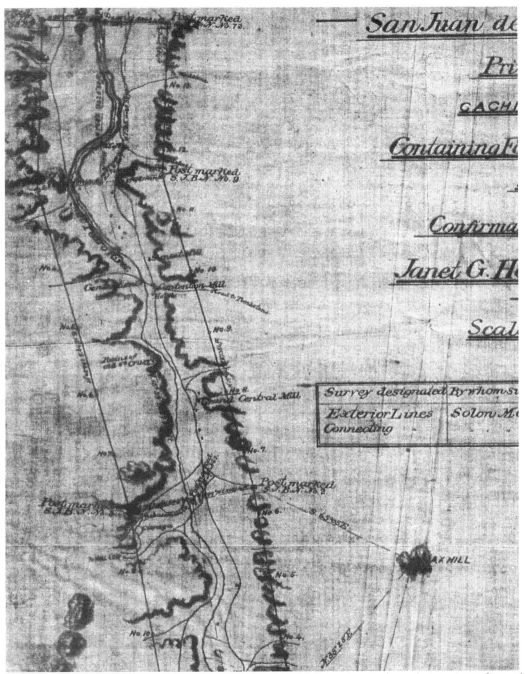

A portion of Solon Allis' map of the Boquillas Land Grant, showing its boundaries. Copy from the collections of John D. Rose.

WHALING MUSEUM

AND

OLD DARTMOUTH HISTORICAL SOCIETY

18 Johnny Cake Hill — New Bedford, Mass.

March 15, 1960.

Mr. Alfred L. Paul,
2805 Larkfield Ave.,
Arcadia, Calif.

My dear Mr. Paul:

In answer to your letter of March 8 regarding Robert Havlin Paul, the following information was obtained from crew lists:-

	Age	Height	Color	Hair
July 20, 1842 -				
Robert Paul, Lowell - Returned in the ship Master was Shubael Hawes	12	4-9	L	Br.
(Also with above) John Paul, Lowell Probably a brother	17	5-3	D	Br.
Sept. 30, 1844 -				
Robert Paul, Lowell Master was Shubael Hawes	14	4-9	L	Br

We have no further knowledge of this man. I would suppose Mr. Paul's education was no more than of a common grammar school.

Yours sincerely,

Philip F. Purrington

Philip F. Purrington
Curator

P:R

A research inquiry by Alfred Paul into the early adventures of Bob Paul at sea. Copy of which from the collections of John D. Rose.

Legendary lawman Bob Paul in his later years. Copy photo from the collections of John D. Rose.

Original Billhead for a funeral and burial at Fairbank, from the collections of John D. Rose.

Two original Arizona & Southeastern railroad passes, signed by James Douglas, from the collections of John D. Rose.

Images of working cattle on the Boquillas ranch, which also included another area where Contention City had once been, from the collections of John D. Rose.

Cowboys branding at the Boquillas, into the 20th Century.

Above copy images from the collections of John D. Rose.

Coal bins at Benson.

A luxury railroad car for the E.P. & S.W., the first train to Tombstone. Above images copy photos from the collections of John D. Rose.

Riding the Arizona & Southeastern, Bisbee picnickers head form Lewis Spring, 1894.

Ca. 1907, train arrival in Benson. Above copy photos from the collections of John D. Rose.

J. O. DUNBAR,
County Treasurer Cachise County, Arizona.

LOCK BOX 256.   *Tombstone, A. T.,* _____ *1881.*

Original printers sample of John Dunbar's stationary, from the collections of John D. Rose.

An original supply order dated July 14th, 1874 at Tres Alamos. From the collections of John D. Rose.

School house at Tres Alamos, ca. 1920's. Copy photo from the collections of John D. Rose.

No. 386   Tombstone, A. T. Jany 25   1883

I, J. H. BEHAN, *Ex-Sheriff and ex-officio Tax-Collector of the County of Cochise, Territory of Arizona, do hereby certify, that by virtue of an Act entitled "An Act Amendatory to Chapter XXXIII of Compiled Laws of Arizona Territory, to provide revenue for the Territory of Arizona, and the several counties thereof, approved April 12th, 1875," approved March 10th, 1881, I have this day sold for taxes to* Territory of Arizona _____ *for the sum of* 147.08 _____ DOLLARS. *the following described property* Hotel, Lands & Imps 160 acres Contention 4000 Liquors & Bar fixtures 300 Horse 50 Harness 15 Hotel and Restaurant Furniture 500

Said property was assessed to L. Meyers & Son *on the Assessment Roll of Cochise County, A. T., for the year 1882, in the sum of* $ 4.865 ____, *the taxes and costs on which amount to* $ 147.08

And the said property is subject to redemption in six months, pursuant to the Statute in such cases made and provided; and that the said Territory of Arizona _____ *is entitled to a deed for said property on the* 25 *day of* July _____, 1883.

                                        J H Behan
                    Ex-Sheriff and Ex-officio Tax-Collector Cochise County, A. T.

384

Meyer's opulent Hotel and real estate investments aided in his tardy taxes. Courtesy of the Cochise County Archives.

Fairbank, 1995. Photo by John D. Rose.

Fairbank School house, today a well restored museum by the BLM. Copy photo from the collections of John D. Rose.

J. GOLDWATER. A. A. CASTANADA J. QUINDANI.

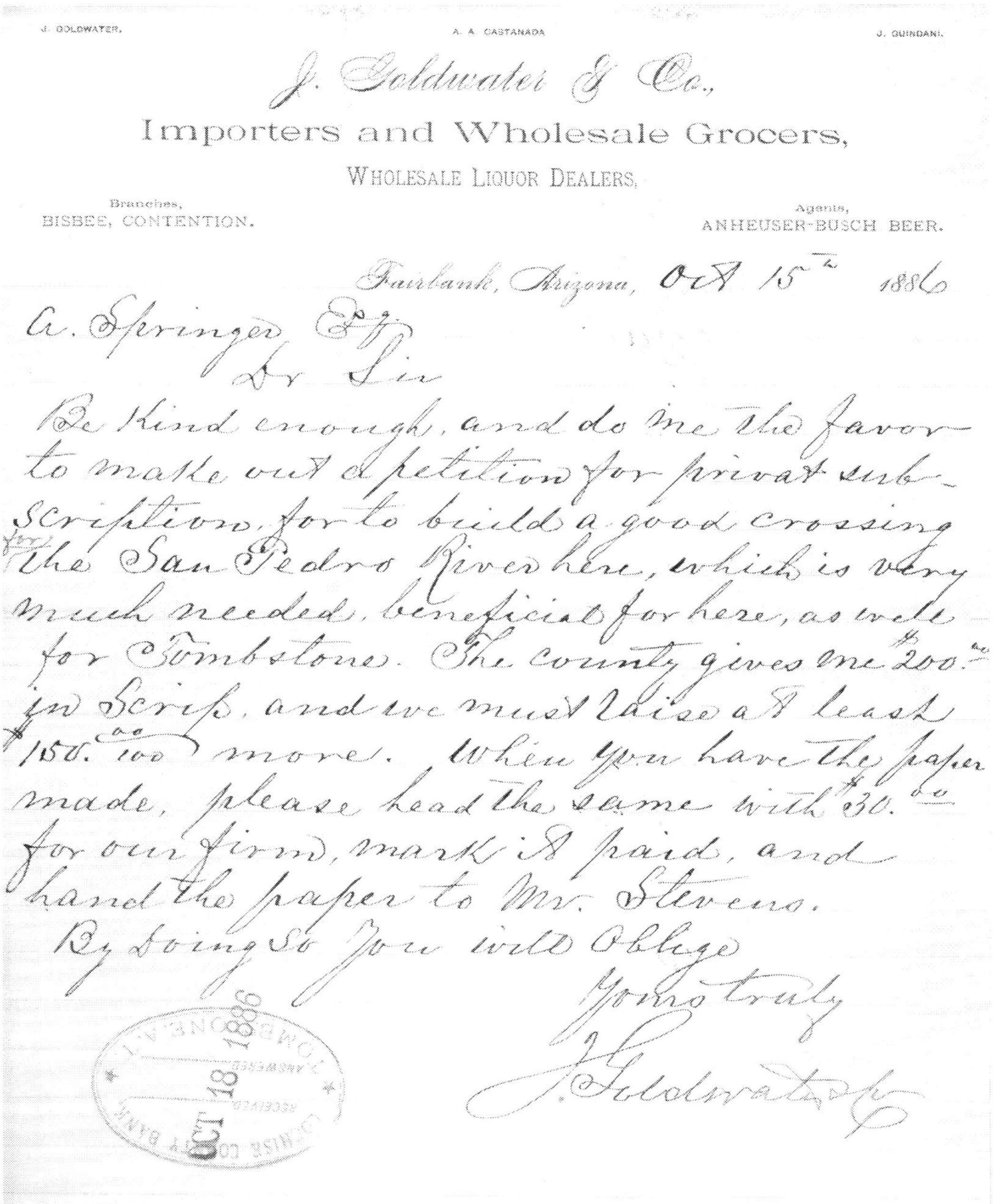

J. Goldwater & Co.,

Importers and Wholesale Grocers,

WHOLESALE LIQUOR DEALERS,

Branches, BISBEE, CONTENTION.

Agents, ANHEUSER-BUSCH BEER.

Fairbank, Arizona, Oct 15th 1886

A. Springer Esq

Dr Sir

Be Kind enough, and do me the favor to make out a petition for privat subscription, for to build a good crossing for the San Pedro River here, which is very much needed, beneficial for here, as well for Tombstone. The county gives me $200.00 in Scrip, and we must Raise at least $150.00/100 more. When you have the paper made, please head the same with $30.00 for our firm, mark it paid, and hand the paper to Mr. Stevens.

By Doing So You will Oblige

Yours truly

J. Goldwater & Co

OCT 18 1886 RECEIVED ANSWERED COCHISE COUNTY BANK

Original letterhead written by Joe Goldwater attempting to raise support for bridging the San Pedro at Fairbank. From the collections of John D. Rose.

OFFICE: 209 EIGHTH STREET.

Tombstone, A. T., ... 188

M ....

To FULLER & FULLER, Dr.

To .... Gallons of Water, at ....

From ....

Received Payment,

On the evening of March 15th, 1881, Bud Philpot and Peter Roerig were murdered in the wash just south of Drew's Station, and Doc Holiday was implicated as one of the shooters. Given his lack of personal popularity, and local anger over the senseless killings, had there been a provable case against Holiday at the time it most certainly would have been proven. Part of Holiday's alibi is that he rode from the Wells outside of Tombsttone with Old Man Fuller, who owned a water hauling business. This original water bill from the firm of Fuller & Fuller is from the collections of John D. Rose.

Long after neighbors such as Charleston to the south and Contention City to the north, Fairbank would endure, through the end of the 19th century and into the 20th. Copy photo of Fairbank from the collections of John D. Rose.

A FADED FRONTIER IS ALL BUT FORGOTTEN

"He was a man, take him for all in all, I shall not look upon his like again."-Shakespeare

Many had abandoned the San Pedro Valley as it declined; yet occasionally some would return as visitors to these once important locations which had given them opportunity and where they left their own unique marks. After Tombstone, Robert Burnham made his residence in Providence, Rhode Island. "Mr. Burnham is not a stranger to Tombstone having been in charge of the Contention mill in the palmy days…He is here on a visit to his old stamping grounds and meeting several old acquaintances." [506]

Joe Pascholoy, former owner of the Occidental Hotel in Tombstone as well as an associate of Nellie Cashman, paid Fairbank a visit, seeing a local celebrity of the big horn persuasion. "Joe Pascholy, the old Tombstone pioneer was a welcome visitor yesterday from Nogales…Our six horn sheep is quite an attraction to visitors, and as it roams over the street it doesn't seem to think it bears any more honors than any other sheep but it is a general pet. The Montezuma hotel is undergoing a thorough renovation, [a] new dining room, the refreshment room being newly floored, bed rooms arranged and the general manager Jean Larrieu, is leaving nothing out to give satisfaction to the traveling public. Mr. [Nicolai] Anderson, the professor of the cyanide process at the Contention mill, was a visitor yesterday. Mr. L. Larrieu left yesterday for Tucson expecting to be gone for a few weeks." [507] Anderson would die in December of that same year.

"FROM FAIRBANK Jeff Milton, genial Chinese inspector at Fairbank, spent Christmas day in Tombstone with friends." [508]

IF THAT HAPPENED TO ME, I WOULDN'T BRING IT UP

Jeff Milton would leave Fairbank, only to return later. While away at Ajo Milton had an unfortunate incident with his pistol. "JEFF MILTON RECOVERS FROM ACCIDENTAL BULLET WOUND Inspector Jeff Milton, formerly of Fairbank but now of Ajo, came to the city today from Tucson, having just left the hospital, where he has been confined the past week as the result of having been shot in the groin when his automatic pistol was accidently discharged. Mr. Milton was greeted by his many old time friends, and congratulated on his narrow escape. He still suffers a little pain, but expects to be able to return to his post in a few weeks." [509]

The Grand Central Mill had allowed John Clum use of their primitive phone after his midnight walk on December 14th, 1881. Now, 36 years later, a more advanced and comprehensive system was being installed. "BUILDING A NEW LINE A big force of men is at work near Benson installing a new telephone line between that town and Benson via Fairbanks. The construction force consisting of about twenty men, is now camped about a mile and a half out of Benson, on the St. David road, and supplies are hauled as rapidly as possible in motor trucks in order to expedite the work. Besides the new Bisbee-Benson line, the Mountain State

Telephone and Telegraph Company will extend anther from Fairbanks into Tombstone and a branch line extended to Huachuca and Hereford from a point about midway between Fairbank and Bisbee." [510] Conspicuously missing from the listing of cities were Contention and Charleston.

The next century had begun, and with it, a war that few in Fairbank in the 1880's could have imagined. On August 5th, 1917, the Tombstone Epitaph printed "OFFICIAL DRAFT LIST", noting five men from Fairbank who were to be drafted into WWI.

Even 20th century transportation acknowledged Fairbank's continuing presence. In 1913 the "ARIZONA GOOD ROADS ASSOCIATION ILLUSTRATED ROAD MAPS AND TOUR BOOK" was published for the adventuresome traveler who had forsaken horse and wagon for the horseless carriage that was to become the next rage. The Fairbank Commercial Co. gained mention, and Fairbank itself was described: "The Hub Commercial trading point of the renowned San Pedro Valley is situated on the Great State Highway near the banks of the flowing San Pedro River. It has the distinction of being located on the branch lines of the Southern Pacific Railroad from Benson to Nogales and also the branch lines of the El[]Paso and Southwestern Railroad from Benson via Fairbank to El[]Paso, Tombstone to Fairbank, Fort Huachuca to Fairbank, and greatest of them all, Tucson via Fairbank to El[]Paso, over which runs the Golden State Limited. We are also located within a half mile of the great 200-acre vegetable gardens. Livery Stable, Hotel and Restaurant, Telegraph Offices, Long Distance Telephone and U.S Mail in connection. All mail and messages sent in our care will be held for addressee

"Our stock comprises Auto oils and greases, Gasoline, Hardware, camping outfits and a complete line of everything found in an up-to-date General Merchandise Establishment." [511]

By 1922 it appeared the automobile (unlike the steam wagon) was going to stay, so better roads had to be constructed to keep vehicles, men, and materials moving through the valley. "Al Jenkins, project engineer in charge of [the] construction of the Nogales-Tombstone state highway in Cochise county, was in town yesterday and said that from now on motorists could use the completed highway for about two miles…He also stated the he had been delayed for various reasons in moving camp to Fairbank but would do so during the ten days ensuing, having already moved some of the equipment." A reminder of the old days was still at Fairbank-Jeff Milton. "FROM FAIRBANK. Immigration Inspector Jeff Milton was up today from his headquarters in Fairbank." More prevalent to the current economy of Fairbank were cattle shipments and ranching in the area. Drew's Station, Contention City, were no longer running stage coaches and stamp mills, but cows. "FROM FAIRBANK H.K. Street, superintendent of the Boquillas Land and Cattle company, was a business visitor in the county seat [still Tombstone] today. [512]

In the year of 1925, the Arizona State business directory issued made no mention of Contention City or Charleston. They had faded decades ago, but such was not the case for

Fairbank, which was referred to as a small town and post office in Cochise County about 20 miles south of Benson. Given that Fairbank still had railroad access, it was considered an important supply point for surrounding country. The directory told that Fairbank held a population 200. The Boquillas Land and Cattle Co, was a key employer in the area, with Robert Tourr as its superintendent. Surviving businesses included the Fairbank Commercial Co, a general store, and the Fairbank Hotel, owned by A.L. Heney[513]

Although Tombstone did rate mention in the directory, it is indeed ironic that when describing the location of Fairbank, instead of mentioning its proximity to Tombstone, Benson was instead chosen as the nearby city to best orientate the reader as to where Fairbank was located.

WHEN A MAN'S YOUTH BECOMES HISTORY

In his declining years Billy Breakenridge would author *Helldorado*, and make a return trip to his old Cochise County haunts that had been a part of his youth. "During the summer of 1926 I took an automobile trip through Cochise County looking up the old camps and towns that have been abandoned. At Tombstone, we found that a large number of the houses built of lumber had been removed to other mining camps. Fire had destroyed many other buildings, and three fourths of the business houses were empty and boarded up. It looked like a deserted village. From a city

WILLIAM (BILLY) BREAKENRIDGE
In the early 80's Wm. M. Breakenridge was a deputy, under Sheriff Johnny Behan. In the above picture Billy is shown heading a "Helldorado" parade in Tombstone on what is now BROADWAY OF AMERICA (US 80). Helldorado was a word coined by "Billy" as the title of a book he wrote of the early days.

Billy Breakenridge rides in a Helldorado parade, wearing his badge. Original picture postcard from the collections of John D. Rose.

of eight thousand [actually 5,380] it has dwindled to about five hundred…Of [the] Contention and Grand Central, where the two mills were built, with the exception of the tumble-down walls

302

of the mills and the tailing dumps, there was nothing left to show that there ever had been prosperous towns there."

Of Contention's notorious contemporary, Charleston, Breakenridge noted that "We found it was impossible to get to Charleston with a car because the bridge had been washed away, and there were deep washes on each side of it, so we walked in. There was nothing left but the adobe walls of the old buildings, partially fallen down. All the woodwork was gone, and mesquite trees six inches through were growing up inside the walls and in the streets."

Breakenridge also added that of all these vibrant locations, by 1926 "Fairbank is the only town left." In taking the time to write down the story of his life, Breakenridge grew introspective at the end of his writings in Helldorado. He had the advantage of having outlived so many of his contemporaries, but still found value in the experiences that he had spent much of his adult life in pursuit of. "As I look back, if I could live my life over again, I think I should like to live the same kind of life." [514] Quite a statement from anyone who witnessed all the best and the worst that the west had to offer.

THE ROAD TO TOMBSTONE IN THE PAGES OF HISTORY AND LEGEND

The 1920's would see another aging lawman return to the area. Like Breakenridge, Wyatt Earp wanted to tell his story, and he traveled with long term confidant and attempted biographer, John Flood. Earp was now in his seventies, and he drove a borrowed car from an old friend in Benson along the very stage road that had been such a part of his youth. Most of the locations on it were now history. They passed Drew's Station which still had erect walls, but abandoned. From the ruins of Drew's Earp and Flood soon crossed the same wash that Bud Philpot had driven in his final moments of life. They later joined the roadway upon which a grieving Earp had escorted the remains of his brother Morgan to an awaiting train at Contention City. At last they reached their destination, Tombstone.

Wyatt Earp later in life, at a time when telling his story was of paramount importance to him. Only after his death would the story of his life reach levels of fame that even he could not have imagined. Copy photo from the collections of John D. Rose.

Given that Flood was to write Earp's life story, "Wyatt showed Flood all the important sites…so that when they started on the manuscript he could better visualize what had happened….No-one recognized Earp, slightly stooped and dressed in a conservative grey business suit; but then, there was no reason for anyone to expect him to make an appearance. Walking the deserted streets, they lingered at the location of the famous gunfight, Wyatt pointing out the shallow embankment leading into the roadway from the vacant lot where it all began, explaining how his brother Morgan had tripped over an exposed pipe of the Sycamore Springs Water Company, probably saving his life that day. Earp became sadly reflective only once, in front of the spot where Campbell and Hatch's billiard parlor and saloon once stood. It was there, on the evening of March 18, 1882, that Morgan was murdered. With an emotional voice, Earp confided to Flood,

'This is one place I can never forget.' By late afternoon they drove back over the dirt road to Benson, catching the evening coach to Tucson and points west." [515]

For many who care about the west and its transformational impact on the American identity and story, places like Drew's Station, Contention City, Fairbank and Tombstone each qualify in their own way as locations that none of us can ever forget. Nor should we. Those transformational events that shaped the American West forever reshaped the American psyche, and the search for the truth of these events, rather than the intoxicating mythology of them, is a wonderful journey that I hope many choose to take. It has been a life enriching experience that I would not trade, and like Billy Breakenridge, if I could live my life over again, I should think that this quest for knowledge would remain one facet of it that I would not want to change. To borrow from Breakenridge, for differing reasons, I too "think I should like to live the same kind of life."

-John Rose

THE END

Where exactly was and is Drew's Station?

The site of Drew's Station is a location that has long generated a great deal of interest: it was an active stage stop for only a short period of time, it was incorrectly named on a survey, there is limited historical documentation relating to it, and it was located on the larger Drew's ranch which covered 160 acres, with more than one building thereon. The shooting of Kinnear and Company Stage coach driver Bud Philpot near Drew's is a key event in the Tombstone saga, and has only added to the interest in this site. As a researcher and writer, it was important for me to locate every resource possible which would identify the correct location. Luckily, there exist statements from William Drew himself (in the Drew vs. Mason court case) and others who lived and worked in the area, including T.W. Ayles and Bob Paul, which substantiate the site which I have identified in this book and on my website, WyattEarpExplorers.com. (articles entitled "Drew's Station" and "New Drew's?").

The account of Thomas Webb Ayles as cited in Chapter 1 was written in Contention. Ayles would not only understand where Drew's Station/Ranch was in relation to Contention City, but also the location of the point of attack between Drew's and Contention. And Ayles had another first-hand source of information. Eddie Drew personally told Ayles exactly where he found Bud Philpot's body, laying in the wash where he was shot off the top of the Kinnear Stage which he was driving, "...the wash just below Drew's Station..." From the Contention City perspective, this would mean *before* the stage had reached Drew's, or south of Drew's. The Epitaph describes it as follows: "As the stage was going up a small incline about two hundred yards this side of Drew's Station and about a mile the other side of Contention City..." The Epitaph is a Tombstone paper, and in describing the scene to its readers there, "this side of Drew's Station" would be to the south, or the Tombstone side of the station. The "other side of Contention City" would then be to the north of Contention City. The Epitaph estimate of "two hundred yards" from the wash to Drew's Station is in reality underestimated. It is actually 533 yards from the wash to the station, although one of their outbuildings approximately 200 yards from the wash, matching the Epitaph's account.

Also note that Paul's description of the holdup in the Arizona Republican of June 26th,1892 matches the Epitaph description of March 16th, 1881. "A short distance from the ranch was a 'wash' about ten feet deep which lay in the road of the stage. When in its bed Philpott [sic] and Mr. Paul noticed four men, two on each side of the ride, standing on the elevation they were approaching." The stage was coming out of the wash, as the Tombstone Epitaph put it, on "this side" of Drew's station, clearly to its south, as was the wash in which Philpot was killed. In fact, there are no other washes that intersect the north bound stage road between the correct Drew's site and that proposed by TTR/Sosa.

In 2011 it was asserted by Mrs. Nancy Lewis Sosa, on behalf of the group known as TTR, that Drew's Station was farther north than the site I have named and marked on the above maps in Chapter 1. The TTR/Sosa site is 2.43 miles north of south side Contention City, more than one mile farther than the Epitaph report. From the north side of Contention City, the TTR/Sosa site is closer to two miles, still double what Bob Paul stated in his telegram to authorities in Tombstone, on which the Epitaph based the key points of its account.

For support of her site Mrs. Sosa points to the work of 1880's surveyor Solon Allis. Allis was hired to survey and map the San Juan de las Boquillas y Nogales land grant, beginning the project on February 23rd, 1881. While surveying the boundaries of the grant, he also made mention on the resulting map of key points such as Contention City, the Contention and Grand Central mills, and the old ruins at Santa Cruz (de Terrenate) among others. In Allis' notes, he makes mention of other landmarks along his line of measure: adobe house (numerous references to these), new hotel, high gulch, old chimney, etc. On one line of entry he mentions "Drew's House." If one were to use this note to measure Drew's location, it would place Drew's Station closer to the TTR/Sosa site. However, Allis may have mistaken the home of a Morgan or another settler who owned the property north of Drew's, or was simply misinformed as to which homestead was which while working the area. (See Page 285.)

The map pictured by William Carlyle on the following page is for a proposed toll road. The map contains errors. Clearly, the map is not to scale; Billy Ohnesorgan's ranch and stage station at Tres Alamos, aka, the San Pedro Station, is located north of Benson. Still, the map is not without merit, and it does show Drew's as being south of lands claimed by "Morgan." It is in this area that the TTR/Sosa sites are found.

William Carlyle proposed this roadway enterprise to the Pima County Board of Supervisors on November 13th, 1880. This is a different road than the one laid by Robert Mason, William Drew, and H. F. Lawrence, which became what was later known as the "Benson Road," the one that Bud Philpot was traversing when murdered.

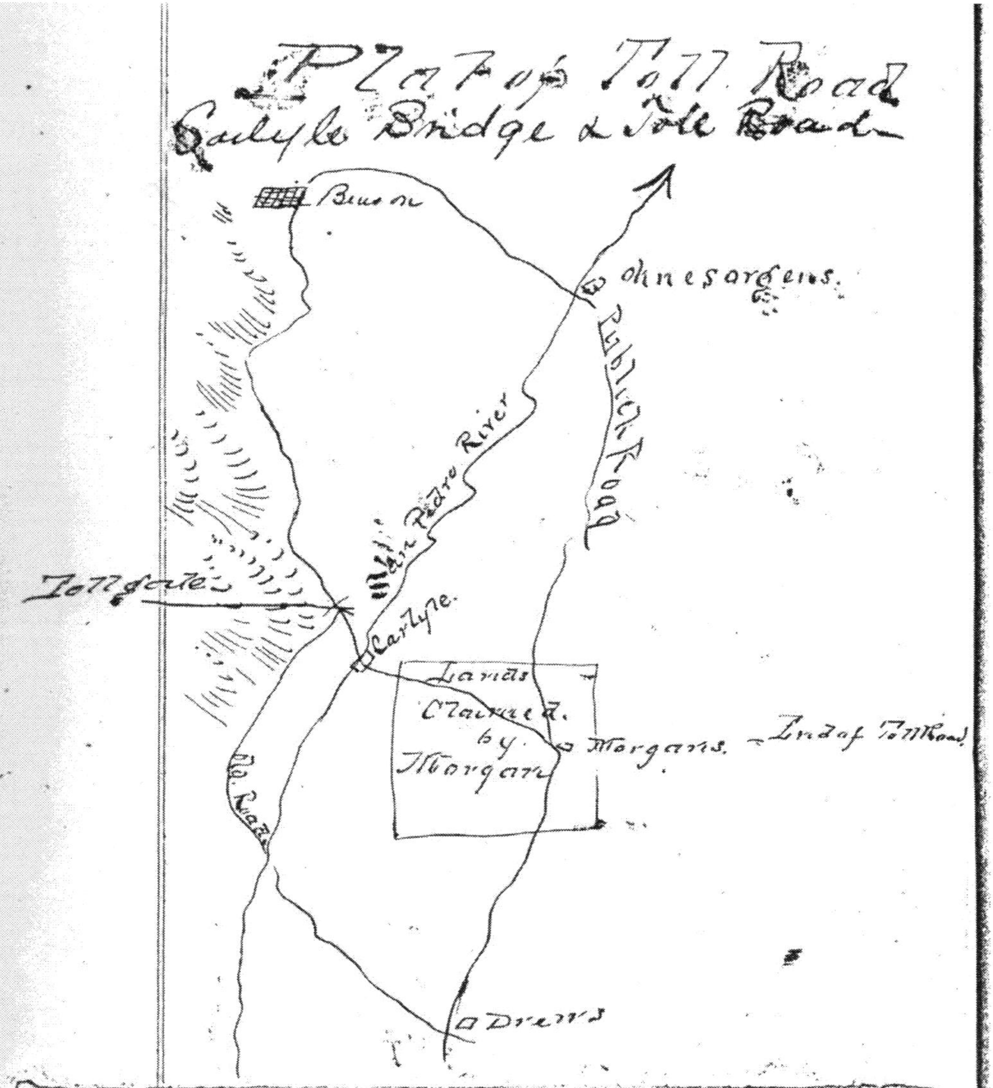

Plat of Toll Road
Carlyle Bridge & Toll Road

Benson

ohnes orgens.

Publich Road

San Pedro River

Tollgates

Carlyle

Lands
Claimed
by
Morgan

Morgans.

End of Toll Road

Drews

Rates of Toll

One Span Animals.	25
Each add. span	12½
Each add. Waggon	12½
Loose Stock pr Head	6¼
Horsman	6¼
Footman	5

308

Allis' key job was defining the true boundaries of the grant, so that the Howard/Hearst partnership knew for certain what lands they had right to as owners. It was not a census to establish the name and location of every inhabitant on the grant, as evidenced by the fact that most buildings are just described rather than specifically identified.

The TTR/Sosa site was actually discovered by BLM employee John Herron, who officially recorded the discovery on October 10th, 1990 by using the Allis survey notes. Since 1990, the Sierra Vista BLM office has widely distributed a contemporary, non-historic, USGS map marking the Herron discovery as Drew's station. This and binders full (along with the Allis Survey) of Drew information are found at the Chiricahua Regional Museum, Willcox Arizona.

San Pedro Riparian
National Conservation Area

Bureau of Land Management
Rural Route 1, Box 9853
Huachuca City, AZ 85616
602/457-2265

December 13, 1990

Mr. and Mrs. Bill Aseltine
~~████████████████████████~~

Dear Bob and Virginia,

I was recently doing some archaeological research and read the notes of a Mr. Solon Allis who did a survey of the San Juan de las Boquillas y Nogales Land Grant in 1881. I located in his incidental description a "Drew House". I plotted his measurements on a USGS topographic map, and went into the field to see if I could locate the house in question. Stumbling through a mesquite thicket at the edge of the San Pedro River I found the corner of an adobe structure. There isn't much left, but I believe this to be the best documented location of the house your family lived in. The location is further north than any of the experts told us it was.

We now have a real location and not just rumors. Best wishes and a Merry Christmas.

John Herron
Archaeologist
San Pedro NCA

A letter from BLM Archaeologist John Herron informing members of the Drew Family that he had discovered a site that he believed to be Drew's Station. Though this site is not Drew's Station, it is the same site which Nancy Lewis Sosa believes is Drew's Station, as well as her discovery. Dated December 13th, 1990, it is clear that Mr. Herron arrived at the site over twenty years before Mrs. Sosa. The address of the family members has been black lined for their privacy.

309

Having interviewed Mr. Herron by phone, I learned that the Allis notes were his only source for identifying this as Drew's Station. I asked him if he had any other primary source for this, and he stated to me that he did not. This means that Mr. Herron made the determination that his site was Drew's Station based on the Allis notes alone. But Mrs. Sosa has the advantage of having a copy of the Drew vs. Mason case, the principle primary source as to the location of Drew's Station. Mr. Herron did not have the benefit of this case when he made his determination. I was the first to publish the existence of this case in 2011 on WyattEarpExplorers.com, under the "Drew Family Scrapbook" article. As previously stated in this book the Drew vs. Mason court papers contain the conclusive information of Wm. Drew's three mile estimate from the ruins. Mrs. Sosa has yet to acknowledge this key information within them, or the fact that this alone disproves the site she claims is Drew's Station.

In his sworn testimony in his trial with Robert Mason, Wm. Drew explained that his homestead was located "about three miles North of the old San Pedro ruins…" The TTR/Sosa site is four miles north of these same ruins. Mrs. Sosa has still not published any of her primary sources that she believes support her argument, which she said she would do in late 2010.

Mr. Kenneth (aka K.t.K) Vail supports Mrs. Sosa on her site, and has made many other errors regarding the location where Philpot was shot, and when and where the wagon roads were established. Vail claims that he has "been unable to find a single contemporary account which places the ambush to fit all the books written about the incident…it dispells [sic] the long-held notion that the ambushed [sic] happened before Drew's rather than after the stage stop". He states, "Correct me if I'm wrong, but if the 'down coach' gets attacked at 'the wash' it means on the Benson side." Vail, in his second statement, is assuming that "down coach" means from north to south. Actually the term "down coach" referred to the stage coach that was coming down from Tombstone (higher in elevation) to Contention, and then on to Benson.

Vail has asserted that since Bob Paul's telegram from Benson to Tombstone was written in Benson, then the directions to the site are reversed, and are written for those traveling from Benson south to Drew's and then to the scene of the shooting. Such a description would only deter the real reason for Paul's sending this all important telegram, on which the Epitaph based its report. It was to recount the route from Tombstone to Contention and beyond that Paul and Philpot had just taken. It is obvious that Paul sent directions to officials in Tombstone for the purpose of directing posses to the scene to start following the tracks of the killers. Bob Paul gathered men to accompany him from Benson to the location of the shooting, so he would not need to give directions starting in Benson. In fact, Paul's directions were so clear that by the time he and his men reached the wash, Philpot's body had been removed.

Vail has also accused Dr. Gary Roberts of misquoting the T.W. Ayles account. Roberts, a respected historian and author, replied, "I've not misquoted Ayles I simply interpret it differently. I have always taken the wash 'just below Drew's Station' to mean the wash on the Contention side od [of] the Station. I would expect him [referring to T.W. Ayles] to have said the wash 'just BEYOND Drew's Station,' were it on the Benson side." Although Roberts added that his mind is not made up on the matter, he was exactly correct. His assertion is backed by Bob Paul's account.

Roberts further added that "...while there is some dispute among the researchers who have worked to locate Drew's Station, most have placed it on the road after passing the wash." Vail's position is summed up as follows: "All I care about is that Cora Drew Reynolds backs Bob Paul on point." Vail and others should care about the fact that the founder of Drew's Station, Wm. Drew, gives a description that shows the TTR/Sosa site to be too far north to be the actual Drew's Station. Cora stated that the shooting took place after Philpot's coach passed their station going north. But Cora was about eight years old at that time. And she does not at all corroborate Paul's description.

Another Vail research error is the following statement: "At this point about August [of] 1879 Drew is nowhere near the place up river from the San Pedro state [station] that would become Drew's Station..." Vail further asserts that "Drew's opened for business June 1880...Before [the] Benson Road' was ever invented there existed the original Tombstone Road direct to Tucson by another route." In the past, Mr. Vail has accepted Cora Drew's accounts without reservation, even though she is recounting them decades after the events occurred, and some of her claims have been proven false by other contemporary sources. Cora was, however correct in saying that her father Wm. Drew helped construct their stage station and home. This is backed by his own testimony in the Drew vs. Mason case. If Vail insists that Drew's did not open until June of 1880, he is actually contradicting Cora here, and has William Drew building his station after his death in November 1879.

Wm. Drew testified that settling and building the ranch began on April 10th, 1878, placing him at that very location for over a full year. He further testified that by the end of 1878, he had built a home, dug a well, built a corral, extended an irrigation ditch to his property, and started raising crops.

Regarding his statements as to the available roadways at the time, Vail further claims the route to Tombstone at that time traversed the "southern end of [the] Whetstone Mts....The stagecoach road from Tucson came by way of Camp Wallen." He is literally on the wrong side of the valley. Vail next states, "there was no such thing as [the] 'Benson Road' before June 1880." It is true that the road that traveled across Drew's ranch was not known as the Benson road until Benson was established in June of 1880, but Vail falsely concludes that this means there was no road that crossed Drew's Ranch and headed toward the area where Benson was about to be founded.

The road in that area did exist, and was improved upon, as proven by the documents published in this book from Mason's ranch in the summer of 1878 when they laid out a newer version of it– the road was not called the "Benson Road", but the established road in the area ran from Tucson to Tres Alamos (Ohnesorgen's stop eight miles north of the future Benson town site) and on to Tombstone. Mr. Vail should take note of the August 13th, 1878 document from Mason's ranch showing the laying out of the roadway from Tucson to the Upper San Pedro Settlements, then across Mason's and Drew's ranch. He should also take notice that on November 19th, 1878, the Pima County Board of Supervisors approved funds for the repair of this road. That this area was well traveled before Benson was established is further confirmed by

John Vosburg's mule ride to Billy Ohnesorgen's, as well as the accounts of Ed Schieffelin and Dick Gird. The travel time and expense of commercial stage coach traffic from Tombstone to Contention to Benson traveling through Camp Wallen and near Whetstones defies reason, and the record. Just because a road ran through Camp Wallen does not mean that it was the road used for commercial stage lines traveling from Tombstone, to Contention, past Drew's and onto the area where Benson would be built.

Vail further advocates the veracity of a reward poster claiming the Philpot robbery happened "at a point about two miles west of Drew's stage station." (See page 209, *Wyatt Earp, Life behind the Legend*, by Casey Tefertiller.) Philpot's route was from Contention to Benson, a south to north route. The stage did not travel west at this point; that would put Drew's and the robbery west of the river. Drew's was clearly on the east side of the river. The poster is in error.

And lastly, Vail supports Cora Drew's claim that Bud Philpot changed his horses at Drew's Station on the night of the March 15, 1881 robbery attempt. Once again, Cora was a little girl, recalling this information decades later, no doubt remembering the past times when Philpot did stop with his team when Drew's was yet a viable station. According to Bob Paul, Bat Masterson was riding that coach that night. "On March 15, a stage left Tombstone with a silver bullion shipment...Bud Philpot was driving, and Bob Paul was riding shotgun...while Philpot changed his teams at the Contention station, the cowboys had ridden cross country to intercept the coach and rob it." (*Bat Masterson, The Man and the Legend*, by Robert K. DeArment, University of Oklahoma Press, page 200.)

In conclusion, it is clear that the stage was travelling south to north from Tombstone to Contention to Benson. The attempted robbery happened south of Drew's Station: "...At Drew's Station the firing and rapid whirling by of the coach sent men at the station to the scene of the tragedy..." The horse team ran out of control after the first shots were fired, galloping at fever pitch past Drew's. Bob Paul's account places Drew's Station two hundred yards north of the second wash north of Contention City as noted in the satellite photo on page 15. This second wash is one mile north of the northern end of Contention City; the TTR/Sosa site is two miles north.

This fact, combined with William Drew's statement that he was located three miles above the ruins, provides definitive proof for the Drew's location that I have published. Solon Allis is the principal primary source as to the boundaries of the Boquillas Land Grant. Wm. Drew is the principal primary source as to where he lived, and built Drew's Station. Drew himself provides clear proof that the site discovered first by John Herron of the BLM, later publicized by Mrs. Sosa as her discovery and supported by Kenny Vail, are not Drew's Station.

312

1 Territory of Arizona }
2 County of Pima } ss
3 District Court }
4 First Judicial District }

5 William H Drew }
6   Plff' } Complaint
7   vs } for Injunc-
8   } tion and
9 Robert Mason } damages,
10   Deft' }
11
12 The plaintiff complains and
13 alledges,
14 First
15 That the plaintiff on, to wit,
16 the 10th day of April A.D. 1898
17 settled upon and improved
18 as a homestead a certain tract
19 of public land of the United
20 States in the San Pedro val-
21 ley in said Pima County
22 Territory of Arizona, about
23 one mile South of what is
24 known as the old California
25 crossing of the San Pedro
26 river, and about three miles
27 North of the old San Pedro
1 ruins,

As this court record from Drew vs. Mason shows, Wm. Drew confirms his home was about three miles from the ruins at Terrenate, and not four miles that the TTR/Sosa/BLM site requires. This disproves the Solon Allis survey notes regarding the location of Drew's Station.

1. *LUZ DE TIERRA INCOGNITA*, Juan Mateo Manje, Unknown Arizona and Sonora 1693-1701, published in limited edition by Arizona Silhouettes, 1954, Tucson Arizona, page 78

2. W.B. Garner, Administrator of the Estate of Thomas J. Bidwell, vs. Richard Gird; deposition of Ed Schieffelin, pages 284, 285.

3. Photo copy of both documents in the collection of John D. Rose. Records indicate that this roadway as surveyed by Robert Mason, Wm. Drew and H.F. Lawrence, went into almost immediate use. On November 19th, 1878, the Pima County Board of Supervisors appointed A.A. Wilt as Road Overseer for the "San Pedro Road District and that the sum of Five hundred dollars be allowed to build [a] bridge and repair [the] road…" The fact that just three months after the Mason/Drew/Lawrence survey, the road was in need of repair, likely means that travelers began using the road in its primitive state, and then the county attempted to improve it once in use, which was often the case in such boom areas. It is likely that Drew began his enterprise of a stage station as soon as travelers began crossing his land, offering him readily available income. The bridge mentioned may be the one noted on Wm. Drew's map. This notation may have referred to where the bridge was planning to be built, or where it had been built. If it was indeed constructed, it may not have lasted long. But if that were the case, then it's less likely that Billy Ohnesorgan's bridge at Tres Alamos to the north would have made any profits, which it did. The bridge may have been built only to be destroyed by flooding, or, it may be that the board was overly optimistic that it could make needed road improvements as well as building a long lasting bridge. Note that the Mason/Drew/Lawrence estimate of the road work alone was $650.00, making the $500.00 appropriation by the Pima County Board of Supervisors underfunded at its inception. Minutes, Pima County Board of Supervisors, November 19th, 1878, courtesy of the Office of the Clerk of the Pima County Board of Supervisors, Tucson Arizona.

4. Arizona Citizen, November 2nd, 1878

5. Arizona Citizen, February 15, 1879

6. Arizona Citizen, September 19th, 1879

7. Arizona Citizen, Friday, June 13th, 1879

8. Arizona Citizen, May 23rd, 1879

9. Transcript, William Drew vs. Robert Mason, 1879, Courtesy AHS

10. Arizona Citizen, August 15th, 1879)

11. My life in the Early West, by Cora Drew Reynolds, copy in the collection of author

12. Daily Epitaph, May 30th, 1881

13. My Life in the Early West

14. Ibid. Further confirmation of Coras' claim that brother Ed Drew had a wood cutting operation is found in the May 3rd, 1882, Daily Epitaph: "Information reached town [Tombstone] yesterday of the killing of two men at Drew's wood camp in the Dragoons, several days ago. Several stories were in circulation about the Contention affair, and while they differ, all agree that it was nothing serious." Nor was the claim that raiding Apaches had killed two men at Ed Drew's wood camp. Although Cora refers to Ed's wood cutting camp as being located in the Chiricahua's, this range is much farther from Contention than the Dragoon Mountain range is, and hauling the wood from the Dragoons as this contemporary account notes would have made Ed's wood cutting enterprise more profitable, and the more likely choice of location.

15. Arizona Citizen, December 19th, 1879, quoting the Tombstone Nugget, December 18th, 1879

16. *Tombstone Travesty*, Frank Waters, 1st Version, Pages 92-94. Allie does not name the stage station, she only says that they stopped at one. Her account reveals that Virgil's horse was injured five miles south of the stage stop where fist fight occurred. After leaving that stage stop, she tells of traveling the stage road until the reach Tombstone. She makes no mention of any stage stops following the one where Virgil fought the offending driver. Therefore, Drew's is the location where this occurred.

17. Daily Epitaph, March 18th, 1881. Thos W. Ayles was of diversified interests. He joined with Bramer Brown to lay claim to a mill site near the Tombstone town site on September 1st, 1879 where they had already constructed a well and tank. Pima County Millsites, Courtesy Arizona State Archives, Phoenix Arizona.

18. AN ARIZONA VENDETTA. (THE TRUTH ABOUT WYATT EARP_ AND SOME OTHERS) By Forrestine C. Hooker. Facts stated to writer by Wyatt S. Earp, page 22)

19. Lotta Crabtree Will Case Papers, Harvard Law School Library, page 318

20. *The Tombstone Stagecoach Lines, 1878-1903: A Study in Frontier Transportation*, by Thomas H. Peterson, Jr., P. 32)

21. Daily Nugget, March 17th, 1881

22. Tombstone Epitaph, July 3rd, 1892, Arizona Republic, June 26th, 1892

23. My Life in the Early West

24. Tombstone Daily Epitaph, March 16, 1881

25. Arizona Republican, June 26th, 1892

26. Garner vs. Gird, testimony of Thomas E. Walker pages 394-395, Garner vs. Gird, exhibit O, page 397, Oxnard Daily Courier, October 31st, 1921; "Charleston and Millville A.T., Hell on the San Pedro, by John D. Rose, page 16

27. Daily Epitaph, March 17th, 1881

315

28. From the discovery and subsequent extensive field research of this road, the exact route is now known, the only one that could have been taken without tremendous delays, additional mileage, and a harder route for the passengers, the animals, and the safety of the coach itself. See "Tombstone Stage Road," WyattEarpExplorers.com.

29. AN ARIZONA VENDETTA, Pages 17 and 18. This may be information that Bob Paul shared with Wyatt Earp, as Earp would join Paul in pursuit of the robbers immediately after the killing. Wyatt Earp was not a witness to this conversation, as he was not on the stage that evening. It is therefore hearsay, an account that might possibly have been passed from Paul to Earp to Forrestine Hooker. It is of note that Wells Fargo, later defended Doc Holliday against the accusation of being one of the shooters.

30. Note that according to Bob Paul, the stage left Tombstone with four passengers, adding two at Watervale, but the Epitaph notes eight passengers. The two accounts differ on this point, although two additional passengers could have been added at Contention.

31. My Life in the Early West

32. Daily Epitaph, March 16th, 1881

33. My Life in the Early West

34. Daily Epitaph, March 16th, 1881; information above also from Arizona Republican, June 26th, 1892

35. Daily Epitaph, March 16th, 1881

36. The Parsons Journal has been published by the W.P.A., also by Carl Chafin, and Lynn Bailey of the Westernlore Press, Tucson, Arizona. The original is at A.H.S., Tucson Arizona

37. In reference to Mr. Roswell ,in another publication, The Daily Los Angeles Herald, March 17th, 1881, the Superintendent for Wells Fargo is referred to as L.F. Powell, who was suffering from malarial rheumatism. In *Wells, Fargo Detective: A Biography of James B. Hume* by Richard Dillon, subject is cited as Leonard F. Rowell, Page 184. Also, regarding the theory that Bob Paul may have been a target, this cannot be proven. Ironically, it's not the first time that it was asserted that a stage coach robbery was really a combined opportunity for stealing money and at the same time killing Bob Paul. Referring to a stage robbery attempt that occurred on February 7th, 1877, outside of Darwin California, author Robert P. Palazzo reports that "It was believed that the highwaymen intended to shoot the Wells Fargo shotgun messenger and detective R.H. Paul. Paul was thought to be on the stage as the guard, and the robbers believed that the stage would have a large amount of money 'intended for disbursement in Darwin.'" "Darwin, California," page 26, Self published by Robert P. Palazzo.

38. Tombstone Epitaph, March 16th and 17th, 1881; Arizona Weekly Citizen, March 20, 1881; Arizona Republican, June 26th, 1892

39. Daily Epitaph, March 16th, 1881

40. Daily Los Angeles Herald, March 17th, 1881

41. Arizona Weekly Citizen, March 27th, 1881

42. Daily Epitaph, March 22nd, 1881

43. Tombstone Nugget, March 29, 1881

44. Parsons journal, March 28th, 1881

45. Daily Los Angeles Herald, April 2nd, 1881; Tombstone Nugget, March 29, 1881

46. Arizona Weekly Citizen, April 3rd, 1881

47. Daily Los Angeles Herald, April 7th, 1881

48. *Helldorado*, Billy Breakenridge, Pages 122,123

49. Daily Epitaph, March 17th, 1881

50. Sacramento Daily-Union Record, March 23rd, 1881

51. My Life in the Early West

52. Arizona Weekly Citizen, March 20, 1881

53. Daily Epitaph, March 18th, 1881

54. Daily Epitaph, March 22nd, 1882

55. Daily Epitaph, March 26th, 1881

56. Daily Epitaph, March 17th, 1881

57. "Wells Fargo Never Forgets" [1987-1988], Reprint, updated bibliography; "Wells Fargo and the Earp Brothers: The Cash Books Talk;" [2001, original article] and "Under Cover for Wells Fargo: A Review Essay [of Fred Dodge, 2000], *California Territorial Quarterly* No. 78 (Summer 2009): 4-19, 20-25, 26-32. Courtesy of Bob Chandler.

58. Arizona Republican, June 26, 1892

59. My Life in the Early West

60. Letter from Wm. N. Miller, to Mrs. Lewis Meyer Royaltey, dated April 11, 1936; M652-4, copy of letter in file of author

61. My Life in the Early West

62. The Weekly Arizona Miner, April 22nd, 1881

63. Arizona Weekly Citizen, April 10th, 1881

64. My Life in the Early West

65. Arizona Republican, July 26th, 1893

66. My life in the Early West

67. The Tombstone Stagecoach Lines, 1878-1903: *A Study in Frontier Transportation*, Page 22

68. Reminiscences of William Ohnesorgen as told to Mrs. George Kitt October 22, 1928-AHS)

69. Ibid

70. On September 12th, a three thousand dollar transaction took place between John B. Allen and his wife, and John S. Carr. In the document, Allen's wife was referred to as "Lola." Whether or not this is the same person that Billy Ohnesorgen referred to as Allen's underage wife is unknown. See Book 2, Deeds of Real Estate, page 4, Cochise County Archives, Bisbee, Arizona.

71. Arizona Citizen, October 28th, 1879

72. Reminiscences of William Ohnesorgen

73. PERSONAL RECOLLECTIONS by John S. Vosburg, as told to Frank C. Lockwood, pages 3 and 7, courtesy AHS.

74. History of the Discovery of Tombstone, Arizona, as Told by the Discoverer, Edward Schieffelin, pages 13, 14, Bancroft Library

75. *Out West*, July, 1907, Vol. *XXVII, No. 1, pages 42-43, original copy in the collection of John D. Rose.

76. Letter dated November 7th, 1878, from Tres Alamos, copy in the collection of John D. Rose

77. Arizona Citizen, August 22, 1879

78. Reminiscences of William Ohnesorgen

79. Arizona Citizen, October 22nd, 1879. Long before building his bridge or entering the cash draining stage coach competition with Kinnear, on August 9th, 1877, Ohnesorgen borrowed $1500.00 from area rancher John Wild. In his promissory note he collateralized his 1500 sheep in the process, promising to repay Wild in one year at the a 24% rate of interest per annum. Chattel mortgages, Book 1, Cochise County A.T. Transcribed from Pima County, A.T., pages 107-108. Courtesy of the Cochise County Archives, Bisbee Arizona.

80. Daily Epitaph, July 20th, 1880

81. Tombstone from a Woman's Point of View, The Correspondence of Clara Spalding Brown, July 7, 1880, to November 14, 1882, Edited by Lynn Bailey, Westernlore Press, page 32

82. Pima County Recorder's Office, Mill Sites, 85.3.5

83. Arizona Daily Star, September 23rd, 1879

84. *Helldorado*, Page 99

85. Arizona Citizen, October 25, 1879.

86. Arizona Sentinel, November 22, 1879

87. Arizona Daily Star, September 23rd, 1879

88. Arizona Citizen, November 29th, 1879

89. Arizona Daily Star, September 23rd, 1879

90. The Tombstone Stagecoach Lines, 1878-1903: *A Study in Frontier Transportation* by Thomas H. Peterson, Jr., P. 36

91. Arizona Citizen, February 28, 1880

92. Weekly Nugget, March 25th, 1880

93. Ibid

94. Ibid

95. Arizona Citizen, March 27th, 1880.

96. My life in the Early West

97. Reminiscences of William Ohnesorgen

98. Copy in the collection of John Rose

99. Daily Arizona Citizen, January 16th, 1880

100. Arizona Citizen, January 17th, 1880

101. Gird letters, transcribed by Carl Chafin, #304. Also see "Charleston and Millville A.T., Hell on the San Pedro," by John D. Rose

102. Chattel Mortgages, Cochise County, Transcribed from Pima County, Book 1, Page 109, courtesy of Kevin Pyles, Cochise County Archives

103. After Walker went solo, he was again in need of funds as the fare war with Kinnear was still taking its toll on his finances. On June 15th, 1880, he borrowed $2500 from Samuel Hughes, who took as collateral Walker's entire stage enterprise, including "Eight Stage Coaches, Eighty four head of horses and sixty setts of stage harness now being for the said mortgagor in its [his] business of operating stage lines from Pantano to Harshaw, from Pantano to Benson and Tombstone, and from Tombstone to Harshaw…" (Chattel Mortgages, Cochise County, Transcribed from Pima County, Book 1, Pages 112-115, courtesy of Kevin Pyles, Cochise County Archives.)

104. Weekly Nugget, March 25, 1880

105. Arizona Citizen April 3rd, 1880

106. Daily Epitaph, July 22nd, 1880

107. Letter from Contention signed by "Idler" dated March 9th, 1880, as published in the Weekly Nugget, March 18th, 1880

108. Weekly Nugget, March 18th, 1880

109. Ibid

110. Pima County Recorder's Office, Mill Sites, 85.3.5

111. Weekly Nugget, March 25th, 1880

112. Ibid

113. Weekly Nugget, April 8th, 1880

114. Weekly Nugget, April 15th, 1880

115. Weekly Nugget, April 29, 1880

116. Ibid

117. Weekly Nugget, June 24th, 1880

118. Ibid

119. See *Charleston and Millville, A.T. Hell on the San Pedro,* John Rose, Pages 110-172

120. Weekly Nugget, July 8th, 1880

121. Ibid. Although newspaper accounts such as this one show Rigg was J.P. at Contention in the summer of 1880, on November 1st, 1879, The Pima County Board of Supervisors had appointed Frederick A. Clifton to the position. It appears that Clifton may have preceded Rigg in this position. Minutes of the Pima County Board of Supervisors, page 380, Office of the Clerk of the Pima County Board of Supervisors, Tucson Arizona. The correct spelling is Rigg, not Riggs, as this account illustrates.

122. Weekly Arizona Miner, July 9, 1880

123. Weekly Nugget, July 15[th,] 1880

124. Daily Epitaph, July 27th, 1880

125. Weekly Nugget, July 29th, 1880

126. Daily Epitaph, August 21st, 1880

127. Walker's continuing financial shortfalls may have necessitated his move into the Cowan Bros. store. On June 15th, 1880, Walker collateralized eight stage coaches, eighty-four head of horses and sixty sets of stage harness that were currently being used on Walker's routes running from Pantano to Harshaw, from Pantano to Benson and Tombstone, and from Tombstone to Harshaw. The four month loan was made at an interest rate of two percent per month. Chattel mortgages, Book 1, Cochise County A.T. Transcribed from Pima County, A.T., pages 112-115. Courtesy of the Cochise County Archives, Bisbee, Arizona.

128. Weekly Nugget, July 29th, 1880

129. Book 3, Deeds of Real Estate, Transcribed from Pima County, page 178, courtesy of the Cochise County Archives, Bisbee Arizona

130. Weekly Nugget, July 29, 1880. On July 23rd, J.[James] B. [Bennet] Smith, and W.H. Furlow entered into a sale agreement for the purchase of R. Mason's Western Hotel in Contention, from Mrs. Maria Mason. The humble appearance of the Hotel is little indication of its contents, and its sale of $150.00 was not even a cash transaction, rather, the two purchasers had until February 6, 1881, to pay off the note in full. The purchasers may have gotten the better end of the deal, as they acquired a largely turnkey operation. The contents of the hotel alone may have approached that value. They included, one No. 9 cooking stove and furniture, two bedroom stoves and related venting pipe, four dining room tables and one side table, two kitchen tables, two dining room lamps, one large coffee boiler, one large porcelain kettle, one meat saw clever and one kitchen lamp, one coffee mill, five dining room castors, four sugar bowls, two dozen knives and forks, three dozen tablespoons, three teaspoons, three dinner plates, three inch pie plates, half inch pickle dishes, three syrup pitchers, three milk pitchers, thirty-three deep vegetable dishes, two dozen large meat dishes, three dozen cups and saucers, four salt cellars, five oil table cloths, two gallon iron buckets, three tin wash basins, two water barrels, eight dining room benches, one large meat block, two butcher knives and carving forks, a half dozen towels, one looking glass, one chopping axe as well as number other articles used in said hotel and boarding house. The transaction was recorded at the request of R. Mason, and was notarized by Wells Spicer. Chattel mortgages, Book 1, Cochise County A.T. Transcribed from Pima County, A.T., pages 117-119. Courtesy of the Cochise County Archives, Bisbee Arizona.

131. Ibid

132. Daily Epitaph, July 28th, 1880

133. Daily Epitaph, July 30th, 1880

134. Daily Epitaph, August 4th, 1880

135. Sacramento Daily Record-Union, July 2nd, 1880

136. Sacramento Daily Record-Union, August 3rd, 1880

137. Arizona Sentinel, July 3, 1880

138. Weekly Arizona Citizen, July 31st, 1880

139. Weekly Nugget, August 19th, 1880

140. Weekly Arizona Citizen, August 21, 1880

141. Weekly Nugget, August 19th, 1880

142. Daily Los Angeles Herald, December 1st, 1881

143. Arizona Citizen, January 31st, 1880

144. Weekly Nugget, August 19th, 1880

145. Reminiscences of Early Days in Tombstone" by C.W. Goodale, April 30th, 1927, published by Mining Journal, Vol. X, No. 28. From the Staunton Collection, University of Arizona Special Collections, Tucson Arizona

146. Daily Epitaph, August 29th, 1880

147. Daily Epitaph, October 20th, 1880

148. Arizona Citizen, November 29th, 1879

149. The Citizen, November 21st, 1879

150. Citizen, November 18th, 1879

151. Citizen, November 26th, 1879

152. Citizen, October 22nd, 1879

153. Special correspondence to the Chicago Tribune entitled "Arizona—1879 by A.H. Noon, AHS. This was also reprinted under the title "TOMBSTONE 35 YEARS AGO AS SEEN BY A TENDERFOOT in the Tombstone Epitaph, August 22nd, 1915

154. Daily Nugget, December 18th, 1880

155. Daily Epitaph, December 17th, 1880

156. Daily Epitaph, September 10th, 1881

157. Tombstone Epitaph, January 23rd, 1882

158. Daily Epitaph, July 16th, 1882

159. Daily Nugget, October 22nd, 1880

160. Weekly Arizona Citizen, October 23rd, 1880

161. Weekly Arizona Citizen, November 13th, 1880

162. Daily Nugget, November 20, 1880

163. Daily Nugget, October 7th, 1880

164. Daily Nugget, October 19th, 1880

165. Tombstone from a Woman's Point of View, The Correspondence of Clara Spalding Brown, July 7, 1880, to November 14, 1882, Edited by Lynn Bailey, Westernlore Press, page 24

166. Daily Epitaph, September 17th, 1880

167. Weekly Arizona Citizen, September 25th, 1880

168. Weekly Arizona Citizen, October 16th, 1880

169. Sacramento Daily Record-Union, July 8th, 1881

170. Weekly Arizona Miner, July 15th, 1881

171. Tombstone Epitaph, February 11th, 1894

172. Sacramento Daily Record-Union, February 28, 1881

173. Arizona Weekly Citizen, February 20, 1881

174. Decoction: an extract of anything made by boiling-Webster's Dictionary, 1877, collection of John D. Rose

175. Daily Epitaph, March 17th, 1881

176. Ibid

177. Weekly Citizen, January 28th, 1883

178. Tombstone Epitaph, March 15, 1881

179. Arizona Weekly Citizen, March 20th, 1881

180. Daily Epitaph, June 25th, 1881

181. Daily Epitaph, June 29, 1881

182. Ibid

183. Weekly Arizona Miner, June 24, 1881

184. Daily Epitaph, June 29, 1881

185. Ibid

186. Ibid

187. Daily Epitaph, July 1st, 1881

188. Daily Nugget, July 10th, 1881

189. Daily Epitaph, June 11th, 1881

190. Book 1, Deeds of Real Estate, page 596, courtesy of the Cochise County Archives

191. Book 2, Deeds of Real Estate, page 55, Cochise County Archives

192. Book 1, Deeds of Real Estate, page 599, courtesy of the Cochise County Archives, Bisbee Arizona

193. Daily Epitaph, June 29th, 1881

194. Ibid

195. Daily Nugget, May 6th, 1882

196. Book 2, Deeds of Real Estate, page 2, Cochise County Archives, Bisbee, Arizona

197. Daily Nugget, December 14th, 1881

198. Daily Epitaph, August 4th, 1881

199. Daily Epitaph, August 6th, 1881

200. Tombstone from a Woman's Point of View, The Correspondence of Clara Spalding Brown, July 7, 1880, to November 14, 1882, Edited by Lynn Bailey, Westernlore Press, pages 35- 36

201. Daily Epitaph, July 17th, 1881

202. Daily Epitaph, August 7th, 1881

203. Daily Epitaph, August 13th, 1881

204. Daily Epitaph, August 14th, 1881

205. Daily Epitaph, September 15th, 1881

206. Daily Epitaph, September 17th, 1881

207. Arizona Weekly Citizen, September 18, 1881

208. This article appeared in the March, 1883 edition of Harper's New Monthly Magazine, but it was written long before it was published. Entitled "Across Arizona," it refers to railroad construction (not actually to Tombstone, but to Contention) and the killing of a stage coach driver. Bud Philpot was murdered on March 15th, 1881 while driving for the Kinnear & Company Stage, which was in competition with among others, the Sandy Bob Stage line, which the writer for Harper's refers to as a competing line to the stage he rode on. He also refers to his driver as the "successor" of the driver who was killed…in all likelihood, this was a published interview with the driver who took the place of Bud Philpot following his shooting death near Drew's Station. That coupled with the construction of the N.M. & A. would imply that this stage ride took place in the late summer or early fall of 1881. (Original March, 1883 Harper's, no. 394, from the collections of John D. Rose)

209. Daily Epitaph, October 15th, 1881

210. Daily Epitaph, November 27th, 1881

211. Daily Epitaph, December 4th, 1881

212. Daily Epitaph, December 13th, 1881

213. Tombstone Epitaph, December 24th, 1881

214. Tombstone Epitaph, December 16th, 1881

215. Daily Nugget, December 15th, 1881

216. Apache Days and Tombstone Nights, John Clum's Autobiography, Edited by Neil B. Carmony, pages 69-70

217. Daily Epitaph, Dec. 16, 1881

218. Tombstone Daily Nugget, December 16th, 1881

219. Daily Epitaph, December 17th, 1881

220. Daily Nugget, December 20th, 1881

221. Daily Nugget, December 28th, 1881

222. Daily Nugget, December 31, 1881

223. Arizona Weekly Citizen, January 15, 1882

224. Tombstone Epitaph, January 23, 1882

225. As published in the Weekly Epitaph, January 16, 1882

226. Weekly Epitaph, January 16, 1882

227. Tombstone Epitaph, January 23, 1882

228. Tombstone Epitaph, January 9th, 1882

229. *Wells, Fargo Detective; A Biography of James B. Hume*, by Richard Dillion, Page 209

230. Tombstone Epitaph, a six page edition from January 9th, 1882, with a page reprinted from the Daily edition of Sunday, January 8th, 1882

231. *Helldorado*, by William Breakenridge, Houghton Mifflin Company, 1928, pages 175-176. Breakenridge also notes that the true name of Alex Arnold was supposedly Bill Alexander

232. Daily Nugget, March 18th, 1882

233. Daily Epitaph, January 29th, 1882

234. Tombstone Daily Epitaph, February 2nd, 1882

235. George Hand's diary, September 27th, 1862, as quoted in the E.A. Rigg bio file at AHS

236. Daily Epitaph, February 5th, 1882. Although the Epitaph spells her last name as Myers, other sources referring to the same family also spell her husband's name Meyers.

237. Daily Epitaph, February 5th, 1882

238. Ibid

239. Daily Nugget, January 31, 1882

240. Daily Nugget, February 1, 1882

241. Flood manuscript, pages 275-276

242. Daily Nugget, February 4th, 1882

243. Tombstone Epitaph, February 11th, 1882

244. Daily Nugget, February 14th, 1882. The appointment of James Bennett Smith, named in the Board Minutes as "J B Smith," can be found in the Minutes Board of Supervisors, Vol. 1, 1881-1885, page 154, Courtesy of the Cochise County Archives, Bisbee Arizona.

245. Hooker Manuscript, pages 42-45. Accounts during this period acknowledge Herring as an attorney, and for a time the manager of the Neptune Mining Company.

246. Hooker Manuscript, pages 42-45

247. Daily Epitaph, February 16th, 1882

248. Parson's Journal, February 15th, 1882

249. Daily Epitaph, October 21st, 1880

250. Lotta Crabtree Will Case Papers Harvard Law School Library, page 317

251. Daily Nugget, October 12th, 1880

252. Daily Epitaph, March 30th, 1882

253. Tombstone Epitaph, January 16th, 1882

254. Arizona Weekly Citizen, January 15, 1882

255. Tombstone Epitaph January 16th, 1882

256. Tombstone Epitaph, January 23rd, 1882

257. Daily Nugget, January 4th, 1882

258. Tombstone Epitaph, January 9th, 1882

259. Daily Nugget, January 12th, 1882

260. Daily Nugget, January 13th, 1882

261. Ibid

262. Daily Nugget, January 28th, 1882

263. Daily Nugget, February 18th, 1882
264. Daily Nugget, April 6th, 1882
265. Tombstone Epitaph, January 9th, 1882
266. Ibid
267. Daily Nugget, January 11th, 1882
268. Daily Nugget, February 4th, 1882
269. Daily Nugget, February 5th, 1882
270. Daily Nugget, February 7th, 1882
271. Daily Epitaph, February 3rd, 1882
272. Daily Nugget, February 8th, 1882
273. Daily Epitaph, Sept. 15th, 1881
274. Daily Nugget, February 15th, 1882
275. Daily Nugget, February 16th, 1882
276. Daily Nugget, February 17th, 1882
277. Tombstone Epitaph, February 27th, 1882
278. Arizona Weekly Citizen, February 26th, 1882
279. Ibid
280. Arizona Weekly Citizen, February 26th, 1882, Tombstone Epitaph, February 27th, 1882
281. Parsons Journal, February 22nd, 1882
282. Tombstone Epitaph, February 13th, 1882
283. Weekly epitaph, March 6, 1882
284. Tombstone Epitaph, February 27, 1882
285. Weekly epitaph, March 6, 1882
286. Tombstone Epitaph, March 6th, 1882
287. Tombstone Weekly Epitaph, October 21st, 1882
288. The Denver Republican, May 22nd, 1882, as published in "John 'Doc" Holliday, Colorado Trials and Triumphs" by Emma Walling
289. Flood Manuscript, page 295, also see the Earp/Flood map published by the U.S Marshalls in conjunction with John Gilchriese
290. EARLY ARIZONA Prehistory to Civil War, pages 193, 486, by Jay J. Wagoner
291. Weekly Nugget, March 25th, 1880
292. Daily Epitaph, June 29th, 1881
293. Tombstone Epitaph, June 10th, 1882
294. Tombstone Epitaph, March 27th, 1882
295. Flood manuscript, pages 277-278
296. Tombstone Travesty, pages 256-257
297. Arizona Weekly Citizen, April 2nd, 1882
298. Tombstone Travesty, pages 256-257
299. Arizona Weekly Citizen, April 2nd, 1882

300. Ibid

301. Tombstone Travesty, page 258

302. Daily Nugget, March 22nd, 1882

303. Next Stop: Tombstone, George Hand's Contention Diary, 1882, transcribed and edited by Neil B. Carmony. Published by Trail to Yesterday Books, Tucson Arizona

304. Daily Nugget, March 26th, 1882

305. Next Stop: Tombstone, George Hand's Contention Diary, 1882. Martin Ruter Peel was murdered by Billy Grounds and Zwing Hunt on March 25th, 1882. See *Charleston & Millville A.T., Hell on the San Pedro*, by John D. Rose, pages 247-249.

306. Tombstone Epitaph March 27th, 1882. This is a six page edition of the Epitaph, which includes information published on March 24th, 1882.

307. Tombstone Epitaph, April 3rd, 1882

308. Daily Nugget, March 30th, 1882

309. Arizona Weekly Citizen, April 2, 1882

310. Reminiscences of William Ohnesorgen as told to Mrs. George Kitt, October 22, 1928-AHS

311. Tombstone Epitaph, April 3rd, 1882

312. Ibid

313. Next Stop: Tombstone, George Hand's Contention Diary, 1882

314. Tombstone Epitaph, April 3rd, 1882

315. Ibid

316. Daily Nugget, April 19th, 1882

317. 1882 Great Register, Cochise County, copy in the collection of John Rose

318. Next Stop: Tombstone, George Hand's Contention Diary, 1882

319. Daily Nugget, April 13th, 1882

320. NEXT STOP TOMBSTONE: George Hand's Contention City Diary, 1882

321. Tombstone Epitaph, May 1st, 1882

322. Tombstone Epitaph, April 17th, 1882

323. NEXT STOP TOMBSTONE: George Hand's Contention City Diary, 1882

324. Daily Nugget, May 5th, 1882

325. Tombstone Epitaph, May 6th, 1882

326. Ibid

327. Ibid

328. Daily Epitaph, May 4th, 1882

329. Daily Epitaph, May 5th, 1882

330. NEXT STOP: TOMBSTONE, George Hand's Contention City Diary, 1882

331. Ibid

332. Daily Epitaph, June 11th, 1882

333. Tombstone Epitaph, June 17th, 1882

334. Daily Epitaph, July 6th, 1882

335. Daily Epitaph, July 11th, 1882

336. The original diaries of George Hand are on file at AHS, Tucson Arizona. The Contention portion has been published by Carl Chafin, under the name of Cochise Classics, and they were also published by Trail to Yesterday Books, P.O. Box 35905, Tucson Arizona, 85740, under the title of "NEXT STOP TOMBSTONE: George Hand's Contention City Diary, 1882."

337. Daily Nugget, May 3rd, 1882

338. Daily Nugget, May 10, 1882

339. Daily Nugget, May 20th, 1882

340. Arizona Weekly Citizen, July 16th, 1882

341. Tombstone Epitaph, July 18th, 1882

342. Daily Epitaph, July 21st, 1882

343. Daily Epitaph, July 22nd, 1882

344. Arizona Weekly Citizen, August 27th, 1882

345. Arizona Weekly Citizen, September 10th, 1882

346. Arizona Weekly Citizen, September 10th, 1882

347. Tombstone Weekly Epitaph, September 9th, 1882

348. Tombstone Weekly Epitaph, September 2nd, 1882

349. Tombstone Weekly Epitaph, September 23rd, 1882

350. Arizona Weekly Citizen, October 22nd, 1882

351. Arizona Weekly Citizen, October 29, 1882

352. Arizona Weekly Citizen, October 29th, 1882

353. Arizona Weekly Citizen, November 5th, 1882

354. Arizona Weekly Citizen, November 19th, 1882

355. Arizona Weekly Citizen, December 3rd, 1882

356. Arizona Weekly Citizen, February 4th, 1883

357. Arizona Weekly Citizen, April 15th, 1883

358. Arizona Weekly Citizen, August 18th, 1883

359. Arizona Weekly Citizen, November 10, 1883

360. Tombstone Epitaph, August 9th, 1908, Sunday Edition

361. Bisbee Daily Review, October 11th, 1908

362. Tombstone Epitaph, March 7th, 1882

363. Tombstone Epitaph, March 6th, 1882

364. Weekly Epitaph, May 13th, 1882

365. Arizona Silver Belt, February 25, 1888

366. Daily Epitaph, May 15th, 1882

367. Daily Nugget, May 18th, 1882

368. Daily Epitaph, May 20, 1882

369. Tombstone Epitaph, June 10, 1882

370. Arizona Weekly Citizen, September 10th, 1882

371. Sacramento Daily Record-Union, December 22, 1883
372. Tombstone Epitaph, December 22nd, 1888
373. Daily Prospector, January 19th, 1889
374. Tombstone Daily Prospector, January 30, 1889
375. Daily Prospector, January 19th, 1889
376. Tombstone Epitaph, February 4th, 1912
377. Daily Tombstone Epitaph, June 4th, 1886
378. Tombstone Epitaph, December 26, 1891
379. Tombstone Epitaph, September 13th, 1891
380. Tombstone Epitaph, September 6th, 1891
381. Tombstone Epitaph, January 24th, 1892
382. Tombstone Epitaph, April 27th, 1902, Sunday Edition
383. Tombstone Epitaph, August 10th, 1902, Sunday Edition
384. Tombstone Epitaph, April 15th, 1906
385. Bisbee Daily Review, December 11th, 1902
386. Bisbee Daily Review, April 14th, 1903
387. Tombstone Epitaph, October 28th, 1900, Sunday Edition
388. Cochise Review, November 20th, 1900
389. Bisbee Daily Review, July 6th, 1905
390. Bisbee Daily Review, July 27th, 1905
391. Bisbee Daily Review, October 10th, 1905
392. Tombstone Epitaph, June 21st, 1908, Sunday Edition
393. Bisbee Daily Review, April 23rd, 1909
394. Original print of "Arizona Place Names" from the collections of John D. Rose
395. Tombstone Epitaph, August 10th, 1902
396. Tombstone Travesty, page 92
397. Arizona Sentinel, May 9th, 1885
398. Arizona Silver Belt, August 4, 1888
399. Arizona Weekly Citizen, June 20th, 1885
400. The Tombstone, July 1st, 1885
401. The Tombstone, July 20th, 1885
402. The Arizona Champion, September 5th, 1885
403. The Daily Tombstone, September 12, 1885
404. Arizona Silver Belt, September 19, 1885
405. The Daily Tombstone, October 29th, 1885
406. The Arizona Sentinel, May 24, 1884
407. Arizona Weekly Citizen, October 16th, 1881
408. Daily Tombstone, January 25th, 1886
409. Daily Tombstone, November 3rd, 1886
410. Daily Tombstone, November 8th, 1886

411. St. Johns Herald, June 2nd, 1887
412. Arizona Silver Belt, June 4th, 1887
413. Arizona Silver Belt, February 1st, 1900
414. Arizona Silver Belt, May 28th, 1887
415. Daily Tombstone Epitaph, January 24, 1886
416. The Daily Tombstone, January 25, 1886
417. Daily Tombstone Epitaph, January 28, 1886
418. The Daily Tombstone, January 27, 1886
419. Daily Tombstone, February 2nd, 1886
420. Daily Tombstone Epitaph, February 3rd, 1886
421. Daily Tombstone, February 3rd, 1886
422. Daily Tombstone Epitaph, April 3rd, 1886
423. Daily Tombstone November 3rd, 1886
424. Daily Tombstone, January 27th, 1886
425. Daily Tombstone Epitaph, June 9, 1886
426. Daily Tombstone Epitaph, February 3, 1886
427. Daily Tombstone Epitaph, February 13, 1886
428. See *Charleston and Millville, Hell on the San Pedro,* John Rose, Page 195
429. Daily Tombstone, February 13, 1886
430. Daily Tombstone, June 21, 1886
431. Arizona Silver Belt, January 19, 1884
432. Daily Tombstone Epitaph, April 13, 1886
433. Daily Tombstone Epitaph, February 10, 1886
434. Daily Tombstone, April 13, 1886
435. The Nogales News, as quoted in the Daily Tombstone, April 12, 1886
436. Daily Tombstone, June 21, 1886
437. Daily Tombstone, September 2nd, 1886
438. The Daily Tombstone, October 13, 1886
439. The Daily Tombstone, October 16, 1886
440. Ibid
441. Daily Epitaph, March 13, 1887
442. Daily Tombstone, March 13, 1887
443. Daily Tombstone, March 19th, 1887
444. Arizona Champion, March 19, 1887
445. Daily Tombstone Epitaph, May 4th, 1887
446. Daily Tombstone Epitaph, May 5, 1887
447. Daily Tombstone Epitaph, May 5th, 1887
448. Tombstone Epitaph, December 10, 1887
449. Ibid
450. Tombstone Epitaph, December 17, 1887

451. Tombstone Epitaph, March 3, 1888

452. Arizona Silver Belt, July 28, 1888

453. Arizona Weekly Journal - Miner, September 19th, 1888

454. *The Goldwaters of Arizona*, by Dean Smith with Foreword by Barry Goldwater. The information cited above comes from the Foreword of the book. Published by Northland Press, Flagstaff, Arizona, in cooperation with Arizona Historical Foundation.

455. Arizona Weekly Citizen, February 20th, 1881

456. Original Joe Goldwater letter dated October 15th, 1886, from the collection of John D. Rose

457. Tombstone Daily Prospector, February 11, 1889

458. *The Goldwaters of Arizona*, Dean Smith, Pages 79, 80

459. Daily Tombstone Epitaph, January 24, 1886

460. Arizona Sentinel, February 28, 1885

461. Arizona Champion, February 13, 1886

462. Daily Tombstone Epitaph, March 19, 1887

463. Arizona Champion, June 9th, 1888

464. Arizona Silver Belt, June 30, 1888

465. Arizona Silver Belt, Saturday, August 11th,1888

466. Tombstone Epitaph, July 1st, 1894

467. Arizona Sentinel, June 9th, 1888

468. Arizona Silver Belt, June 16, 1888

469. Arizona Silver Belt, October 6th, 1888

470. Arizona Silver Belt, September 1st, 1888

471. Tombstone Epitaph, December 22nd, 1888

472. Tombstone Daily Prospector, February 11th, 1889

473. Tombstone Daily Epitaph, August 17th, 1889

474. Daily Tombstone, June 18th, 1886

475. Tombstone Daily Epitaph, August 7th, 1889

476. Arizona Silver Belt, June 8th, 1889

477. Ibid

478. Tombstone Epitaph, January 25th, 1890

479. Tombstone Epitaph, August 2nd, 1890

480. Tombstone Daily Prospector, July 30th, 1890

481. Tombstone Daily Prospector, August 5th, 1890

482. Tombstone Daily Prospector, August 8th, 1890

483. Tombstone Daily Prospector, August 14th, 1890

484. Tombstone Daily Prospector, August 11th, 1890

485. Tombstone Daily Prospector, August 29th, 1890

486. Arizona Silver Belt, August 30th, 1890

487. Arizona Silver Belt, August 11th, 1894

488. Tombstone Daily Prospector, August 11, 1890

489. Tombstone Daily Prospector, August 29th, 1890

490. Tombstone Daily Prospector, November 1st, 1890

491. Tombstone Daily Prospector, September 23rd, 1890

492. The Arizona Champion, June 21st, 1890

493. Tombstone Epitaph, December 16th, 1900

494. JEFF MILTON SHOOTS IT OUT And the curtain Falls On The Styles-Alvord Gang, by Mildred Taitt Milton. MS 500, Milton papers, Box 2 of 2, AHS

495. JEFF MILTON, A Good Man with a Gun, J. Evetts Haley, Page 308

496. JEFF MILTON SHOOTS IT OUT

497. JEFF MILTON, A Good Man with a Gun, Page 308

498. JEFF MILTON SHOOTS IT OUT

499. Tombstone Epitaph, February 18th, 1900, Sunday Edition

500. Tombstone Epitaph, March 4th, 1900, Sunday Edition

501. Tombstone Epitaph, April 1st, 1900, Sunday Edition

502. Tombstone Epitaph, Sunday Edition, April 8th, 1900

503. Arizona Silver Belt, May 3rd, 1900

504. Tombstone Epitaph, June 3rd, 1900, Sunday Edition

505. Tombstone Epitaph, Sunday Edition, October 14th, 1900

506. Tombstone Epitaph, November 25th, 1900, Sunday Edition

507. Tombstone Epitaph, May 25th, 1902, Sunday Edition

508. Tombstone Epitaph, January 2nd, 1916

509. Tombstone Epitaph, April 16th, 1916

510. Tombstone Epitaph, April 8th, 1917

511. Reprinted by Arizona Highways Magazine in 1976 for the U.S. Bicentennial and in 1987 for Arizona's Diamond Jubilee of Statehood. Fourth printing 1992, page 85

512. Tombstone Epitaph, May 14th, 1922

513. Arizona State Business Directory, Vol. 1925, the Gazetteer Publishing Company, copy of original in collection of author)

514. *Helldorado*, pages 99, 253-254, 256

515. Introduction to the Johns Western Gallery auction catalogue, written by Wm. Shillingberg. Shillingberg is sharing the quotes of Earp's discussion with Flood as they were related by John Flood after Earp's passing. The 2004 auction was of a miniscule portion of what had been the largest Tombstone/Earp collection ever, once owned by the late John Gilchriese.

Big Jake, aka, Dutch. Contention City troublemaker. 196-197.

Bilicke, Albert. 112, 260.

Bird Cage Academy of Music, located at Tombstone. 213.

Bird Cage Theater. 53-54.

Bisbee Massacre. 42, 218, 220-223.

Bisbee, A.T. 100, 120, 185, 214-216, 218, 220-223, 227-229, 234-236, 245, 253-259, 262, 269, 288, 292, 300-301.

Blinn, Lewis W. 202-203, 236.

Boquillas Land and Cattle Co, aka, Boquillas Ranch. 227, 289-290, 302.

Boquillas Land Grant. Correctly known as the as San Juan de los Boquillas Nogales. 74, 112, 114, 181-182, 285.

Boston Mill: 77, 90, 190, 200, 236, 238 image of; 264-265.

Bradley, Billy. Contention City Saloon Keeper who hosted George Hand's Contention visit in 1882. 187.

Bradley, William Franklin. 72, 91, 107, 192,

Bravin, George. Deputy shot by Alvord Stiles gang. 278, 280-282,

Bravo John, aka, Thos Yoea. 279-282.

Breakenridge, William M, "Billy." 35-36, 61-62, 194, 302-305.

Brown, Bob. Charged with being one of the Alvord Stiles gang at Fairbank. 281.

Brown, Mrs. Clara Spalding. 99.

Burnett, James C. 79, 135, 283,

Burnham, R. Superintendent of the Contention Mill, who also worked the Grand Central and Sunset mill sites at Contention City. 66, 74, 89, 300.

Burts, Matt. Member of Alvord Stiles gang. 280-282.

Cable, Daniel N. 6-7, 91, 102, 107, 181.

Calabasas, A.T. 130, 208-209, 211, 215.

Campbell and Hatch Saloon, located at Tombstone. 183, saloon token of; 304.

Carlyle, William. Proposed the construction of a toll road through lands claimed by Morgan, who was located north of Drew's Station and Ranch. 164,307, map drawn by which noted Drew's to the south of Morgan;

Cashman, Nellie. 300.

Castaneda, Amparo Arviso. Wife of Jose Miguel Castaneda, partner of Joe Goldwater. Given the dubious reputation of these two men, they used the initials of Castenada's wife, calling their firm A.A. Castenada so that suppliers would be willing to ship to them. Letterhead of said firm, 220. 255.

Castenada, Jose Miguel. Contention City Merchant. 192.

Charleston, A.T. 21-22, 27, 33, 42, 51, 59, 61-62, 64-65, 75-76, 79-80, 87, 90-91, 94, 98-99, 101, 103, 105, 108, 119,-120, 132, 135, 138, 143, 172, 175, 181-182, 188, 200, 205, 215,-218, 226, 236-240, 243-248, 253, 263-264, 266, 268-269, 283, 299, 301. 303.

Chase, Alexander Wells, offered to survey Contention City. 192.

Chase, Capt. A.W.. Excavated near Contention City for prehistoric artifacts on behalf of the Smithsonian Insitute.

Chinese Gardens. 264.

Chinese. 63, 195,212, 244-245, 249, 264-265, 300.

Christiansen, Hans M. Accused at Contention City of petty theft and arson, and publicly urged to leave town by many leading citizens. 91.

Clanton, Joseph Isaac "Ike." 39, 42, 135, 142, 145, 185.

Clum, John P. 31, 58, 68, 102, 120, 123-125, 127-128, 142, 160, 176, 300.

Coleman, Walter Coleman, agent for Ingram & Company. 85.

Collections of author, John D. Rose. 3, 14, 24, 26, 34, 40, 54, 56-57, 60-62, 64, 77-78, 83-85, 96, 97, 103, 110, 125-126, 134, 138, 158-160, 163-168, 173, 183, 206, 214, 220-223, 230, 251, 255-257, 267, 276, 270, 278, 280, 283-294, 296-299, 302, 304.

Contention City Depot, N.M. & A. (New Mexico and Arizona railroad.) 51, 111-113, 115, 123, 130, 168, image of Benson Depot; 169, 172, 174-178, 185.

Contention City. 2, 6-7, 15, 18-19, 21-22, 25, 27-29, 32, 38, 40-42, 51, 57, 62-65, 67, 70-71, 73-77, 79-81, 83-88, 90-91, 94, 96, 98-100, 102, 104-109, 111-117, 120-123, 129-130, 135-137, 139-140, 142, 145, 148, 156, 168-169, 172, 174-179, 181-182, 814-188, 190, 192-194, 197, 201-202, 204-207, 209, 212-213, 215-218, 224, 226, 229, 233, 243, 253, 258, 263, 266, 269, 289, 299, 301, 304-305.

Contention Mill. 6, 19, 27, 60-63, 65-66, 71-73, 75-76, 80-81, 89, 96, 102-104, 109, 111, 114, 115, 120, 122, 129, 169, 177, 182, 194, 199, 207, 209, 213, 225-228, 300.

Contention Mine, located at Tombstone. 51, 61-62, 65, 71, 73, 86, 90, 98, 102, 111, 114, 116, 198, 202, 213, 226,

Copper Queen Mine, located at Bisbee A.T. 215, 227.

Cowan, Arthur C. Wells Fargo Agent at Contention City. 30, 82, 91.

Crane, Jim. 42.

Crittenden, A.T. 204, 208-211.

Crouch, Robert. (aka, Sandy Bob Crouch) 121, 130, 139, 157, 163, 165, 174, 235, 246.

Cuddy, William. Former hard drinking Tombstone resident who later returned as an evangelist at Fairbank. 260.

Daniels, Billy. 235, killed by Apaches.

Davies, Bill. Robs a Contention City Saloon, along with his partner in crime, Jack Sharp.

Dawson, J.W. Another who experimented with the old tailings at the Grand Central Mill utilizing the cyanide process.

Demartini, Paul. Fairbank shopkeeper. 241, 247.

Dodge, Frederick. 132.

Dolan, Peter. Murdered Peter Smith at a railroad camp along the Babacomari. 189-190.

Dole, L.E. Tombstone area teamster working for Blinn Lumber Company, who thought he saw an Apache. 202. Public ridicule of, 203.

Douglas, James., Dr. Ran Phelps Dodge and Company to great success at Bisbee, and spearheaded the building of the Arizona and Southeastern railroad from Fairbank to Bisbee. 257-258, 269, 288.

Dragoon Mountains, A.T. 199, 204, 210, 243, 271.

Drew, Cora. 1,18 photo of as a young lady; 19, 25, 29, 38, 41-43, 44 image of later in life; 66, 192, 235.

Drew, David Stuart. Image of, 46.

Drew, Ed, aka Eddie. 42 finds Philpot's body after shooting south of Drew's Station, 44 image of in group photo; 46,Image of working horses at the Sierra Bonita Ranch; 47 image of at Ray A.T and also a note written by him.; 48-49 death of and related photo and documents.

Drew, George Harrison. 16, testifies during Drew vs. Mason re Mason's pulling a weapon on his father; 18, helps his father and laborers in the construction of Drew's Station; 50, interior image of his own home later in life; 192.

Drew, Georgiann, aka, Anne. 44, image of.

Drew, William Charles. Image of, 45.

Drew, William H. 1, photo of, 2, 4 listed on survey bill for roadway; 5 assaulted by Robert Mason; Drew vs. Mason 5-17, 18, 19, 57, 66, death of; 102.

Drew's hand drawn map of his and nearby ranches. 7-12.

Drew's Ranch and Stage Station. 1-25, 27-30, 32, 38, 40 photo of author at Drew's Station, 14-43.

Drew's Station. 1-2, 6-7, 13-15, 17-20, 22, 25, 27-30, 32, 38, 40-43, 50-52, 57, 60, 66, 104, 123, 174, 178, 192, 229, 234, 263m 285, 289, 301, 304, 305. Location of, 306-312.

Dunbar, John. 33-34,293.

Dunbar, Thomas. Brother of John Dunbar. 58, was visited by and served dinner to John Clum on August 3rd, 1875.

Dunlap, "Three fingered Jack." 273.

Durand, Dick. Drunk from Tombstone who frequented Contention City. 204.

Durkee, Julius Emmons. Tombstone teamster hauling to Millville and Contention City, among other destinations. Owner of a substantial corral in Tombstone near the homes of Wyatt and Virgil Earp. 139, 213, 265.

E.P. & S.W. (El Paso and Southwestern railroad, the train to Tombstone.) 228, 234, 269,

Earp, Allie. 1, 19, 181, 185,-186, 234.

Earp, James, aka Jim. 19, 20-21, 184, 188.

Earp, Mattie. 19.

Earp, Morgan. 35-36, 125, 132, 142-143, 183, 186.

Earp, Virgil. 20, 35, 37-38, 81, 91, 102, 125, 140, 142-143, 145, 160-161, image and oath of; 184-185.

Earp, Wyatt. 22-23, 39, 54, 87, 133, 135, 140-145, 159, 178, 180, 184-188, 304.

Earthquake of May 3rd, 1887. 226, 248,

Effrein, Peter. Copper Queen for who tore down the old Contention Mill. 227.

Effrein, Peter. Copper Queen foreman who supervised the dismantling of the old Contention Mill. 227.

Emanuel, Alfred H: 235.

Fairbank Gardens. 265.

Fairbank Rioting. 259.

Fairbank. (also spelled Fairbanks in the historic period) 2, 52, 57, 90, 94, 115, 142, 169, 172, 181, 211, 214-216, 218-219, 224-225, 228, 232-266, 268-271, 274, 276, 279, 281-284, 288, 296-297, 299-305.

Fairbank. 2, 52, 57, 90, 94, 115, 142, 169, 172, 181, 211, 214-216, 218-219, 224-225, 228, 233-266, 268-271, 274, 276, 279, 281-284, 288, 296-297, 299-303, 305.

Farish, Thomas E. 70, 96, 103, signature of on Head Centre billhead.

Felter, Lizzie. Daughter of Judge Felter, and public school teacher at Drew's Station. 18.

Flood, John H. Jr. Confident and attempted biographer of Wyatt Earp. 180, 184, 304.

Flooding. 58, 66, 117, 209, 262-263, 265, 271.

Fort Huachuca. 181, 198, 205, 236, 249, 301.

Fuller and Fuller. 298.

Gage, E. B. 74-75, 99, 178, 232.

Gird Mill, located at Tombstone. 114-115, 123, 224.

Gird, Richard. 1, 6, 21,26, 55-57 including image of, 59, 62, 65 Gird's Mill; 69-70, 75, 80, 92, 98 Gird's Mill; 99, 117, 130, builds Huachuca Aqueduct; 213, 226, Gird's Mill 232.

Herron, John. BLM Archeologist who discovered and misidentified an historic site north of the actual Drew's Station, as Drew's Station. 309-310, 312.

Hillman, J.W. Focus of a nationally known insurance fraud, who was finally arrested while hiding out in Fairbank. 260.

Holliday, "Doc," John Henry. 32, 37-38, 40, 42, 91, 102, 140,142-147, 179, 184, 186.

Howard, James. G. Contemporary accounts also refer to him as George Hill Howard. Partner with George Hearst for the San Juan de dos Boquillos Nogales. 112-114, 181-182,

Huachuca Moutains. 268, 185, 235, 268.

Huhn & Luckbardt, San Francisco Mining Engineers visit the Contention Mill. 65.

Hume, James B. Wells Fargo Detective robbed while traveling via stage from Contention City to Tombstone. 131-132.

Humphries, Williams. Murdered J.R. Mason at Fairbank. 239.

Hurst, Captain, Joseph H. Made a matter of record the false claim by Henry Niven that Apahes had raided Helm's ranch. 197-199.

Ingram & Co. Opposition Line. 85-86.

Iron Spring, Whetstone Moutains, where Wyatt Earp claimed to have shot down Curly Bill Brocius. 133, 178, 180.

Isaacs, Ike. Tombstone firefighter and gambler and witness to the assassination of Morgan Earp.34, 195.

Judge French, who presided of Drew vs. Mason case. 17.

Judge Mills. Becomes J.P. at Fairbank following the death of J.B. Smith. 247.

Judge Underhill. Sent by Charles Crocker of the Southern Pacific railroad to assess a possible route south toward Tombstone. 93-94.

Junction City.(Early name for the area which would later known as Fairbank. Also see Kendall and Kendall's Camp.) 172, 176-178, 215, 234.

Katzenstein, Sam. Charleston merchant moved to Fairbank. 245.

Kendall. (also an early name for the area that would later be known as Fairbank.) 182, 200, 215-216, 234.

Kendall's Camp. 215, 234.

King, Luther. 33-34, 42.

Kinnear, John D. 23-25, 31, 38-39, 42-43, 51, 64, 66-70, 85-86, 88, 127, 187, 240, 246.

Kinnear, Mrs. 70.

Kong, Wong. Tombstone restaurateur. 278, bill for meals for prisoners doing street maintenance.

Laing, Arthur. Occasional Contention City correspondent for the Arizona Weekly Citizen. 102, 104.

Larrieu, Leon. Contention City Hotel keeper and owner of the local French Restaurant. 207, 300.

Lawrence, H. F. 4, aids Robert Mason and William Drew in laying out stage road; 19,

Leonard, Bill. 42, 106.

Leslie, Nashville F, "Buckskin Frank." 35-37,

Letson, James. Constable at Fairbank. 238, 240, 242-243.

Levi. Friend of Joe Goldwater who attempted to prevent his arrest by Bob Paul. 254.

Ludwig, John Baker. Deputy Sheriff at Contention City. 101, 108, 190, 194, 196, 199-201, 210-211.

MacDonald, Mark. San Francisco Stock Broker who rode with A.H. Noon in a stage to Tombstone, and promised a railroad would reach Tombstone twenty years before it did. 96.

Macia, Bert, whose decedents operate the Rose Tree Museum, Tombstone Arizona. He worked the old Grand Central tailings along with partner W.W. Poindexter. 233.

Malcom's Water Station. Located on the road from Tombstone to Contention City, it was the last landmark before the stage driven by Jimmy Harrington was fired upon, which included passenger John P. Clum. 123.

Malter & Lind. Stamp Mill construction contractors. 81, 88, 190.

Mandibles, Carmen. Killed Thomas Salcido at Fairbank, captured at Nogales. 248.

Manje, Captain Juan Mateo. Vii, visits what will become the Contention and Fairbank area November 9th, 1697 with Father Kino.

Marks, Simon. German born Contention City Merchant. 70, 82, 84, 91, 107, 116, 210, 244.

Martyn, A.J. Murdered by Charles Williams and his wife Tommy Martyn. 252-253.

Mason, J.R. Murdered at Fairbank by Williams Humphries. 239.

Mason, Robert. 2, marks out roadway in the summer of 1878 along with Wm. Drew and H. Lawrence; 4, bills Pima County for roadway related services; 5-6 temper of and Drew vs. Mason; 7-9 mentioned on map drawn by Wm. Drew; 16-17, cuts off irrigation to Drew's crop fields and defies a court order to desist; 19, 61 witnesses the signing of the Contention Mill land claim; 80, succeeds in saving the dam belonging to the Upper San Pedro Ditch Co during flooding; 84 along with his wife sells R. Mason's Contention Hotel to J.B. Smith,(Smith was later to become a Contention and Fairbank Judge; 90 victim of horse thieves; 102 sues partner D.N. Cable in the Upper San Pedro Ditch Company; 285 Mason's Ranch.

Masterson, William B. "Bat." 26, 32.

Maxson, Hubert Burdell. Surveyor of the second Contention City. 112-113, 169, 192.

McCauley, Wm. Prospoector and murderer of Charles Helm. 203-204.

McDermott, John C. 5, one of three jurors for Drew vs. Mason; 63 sells Contention City lots with D.T. Smith; builds hoisting works for the Contention Mill; 64, signature of on a delinquent loan; 72 referred to as "Mayor McDermott; 74 begins work on the Grand Central Mill; 75, criticized for water use by those in Charleston who have access to the water before he does; 77, becomes Contention City Postmaster; 81, sells mill-sites; 82, McDermott's Exchange Saloon; 91 signs petition urging Hans. M Christiansen that he has over stayed his Contention City welcome; 99-100, active in local politics and his horseback accident; 105 real estate activities of; 107, McDermott's Hall; 204 deals with a drunk.

McMenomy. A sheep rancher outside of Contention City, murdered. 189, 194,

Meyers, Louis Wheeler. Also spelled Meyer in contemporary records. Contention Hotel keeper and real estate speculator. 91, 111, 116, 120, 129-130, 138, 206, 217,

Meyers' Hotel. (aka, Meyers' House, also Myers' House) 129-130, 156, 169, 177, 206, 217, 295.

Mills, Joseph L. Replaced Fairbank Judge J.B. Smith after his death. 247.

Millville, A.T. 26, 55, 59, 70, 75, 77, 80, 91, 98-99, 109, 117, 122, 181, 188, 194, 196, 213, 216, 232.

Milton, Jeff. 192, 270-274, 276-279, 282-283, 300-301.

Mitchel, Alexander J. Surveyor of the Head Centre Mill (aka, Sunset Mill) at the north edge of Contention City, as well as surveyor of Charleston, where Mitchel Street was named in his honor. 61.

Montezuma hotel, Fairbank. 263, 265, 300.

Mungie, Jose. One of four men who had been drinking heavily at Fairbank for two days non stop, when his three companions viciously turned on him with brutal assault. 259.

N.M. & A. (New Mexico and Arizona railroad.) 94, 97, 111, 114-115, 168, 170, 172, 175, 211, 234, 246, 248, 258, 265, 269, 271, 276, 284.

Niven, Henry. Spread false report of Apache raid at Helm's ranch. 199.

Noon, Dr. Adolphus Henry. 95-96,

Ohnesorgen, Billy. 1, 51, 54-56, 58-60, 67, 69.

Owings brothers, George and Louis.. Arrested along with Alvord Stiles gang. 282.

Page, Sid. Member of the Alvord Stiles gang who chose not to join the jailbreak engineered by Billy Stiles. 281.

Pantano, A.T. 56, 78, 86-87, 187.

Papagoe Indians. 197.

Parsons, George W. 31, 35, 56, 145, 176.

Pascholoy, Joe. 300.

Patton, John J. Tombstone saddle and harness maker. 235.

Paul, Robert H, "Bob." 13, 15, 26-27-28, 30-32, 35, 39, 42, 166-167, 174, 205, 252, 286-287,

Penwell, E.S. Special Deputy who served Robert Mason and testified against him in Drew vs. Mason. 17.

Phelps Dodge. Bisbee Mining company of great success. 215, 256, 257-258, 269.

Philpot, Eli P. "Bud." 15, 25-31, 35, 37-43, 48, 101, 104, 117, 123, 166-167, 192, 298, 304,

Poindexter W.W., partner of Bert Macia working the old Grand Central tailings. 233.

Posse. 30-33, 35-37, 42, 87-88, 100, 138, 145, 172, 178-179, 186-189, 198, 204, 210, 213, 218, 229, 238-239, 252-253, 261, 265, 271, 273, 276, 278-281, 310.

Redfield, Len, Redfield's Ranch. 32-34, 39.

Rigg, E.W. [Edwin Augustus] 79, Justice of the Peace at Contention as well as postmaster; 91, less tolerant of criminals than Jim Burnett and Charleston; 100; 106, serves as election inspector; announces the first wedding in Contention history; 108 acts as coroner; 123, visits Tombstone; 129, acts as coroner again; 135 death of; 136, handwritten letter to County billing expenses; 137, funeral of; 138, George Hand visits grave of; 145, politics of; 147, 201.

Roberts, Dr. Gary. Historian. 310.

Robles, Manuel. An active outlaw, killer and train robber, who escaped badly wounded from a gunfight with Sheriff John Slaughter and his deputy, Burt Alvord, later himself an accomplished outlaw of the train robbing specialty. 108, 259.

Roerig, Peter. 25, 27, 29, 31, 35, 37-38, 298.

Rogers Brothers. Benson firm also operating at Fairbank, and foreclosed on Jerry Barton. 245-246, 266, 267.

Rose Tree Museum, Tombstone Arizona. 233.

Rupert, Elmer Ellsworth, aka, Fatty Rupert, Contention City resident. 200, 206, threw a going away party for himself at Myer's Hote, 206-207.

Salicido, Thomas. A boy killed at Fairbank over a girl by Carmen Mandibles. 242.

San Pedro River. 1, 5-6, 13-14, 18-19, 21-22, 41, 51, 55-56, 59-62, 64, 67, 75, 86, 90, 93, 96, 98-100, 102, 104-105, 108-109, 113-114, 117-122, 129-130, 169, 172, 177-179, 182, 188, 203, 206, 213, 216, 232, 234, 237, 252, 254, 258, 262, 301.

San Rafael del Valle land grant. Located on the San Pedro River south of Charleston. 182.

Santa Cruz de Terrenate-see Terrenate.

Schieffelin, Al. 6, 57 image of; 61.

Schieffelin, Ed. 1, 56 image of; 57, 181.

Sharp, Jack. Robs a Contention City Saloon, along with his partner, Bill Davies. 210.

Sheldon, Jack. Stage driver for Sandy Bob Crouch the night that passenger J.B. Hume was robbed along with other passengers between Contention City and Tombstone. 132.

Sheriff Ward. 218-219.

Sherman, General William T. 195-196.

Signal, A.T. 1, Drew family arrives at, 18, Drew family moves from Signal to site of what will become Drew's Station; 26, 56, 255.

Slaughter, Sherriff, John. 235, 248, 252-253, 258-260, 268.

Slimmes Tailing company of Utah. Invest in a cyanide plant at the old Grand Central Mill. 233.

Smith Stage Line. 27-28.

Smith, Charlie. 132, 218.

Smith, D. T. Partner with John McDermott selling Contention City land. 42, 63, 72, 74, 76, 91, 105.

Smith, J.B. (James Bennett) 84, 91, 135, 142-143, 147, 189-190, 197, 210, 240, 269.

Smith, P.W. Tombstone Merchant who later goes bankrupt. 39, 186.

Smith, Peter. Railroad construction worker murdered along the Babacomari by Peter Dolan. 189-190.

Smithsonian Insitute. Excavation near Contention City performed by Capt. A.W. Chase. 100.

Sonoita, A.T. 210-211.

Sosa, Mrs. Nancy Lewis. 307 misidentifies the location of Drew's Station, advocating a site too far to the north; self-described discoverer of this site. As shown on page 309, this site was actually discovered by John Herron of the B.L.M (Bureau of Land Management); 307,309-312.

Southern Pacific railroad, aka, S.P. 51, 78, 86, 94, 262.

Spicer, Wells. 74, 91-93, 142, 178.

St. David, A.T. 96, 182, 188, 247, 253, 300.

Stage Coach Road to Tombstone. 3-4, 19, 21, 26-27, 30, 57, 59, 125, 142, 264, 304.

Sterling Silver Mining Company. Successors to the Vizina Mine located at Tombstone. 224.

Stiles, William, aka "Billy." 271, 278, 279-282.

Stilwell William H. Judge. 140-141..

Stilwell, Frank. 185-187.

Sunset Mill. (aka, Head Centre mine and Mill, also spelled Head CENTER is historic references) 13, 76, 81, 89, 98, 103, 190, 224.

Swift, E.J. Beaten to death at Fairbank by Jerry Barton. The case against him was complicated when one Mr. Crane, a key witness to the case against Barton, was suddenly not be found. 239-240.

Made in the USA
Charleston, SC
29 September 2013